GW00656500

MAY TYRANTS TREMBLE

In memory of Philip Casey, 1950–2018,
poet, novelist and friend.

MAY TYRANTS TREMBLE

THE LIFE OF WILLIAM DRENNAN, 1754–1820

Fergus Whelan

IRISH ACADEMIC PRESS

First published in 2020 by
Irish Academic Press
10 George's Street
Newbridge
Co. Kildare
Ireland
www.iap.ie

© Fergus Whelan, 2020

9781788551212 (Cloth)
9781788551229 (Kindle)
9781788551236 (Epub)
9781788551243 (PDF)

British Library Cataloguing in Publication Data
An entry can be found on request

Library of Congress Cataloging in Publication Data
An entry can be found on request

Typeset in Garamond Premier Pro 11/14 pt

Jacket front: William Drennan's sketch of Blaris executions.
Courtesy of the National Archive of Ireland.

Jacket back: William Drennan (c.1790), Robert Home, 1752–1834
© National Museums Northern Ireland, Collection Ulster Museum.

Cover design: edit+ www.stuartcoughlan.com

CONTENTS

ACKNOWLEDGEMENTS

I wish to thank Sheila Hanley, Theresa Moriarty, Dr Sylvia Kleinman, Dr Patrick Walsh, David O'Brien, Raymond O'Regan, Aaron McIntyre, Ray Naughton and Dr Jim Smyth for their help. I wish also to thank the staff of the Royal Irish Academy, the National Archive of Ireland, the National Library of Ireland and the staff of Trinity College Library, particularly the very helpful people in Early Printed Books.

INTRODUCTION:
BRAZEN WALLS OF SEPARATION

This is an account of the life of William Drennan (1754–1820) physician, poet and political radical. Drennan was a founding member of the Dublin Society of United Irishmen in 1791. The new Society lamented 'the brazen walls of separation' which had been erected amongst the inhabitants of Ireland by distinctions of rank, property and religious persuasion.[1] Drennan composed the Society's test which had as its purpose 'the forwarding of a brotherhood of affection, a communion of rights and a union of power amongst Irishmen of every religious persuasion'.[2] Many of the Society's addresses were drafted by Drennan and he was a prolific writer of prose, poetry and pamphlets. He was by far the most active and able literary propagandist with no equal in the Dublin United Irish Society.

Drennan began his writing career in 1780 with an open letter to Edmund Burke (1729–1797) condemning the Irish-born English politician for his hostile reaction to the trade concessions Lord North's government had made to Ireland. Time and again for the rest of his career Drennan used the device of an open letter to prominent public figures as a way of getting attention for his radical ideas and enhancing his literary reputation.

He established himself as a leading writer in the radical cause with the publication, in 1784, of his *Letters of Orellana: An Irish Helot*, in which he attempted, with limited success, to breed new life into the flagging Volunteer reform campaign. His letters from this period to his friend Reverend William Bruce tell us a great deal about Drennan's zeal for Volunteering. He expressed his contempt for the aristocratic leadership of those such as Lord Charlemont and the Whig opposition in the Irish House of Commons whom Drennan did not consider sincere about reform.

Drennan maintained a regular correspondence with his sister Martha McTier (1742–1837) from 1776 to 1819. Brother and sister were accomplished writers and their letters contain fascinating details, insight, observations and commentary on their lives. William Drennan and Martha McTier lived in interesting times and took a keen interest in public affairs and the politics of

Ireland, Britain, France and America. They were enthusiastic supporters of the American and French Revolutions. Drennan rejoiced when the Americans defeated the British at Saratoga in 1777 and Martha sang 'Over the Hills and Far Away' when the Duke of Brunswick was defeated at Valmy in 1792. Even before the King of France was executed, Drennan believed that the Revolution 'ought to be cemented and consolidated with his blood'[3]

As the foremost propagandist of the United Irish Society, Drennan was an influential figure in Dublin and, through his correspondence with Martha's husband Sam McTier, he had a profound influence on the policy and strategy of the Belfast United Irishmen.

Although Drennan advocated a brotherhood of affection involving all religious persuasions, a consensus persists amongst historians that he was an anti-Catholic bigot with an obsessive dislike and mistrust of Catholics 'based on petty or superficial motives'.[4] The validity or otherwise of charges of bigotry are carefully examined in this book in the light of the available evidence.

Drennan's friend Archibald Hamilton Rowan escaped from Newgate prison in 1794 after becoming entrapped in a treasonable conspiracy with Reverend William Jackson, an agent of revolutionary France. Drennan denied all knowledge of the affair. Yet he had read the document which Rowan had passed to Jackson and he also had accurate information about how Rowan had managed to escape from the prison and the country. A few weeks later, Drennan was acquitted on charges of seditious libel. We are told that after the experience of his arrest and trial, 'he was considerably chastened and from that point on gradually withdrew from the United Irish movement'.[5] It is also said that he had developed a distaste for the more extreme views in politics.[6] In fact, after his trial, Drennan continued to produce literary propaganda including writing and publishing an open letter to the Earl of Fitzwilliam. With a prudence dictated by the climate of oppression, some of his work appeared anonymously. Some of the most seditious material to appear in the *Press*, the United Irish newspaper suppressed in early 1798, was written under the pseudonym Marcus. This book will present significant evidence to suggest that Drennan was Marcus.

In the spring of 1798, when 'most of Drennan's friends were in prison, he compared himself to a solitary ninepin when all around him had fallen'.[7] He did not condemn those of his associates who had absconded to avoid arrest but he assured Martha 'I am still at my post and here I shall remain.'[8] Although informers were accusing him of working with people who had been arrested or fled to avoid arrest, the authorities did not molest him in any way in the run-up to or the aftermath of the 1798 Rebellion.

By early January 1799, Drennan was hurriedly composing an open letter to William Pitt opposing his proposals for the union of Great Britain and Ireland. The letter appeared in print on 24 January 1799 and sold 300 copies in the first morning.[9] Later that year, Drennan set about making his own union with England when he travelled to Wem in Shropshire to renew his engagement to Sarah Swanwick. Sarah was from a Unitarian family and 'liberal in her mind and of a democratical turn in politics'.[10] The couple were married in Dublin in February 1800 and set up home in Marlborough Street.

Drennan had been close to the Emmet family but was very much surprised when Robert Emmet's Rebellion broke out in Dublin in July 1803. Much to Martha's distress, her dear friend Thomas Russell was executed for his part in the Rebellion. Drennan wrote two epigrams relating to Emmet's Rebellion. The first was aimed at William Plunket, the prosecutor who had gratuitously and needlessly insulted Emmet at his trial. The second was aimed at Dr James McDonald who had offered a reward for the capture of Thomas Russell who had been his close friend.

Drennan had always held 'the vain-glorious and venal' Edmund Burke in utter contempt. He denounced him as the 'trumpeter' for the totally unnecessary and long-drawn-out war between France and England.[11] He was convinced that Burke was doing his utmost to prevent the alliance the United Irish Society sought of 'three million discontented Catholics and a half a million disaffected Presbyterian republicans'. When Drennan read Burke's pamphlet *Letter to a Noble Lord* he thought Burke had joined 'insanity with the wiliness of a crafty politician' and that he was 'as coarse and vulgar as one of Robespierre's hirelings'.[12]

The Unitarian religious tradition which Drennan had inherited from his father was important to him. When defending himself against charges of sedition, Drennan asserted that he 'gloried to be a Protestant Dissenter and to the best of fathers and the best of religions he was indebted for his veneration of the rights of mankind'.[13]

Although his father had been a clergyman and Drennan considered himself 'rigid rather than loose' in the Unitarian persuasion, he had little time for clergymen in general.[14] He once observed that 'the priesthood in all ages had been the curse of Christianity'. In this he included those Unitarian clergymen with whom he was on friendly terms. He described the *Regium Donum* as a slow poison injected into the Protestant Dissenting churches and that ministers had become 'nothing more or less than the pensioners of government'.[15] In the aftermath of the Rebellion, Lord Castlereagh introduced a new *Regium Donum* scheme to create 'a considerable internal fermentation perhaps even a schism to change the temper' of the Presbyterian Synod.[16] His objective was to weaken what he deemed to be the democratic party within the Synod whom he believed were deeply infected with the principles of the Rebellion. Castlereagh had two allies in the Synod, Reverend Robert Black of Derry and Reverend William Bruce. Drennan denounced what he described as this 'pensionary establishment' and Castlereagh's scheme as an attempt to create a Presbyterian hierarchy.[17]

When William Pitt died in 1806, Drennan hoped that the new regime might lead to an improved climate in politics. Charles J. Fox, the leader of the Whigs, had joined 'The Ministry of all the Talents'[18] and Drennan wrote him an open letter. He expressed the hope that the race of informers would perish in infamy and famine, that the prison doors would be unbarred and the United Irish prisoners be released and that the unfortunate rebel emigrants would be pardoned and allowed to return. He also looked forward to a free press and Catholic emancipation. Even as he wrote, he knew that Fox was dying and that all his hopes were unlikely to be realised.

In 1807, Drennan became financially independent following the death of a relative who bequeathed him a substantial legacy.[19] Within a few weeks, he returned to Belfast where he lived henceforth in moderate affluence. He was unburdened at last of the drudgery of his less than lucrative medical duties. He was now free to do what he most enjoyed and he founded a literary magazine, the *Belfast Monthly Magazine*. Through the six years of the magazine's existence, Drennan wrote consistently in favour of the reform of Parliament, Catholic emancipation, against the war with France, in favour of freedom of the press and abolition of the slave trade. These issues had all been part of Drennan's agenda as a United Irishman but now he pursued them in the context of the Union parliament at Westminster.

Drennan denounced the Union between England and Ireland in print. He thought the corrupt way it had been effected to be most disgraceful. Yet, by 1810, Drennan had a more positive view of the Union and accepted that it 'had a tendency to ally party feuds and relieve us from the rough riding of some of our Irish unprincipled jockeys'.[20] Gerald R. Hall tells us that now 'Drennan believed that any agitation for repeal was misguided and that reformers in England and Ireland should join forces.'[21]

Shortly after his return to Belfast, Drennan became involved in what was to prove the most successful and enduring of his public projects, the founding of the Belfast Academical Institution. It would be another battleground where he had to fight Castlereagh, Black and Bruce for the soul of Irish Presbyterianism. The school, which became known colloquially as the 'Inst', was an 'astonishingly ambitious' project and was the 'first university established in the British Isles since Trinity College Dublin at the end of the sixteenth century'.[22] The Inst was founded and, to some extent, run by former United Irishmen and their sympathisers.

Some of those most closely associated with the school held a dinner on Saint Patrick's Eve 1816 where, after the speeches, many unashamedly radical toasts were raised including one to the United Irishmen who had escaped to America in '98. Castlereagh saw this as an opportunity to wrest control of the Inst from Drennan and his friends but he overplayed his hand and did not succeed.

Drennan became terminally ill in late 1819 and died in February 1820. The letters written in the last active year of his life show us clearly that Drennan's radical principles which inspired his great zeal in Volunteering and his enthusiasm for the United Irish Society and its principles remained with him to the very end.

1

SON OF THE MANSE

William Drennan was born in the manse of First Presbyterian Church, Rosemary Lane, Belfast, on 23 May 1754. He was the son of Reverend Thomas Drennan (1696–1762) and Anne Lennox (1718–1806). Thomas Drennan was a 'New Light' Presbyterian Minister and Anne Lennox was a co-heiress, with her elder sister, to a moderate estate in County Down.[1] Little is known of Thomas Drennan.[2] It appears 'he was the clever son of a poor family, probably first generation emigrants to Ulster from Scotland'.[3] He has been described as an 'elegant scholar, a man of fine taste, overflowing benevolence and delicate sensibility'.[4] His father 'was induced by the early promise of his son's abilities to spend on his education more than came to his share'.[5] Thomas made excellent academic progress and graduated from Glasgow University in April 1717.[6] He met Francis Hutcheson (1696–1746) at Glasgow and the two became firm and life-long friends. Hutcheson, who was born near Saintfield in County Down, would eventually establish himself as the greatest Irish philosopher of his own or, perhaps, any generation. He is universally acknowledged today as the Father of the Scottish Enlightenment.

At Hutcheson's invitation, Thomas Drennan moved to Dublin *circa* 1720 where together they ran an academy for Protestant Dissenters in that city.[7] Hutcheson's and Drennan's Presbyterianism had Scottish roots but the families who sent their sons to the Dublin Academy were of English descent and most were members of the Protestant Dissenting congregation based at Wood Street. Some of them had come to Dublin with Oliver Cromwell's army in 1649 or as settlers in the wake of the Cromwellian invasion of Ireland. Despite the fact that these Cromwellians were a community of Protestants in a Protestant city, they were regarded with suspicion by the Irish government and the Established Church authorities. Like their Dissenting brethren in England, from the Restoration of Charles II in 1660, they faced legal disabilities arising from their refusal to conform to the Established Church.

In their Dublin years, Hutcheson and Thomas Drennan formed an intellectual circle under the patronage of Robert Molesworth (1656–1725), who had been a supporter of William of Orange during the Glorious Revolution and had acted as his Ambassador to Denmark. This group, which often met at Molesworth's home in Swords, County Dublin, included Hutcheson's cousin William Bruce, Reverend John Abernethy (1670–1740) and Reverend James Duchal (1697–1761). Bruce was an editor and book publisher by profession and was an elder at Wood Street. Abernethy was called to Wood Street as Minister in 1730 and Duchal was his successor there.

Back in 1705, Abernethy had formed a philosophical, study and reading group in Belfast, which became known as the Belfast Society. This group became notorious to orthodox Presbyterian historians for allegedly opening the door to heresy and schism.[8] The Society became the nucleus of a group of ministers who became known as New Light Presbyterians. The central message of New Light sermons and theology was the right to freedom of conscience and private judgement and that religious persecution violated the natural genius of man.

Caroline Robbins in her classic work, *The Eighteenth Century Commonwealthman*, identifies Molesworth as having begun the agitation for reform, which went further than that offered by the Bill of Rights and the Toleration Act with the appearance of his *Account of Denmark* in December 1693.[9] Robbins suggests that there is no doubt that Hutcheson, Drennan, Abernethy and Bruce shared the politics of the Molesworth connection. She had this to say of them: this 'New Light group preached and published sermons that were widely read, had contributed a quota of tracts and pamphlets to contemporary controversy, and handed to a second generation a patriotic spirit that included all Irishmen in its loyalties, and diffused a liberal philosophy throughout more than one city or country'.[10]

The New Light Presbyterians referred to themselves as Protestant Dissenters and formed the most intellectual and radical wing of the Presbyterian church.[11] They described themselves as:

Created by a love of freedom, [they claimed] they have ever championed the cause that gave them birth. Whether the freedom was that of the coloured slave or the honest religious enquirer, they have fearlessly taken the side of justice, and resisted every attempt to stifle private judgement. An ardent desire to bring about the brotherhood of man has led them to generously support many charitable and benevolent movements of a non-sectarian nature.[12]

This New Light background has been described as of great importance to William Drennan's intellectual development.[13] The love of freedom, an end to slavery and the slave trade, the right to private judgment in religion, the pursuit of brotherhood and an end to sectarian divisions were important themes of Drennan's life and work. When he faced one of the major crises of his life, as he stood trial on charges of writing and publishing a seditious libel in 1794, he claimed his father, with Bruce, Ducal, Hutcheson and some of their circle, as the source of his political principles.

While a member of the Molesworth circle, Francis Hutcheson wrote *The Original of Our Ideas of Beauty and Virtue*, which established his international reputation. Thomas Drennan remained at the Dublin academy after Hutcheson moved to Glasgow to occupy the Chair of Moral Philosophy in 1730. In 1736, Drennan was appointed assistant minister to the First Presbyterian Congregation, Belfast. After he left Dublin, Thomas maintained strong ties with the ministers and elders at Wood Street. The complex theological, historical and political significance of these connections will be explored in more detail later. However, a straightforward aspect of the connection was that it led to Thomas Drennan's marriage to Anne Lennox. Anne's father had been a prosperous merchant in Belfast. Her mother was a descendant of the Scottish Hamilton who had persuaded James I to grant him the O'Neill's land in North Down.[14] When Anne was just twenty-three, she had occasion to travel to Dublin. As her parents were both dead, her wealthy Presbyterian relations were anxious to find a suitable chaperone for her. Thomas Drennan travelled to Dublin regularly to preach at Wood Street. What could be more suitable than the company of a forty-five-year-old clergyman, who was regarded by his friends as a confirmed bachelor? In the event, the family tradition has it that, before their carriage reached Swords, in County Dublin, the couple were engaged. They were married on 8 August 1741.[15]

Anne 'brought a respectable marriage portion and, for some years, the couple appeared to live happily and in moderate affluence'.[16] Thomas was not good at keeping in touch with his friends and this aspect of his character, along with his reputation as a bachelor and Anne's relative prosperity, brought forth a somewhat mischievous letter of good wishes from Francis Hutcheson:

Dear Thom

Tho' I have often heard the rumour of your courtship without believing it, as I never thought your Talent lay in Fortune hunting; yet as late I have had such assurances that you are actually married, as I could not question it any longer. My wife and I congratulate you most heartily and wish you all the joys of that new Relation and wish the same to Mrs Drennan, who shows a much more valuable Turn of Mind in her conduct than most young Ladies in such circumstances.[17]

The Drennans had eleven children, only three of whom, Martha (1742–1837), Nancy (1745–1825) and William (1754–1820) survived infancy.[18] We know a great deal about Martha and William because of their regular correspondence from 1776 until 1819.[19] We know almost nothing about Nancy as she was withdrawn and silent and seems to have suffered from life-long depression.[20] We do know that, unlike her brother and sister, she took no interest in public or political affairs and she lived to the age of eighty.[21]

William was educated first by his father and later by the Reverend Mathew Garnet, a Church of Ireland vicar who ran a school at Church Lane, Belfast. Under their guidance, William became a classical scholar of some ability.[22] Thomas Drennan was a kindly man.[23] Young William loved his father dearly while he lived and venerated his memory after his death. Thomas Drennan died when William was just fourteen years old. A.T.Q. Stewart tells us that all through his life thereafter, William walked with the ghost of his father, whose 'beckoning shade constantly exhorted him to a high level of virtue, public and private'.[24] William himself says that in his later life, 'in every trying situation', he 'was accustomed to look to this best of fathers', who had, 'to his last hour desired him never to forsake his political principles'.[25]

At the age of fifteen, just a year after the death of his father, William went to Glasgow University. He was following in the footsteps of generations of Irish Presbyterians who were debarred from Trinity College Dublin, Oxford and Cambridge on religious grounds. He arrived at Glasgow in 1769. That year, ninety-six students were admitted to the university, twenty-six of whom were Irish. It must have been a difficult time for such a young man, not long after the death of his much beloved father, to find himself away from his family in a strange city. We know little of his life as an undergraduate but he seems not to have had happy memories of his time in Glasgow. Looking back in later life, he told of how the Irish students were in 'a humiliated and dispiriting situation' and that they were regarded as nothing more or less than a degraded class.[26] He took his MA in 1771 and moved to Edinburgh to study medicine in 1773, graduating from there as an MD in September 1778.

He does not appear to have enjoyed his early years in Edinburgh any more than he did in Glasgow. His family began preserving his correspondence from

1776, seven years after he had left Belfast. At this point, he was still homesick and declaring, that 'never was there a person who loved Ireland and hated Scotland more than I do'.[27] In one of the earliest preserved letters he told Martha:

> Never, never had a man a more burning affection for relations, for friends, for country than I have and the pleasure I used to feel on the first day of my return to Ireland is sufficient reward for the pains of purgatory which I suffer here ... I cannot read two pages without thinking of Belfast. I am a continual joke of the lads here for making Belfast the eternal subject of my conversation.[28]

In the same letter, he mused about his capacity for empathy with his fellow man. He fondly remembered walking with his father and being gently rebuked by the older man for striking down a plant with a stick. He hoped that he had, since that time, caught some of the sympathy which his father felt so much for the fall of a flourishing vegetable.[29] He clearly cherished this memory, for very many years later he wrote a poem in veneration of his father which contained these lines:

Not on an insect would he tread nor strike the stinging nettle dead
who taught at once my heart and head? My father![30]

Dugald Stewart (1753–1828), although only one year older than Drennan, was one of his teachers at Edinburgh and they became firm friends. Stewart was appointed Professor of Mathematics at the age of only twenty-two. He is regarded today as one of the most important figures of the later Scottish Enlightenment. He became a renowned populariser of the work of Francis Hutcheson and Adam Smith and was one of the most admired lecturers and famous Scottish teachers of his day.[31]

From the time of Drennan's arrival in Edinburgh, he had breakfast or dined with Stewart frequently and his great admiration for him grew over time. Drennan's father's close connection to Francis Hutcheson might have helped cement their relationship and 'it is not unlikely Stewart may have stimulated Drennan's own interest' in Francis Hutcheson.[32] It is said that it was under the tutelage of Stewart that Drennan: 'imbibed the classical tradition of republican theory, in its most famous English embodiment in the works of John Locke, and its contemporary reincarnation in the works of Richard Price and Joseph Priestley.'[33]

Stewart and Drennan's friendship continued long after Drennan graduated from Edinburgh. Stewart was in Paris in the summer of 1789 and witnessed the storming of the Bastille. Like Drennan, Stewart became a firm supporter of the

French Revolution. He was to pay a price for his unpopular opinions and was eventually virtually ostracised from Edinburgh society.[34] Stewart's reputation as a philosopher eventually undermined this hostility and today an elaborate monument on Calton Hill, Edinburgh, commemorates his contribution to the Scottish Enlightenment.

It is likely that if Drennan and Stewart discussed politics at their breakfast meetings, their focus would have been on the struggle between Britain and America. The American war was raging by this time and Drennan had the pleasure, once a week, of addressing a college literary and public speaking club, the Speculative Society, 'venting his rancour' in favour of the Americans. He confided in Martha, 'poor America – how much do I fear for it – if it be conquered – let us prepare for a universal conflagration. Was not Montgomery vanquished superior to Wolfe the victor? I suppose you have seen his epitaph by order of Congress – it is very good, but he deserves better.'[35]

Major-General Richard Montgomery (1738–1774) had been killed while attempting to capture Quebec for the American forces on 31 December the previous year. Dublin-born Montgomery was the highest-ranking soldier to die in the American Revolution. Montgomery's family was connected to the Wood Street/Strand Street congregation, with which Drennan's father had been connected in the 1720s and 1730s and with which William would also be connected in his Dublin years. Richard Montgomery's brother, Alexander, was a member of the Irish Parliament for thirty-two years from 1768 and was a supporter of the Volunteer and United Irish movements.

Drennan needed to be careful regarding his support for the American cause. He was aware that one of his fellow medical students had been denied his degree because he had dedicated his thesis to his uncle, John Zubly (1724–1781), a delegate to the American Continental Congress. By January 1778, 'nothing was going on [in Edinburgh] but the raising of regiments to be devoted to the destruction of America'.[36] Drennan observed that every order of men from the lowest to the highest are emptying their pockets in support of the war. Even the Speculative Society, of which he was a member, donated 100 guineas. Drennan absented himself from the meeting and donated nothing.

Martha recommended that William read Dr Richard Price's *Observations on Civil Liberty and the Justice and Policy of the War in America* (1776). She told him that with this pamphlet in his 'hand, or head, he could bid defiance to all the slavish [anti-American] arguments the greatest Scottish genius can oppose to you'.[37] This is the same Dr Price who would be the target of Edmund Burke's *Reflections on the Revolution in France* some fifteen years later.

One Sunday, William was shocked to hear a clergyman pray against the colonists as he was sure that his clergyman father would never have behaved so:

> I heard this morning a most virulent prayer to the Father of Mercies against poor America – oh how I pity such – Pray on ye men of blood – but if I ever forget thee O Jerusalem may my tongue cleave to the roof of my mouth, may this right hand forget its cunning. Spirit, gentle spirit of my father, wouldst thou have prayed so?[38]

Drennan complained that in their race to display their loyalty, 'every minister in the city have [*sic*] given what they could spare, to edge the sword of war' except for Dr Dick of Greyfriars. To bolster support for the war against America, the government had ordered fast days, on which the clergy were expected to promote loyalty to the king and denounce the American rebels from the pulpit. On one such fast day, Dr Dick, 'this worthy clergyman', preached 'how shall I curse whom the Lord has not cursed? How shall I judge whom the Lord had not condemned'?[39] Dr Dick may have been in a minority in Edinburgh but it is likely that Drennan would have been aware that many Protestant Dissenting clergy in his native Ulster, and in many other parts of Ireland and England, used their fast-day sermons to denounce the war and support the Americans.

During the early stages of the war, both William and Martha were worried for the Americans, particularly when they heard rumours such as the defeat of Washington with a terrible slaughter on both sides.[40] However, the war turned decisively in favour of the Americans, with their victory in the second battle of Saratoga in October 1777. Drennan was delighted and he told Martha, 'I congratulate the people of Belfast and all mankind for the late victory over Burgoyne.' He was anxious to know how the news was greeted in Belfast and believed the British defeat would have profound long-term implications for the Empire:

> I am persuaded that the event of the war will turn on this great event, and it is probable that future historians will date the fall of the British Empire from the 16th October '77 – No object can be thought of more melancholy, than a great empire that has thus outlived itself and is now degenerating into a state of political dotage, prophetical of its final dissolution. Was it for this shameful day that Sidney suffered, and that Hampden bled? Were all the glories, triumphs, conquests, spoils, this nation has acquired in the defence of liberty, thus meanly to be blasted in a traitorous attempt to destroy it.[41]

The statement gives us a clear indication of Drennan's extremely radical political outlook. He invokes Sidney and Hampden, two heroes of the Real Whigs or Commonwealth tradition of the early eighteenth century. John Hampden had challenged Charles I over the introduction of 'ship money' and had died fighting on behalf of Parliament in the English Civil War. Algernon Sidney was a republican theorist, who was executed for treason by Charles II in 1683. Drennan invoked their names to accuse the British government of a traitorous attempt to destroy liberty. In some of his later writings, Drennan used what he called, 'the sainted name' of Sidney as a pseudonym.[42]

Within a short time of his hailing of the American victory at Saratoga, in his letter of 30 January, Drennan appended the date with the words 'and may the tyrant tremble at the day'.[43] This was the anniversary of the execution of Charles I in 1649 and had long been designated by the Anglican Church as the Feast of Charles the Martyr. At church services on the anniversary, the clergy were expected to preach loyalty to the King and to denounce rebellion as sinful. The sermons often involved reminding listeners of the role Protestant Dissenters had played in the overthrow and execution of Charles I. It was rumoured that, as Tories and Anglicans mourned their saintly king, Dissenters secretly celebrated the execution of a tyrant.

On the next government-appointed fast day in March, 'the Scotch spent in humiliation and prayer', Drennan and his Irish friends spent the evening 'making many excellent toasts on the subject of politics'. He told his sister, 'we concluded with unanimously wishing that all the tyrants in Europe had but one neck, that neck laid on the block and one of us appointed executioner'.[44]

Toasts in favour of tyrannicide had a long-established provenance, real and imagined, in radical circles. From the Restoration of Charles II in 1660, it was common for Tories to accuse Protestant Dissenters of being covert republicans and regicides. Tory accounts of the Calves' Head Club, which some suggested was founded by John Milton and celebrated on 30 January by drinking wine from a calf skull, may have been a gothic horror fantasy. However, we know that Drennan's Belfast friends held an annual celebration each year on 30 January. In 1793, at an event held in the Washington the attendance 'was very thin'.[45] This is not to be wondered at, as the event took place just as news of the execution of Louis Capet,[46] just nine days earlier, had reached Belfast.

Edmund Burke had predicted the execution of Louis long before the King was placed under arrest and many commentators have put this down to his keen foresight, which amounted almost to a gift of prophecy. However, Burke would have been very familiar with the accusations of republicanism and regicide often levelled at Dissenters. Sometimes such accusations were unfair Tory propaganda. The annual celebration in Belfast suggests that accusations of support for regicide amongst Dissenters were, in some cases, true, however. Nor can we put the toast of Drennan and his friends down to drink-induced hyperbole. He was presumably sober when he reported the toast to Martha.

Drennan's enthusiasm for the execution of tyrant kings was not just a foible of youth. Many years later, in December 1792, Drennan met his friend Isaac Corry in the street, who asked him, 'My dear Drennan, how are you? How many kings have you killed this morning?'[47] Drennan does not appear to have been surprised or put out by the question. That same month, just before Louis' trial commenced, Drennan ventured his view on the affair to Sam McTier: 'As for Louis it is my opinion in two words [sic], that if he not be executed there will be another massacre, and in mercy to the people, in mercy to the constitution it ought to be cemented and consolidated with his blood.'[48]

Many of the Irish and British radicals who had welcomed the French Revolution were appalled by the execution of the King. Others such as Wolfe Tone, regarded it as a sad necessity. William Drennan regarded the execution as not only necessary but desirable.

In his student days, Drennan did not let his regicidal revels, nor his support for America, interfere with his medical studies. However, in early 1777, he left Edinburgh temporarily due to his poor state of health. He went to Castlecor, in County Cork, to recuperate from a bout of illness and remained there for most of that year. He drank the spa waters from nearby Mallow and, weather permitting, he went horse riding as his preferred method of taking exercise. Throughout his recuperation, he continued to pore over his medical books. By the end of the year he was back at Edinburgh and applied for permission to graduate. His application was successful and he decided he would submit his thesis with a view to qualifying as a doctor in September 1778.[49]

2

NON-SUBSCRIBING PRESBYTERIAN

The meeting house at First Presbyterian Rosemary Lane, Belfast, Drennan's birthplace, was the very cradle of non-subscribing Presbyterianism. In 1720, at the installation of the Reverend Samuel Haliday (1685–1739), the new minister refused to subscribe to the Westminster Confession of Faith leading to what has been described as the first subscription crisis. Haliday was supported in his stance by other ministers and congregation elders including Reverend Thomas Drennan, Reverend John Abernethy, Reverend James Duchal, Francis Hutcheson and William Bruce, all of whom Drennan was to mention in his proposed defence when he stood trial accused of sedition in 1794.

Abernethy had founded his Belfast Society in 1703 of which A.T.Q. Stewart had this to say:

> Orthodox Presbyterian historians have little good to say about it. While reluctantly recognizing the intellectual abilities of its members, they have deplored their ecclesiastical indiscipline and accused them of opening the door to Schism and heresy. Undoubtedly it created the nucleus of ministers who would come to be called 'New Light' and through them it precipitated the great storm over doctrine which would soon break over the Synod.[1]

It is perhaps of some significance that Haliday's 'unusual early career had taken him well outside the bounds of provincial Presbyterianism, and he studied theology at the university of Leyden in the Netherlands.'[2] He was licensed at Rotterdam in 1706 and subsequently ordained at Geneva.[3] Haliday's stance at Rosemary Lane was not just another local schism over obscure points of doctrine to which all shades of Ulster Presbyterianism are so prone. Though the controversy had been in gestation in Ireland from nearly twenty years earlier, the issue at stake had been fought over in England in the previous decade from the Glorious Revolution of 1688. The conflict had, in a sense, been imported into

England from the Netherlands and had been promoted by two philosophers both of whom had spent time in the Netherlands. The towering figure in the controversy was the philosopher John Locke whom William Drennan often claimed as the inspiration for his political ideas. The other philosopher involved was the flamboyant, irreverent and enigmatic young Irishman John Toland (1670–1722).

Locke had been in exile in Holland in the wake of the Rye House Plot of 1683 which was an attempt to overthrow Charles II and assassinate his brother, the avowed Roman Catholic James Duke of York. Holland was a staunchly Protestant State but probably the only place in Europe where the different sects were free to worship as they pleased and propagate their opinions. Locke's time there was a period of great intellectual upheaval. Christopher Walker has described what was happening. Essentially, hard-line Calvinism was crumbling as post Calvinists began abandoning the severity and intolerance of the Genevan master and discovering different types of Protestantism in the more humane, tolerant and rational versions of Arminianism and Socinianism.[4]

The heresy that Reverends Haliday, Abernethy, Drennan and their friends were suspected of was Socinianism. To understand the world view of the non-subscribers, one needs to know a little of the nature of this heresy. Faustus Socinus was born in Sienna in 1539. He was a wandering scholar who had been profoundly influenced by the Humanism of Erasmus. When he arrived in Krakow in the 'tolerant Kingdom of Poland' in 1580 he encountered a growing anti-Trinitarian movement styling itself the Minor Reformed Church.[5] Though he never joined this sect, he soon became its spiritual leader. The sect eventually moved to the town of Rakow where it flourished for more than thirty years. They established an academy there whose pupils, at one point, numbered one thousand.[6]

The Socinians believed in a 'scrupulous and vigorous Biblicism and the right to reason in religion'.[7] As there is no reference to the Blessed or Holy Trinity in the Scriptures, Socinians believed in only one God and did not regard Jesus as God but as a moral, human, teacher. They refused to believe in anything they could not understand. Socinus wrote in favour of the separation of Church and State and declared himself against civil punishment of heretics by exile, prison or execution. He was writing at a time when many of the states of Europe, Catholic and Protestant alike, used the stake, the executioner's block, inquisitions, torture and forced mass exile of populations to punish such crimes as believing in, or refusing to believe in, transubstantiation.

Socinus died in 1604 and thirty-four years later, in 1638, the Socinians were forced to leave Poland or to conform to Roman Catholicism. Many fled to Transylvania, East Prussia and the Palatinate, while others found asylum in Holland, in Amsterdam and Leyden. Their printing press moved to Holland and an imposing series of volumes containing all the main Socinian writings was printed in Amsterdam in 1665–6.[8]

The lapse of the Licensing Laws in England in 1695 gave Locke and Toland the opportunity to publish their controversial views. Locke published *The Reasonableness of Christianity as Delivered in the Scriptures* and Toland published his *Christianity not Mysterious*. Both books promoted similar ideas though they were written in somewhat different styles. Locke was careful and prudent whereas Toland loved to provoke. Both works were an explicit attack on orthodox Christian priest-craft and advocated a return to a simple moral Christianity. Each Christian should be free to come to their own views without persecution by Church or State. Locke denounced those who would try to enforce religious orthodoxy: the Protestant Reformation challenged not only Roman orthodoxy but also the very idea of orthodoxy. From its beginning, the principal goal was to transform Christianity from a religion of priestly orthodoxy to one of freedom of conscience.[9]

Locke published his *Essay Concerning Human Understanding* and *Two Treatises on Government* in 1690. He had published his *Letter on Toleration* the previous year. In his *Letter* he said: 'The heads and leaders of the Church, moved by avarice and an insatiable desire for dominion, making use of the immoderate ambition of magistrates and the credulous superstition of the giddy multitude, have incensed and animated them against those that dissent from themselves, by preaching ... that schismatics and heretics ... are to be destroyed.'[10]

Orthodox churchmen grasped instinctively that many of Locke's ideas were Socinian. Locke denied this, declaring that there was 'not one word of Socinianism in his work'.[11] Yet this did not cut much ice with his contemporaries, some of whom argued that Locke 'might pass for the Socinus of his age or that he was Socinianized all over'.[12] One modern historian has taken his cue from Locke's detractors and branded him with the title 'the Socinian John Locke'.[13] Whether this is fair or not, it was grossly unfair for Locke's contemporary Edward Stillingfleet, the bishop of Worcester, to attack Locke for what John Toland had written. The bishop alleged that Locke held Unitarian views because he believed him to be the source of the ideas expressed in Toland's *Christianity not Mysterious*.

Toland was born in Donegal in 1670. He was probably the son of a Roman Catholic priest and his first language was Gaelic. In his early years, he became a Presbyterian and was educated at Glasgow, Edinburgh, Leyden and

Utrecht.[14] His education in Holland was paid for by Reverend Daniel Williams (1643–1716) who, for twenty years, ministered to the Dublin Wood Street congregation, until 1687.

During his studies and travels Toland acquired nine languages. He was a strident spokesperson for republican virtue and, in his lifetime, he published over one hundred books.[15] *Christianity not Mysterious* was published between December 1695 and June 1696. Draft papers for the work 'had possibly been sent to John Locke in late March 1695'.[16] In *Christianity not Mysterious* Toland: 'applied the Lockean theory of the meaning of religious mystery, arguing that since mysteries such as the Holy Trinity do not stand for distinct ideas, Christianity must either employ meaningless doctrines, or else be non-mysterious ... for', writes Toland, 'if we have no idea of a thing, it is ... lost labour for us to trouble ourselves about it'.[17]

Shortly after his book was published, Toland arrived in Dublin to find that a great clamour had been raised against him and it. He was attacked from the pulpits and in the press. His book was arraigned by a Dublin Grand Jury none of whom had read one word of his work. Finally, it was declared heretical by the Irish House of Commons. It was to be burnt twice (once before Parliament and once before the civic buildings).[18] Toland claimed that one member of Parliament suggested that the author should be burnt along with his book.[19] This was no small matter as Thomas Akenhead, an eighteen-year-old student at Toland's alma mater at Edinburgh had been hanged the previous January for mocking the doctrine of the Trinity. Akenhead had retracted but to no avail. All copies of Toland's book were seized and further imports banned. Toland fled Dublin to avoid arrest and was never to return to his native land.

Toland rescued the works of the English Commonwealth republicans such as John Milton, Edmund Ludlow, Algernon Sidney and James Harrington and 'fashioned them so they would be acceptable to a later generation'.[20] The first edition of Harrington's republican classic *Oceana* was published in 1656 and dedicated by the author to Oliver Cromwell. Toland republished it in 1702 with an account of Harrington's life. Harrington was always a great favourite of Francis Hutcheson who, in his lectures to students, endorsed many of Harrington's suggestions. When William Bruce was preparing a reprint of Toland's *Life of Harrington* in Dublin in 1737, he wrote to Reverend Thomas Drennan: 'Our subscription to Harrington goes on apace. It will be the prettiest and cheapest book that will be printed in Ireland.'[21] When the book appeared, the subscription list included the names of Reverend Haliday, Reverend Abernethy and Professor Francis Hutcheson.

The prosecution of Thomas Emlyn

In June 1702, less than four years after Toland left Dublin, Reverend Joseph Boyse, who was then the Minister in charge at Wood Street, with one of the elders, approached his assistant minister Thomas Emlyn at his home. Although Emlyn had never expressed any anti-Trinitarian views, the elder was correct in suspecting that his friend had indeed lost his belief in the Trinity. When Emlyn confirmed the suspicion, he offered to leave the congregation, which he had served for eleven years, for the sake of peace. He was forced to leave for England but while there, he heard that he was being denounced from the same pulpits which had attacked Toland a few years previously. He published a defence of his position which left him vulnerable to charges of blasphemy. He returned to Dublin to settle his affairs and was promptly arrested.

His trial began on 10 June 1703 and before the court sat, Emlyn claimed that he had been 'informed by an eminent gentleman of the Long Robe' that he would not be permitted to speak freely but it was designed to run him down like a wolf without law or game.[22] That was how the trial was conducted. There were seven or eight bishops present of whom two, Dublin and Armagh, took the bench. Emlyn observed that a jury of tradesmen was being asked to decide on 'abstruse points of divinity of which there were many disputes among the learned of the age'. The Queen's Counsel behaved with 'great heat and fury' and when he made the ludicrous assertion that 'presumption is as good as evidence he was seconded in this by the Chief Justice'. Emlyn's Counsels were intimidated and were 'interrupted, contradicted and so brow beaten that they eventually withdrew'.[23] When Emlyn tried to speak for himself, the Chief Justice cried 'speak by your Counsel' even though by this time he had none. The Chief Justice warned the jury that if they were of a mind to acquit the defendant 'my Lord bishops are here'.[24]

After his inevitable conviction, Emlyn was asked to retract his opinions and when he refused, he was sentenced to a year in prison and a £2,000 fine. This was so beyond Emlyn's means that it amounted to an indefinite prison sentence. Emlyn was to spend two years and one month in the common gaol and in all that time, none of the bishops who had taken such an interest in him came to see him to rescue him from his error.[25]

Boyse began to regret his role in the affair and worked for Emlyn's release, finally achieving it in late 1705. Emlyn left Ireland never to return. In a caustic review of the affair, the Whig bishop Benjamin Hoadley concluded: 'The nonconformist accused him, the conformist condemned him, the secular power was called in and the cause ended in an imprisonment and a very great fine, two methods of conviction about which the Gospel is silent.'[26]

Two matters relating to the persecution of Thomas Emlyn contributed to the schism which would reveal itself at Reverend Haliday's installation at Rosemary Lane nearly two decades later. Firstly, the Synod of Ulster, running scared of further accusations of heresy, imposed acceptance of the Westminster Confession on all newly ordained ministers. It was probably in reaction to the Synod's decree that Abernethy founded his Belfast Society. He and his fellow Society members would never accept the Westminster Confession or indeed any other man-made confession of faith. Many orthodox Presbyterians suspected that this was because Chapter II of the Confession restates the traditional doctrine of the Trinity and three persons in one God. However, Abernethy's view was that all confessions of faith are man-made and therefore might contain human error. For him, it is the duty of every Christian to seek truth in the Scripture and not allow one's conscience to be bound by what others have decided is truth.

Abernethy, Haliday, Drennan senior and their fellow non-subscribers recognised no earthly authority in religious matters and believed no one should suffer penalties for holding particular religious opinions. The latter point goes a long way towards explaining why many non-subscribers, including William Drennan himself, were opposed to the Penal Laws against Roman Catholics.

3

DRENNAN'S RELIGIOUS OUTLOOK

William Drennan was only fourteen years old when his father died but he would have been familiar with the non-subscription controversy and his father's Unitarian theology. In his later life, Drennan claimed that he was always 'rigid rather than loose in that persuasion'.[1] It is likely that the Drennan family library would have held copies of John Locke's work as well as Abernethy's sermons and Hutcheson's works published by William Bruce. When Drennan senior's generation had passed on, the mantle of the intellectual leadership of Protestant Dissent devolved to England, to figures such as Dr Richard Price, Joseph Priestley and John Jebb.

Price, Priestley and Jebb were greatly admired by William Drennan and many Irish Protestant Dissenters, particularly the Non-subscribers. They were regarded by their contemporaries as Socinians. Because Unitarianism was illegal and because Socinian had become a pejorative term, Price, Priestley and Jebb described themselves as Rational Dissenters. On occasion, the Northern Dissenters wrote to Dr Price for advice on political matters. He advised the Belfast committee of the Volunteer movement in 1783 that they should seek to extend the franchise to 'Papists of Property' and argued that any danger from Catholics was more likely to be the result of alienating penal laws rather than religion.[2] We have seen previously that Price and Priestley had written in support of the American Revolution and been attacked savagely for their support for the French Revolution.

It may be presumed that, as the son of a clergyman, Drennan, when a child, was in the habit of attending Sunday services. In adulthood, he was asked to be an elder of the Newry congregation due to his punctual attendance at public worship there.[3] In his Dublin years, he served as an elder at Great Strand Street and took a deep interest in the affairs of the Presbyterian Synod.

His sister Martha was impressed when, in early 1796, she read Thomas Paine's *The Age of Reason*. She thought Paine 'a smart, impudent imposing writer who ought not to be despised'. Most of what Paine had said on the Old Testament had been Martha's thoughts in childhood and what he said 'on the *New* could not stagger any rational Christian'. Martha's use of the qualification 'rational' is important. *The Age of Reason*, most of which Paine 'had composed in the shadow of the guillotine in Paris in 1793 was a sustained invective against State religion and all forms of priest-craft'[4] and had indeed staggered many orthodox Christians. Many Roman Catholics and Anglicans were enraged but E.P. Thompson has observed that 'for all the brash provocations of its tone, Paine's work contained little that would have surprised the eighteenth-century Deist or advanced Unitarian'.[5]

Although impressed by Paine, Martha saw an opportunity for her brother to gain some public credit by publishing a response to him. She saw weaknesses in Paine's polemic particularly in relation to his dealing with the New Testament. 'He appeared to hurry over his subject as if predetermined to laugh at it rather than confute it.' She suggested to her brother that he could answer Paine 'well with wit and humour – the only way that would secure readers'. She had enlisted a Biblical scholar, Reverend William Bryson (1730–1815), who was prepared to help with dates, proof, authors etc. and though she invited her brother to laugh at her suggestion, she felt he 'could clear his character and do himself honor by enlisting early as the religious adversary of T[om] Paine'.[6]

Drennan said he would be glad to see what he called the Presbyterian Patriarchs[7] answer to Paine but he did not trouble his heart and his head much about the question. When he went into detail about his own religious sentiments, he was at least partly in sympathy with Paine:

> The Romish church are consistently politic in ... denouncing knowledge, and debate, and disquisition, for the restless power of reason once introduced brings in doubt and is apt to beget incredulity in the place of that serene and all confiding faith which makes everyone a Christian in the same degree, and thus preserves the unity and the peace of the church universal. Trust like a Papist for if you doubt as a dissenter the same restless faculty that rejects the Athanasian creed ... will begin to nibble at the incarnation, the miraculous conception etc., and thus Priestley lifts the latch for Paine to enter.

> I like the morality of the gospel so well that I have not the least occasion for the supplementary proof of miracle: perhaps the ignorant and stupid may be alarmed into belief and chilled into conviction, and for this purpose perhaps they were from time to time invented.[8]

For Drennan, miracle in the proper sense of the word was God contradicting himself and he agreed with Isaac Newton and Priestley after him, that it was 'necessary for the scythe of infidelity to clear off the weeds of superstition to prepare the soil for the growth of new Christianity'.[9] He thought his own sect of Protestant Dissenters was the best acquainted with the principles of religion but the Quakers were the best practitioners, in their simplicity, their fraternity, their equality and their charity to each other.

In 1799, Drennan made a comprehensive declaration of his beliefs in relation to the Christian religion as follows:

> It is a pure system of morality not beyond man to discover or enounce, not so much beyond man as the discoveries of Newton appear to be, particularly when very pure systems of morals had gone before in almost all nations and I believe Christianity properly called has scarcely appeared on this earth since the death of Christ, and that the very first and noblest principle of religion the unity of God, has been scarcely ever generally and never nationally acknowledged by Christians, though the foundation article of the Mahometan religion. I believe the priesthood in all ages has been the curse of Christianity, and I believe there will never be happiness or virtue on the face of the earth until that order of man be abolished and until there be a greater equality of property which may deliver the rich and the poor from the vices incident to their conditions.[10]

He had friends in the Presbyterian ministry but even they were not spared his strident anti-clericalism. Drennan was always opposed in principle to the *Regium Donum*, the royal bounty bestowed on the Presbyterian clergy by the government. He once described it as slow poison pouring into the Protestant Dissenting church. He told Martha:

> In our churches I always considered the increases of the *Regium Donum* as hush money, a bounty to be quiet and to have very tolerably answered its end. I think them [the Presbyterian clergy] nothing more or less than pensioners of government, these once formidable puritans in name and nature, these upright independents now depend and bow in exact ratio which the bounty bears to the sum of their income.[11]

In 1792, Reverend Robert Black of Derry came to Dublin seeking an increase in the payment. Drennan believed that if Black was successful, the Presbyterian religion would 'be contaminated by the corruption of our pastors'.[12] Black had been threatened with being tarred and feathered and accused of coming to Dublin 'to sell the Presbyterian clergy to the government for a pension, on condition of their repudiating the Catholics'.[13] Drennan felt that the clergy of the North might lose some of their influence 'by courting dependence on a rascally government'.[14]

In the aftermath of the 1798 Rebellion, Lord Castlereagh created a new *Regium Donum* scheme with three objectives. Firstly, he wished to reward, those who had committed themselves in support of the State against what he regarded as the democratic party within the Synod. He believed that many of those he deemed the democratic party 'if not involved in the rebellion were deeply infected with its principles'.[15] Secondly, he wished to create 'a considerable internal fermentation perhaps even a schism to change the temper of the Synod'. Finally, he wanted to buy and consolidate support for the Union amongst the Presbyterian clergy.[16]

Castlereagh believed that making 'the Presbyterian clergy less dependent on their congregations for their subsistence would make them better subjects than they have of late years proven themselves'.[17] His scheme involved different amounts being paid to differing classes of minsters depending on seniority or the size of their congregations. Drennan and some of the Presbyterian elders and clergy saw this as an attempt to create a dissenting hierarchy.[18] Martha agreed with her brother and she denounced the ministers who accepted the bounty as:

Fallen – fallen men – Yes they had a station, a high one for which it was necessary for government to overset them and a hundred a year has done it, without one honest soul daring to spurn the bribe. Neither they nor their families will be half so respectable nor do better than those of their cloth who, not having the third of the sum, could refuse assistance from the contentment produced by £50 at interest. All vanity, all desire of a good name, or the praise attending a disinterested action seems fled. How proudly I would have been the one to refuse this bounty.[19]

Castlereagh's allies in the Synod, Reverend Black and Reverend William Bruce, were non-subscribers from the same New Light tradition as Drennan. Both had been active in the Volunteers but both had opposed the United Irish society from the outset. Bruce and Drennan had been close friends but their friendship cooled somewhat, though it was not irrevocably fractured, over Bruce's denunciation of Drennan's United Irish test. When Drennan became aware of

Black's and Bruce's contacts with Castlereagh, he described Bruce as a presbyter bishop and said that Bruce and Castlereagh were 'walking hand in hand in a new alliance of church and state'.[20] He again invoked the names of the great stalwarts of non-subscription of an earlier generation:

> Is all this possible? And can the dissenters repair to their meeting house after such a business is completed ... Is it possible that any lay dissenter who preserves or is preserved in the salt of his sect can set his foot into a house corrupted with such a pensionary establishment? What would Abernethy, Duchal and Hutcheson have thought of their descendants? But it is a link in the chain of events which is tending to the abolition of such an order of men in the world. Infected, corrupted, papisticated, mankind will grow disgusted with their selfishness and hypocrisy, as they have already done on the continent, and the tyranny of the priesthood will no longer usurp the throne of God or stand between man and his maker.[21]

Martha heard reports that the laity and elders of the Synod were opposed to accepting Castlereagh's new scheme and had managed to get it rejected at the Synod. She urged her brother to write a pamphlet to rouse the Presbyterian laity 'into some sense of justice and honor' that they might make better provision for their 'ill-rewarded pastors'. Martha felt that some congregations had treated their ministers so poorly that some poor ministers felt compelled to accept Castlereagh's scheme. If the people did not reform the manner in which they treated their clergy, 'the dissenters would soon cease to be the respected and feared body, they had hitherto been'. She asked her brother to consider 'what pen would have a better chance of effecting this worthy purpose than Drennan's the acknowledged son of a preacher not yet forgot'.[22]

Drennan was not inclined to write on this subject because he felt 'that that order of men [the clergy]' were 'losing all hold of the people' and he therefore thought it 'improbable that their stipends would be raised by the people'. The *Regium Donum* would 'accelerate the beginning schism between laity and clergy'. He thought it probable that most lay dissenters would soon become Deists or Methodists and he imagined that Paine's *Age of Reason* had 'increased indifference to Christian instruction, and the neglect of Christian pastors'. There appeared to be an affinity between democratic and deistical doctrines but Drennan saw no solid foundation for this in reason. 'The life and doctrines of the unlettered prophet Christ are of a nature that I think would perfectly assimilate with the equality and fraternity of real republicans.'[23]

Drennan asserted that the priesthood in all ages was the curse of Christianity. There would be no virtue or happiness in the world until the priesthood was abolished. He believed he was living in an era where that order of men were losing influence. He had read Paine's *Age of Reason* and he accepted that Christian miracle stories had been invented to chill the ignorant and stupid into belief. Yet William Drennan remained a Protestant Dissenter and regarded himself as a Christian. However, his regular attendance at public worship did not protect him from charges of being a Deist or an infidel for, as he once told his sister, 'take notice an Unitarian and a Deist here [in Dublin] ranks as the selfsame character and if you deny the Trinity, you will be set down to deny there is a God'.[24]

Reverend Thomas Drennan had a significant lifelong influence over his son's religious principles. There is no earthly authority in religious matters and no man should suffer penalties for his religious opinions. These guiding principles led to William Drennan's activities within the United Irish movement. Drennan regarded the *Regium Donum* as an attempt by the State to wield influence and authority where it should have none.

4

THE VOLUNTEERS

In February 1778, as Drennan prepared for his graduation, he heard the news that France had recognised American independence and agreed to join the war against the British. Ireland and Britain were swept by fear of a French invasion. Drennan had mixed feelings about the unfolding events. He was delighted that Benjamin Franklin had been well received by the French and that, 'Persecuted Liberty has sought for and found refuge in the French and Spanish courts.'[1] Although he continued to support the Americans, 'he detested the Bourbon regimes of France and Spain.'[2] Determined to fight in the event of a French or Spanish invasion, he joined the militia. Along with six other Irish lads, he received training in musketry from the Sargent at Edinburgh castle.

He planned to return to Ireland after his graduation. When he heard that an Irish militia was forming there, he expressed a wish to have some rank in it. He was misinformed about the militia. The Irish administration could not afford to raise and equip a militia at this point.[3] Many of the regular troops who garrisoned Ireland had been sent off to fight the war in America. In response to the threat of invasion in many places around the country, independent companies of Volunteers were established. Ulster and Belfast took to volunteering with enthusiasm. In Belfast, on Saint Patrick's Day 1778, a corps was established which became known as the Blue Company because of the colour of their regimentals. The Blue Company publicly declared its refusal to accept commissions or pay under the Crown or to take any military oath.[4]

By April, 15,000 men had joined up nationally but as invasion fears heightened, the number of recruits rose exponentially and by mid-1780, some 60,000 had enrolled almost half of them in Ulster.[5] Sam McTier, Martha's husband, was elected as a commander in the Blue Company which Martha told her brother was 'very inconvenient because an expensive honour'.[6]

In August, Drennan took his degree and returned to Belfast. He immediately joined the Blue Company and from there began his keen interest in Volunteer politics.[7] Because his correspondence with his sister ceases at this point, we do not know much about his professional life in Belfast over the next four years. It appears that he found it difficult to establish a practice as the town was already well supplied with physicians. He had a significant involvement with a public health campaign in cooperation with the infirmary run by the Belfast Charitable Society.[8] In March 1782, he read a paper to the board of the Society suggesting that the Poor House premises be used for a smallpox inoculation campaign. He must have used a direct arm-to-arm infection technique as Edward Jenner did not propose inoculation using cow pox until 1798. The board of the society passed a vote of thanks to Drennan for his efforts.[9]

We do know from his correspondence with Reverend William Bruce in Dublin that, politics and Volunteering aside, he was not particularly happy either in his native town or his chosen profession.

> If I leave Belfast, I will never return to it. Do not mistake me I do not like this town. Why should I like what never has behaved as if it liked me? I have not a single friend except among my nearest relations. I have never received a smallest instance of real regard from the friends of my father. Who though they could have no reason to fear me as a rival or dislike me as a man have always been professional friends to me. I know that every profession has a certain portion of servility attached to it. But there is a parasitical species of servitude to men of eminence in our profession which I never will and never can conform to.[10]

Whatever about feelings of personal isolation and professional dissatisfaction, Drennan did find solace in his involvement with the Volunteers. He was not content with donning his blue uniform and attending marches, reviews and meetings. He was determined to establish himself as a leading writer in the Volunteer cause.

The year 1779 proved a very successful year for the Volunteers of Ireland. As the numbers in their ranks grew, they were thanked in the Irish House of Commons for their endeavours in defence of the country. Their crowning achievement that year was the concession by the British government of Free Trade for Ireland. Through their shows of military strength at rallies and marches, the Volunteers had pressured government into this concession. Edmund Burke (1730–1797), the Irish-born British parliamentarian, denounced Lord North for conceding Free Trade and this provided Drennan with the opportunity for his first foray into literary propaganda.

In April 1780, he published an open letter to Edmund Burke. He was embarking on what was to be a long literary career in which he would, time and again, use the device of writing to well-known public figures and publishing the letters as a way of propagating his radical ideas. In the years that followed, Drennan published letters to King George III, the Earl of Fitzwilliam, William Pitt and C.J. Fox. The purpose of these letters was not to communicate with the recipients but to influence reformist and radical opinion and to establish his literary reputation.

Burke had been a member of the British House of Commons since 1765. At this point, he was fifty years old and although not in ministerial office, he was one of Britain's most prominent statesmen. The letter was published at a time when, as one of Burke's recent biographers suggests, 'the conflict in the colonies was reaching the apogee of crisis, discontent in Ireland was contributing to popular militancy and public protest was affecting confidence in the British system of government'.[11]

Drennan was encouraged by the progress the Volunteers and reform movement was then making in Ireland. However, in his open letter, he condemned Burke because of the latter's hostile reaction to the positive developments in their native land. Burke had denounced recent British concessions on Irish trade as 'an unqualified surrender on the part of Lord North's government'.[12] John Bardon succinctly summarised the developments which so encouraged Drennan and alarmed Burke:

By November of 1799 the Government was helpless before menacing demonstrations of Volunteers, a vigorous campaign against British goods, and a united patriot majority. At the end of the year a beleaguered Tory ministry at Westminster reeling from news of disastrous defeat in America responded ... to appeals for immediate concessions. Laws imposed by England on Ireland forbidding the export of Irish wool, glass leather and other goods were removed.[13]

Drennan began his letter by accusing Burke of being 'too patriotic, in other words too much of an Englishman to wish for equality of rights and privileges in every part of the British empire'. He told Burke that his ill-timed and inconsiderate expressions were highly injurious to his native country.[14] He accused Burke of being a party man, 'The party may aim at nothing more than local or partial liberty, a liberty which includes not only the desire for a free government at home but the power of arbitrary rule over every country that might have the misfortune of being connected to Britain.'[15]

Drennan declared that there was now 'a revolution of opinion' in Ireland which he predicted would force the legislature of Britain 'ere long to perceive the necessity of getting clear of that wonderful paradox' which 'disenfranchises the descendants of Englishmen and robs them of their just interest in the legislative power'.[16] It was the common people of Ireland who were leading this revolution in public opinion. 'The lower ranks of the community [now has] an independence and republicanism of spirit which will have much influence on their future conduct; which will serve to remove that servile awe of estated tyrants which is incident in the lower orders of men; and will secure the free and unbiased election of the representative body.'[17]

Given what we know of Burke's attitude to the lower ranks of the community, Drennan's boast of the leading role of the lower orders in the agitation for reform would have horrified the honourable member for Bristol.[18] It must also have horrified many of Drennan's comrades in the Volunteer army who regarded themselves in Henry Grattan's famous phrase as 'the armed property of Ireland'. Drennan went on to suggest that Burke was among 'the men in high places of trust who repeatedly and publicly declare that all interference of the people in matters of legislation is libellous and leads to rebellion'.[19]

The Irish people would now do one of three things depending on how the Dublin Parliament behaved in this 'momentous season'. 'For the people would either guide themselves, or choose new leaders, or repose full confidence in the representative body.'[20] However, even if the Dublin Parliament 'proved sensible to the opinions of the people of Ireland in this crisis they, the people, would not trust all to their senate'.[21] No statement could have been more calculated to incense Burke. He never accepted that people had a right to choose new leaders or have any say in how they were governed. For Burke it was for King, Lords and Commons to rule and legislate and for people to obey and do as they were bid by their betters.

Perhaps Drennan was taunting Burke when he told him, 'The people have been the prime or rather the sole agents of "the revolution of – 80"'[22] which he declared was 'founded on a broad popular base. Necessity had been the stern rugged nurse' of Irish patriotism amongst the common people. 'It grew up in the cottage and the hovel amid sickness and sorrow. Its cradle was tended by famine and it listened to the bitter and unremitting cries of human misery.'[23]

Burke always had a horror of the common people whom he infamously referred to in his *Reflections on the Revolution in France* as 'the swinish multitudes'.[24] However, Drennan expressed enthusiasm for the revolutionary potential of the lower orders and clearly expressed sympathy for their suffering. In this, he was unique even amongst his fellow radicals. Most radicals and reformers sought political rights for the middle classes and the self-made men of trade and religious freedom for oppressed religious sects or confessions. They rarely, if ever, mentioned the conditions of the common people nor suggested reforms that would extend political rights to the poor. Drennan was to make the need to improve the miserable conditions of the lower ranks of people, and their right to involvement in politics and universal education, a consistent theme of his polemics for the rest of his life.

Burke would have agreed with Drennan's view of the short-sightedness of England's traditional approach to Irish trade. 'It is indeed full time that this great people should relinquish the mean and unenlightened jealousy of a petty shopkeeper and begin to display the amplitude of thought and mercantile sagacity, which can make not only the welfare of friends but even the prosperity of enemies, instruments for promoting its own opulence and grandeur.'[25]

They both would have accepted the thrust of David Hume's famous argument 'the increase of riches and commerce in any one nation, instead of hurting, commonly promotes the riches and commerce of all its neighbours'.[26] Burke had followed this contention in a speech he made on Irish trade two years earlier.[27]

There is some validity in Drennan's claim that Burke was behaving as a party man. Burke had criticised Lord North for conceding what he knew to be a laudable measure in Ireland. Yet he had consistently attacked North for relying on force and refusing concessions in America. There was, however, a far more deeply held concern behind Burke's negative reaction to North's concessions in Ireland.

The trade concessions had been made in the context of thousands of Volunteers in arms, some parading with cannons festooned with the slogan 'Free Trade or This'. To Burke, the Volunteers constituted an illegal military force.[28] He was dismayed by the potential for the Volunteers to provoke a popular insurgency, noting darkly that the troops were electing their own officers.[29] Burke believed that the principle of free trade should have been accepted by the British Parliament but that for the Irish to extract national benefits by the threat of military force was illiberal and potentially subversive to the constitution.[30]

The purpose of Drennan's letter was not to change Burke's mind but rather to urge his fellow Volunteers to greater efforts to build on their achievements.

He reminded them that they had joined the Volunteers 'with ardent zeal' in 1778 when 'the common danger united all ranks whom the feeling of a common country could not unite before'.[31] He hailed what he called 'that ever memorable institution' and claimed the Volunteers had 'Saved the island from invasions, secured domestic tranquillity, advanced civil liberty, laid the foundations of national independence ... taught the administration a lesson ... [and achieved] everything great and good, everything auspicious to the hopes, most connected to the best interests of the country.'[32]

Drennan next informed Burke that the rise of the Volunteers had led to a change of opinion in Ireland and that political independence was now the aim of the kingdom. There were four different means according to Drennan which the country relied upon for obtaining this great end. These were the benevolence of the sovereign, the policy of the British legislature, the wisdom of parliament and the spirit of the people. Burke was utterly opposed to any extension of independence to Ireland. However, he could have no argument that the first three means for achieving political change were unconstitutional. Drennan's suggestion that the spirit of the people could be relied upon was an entirely different matter.

What Ireland was demanding was nothing less than 'the repeal of that odious statute the Sixth of George I relative to Ireland'.[33] This was the Declaratory Act of 1720 which established the legislative subordination of Ireland.[34] Drennan finished his letter with a flourish, suggesting that 'Ireland will no longer sit at the gate in wretched apparel but will take her place amongst the mighty of the earth.'[35]

Burke was appalled when, less than two years later in 1782, Drennan's prediction came to pass and the Declaratory Act was repealed. Burke believed that the measure threatened to 'tear asunder the connection between England and Ireland'.[36] He had no desire to see the Irish legislative process separated from British parliamentary proceedings.[37]

An Address to the Volunteers of Ireland

It is not clear what effect the *Letter to Burke* had on Drennan's literary reputation. It was printed in Dublin and, presumably, circulated to Volunteer corps around the country. He did not sign his name to the first edition but he had clearly enjoyed seeing his work in print. In early 1781, his next epistle appeared. This was entitled *An Address to the Volunteers of Ireland by the Author of the Letter to Edmund Burke Esquire containing Reflections on Patriotism, Party Spirit and the*

Union of Free Nations. It would appear from this choice of title that his *Letter to Burke* might have had some impact on the reading public.

The aim of the *Address* was to focus the Volunteers on the next phase of the struggle. He began by telling them that they 'deserved well of their country' but went on to say that 'the virtue that has done much brings on itself [the obligation] to do more and much more is there to do. The liberty of Ireland is as yet eventual'.[38] He continued by asserting that 'liberty depends on power and that it is union that gives that power'.[39] Drennan was aware that there were different attitudes to the American war amongst the Volunteers. While he and many in Belfast and Ulster were strong supporters of the Americans, other Volunteers had joined up to defend Ireland against America's European allies. He therefore suggested, in the interest of unity, that the Volunteers drop all discussion about America.[40]

He stressed the importance of perseverance and proclaimed that 'if Ireland has not the perseverance sufficient to wrestle for a few years for a free constitution she does not deserve a free constitution'. Once more Drennan tried to finish on a high note, by declaring. 'Forward armed countrymen – Forward – Be cool and confident, silent and determined, patient and persevering. Blend the prudence and foresight of a citizen with the spirit and sinew of a soldier. Watch your enemies and your friends. Trust only to yourselves.'[41]

The most significant aspect of Drennan's second venture into print, was that he suggested that the Volunteers should adopt a test. He took it upon himself to draft what he regarded as a suitable text:

I, A. B. Citizen and Volunteer in the presence of my fellow countrymen, declare my loyalty to the King, my love to my country my obedience to its laws. I am ready to defend my country from foreign and domestic enemies. I declare, and will when called upon with my life and fortune that the right of the Kingdom of Ireland is to be free. I maintain that to be free is to have the power of making our own laws. I maintain that the power of making laws for Ireland assumed by Great Britain is not a rightful power and ought to be renounced by every Irishman. I will also be obedient to all lawful commands of my officers.[42]

He suggested that this test should be taken annually at a public ceremony. It is not clear if any attention was paid to this test or whether he or anyone else in the Blue Company took it. Even at this relatively early stage of his political involvement, he believed that committing oneself in ceremonial fashion to a set of objectives was an effective way to foster unity of purpose and fellowship amongst comrades. Later, Drennan would compose the United Irish test and vigorously defend it when it was attacked by his friend William Bruce. Drennan took immense pride in his authorship of the United Irish test and took many opportunities to quote it verbatim in his later written work. He was still publicly claiming credit for it years after the organisation for which it had been drafted had been destroyed by torture, suppression, massacre and executions.

Drennan's correspondence with William Bruce gives us insights into the many controversies which arose within the Volunteer movement in those early years. One controversy which caused Drennan some personal disquiet arose from the government decision to raise Fencible regiments to defend the country against invasion. It was hoped that these regiments would be used to fill the place of the regulars serving in America. They would not be required to serve overseas. Lord Portland's plan was to use the fencibles as a way of weakening the Volunteers or at least bringing some of them under military discipline.[43] Most volunteers saw through the plan and one newspaper suggested the scheme was one of 'the deepest strokes against the power and consequence of the Volunteer army of Ireland'.[44] For his part, Drennan 'beheld the scheme of fencibles with detestation' and was greatly concerned that it might succeed.[45]

The problem for Drennan was that his brother-in-law, Sam, had been reduced to penury after a fire at his tan-yard premises in Belfast. He announced his intention to accept a commission in the fencibles. Several Volunteer corps, including the Blue Company, passed resolutions rejecting the government's fencible plans. One resolution declared that 'we consider any volunteer who shall accept a commission in any regiment of Fencibles to be raised in Ireland justly entitled to our severest censure'.[46] This led to an acrimonious debate in which Sam found himself isolated within the Company. He resigned his position in the Volunteers and as the government soon dropped its fencible plan, he ended up with the worst of both worlds.

Drennan was fortunate that he was absent from Belfast when this dispute arose. He had taken Martha to Scotland to consult with his former teacher, Professor Cullen, regarding Martha's poor health. In fact, her condition had improved on the journey over and the professor diagnosed a nervous complaint which would respond well to exercise and a change of air.[47] Martha was hurt when she heard from Sam that he was no longer a Volunteer. Yet her support for her beloved husband appeared to be somewhat qualified when she told him:

I am perfectly assured that in such a case you would consider and act right, but be cautious of throwing blame on the company, though you are right it does not prove them wrong. If they are in error, it is an excusable one and what I am inclined more to admire than condemn – perhaps their country may yet thank them for it. I cannot blame them in regard to the Fencibles – although I would never blush for you being one.[48]

Drennan's sojourn in Scotland made it possible for him to avoid having either to support or oppose Sam, though he was secretly in sympathy with the majority. He believed that Sam should have resigned from the Volunteers once he had decided to seek the commission in the fencibles.

There was another controversy which shook the unity of the Volunteers and did much damage at this crucial time. A very successful convention of the Ulster Volunteers held in Dungannon in February 1782 passed a number of pro-reform resolutions, including one strongly condemning 'the legislation for Ireland by any body but the King Lords and Commons thereof'.[49] Over the next couple of months, many Volunteer corps throughout the country threw their weight behind the Dungannon resolutions. The American war was going badly for the British and Lord North's administration fell in March. Henry Grattan, a leader of the opposition in the Irish House of Commons, who had secretly helped to draft the Dungannon resolutions, was hailed as the hero of the hour when the British were compelled to concede repeal of the Declaratory Act in May 1782.

Henry Flood, Grattan's opposition rival, very quickly declared that Grattan's triumph was illusory and what was required was for Britain to renounce forever the power to legislate for Ireland. This was to be the cause of division that side-tracked the Volunteers in a crucial year. Most of the Belfast Volunteers supported Flood but Drennan did not trust his motives. He told Bruce: 'Mr. Flood has certainly gained many converts in this county-amongst the rest Dr Haliday is rather on his side. Bryson the only man in the Company against him except W. Cunningham – I humbly conceive Flood uses his great abilities at present for the worst of all purposes, yet his argument is a strong one.'[50]

Drennan could see that even if Flood's 'strong argument' was accepted, he would hardly be successful when demanding Great Britain concede something 'we forgot to ask for at our last meeting together and before we sign and seal you must give us something more'.[51] Drennan felt that the dispute about repeal or renunciation was pointless and purely verbal. He could not vote for either Grattan or Flood without reproach to his heart.[52] Much more fundamentally, he was concerned that this dispute was diverting attention away from what, for Drennan, was the most important task for the Volunteers. In his view, that task was now to secure a more equal representation of the people in parliament. In June, Sir Edward Newenham gave notice in Parliament of his intention to move a bill to increase the weight of city and county representation in parliament.[53] Drennan believed that the repeal renunciation dispute was sapping the energies that should have been supporting Newenham. 'Let them all talk but I believe Newenham's Bill for adequate representation of the people is of more importance than the question that is agitating the mind of the public – yet it is scarce heard of and without the backing of the people it can never prevail.'[54]

One of the driving forces behind the Dungannon Convention and, by extension, the key figure behind Grattan's success with the Declaratory Act was Francis Dobbs (1750–1811). Dobbs was a barrister possessed of great organising skills. He now attempted to combat Flood by organising a second Dungannon Convention on 21 June, at which he succeeded in getting the Volunteers approval for Grattan's settlement.[55] He had himself represented the Belfast Volunteers at the convention and some of them demanded an explanation about why he had cast their vote without referring to them for a mandate.

Dobbs was summoned to Belfast to answer for his conduct. The Blue Company met in the Market House and Dobbs was asked to account for himself. His long-winded attempt to vindicate his action did not impress the meeting. Drennan described his rambling defence as: 'A most verbose oration that lasted nearly an hour, touched upon every point that lay in the whole compass of Irish politics, contained his conferences with every minister in the Cabinet, their opinions, his opinions, plentiful abuse of Flood, plentiful praise of Grattan and Charlemont, and plentiful paucity of argument.'[56]

Dobbs' performance succeeded only in further infuriating the angry Volunteers. He withdrew to the New Inn while the Company considered a motion of censure. Drennan moved the motion and it was carried unanimously. However, he was 'astonished at the unjustifiable and excessive punishment aimed' at Dobbs and believed some of it was 'motivated by personal pique and animosity'. He therefore proposed, as Dobbs had admitted his error, that while the censure should stand, it should not be published in the press. When this was carried by a margin of forty-three to thirty-three, the minority withdrew 'in paroxysms of rage'. They left the meeting and went to join a crowd who were already besieging the New Inn. Some of the crowd cried out 'Let us see him, the villain has sold his country.' Drennan and his friends rushed to the New Inn to protect Dobbs. He told William Bruce: 'I saw and I know this man is singled out as an object for vengeance. He is weak, vain [but] honest ... I would never wish to countenance private pique in its extremity of wrath against a sinking man. It is ungenerous. It is cruel.'[57]

5

IF YOU SLEEP YOU DIE!

In December 1782, Drennan moved to Newry and set up in medical practice. He hoped to take advantage of the fact that Dr James Moody, one of the local physicians, had moved to Dublin and Drennan anticipated that he might be able to attract the custom of Moody's former patients. He arrived in Newry with letters of introduction to a dozen principal inhabitants of the town. He took 'genteel, commodious lodgings at Mrs. Maxwell's in Market Street'. He soon made friends with the departing doctor's brother, Reverend Boyle Moody (1752–1799), the local non-subscribing minister.[1] He told William Bruce: 'I consider myself as very happy in acquaintance or rather intimacy with Boyle Moody – he is one of those agreeable, lively well-informed men with whom it is always a pleasure to be connected particularly in a county town where the seeds of rational society are but thinly scattered.'[2]

Boyle Moody and his older brother, the Reverend John Moody, a Minister at Strand Street, Dublin, had both been educated at Dr Joseph Priestley's Warrington Academy. William Bruce, who was at this time working as assistant minister to John Moody at Strand Street, had also been educated at Warrington. Drennan admired Boyle's singing voice and his preaching ability. A few months later, when Sam McTier had occasion to meet Boyle Moody, he formed a somewhat different view of Drennan's new friend. After Sam had spent an evening drinking with him in the tavern, he described Moody as, 'a very great coxcomb and an empty fellow', who did not 'live as a clergyman ought'.[3] Empty fellow or not, Boyle Moody had been an active member of the Volunteers and later the Society of United Irishmen. He was imprisoned during the 1798 Rebellion and died the following year from a fever contracted in prison. A Dr Campbell quotes a letter dated 1800, which goes some way towards explaining the reason for the arrest and subsequent death of Boyle Moody. 'His crime was his profession, his liberal principles, his avowed friendship with the Catholics, nothing else is alleged.'[4] The Non-subscribing Presbyterian congregation at

Newry still exists and they display a plaque which, while it acknowledges Boyle Moody's service as its minister from 1779 until 1799, makes no mention of why or how his ministry came to an abrupt end.

Other than Boyle Moody, Drennan found the young men of the town genteel and dressy, not much cultivated by education but very civil and obliging to himself. The young women Drennan encountered were 'not much inferior to those in Belfast. They were exceedingly affable and conversable, and he was sure all of them improvable on acquaintance.'[5]

Fortunately, Drennan's and Martha's correspondence resumes at this point. She kept her brother 'Will' informed of the fluctuations in her precarious state of health. She constantly reassures him that all the reports of his progress in Newry reaching Belfast are positive. For his part, Drennan kept Martha appraised of his efforts to court the acquaintance of those local families whom he hoped might employ him as their physician. Martha told him of his family's efforts to ensure that he would have a wardrobe suitable for a respectable young Doctor of Medicine. His sister Nancy had taken his Volunteer coat to the tailor to have the gold braid removed and new lining and lapels sewn on. However, the tailor must have been a Volunteer, for 'he refused to perform this [sacrilegious] operation.'[6]

It is perhaps not surprising that one of the established local medical doctors, John Templeton, did not welcome Drennan to town and maintained a hostile attitude towards him. This hostility resulted in a very unpleasant stand-off between them, when Drennan was called to the sick bed of an elderly gentleman, a Mr Montgomery, one of Templeton's patients. Usually in such a situation, doctors would be expected to consult each other in terms of comparing opinions and ensuring prescriptions and treatments were compatible. This Templeton resolutely refused to do.

Montgomery died and it is far from clear whether Drennan was appalled or amused by how the burial of the deceased was conducted. He told Martha:

> I attended Mr. Montgomery's public funeral and walked before the rest in a very disagreeable procession, preceded only by a ragged beggar-looking fellow who kept jingling a little bell in his hand as if to appraise the whole town that the deceased and the doctor were just a coming. This is a constant ceremonial in funeral solemnities in this place, and not satisfied with this, there is always one of these bell ringers informing everyone by their papistical bell, who had died and what hour and when he is to be interred. I observe that these fellows always pull off their hats most respectfully on

meeting me in the street, as if certain of my being a future friend of theirs, and looking upon themselves as acting pretty much in the same vocation.[7]

About this time, William Bruce informed Drennan that Dr Priestley's dissenting academy at Warrington had closed for want of pupils. Drennan suggested to Bruce that this provided an opportunity to draw up a plan to open such an academy in Belfast. Nothing came of this at the time but obviously the idea stayed with Drennan for a very long time. Over thirty years later, Drennan succeeded in opening the Belfast Academical Institution and ironically, one of the most vehement opponents of the project would be William Bruce.

Martha was ambitious for her brother and often urged him to resume his political writings with a view to enhancing his public reputation. Her aspiration was that one day he might be a Member of Parliament and she looked forward to him being referred to as 'Sir W[illiam] D[rennan]'. He considered a writing comeback in 1783 when he witnessed a massive increase in emigration, which apparently resulted from the end of the war in America, coupled with the effects of a major economic downturn. He considered writing a series of open letters to Lord Charlemont, 'on the questions of emigration, Volunteering etc'. He was preoccupied with his medical duties at this point and suggested that if he was to resume political writing, he would confine himself to short pieces. He felt that, 'a natural interruption of letters might give relief to the reader who has not even the patience to finish a sixpenny pamphlet and assist the writer when he became tired of his subject or his subject tired of him'.[8]

He sent a draft paper to Martha but she was not impressed. She felt it lacked design and it was not clear in its conclusions and she felt that Drennan was arguing against his own feelings. Nor did Martha feel it was a 'fit' subject for a patriot and suggested he should find another topic. If, and when, he should find such a suitable subject, he should attach a flattering introduction to Lord Charlemont. She strongly advised him not to claim authorship at first. Rather, he should wait till the work gained recognition and then claim it. The heavy workload in his medical practice prevented him from acting on her suggestions at the time.

An unforeseen circumstance not only delayed his return to writing but nearly terminated his writing career and his life. He was suddenly stricken with a serious illness which he was fortunate to survive. It would be more than a year later, when he had fully recovered his health, that he had found his 'fit' subject to resume his writing. He then employed his 'natural interruption of letters' formula and Martha's concealed authorship stratagem, for the new work. He sent seven relatively short letters anonymously to the *Belfast Newsletter*, which he later published as a pamphlet under his own name. The title of the pamphlet was *Letters of Orellana, an Irish Helot*, the work that was to establish his national reputation.[9]

Although Will and Martha both often expressed worry about their respective poor health, it was Martha's ongoing illness which caused them both the most concern. In May 1783, Martha and Nancy stopped at Newry on their way to Bristol via Dublin. They hoped the change of air and the spa waters of Bristol might be beneficial to them. After a pleasant stopover at Drennan's lodgings, the sisters endured a most unpleasant coach journey on the road to Dublin. They arrived, 'sick, sore, crammed and sorry at the Man of War Inn', fifteen miles north of Dublin city. They both felt so miserable that they quit the coach and spent the night at the Man o'War. The following day they made their way to Dublin where they were warmly received by William Bruce's family. They were frustrated by having to delay in Dublin awaiting the departure of their ship but enjoyed their time with the Bruces. When they finally embarked on 2 June, they were accompanied by William Bruce's brother, Sam.[10]

In Belfast three days later, on Thursday 5 June, Anne Drennan received a letter from Newry pressing her to come immediately, as her son was dangerously ill with a fever. At three o'clock, within an hour of receiving the summons, she and Sam McTier set out on the road, reaching Newry after midnight. The next morning, they found Will in a terrible condition in the seventh day of his fever. They greatly feared for his life. They nursed him through several nights as his condition continued to worsen. Sam described to Martha how very ill her brother was, on the Sunday following their arrival:

> What a melancholy object poor Will is this day, shouting with pain and trembling so that in the drawing room I hear his teeth gnashing together. We have a nurse keeper to assist us, George [Will's man servant] and I can do no longer without one, and your mother is so affected she is of little use. He purges greatly without being sensible to it. We have terrible work watching and cleaning him, not the smallest trifle can he do for himself, even when we lift him to the close stool George or I were obliged to wipe for him.[11]

Eventually the crisis passed and Drennan began a slow recovery and to regain his strength. Dr Haliday had warned Sam that the patient would continue to rave a little until he was fully recovered. Will at first proved troublesome and cross, accusing Sam of trying to starve him when he discouraged him from eating solid food before he was ready. Sam and Mrs Drennan stayed in Newry until early July. Just before they set off for Belfast, Mrs Drennan wrote to Martha enclosing a short note she had encouraged Will to write. He told his sister:

> My mother has asked me to add a few lines if I am able. I am just newly arisen from the dead after an interment (for such surely is a gloomy bed surrounded by three physicians, a surgeon, an apothecary and two nurses) which has lasted no less than five weeks on Saturday. I am gathering strength daily and my head is grown more clear and serene.[12]

Sam and Dr Haliday could see some silver lining in the cloud of Drennan's suffering. Sam had no doubt that 'the attack would add vigour to his constitution that before it was a stranger to' and that he would possibly be stronger than ever. Dr Haliday observed that 'it was worth Will's while to have fever for the sake of those unaffected testimonies of regard his situation drew from the good people both in Newry and Belfast'.[13]

When Mrs Drennan and Sam were leaving Newry, there was heavy election canvassing going on in relation to filling two seats in the House for County Down. The mobs were gathering each night but the quarrelling and breaking of heads (which Sam liked), was yet to begin.[14] The contest was a three-cornered fight, involving Edward Ward, son of Lord Bangor, and the two sitting MPs, Robert Stewart of Mount Stewart, supported by the Whigs and dissenters, and Lord Kilwarlin, son of the Earl of Hillsborough, supported by the High Church interest and the Tories.[15]

When fully recovered from his illness, Drennan wrote some squibs and letters to the freeholders of County Down in support of Stewart. As well as his political commitment to the independent interest, Sam was hoping for employment through the patronage of Stewart. He arranged to have Drennan's letters printed in Belfast and worked hard in Downpatrick as Stewart's election agent.

To preserve anonymity, Drennan signed himself 'Sidney', after Algernon Sidney the republican theorist and Whig martyr. Martha reported that Sidney's letters were much admired in Belfast but many thought William Bruce was the author.[16] Others were touting the names of Crombie and Haliday as Sidney's identity. The dilemma Drennan now found himself in was one which was to dog him throughout his writing career. He felt he needed to balance his desire for literary fame as a radical propagandist with his anxiety not to alienate and lose the custom of his more conservative patients. He told Martha, 'it might perhaps be of service to me to be known as the author by the Stewart party here but would not at all with the other. They are indeed so unconnected with each other that the one would scarcely know anything that the other did'.[17]

The latter remark shows how polarised politics were amongst well-to-do Protestants, even in a relatively small town like Newry. Martha warned him not to reveal himself as Sidney for, in her view, 'Newry or its people are not to be trusted.'[18]

Stewart ran a very lacklustre and disorganised campaign. Martha, William and their friends, who were Stewart's natural supporters, were appalled when, after promising to stay independent, he tried to do a deal and made commitments to Lord Kilwarlin. Martha regarded those commitments as 'full of madness and folly' and she believed that he had no right to give them. Stewart's conduct was such that Martha felt he deserved to lose the election.[19]

Drennan was also disgusted at Stewart's behaviour:

I sicken at the Down elections. I like none of the candidates. Stewart as little as any. Had it not been for his nauseous neutrality which is not to be forgiven he and Ward, I believe would have had the country. I don't believe he regards the independent interest a fig and his whole ambition was to please both parties and to be returned by both. He has nearly met with his merited punishment.[20]

In the event, Kilwarlin and Ward defeated Stewart and Sam was left disappointed and unemployed but not greatly surprised.

While sister and brother shared their dismay regarding the conduct of the Down election, Martha reported on what she felt were more interesting political goings on in Belfast. In preparation for yet another Volunteer convention in Dungannon, a committee was sitting to consider appropriate resolutions that might form the subject for deliberation at the forthcoming convention. Letters were sent to prominent reformers both at home and abroad. Amongst those whose advice was sought were the Duke of Richmond, Dr Price, Dr John Jebb and Christopher Wyvill in Britain, Dr Franklin and Abbé Raynal in Paris and Charlemont, Flood and Grattan in Ireland. Martha thought the responses of Richmond and Dr Price were very satisfactory and useful. They had not heard from Paris by the time she reported but she felt that the Irish responses were poor, trifling, polite, short and unsatisfactory.[21]

The reason the Irish responses were so cool was because Charlemont and Grattan had no enthusiasm for further political involvement of the Volunteers. Flood was anxious to keep the Volunteers onside as part of his rivalry with Grattan but he had never been a supporter of reform or broadening the franchise, much less the extension of political rights to Roman Catholics. The third Dungannon Convention was held on 8 September and 272 corps attended, as did fifteen MPs. Charlemont and Grattan stayed away. Flood started out for Dungannon but never made it due to an attack of gout. In the event, the Convention 'achieved little beyond issuing the summons for a National Reform Convention in Dublin for 10th November'.[22]

In November, the National Reform Convention of the Volunteers met in the Exchange Rooms in Dublin but, because of the large attendance, it had to move to the much larger venue at the Rotunda. The earlier successful convention in Dungannon in 1782 ended in one day, having agreed several resolutions and a way forward. The Dublin Convention ran for three weeks with no such positive outcome. Many factors contributed to making this a chaotic and confused failure. Grattan was not prepared to help on this occasion as he now wanted the Volunteers to leave politics to the parliamentarians. Charlemont and his allies attended the Convention only to ensure that Frederick Hervey, the Bishop of Derry, who they regarded as an extremist and a maverick, should not unduly influence the proceedings. The bishop was an unequivocal supporter of Catholic rights. The government took the precaution of having several of its friends, including the staunch Protestant George Ogle, attend with a view to sowing division, particularly on the Catholic question.[23] One of Ogle's spoiling tactics was to mislead the Convention by stating falsely that the Catholic leadership had told him they were not seeking any relief of grievances at this time.

The Bishop of Derry tried to keep the rights of Catholics to the forefront but he was frustrated by the Charlemont moderates and the Ogle spoilers, and it looked like the Convention might have to adjourn having agreed to nothing. In desperation, the Bishop suggested that Henry Flood, who had stayed away from the Convention, should be called in to help mediate an agreed programme. Flood duly arrived and saved the day by convincing the Convention to adopt a superficial reform programme that said nothing about the Catholic question. Charlemont was hoping that Flood's programme would be referred back to the country which could then petition parliament through constitutionally convened county meetings.[24] However, Flood suggested that he and another MP, William Brownlow, would go straight over to the House of Commons and present the programme in the form of a Bill.

When Flood stood up in the House to introduce his Bill wearing his Volunteer uniform, he gave the government just the opportunity they were waiting for. The Attorney General set the tone for the government response by declaring, 'I do not intend to go into discussion of this Bill ... if it originates with an armed body 'tis inconsistent with the freedom of debate for this House to receive it. We sit here not to register the edicts of another assembly, or to receive propositions at the point of a bayonet.'[25]

When Flood reported back to the Convention, the more radical element within it wanted to denounce the House of Commons. Charlemont managed to convince the majority that the Convention should adjourn and refer the reform programme to the county committees. The Volunteer movement never recovered from the fiasco that was the Dublin National Reform Convention of 1783.

Drennan did not attend the Convention but he was apparently given a comprehensive report on the proceedings from William Bruce. No record of Bruce's report seems to have survived but Drennan's trenchant reaction prefigures differences that would later emerge between his radicalism and Bruce's moderation. Drennan told Bruce:

You have been wise dearest friend, very wise and you admire Flood because you are a transcript, not a faint one, of his prudence and wisdom but I almost fear to say it – times of reformation require impetuosity of spirit. Our religious reformation required such a man as Luther. Flood is too wise, to cool, perhaps too selfish to be a Luther in civil reform.

I was going to say that your assembly would have been less wise by adopting the passions as well as the reason that characterize every popular assembly but perhaps more successful than it has been as Mr. Flood's convention. – I am presumptuous in saying so to anyone but a friend – It is the people which government fear – the rude illiterate voice of the people not Mr. Flood. You have not represented the people.

When Mr. Flood said 'stay here in solemn convention until I return from Parliament' was there not one high sounding enthusiastic voice to cry aloud 'and why not go along with you – let us in the name of the just God – Let us the delegates of the people go up to the House of the People – Let us go up in slow and peaceable procession, and let the acclaim of the surrounding multitude re-echo the justice of our cause and their cause in the ears of our enemies – Let us march unarmed but undaunted into that House which is our own and in awful and terrible silence wait until the voice of the People and the voice of God was uttered by that man and then with a shout that would reverberate thru' those polluted walls call upon them to give us our rights – I am sometime so enthusiastic as to think that more might have been obtained by some showy method as this without losing one drop of blood. We are the slaves of our eyes and our ears – The hearts of the ministers would have withered within them and 60,000 Volunteers would not have been insulted by quondam usher of a boarding school.'[26]

The final barb was directed at Barry Yelverton the Attorney General who had once been an assistant master at the Hibernian Academy.

Just how much damage had been done to the morale and status of the Volunteer movement by the debacle that was the National Reform Convention of 1783 became all too apparent a year later when yet another Volunteer Convention gathered in the Exchange Rooms, Dublin, on 25 October 1784. There was no need to adjourn to a bigger venue on this occasion. There were only thirty-six delegates present. Just fourteen counties and eight towns were represented. Even more indicative of decline was the lack of interest from Ulster. Only two counties, Antrim and Donegal, and two towns, Belfast and Lisburn, sent delegates. The small delegation from Ulster included 'Rev. Sinclair Kelburn of the Belfast Third Congregation, Rev. William Bruce of Lisburn and William Drennan'.[27] The best this meeting could rise to was to adjourn until January 1785 and circulate resolutions urging those counties who had not nominated delegates to do so for the next meeting.

Immediately on returning to Newry, Drennan put pen to paper. During November and December, a series of letters appeared in the *Belfast Newsletter* signed 'Orellana an Irish Helot'. Later, Drennan published the collection as a pamphlet. Even in an era when pamphleteers were not shy about loquacious titles, Drennan's title was as enigmatic as it was long-winded. The title he chose was: *Letters of Orellana, an Irish Helot, to the seven northern counties not represented in the National Assembly of Delegates, held in Dublin, 1784, for obtaining a more equal representation of the people in the Parliament of Ireland.*

One plausible explanation for *Orellana* has been posited by A.T.Q. Stewart. He suggests that it represented a play on the title of a book that Drennan would have read and admired. This book was *Oroonoka: The Royal Slave* by Aphra Behn. Stewart tells us:

In eighteenth century atlases, the river which we now call the Amazon was marked as the Orellana ... thus, the two great rivers of South America were the Orellana and the Orinoco. In Mrs. Behn's novel (published in 1678) Oroonoka was the grandson of an African king, captured by the master of an English trading vessel and carried off to Surinam ... There he stirs up the other slaves to revolt and escape from their miserable condition. The novel is remarkable as the first expression in English literature of sympathy for the oppressed negroes.[28]

The use of the term 'helot' had been described as 'nicely provocative', because in ancient Sparta, helots were state slaves who could neither be sold or set free. Kenneth R. Johnson tells us 'As the helot population outnumbered the Spartans by more than ten to one, the government lived in fear of a helot revolt so much so that each new magistrate opened his term by formally declaring war on them, which allowed them to be summarily executed in case of any disturbance.'[29]

Drennan's objective in *Orellana* was to encourage, to provoke and to shame the seven Northern counties who had stayed away from the recent convention in Dublin to attend the next meeting scheduled for 20 January 1785 and to reassert their demands for reform of Parliament. Drennan addressed his readers as 'fellow slaves'. He blesses his God because he is sensible to his own condition of slavery, for he says 'bondage must be felt before the chains can be broken'.[30] 'Every nation under the sun must be placed in one of two conditions. It must be free or enslaved.' The first letter ends with the slogan, 'Awake, arise for if you sleep you die!' All seven letters carry a similar message that if a people wishes to be free, it must show that it is determined not only to gain freedom but to maintain that freedom when achieved. However, the letters are not without self-contradiction. One stark example of this is the treatment of the issue of the political rights of Roman Catholics. At one point Drennan calls for unity across the confessional divide and an end to religious animosity: 'I call upon you Churchmen [Anglicans], Presbyterians, and Catholics to embrace each other in the mild spirit of Christianity and to unity as a secret compact in the cause of your sinking country – For you are all Irishmen.'[31]

Yet in his fifth letter, he states that 'the Catholics of this day are absolutely incapable of making a good use of political liberty'. He goes on to state, almost in the fashion of George Ogle, that the most enlightened amongst the Catholics 'are too wise to wish for a complete extension of civil franchise to those of their own persuasion'. He is not suggesting that Catholics should be forever denied political rights, rather that 'it must require the process of time to enlarge their minds and meliorate their hearts into the capability of enjoying the blessing of liberty'.[32]

Michael Brown is correct to identify this argument as a trope of the Scottish Enlightenment, that only involvement in commercial society fits people for democratic government.[33] However, Brown's suggestion, that Drennan's analysis amounts to 'a static rendition of Catholic history',[34] is hard to accept. Drennan's suggestion that, in time, Catholics will be capable of enjoying the blessings of freedom hardly amounts to a static rendition of history. Brown's assessment of *Orellana* is that Drennan is guilty of conceptional confusion and contradiction. His summation of the reasons for this is convincing. 'Such contradictions were necessary in covering over the cracks in the coherence of Drennan's argument. He was struggling to hold together a Volunteer movement which was made up of a disparate alliance of interests.'[35] Drennan knew that the movement could split on the Catholic question. He knew also that many Irish Protestants did not share the radicalism or liberalism of the advanced Presbyterians and that his own views on the constitution and the American war were not shared by at least some of his fellow Volunteers.

Drennan was not engaged in writing a coherent work of political philosophy. He was engaged in producing literary propaganda which had a primary and a secondary objective. He was prepared to use any argument, regardless of inconsistency, which he thought might appeal to his politically heterodox target audience. He admitted that some of *Orellana* was a rant but he felt justified that a writer should 'suit oneself to the temper of the readers'.[36] The primary objective was to encourage a good Northern response to the January 1785 meeting. His secondary object was to enhance his reputation as a political writer. He was remarkably successful in relation to both objectives. When it became apparent that attendance at the convention was going to be full and respectable, his family friend Dr Haliday said the success was fully owing to the *Irish Helot*. When the Convention met, there were twenty-seven counties and thirteen towns represented at the meeting held on 20 January and all nine Ulster counties were represented.[37]

In relation to his literary reputation, he was prepared to hasten slowly and he heeded Martha's earlier advice about claiming his work only after it had gained recognition. In fact, he did not even tell Martha that he was the 'Helot'. When she became aware he was the author, she assured him the letters were well-received in Belfast but she expressed her disappointment, perhaps because he had not been direct or hard hitting enough. She seems to have been disappointed that he did not call for the withdrawal from Parliament of those politicians who were supported by the Volunteers. Martha told him:

> They [the letters] were read with eagerness and pleasure and more than your partial sister were disappointed by the last newspaper. I did suppose that by the great care you had taken not to be known, even by me, that something was yet to appear to make this great caution necessary – an address perhaps to some well-known character a call upon Lord C[harlemont], Flood, or the benumbed Robert Stewart to speak to the people and direct them out of the House.[38]

Martha went on to suggest that if he wanted to be known, 'now was the time to reap any benefit from the discovery which may be made by a single whisper'.[39] Drennan was not at all concerned by Martha's criticism because his work was being praised by many, including the Bishop of Dromore. The Constitutional Society of Dublin had resolved to reprint it. He could also see that his work had a positive effect in Newry, where over sixty people signed the requisition for a meeting with a view to selecting delegates for the Convention. As he still wished to keep the custom of his more conservative patients, he was pleased that he was scarcely known as the Helot in Newry. However, his desire for public recognition eventually won out and he permitted the editor of the *Newsletter* to disclose the author's identity.

Drennan's ambivalence in relation to the question of the political rights of Catholics arose from the conflict within himself as well as a desire to please both the liberal and conservative Protestants within the Volunteers. He had been educated in the stadial theories of the Scottish Enlightenment which held that involvement in commercial activity made men fit for political liberty. He believed that without education and without the guidance of an enlightened middle class, the lower orders would be prone to, at best, manipulation by their landlords and priests and, at worst, might descend into sectarian barbarism. Yet he also knew enough about the attitudes of his fellow Protestants and Presbyterians that he foresaw that the greatest barrier to unity among them was 'the rock of religion and indulgence of Catholics'.[40]

When the rights of Catholics were debated at Newry, Drennan supported Captain Black, a voting delegate of the Roman Catholic [Volunteer] company. They managed between them to get a slim majority in favour of the Catholics. Drennan had feared that a positive resolution against the Catholics might have been proposed by a Mr Dawson and may have been easily carried, had not the delegates listened to Drennan's argument with much greater attention.[41]

We shall see presently that Drennan's political expedient in *Orellana*, that Catholics were 'incapable of a good use of liberty',[42] would come back to haunt him. Some years later when, as a member of the Society of United Irishmen, he argued trenchantly for male suffrage[43] to include Roman Catholics, his then protagonist, his erstwhile friend William Bruce, reminded him that the author of *Orellana* had held a different point of view.

Notwithstanding the obvious inconsistencies contained in *Orellana*, Drennan was successful in both his primary and secondary objectives. Despite government hostility and threats of prosecution, the Dublin Convention of January 1785 was well attended and widely representative. Many observers gave Drennan the credit for the triumph. He was chosen as a delegate from Belfast because of the prestige he had garnered by being acknowledged as the 'Helot'. When he arrived in Dublin for the Convention, he was told that '*Orellana* had fixed the admiration of the nation.'[44] One of his chief flatterers was the author, Richard Lovell Edgeworth (1744–1817). He had many invitations which he could not accept and had he been able to stay longer he would have had the honour of seeing and talking with great men.[45]

Despite Drennan's personal success, the Convention accomplished nothing and it would soon become clear that the tide had turned against the Volunteers. Throughout 1785, Lord Charlemont made sure that pro-reform and pro-Catholic resolutions were avoided by the Volunteers. Thanks to his Lordship's efforts, the Volunteers became politically irrelevant. At a Volunteer review held on the Plains of the Falls in Belfast on 13 July, Charlemont refused to accept an address from the Killyleagh corps calling for reform of parliament and relief for the Catholics. Charlemont told them politely that he could not agree on the elective franchise for Catholics but assured them that they would shortly meet in a civil capacity and pass an address to parliament on the general reform question.[46] This response did not impress Archibald Hamilton Rowan, a relatively recent recruit to Volunteering, who had drafted the address. Rowan bluntly informed Charlemont that 'citizens with Brown Bess[47] on their shoulders were more likely to be attended to.'[48]

Within a few days of his disagreement with Charlemont, Hamilton Rowan gave an account of the affair directly to Drennan at Newry. The pair had first met earlier that year when Rowan stopped at Newry on his way to visit his father Gawen Hamilton at their ancestral home at Killyleagh castle. Rowan was an independently wealthy man who had been born, raised and educated in

England but had always considered himself an Irishman. He had recently settled in Ireland with his wife, Sarah, and their young family, having lived in France for the previous few years. His father, Gawen, was renowned for his radical politics and had been closely associated with an earlier generation of English and Irish radicals, such as the celebrated English radical John Wilkes and Charles Lucas of Dublin who was sometime called 'the Wilkes of Ireland'.[49] Gawen Hamilton had sent his son to Cambridge and placed him under the care of John Jebb, probably after Wilkes, the most famous and certainly the most able of all the English radicals. Rowan had also spent some time at Joseph Priestley's Warrington Academy and considered himself a life-long friend of the good doctor.

It is not surprising, therefore, that on arriving in Ireland in 1784, Rowan joined his father's Volunteer Corps at Killyleagh. Rowan had sought and received John Jebb's advice on the content of the address which Charlemont had quashed. What perhaps offended Charlemont the most was Jebb's advice to Rowan that 'no reform can be justly founded which does not admit the Roman Catholics and does not restore to the people their full power'.[50] Rowan told Drennan that he believed Charlemont was nervous and surrounded by other tremulous advisors.[51] Drennan had already come to that conclusion. He had lost respect for his Lordship but was very impressed by Archibald Hamilton Rowan. He told Bruce, 'I do not like Lord Charlemont ... He is not a man of nerve – I like Rowan better – he has somewhat of the Long Parliament in his countenance, some of the republican ferocity.'[52]

The Long Parliament referred to the English radicals who had defeated Charles I and helped to bring about republican government in England under Oliver Cromwell. Drennan's political friendship and admiration for Rowan which began with those brief encounters in Newry in 1785 was to have very significant implications for both men and for the radical politics in Ireland in the following decade. They would each play an influential role in the foundation and development of the United Irish Society in 1791. Many of the formative documents issued by the Dublin Society of United Irishmen in the early 1790s were drafted by Drennan and appeared under the names of William Drennan and Archibald Hamilton Rowan. Rowan escaped the gallows by absconding from Newgate in 1794, having been sentenced for distribution of a seditious libel written by Drennan. That same year, Drennan would be acquitted on charges of publishing the same seditious libel.

William Hamilton Drummond, Rowan's first biographer who knew both Drennan and Rowan, was much struck by the remarkable contrast between them. 'The one being of Herculean size, warm impetuous, but highly polished withal; the other low in stature, cold in manner, slow deliberative, but lodging in his breast the element of a lofty and noble spirit.'[53]

Rowan has been described as a handsome giant who could have been a model for Hercules. Drennan's son William said his father stood only five foot five and would have been considered plain.[54] Despite these obvious physical and personality differences, there were less obvious but far more fundamental similarities between them which enabled them to work well together in a common cause over a prolonged period. They shared a background in Ulster New Light Presbyterianism. Neither had compunction about acknowledging their Unitarianism when it was still illegal to do so. They would have regarded themselves as the inheritors of the traditions of Francis Hutcheson and the New Light clergy of Drennan's father's generation. They had both been enthusiastic supporters of the American Revolution and would have been avid readers and admirers of the English Unitarian radicals, Doctors Price, Priestley and Jebb. Drennan admired the writings of Price, Priestley and Jebb from afar, whereas Rowan had been a friend of Priestley while Jebb had been his teacher and political mentor. Jebb kept up an active correspondence with Rowan and one of the last letters he ever wrote, dated September 1785, consisted mostly of advice on how his former student should fight for reform amongst the Volunteers.[55] John Jebb died in 1786 and his *Political Works* were published posthumously in London the following year. Drennan was pleased to see that, in the last of his published letters, in August 1785, Jebb mentioned *Orellana* with approval.[56]

Drennan's other positive impression of Rowan is illustrative of the way his thinking was evolving regarding the next stage of the struggle for reform. He told his sister, 'Rowan is a clever fellow, looks just the thing for a constitutional conspirator.'[57] It was clear that now Drennan was contemplating a totally new approach. His mind was now turning to a conspiracy involving 'sincere and sanguine reformers'. He felt that the political part of Volunteering had been stifled by Charlemont and that all thoughts of reform had been banished from the public mind. Two weeks after the January Convention, he had told Bruce:

> I should like to see the institution of a society as secret as the Free-Masons, whose object might be by every practicable means to put into execution plans for the complete liberation of the country. The secrecy would surround the proceedings of such a society with a certain awe and majesty and the oath of admission would inspire enthusiasm into its members ... The laws and institutes of such a society would require ample consideration, but it might accomplish much.[58]

At about this time also, John Chambers, a Dublin-based printer, wrote to Drennan seeking permission to republish *Orellana* in the capital, a request to which Drennan was happy to accede. This contact was to have significant implications for the future of Drennan's literary career. John Chambers would later be an important member of the United Irish Society. He printed and distributed many of Drennan's later works. He also printed other radical and even seditious materials throughout the 1790s, including the United Irishmen's most incendiary publication, the *Press*. This paper, to which Drennan contributed, was founded in September 1797 and suppressed in March 1798. Chambers, like many of Drennan's United Irish comrades, was imprisoned at Fort George in Scotland from 1798 until 1803 and thereafter exiled from Ireland under the Banishment Act.

6

OF PIGS AND PAPISTS

In May 1785, Bruce told Drennan of plans to establish a Whig Club in Dublin, which was to have a blue uniform with silver buttons and the motto 'persevere'. He asked if Drennan was prepared to put his name forward for membership. Drennan's response was a scathing repudiation and utter rejection of the idea of what he saw as 'a club of little gentlemen'. He believed the club was hostile to Volunteering and saw the members as a jovial crew in blue coats, mere prattlers who would achieve nothing.[1] More importantly, Drennan saw that one of the motives for the formation of the Whig club was to separate 'all the gentlemen and the chaff of the Volunteers leaving the mechanics and the yeomanry who are the weighty grain to themselves'. He responded to Bruce:

> You bid me send my name to be inserted in the Club. My name is William Drennan. But don't think I will put myself to the expense of a suit for such a purpose if that be a sine qua non. For my part I am more eager than ever in the reform business ... I can't find men that would form a serious Association – a sacred compact about the matter. I would sign such a Confederation of Compatriots with my blood.[2]

The establishment of the Whig Club in Dublin was followed by another in Belfast and though many of Drennan's friends became active in both, he stayed aloof, though he did continue to attend Volunteer reviews in Belfast over the next few years. However, his time in Newry, though eventually lucrative in terms of his medical fees, passed in political inactivity and tedium. The local MP, Isaac Corry, offered to make use of Drennan's writing talents and Martha encouraged him to accept the offer. After considering the matter, 'his obstinate republican honesty won the day' and he refused the proposal.[3] He admitted to Bruce that he missed the admiration that came from well-received political commentary. 'Praise to me is everything but a place like this is as cold as a cucumber.'[4] He was candid about his misery and dejection. 'I lead in this place a very insignificant and I had almost said a disgraceful life – I read little or none – I wish nothing – I correspond with none – I hear nothing but the babble of the day. I haunt after company to deliver me from an ennui and a brooding over maladies some imaginary and others real.'[5]

Drennan's sense of isolation seems to have increased when Martha was overcome by depression and lost her zest for writing. Only one letter from her to William survives from 1786. His correspondence with William Bruce also seems to have slackened, as he had little to report from Newry. He seemed desperate for political news from elsewhere. On two occasions, he began his pleas to Bruce for interesting news by saying, 'there is nothing stirring here [in Newry] but pigs and papists'.[6] To put it at its mildest, this was an unfortunate phrase from a man who only a short time previously had called on his fellow Irishman 'to embrace each other in the mild spirit of Christianity and to unite as a secret compact in the cause of your sinking country'.[7]

Twentieth-century historians have used this statement as a foundation on which to construct a case against Drennan, that he was a bigot with an obsessive dislike and mistrust of Catholics, which was 'based on petty or superficial motives'.[8] One of Drennan's main accusers in this regard was L.M. Cullen, who described Drennan as a bigoted anti-Catholic individual and branded him 'the Wretched Drennan'.[9] We will proceed to examine the case against Drennan and assess whether he is guilty as charged. In order to give a fair account of Drennan's attitudes, we require a review of his entire career including his time as a member of the United Irish society and beyond.

A decade after Drennan's 'pigs and papists' remarks,[10] further evidence of Drennan's alleged anti-Catholic bigotry emerged. The informer Leonard McNally wrote a detailed report to Dublin Castle dated September 1796. McNally states that the Catholics were becoming more extreme in their demands and were forming committees to negotiate with the French in the event of an invasion. McNally identified John Keogh (1740–1817) and Richard McCormick (d. 1827) as leaders of the Catholics. In the last line of his report, McNally states, 'Drennan declares his hatred of the Catholics charging them with duplicity and ingratitude.'[11]

Drennan and the United Irish Society had, from the beginning, supported political rights for Roman Catholics. However, as we have noted, back in 1785, while Drennan was prepared to support Catholic claims in debate, in writing he was denying that they even had such claims. Drennan's comment in *Orellana* stated:

the Catholics of this day are absolutely INCAPABLE of making a good use of political liberty, or what is the same thing political power. I speak of the sentiments of the most enlightened amongst them ... are too wise to wish for a *complete* extension of the civil franchise ... it must require the process of time to enlarge their minds and ameliorate their hearts.[12]

Later, when Drennan's fellow United Irishmen were prepared to demand a complete extension of the franchise to all males, including the lower orders of Catholics, he insisted that a national education system was an essential element that must accompany the measure.[13] He felt that the lower ranks of the different religious persuasions 'have strong antipathies' and he felt that 'the middle ranking members of each sect can instil into the mind of those beneath them the milk of human nature'. He seemed to believe, in 1785, that the Catholic middle class were too few to do this.[14]

Drennan's assertion of the incapability of Catholics to make good use of political liberty was greatly resented by Catholics at the time and was remembered for a long time afterwards. Eight years later, in January 1793, when Martha suggested that Drennan should republish the *Helot*, he told her:

> There is one letter asserting the incapability of the Catholics of Ireland for political liberty or power which was infused in my ear by H. Joy as I well remember and as I could testify from his letters. This displeased many of the Catholics at the time and you may recollect ... W. Jones who has indeed been their oldest and most consistent friend, taking me up on this very account in the Belfast paper under the title Zealot. I am apt to believe that the Catholics still owe me a grudge for this and think that my late conversion since I came to Dublin has been brought about by views of interest rather than upon principle, and this with an instinctive horror of republicanism which inspires them, has occasioned rather a dryness and want of confidence respecting me.[15]

The opinions expressed by Drennan regarding the superior enlightenment of Presbyterians over Catholics and hence, the incapability of the Catholics to use political liberty, was probably shared by many Presbyterians at the time. It was most certainly the view of William Bruce, to whom Drennan had made his 'pigs and papists'[16] comments. Bruce never wavered in this opinion and it is not clear what changed Drennan's mind. It might have been the French Revolution which showed Catholics to be capable of making a revolution. It may also have been the argument put forward by Wolfe Tone (1763–1798)[17] in his *Argument on Behalf of the Catholics of Ireland* when he addressed the idea that Catholics are not prepared for liberty. He asked 'Were the Polish? Were the French? Peasantries were the same the world over, but the French Catholic gentry are as enlightened as any gentry. Catholic emancipation is not a disease we prepare for by inoculation. Liberty is the vital principle of man: he that is prepared to live is prepared for freedom.'[18]

Whatever the reason, from the formation of the United Irish Society until the end of his life, Drennan was a passionate advocate of Catholic political rights. However, at the time McNally was reporting, Drennan was far from pleased with his Catholic allies. When 'a Catholic of some consequence' asked Drennan to join one of the new committees he refused.[19] He had been trying to live on his modest professional income which he believed had suffered because of his very public attachment to the Catholics' cause. Martha had told him that because of his trial he had lost his expected inheritance from the Hamilton family of Mount Collier and that 'from that moment Hamilton had never called on one of us'.[20] He also felt that his political enemies were trying to ruin him professionally.[21] In all the years Drennan had worked in Dublin, he 'had not received one guinea in professional income as a doctor from any of the Catholic persuasion'.[22] He was struggling to make a living and was very resentful that the Catholics, whose political cause he believed had cost him much, had not used his services.

His resentment or 'hatred' could not have extended to the entire Catholic community but rather to the well-to-do Catholics of the Catholic Committee who could have afforded his services but chose not to employ him. The unidentified 'Catholic of consequence' was surprised, as he had believed that as Drennan lived in expensive lodgings, he was 'a man of few wants', yet 'he affected concern and gave hope of better times'.[23] Those better times never came.[24] Nonetheless, when the Catholic leader, Richard McCormick, absconded to avoid arrest in March 1798, Drennan described him as one of his friends and expressed the hope that he and his fellows would be successful in escaping.[25]

As further evidence of Drennan's anti-Catholic prejudice, some writers point to his observation that, although the Roman Catholic bishop, Thomas Hussey, was 'someone of the most ancient strain of Ireland and in foreign Courts all his life, [it was strange that he] should smack so strongly of the bogtrotter'.[26] This comment has been described as shading into 'unreconstructed racism'.[27] This is a gross distortion of what Drennan had to say about the bishop. He was merely commenting on Hussey's bucolic accent. Drennan's remarks were made in an account of a dinner engagement he had had with Hussey and General O'Connell, also a Roman Catholic, formerly in the 'French service'. He had clearly been very impressed with both men. Drennan observed, they were both shrewd, very generally informed, very pleasant.[28]

Another writer tells us that, having reviewed Drennan's correspondence in the period 1791 to 1794, 'Drennan mistrusts the Catholics who he thought to be a self-seeking and aristocratic party. It was apparently very difficult to retain them as allies after the terms of the United Irish Test with its obvious echoes of the French Revolution had been made public.'[29]

Drennan believed that many Catholics were much attached to the writings of Edmund Burke who had trenchantly denounced the French Revolution.[30] However, many of the negative comments that Drennan made about 'the Catholics' were not directed at members of the Church of Rome. Rather, they were directed at leading members of the Catholic Committee. Drennan believed that great efforts were being made to detach them from the United Irish Society. He believed that Edmund Burke was working for a coalition between the 'Protestant gentry and the Catholics of consequence to keep everything much as it is'.[31] This belief had a solid foundation, for we know that Burke had asserted:

> To resist the revolutionary contagion, it was necessary to rally in defence of the established order and civilisation all men of sound principle. The Irish Catholics, whether 'the old gentlemen who still retain their old religion and estates' or 'the new race of Catholics who have risen by their industry and their good fortune to considerable opulence' were clearly from 'their religious principles, church polity and habitual discipline,' natural conservatives.[32]

The administration in Dublin Castle did not take Burke's advice and instead chose the path which Wolfe Tone described as 'oppression and persecution' which he believed had radicalised 'the great mass of Catholics'.[33] No one has suggested that Burke's assertion that Irish Catholics are natural conservatives is an indication that he was an anti-Catholic bigot. However, the fact that Drennan suspected that Burke might be right is one of the reasons which has resulted in Drennan being labelled a bigot. For his own part, Drennan felt that, in him, the Catholics of Ireland 'have not had a more constant friend'.[34]

Despite Drennan's doubts about the Catholic Committee's commitment, he was fair minded about their each-way bet. He observed that 'the truth was and is, the Catholics [Committee] wish to have two strings to their bow, a part to treat with government, a part to allay with us, and if one string cracks, why try the other. This is good and perhaps fair archery'.[35]

One historian has made the erroneous claim that when Drennan wrote in favour of Catholic Emancipation in the *Belfast Monthly Magazine* in 1808, this represented a shift in his position. This writer claims, 'like many Protestant reformers of the 1790s [Drennan] had doubts about Catholics'.[36] Here we come to the kernel of the question. To have doubts about the sincerity or steadfastness of one's allies has nothing to do with prejudice, bigotry or racism. Far from shifting his position in 1808, Drennan could point back nearly a quarter of a century when he sowed the seed of Catholic and Protestant union in Newry in 1784.

> We associate although differing in religious opinions because we wish to create a union of power and to cultivate that brotherhood of affection amongst all the inhabitants of this island ... We are all Irishmen. We shall ever think an association deserves well of its native land whose chief objective is to unite the different religions in the cause of our common country.[37]

In 1805, Martha heard rumours that the Catholics had unanimously, but in secret, agreed a new petition to the British House of Lords seeking emancipation. She suggested to her brother that this seemed like a time he might again write a pamphlet in the Catholic cause:

> If there is a man who once stirred up an ardent love of reform, who first pleaded for and brought forward the Catholic rights, if still consistent he ceases the favourable moment and with truth, energy, propriety and eloquence forces a healing, perhaps redress – the Catholics ought to erect a statue to him and what would be far better make him independent for life.[38]

She knew, however, that if he took her advice, he would require great prudence as he would likely be involving himself in 'an odious, dangerous business' where he would be cast as a rebel and a lover of blood. Drennan did not expose himself to this danger but he kept a close eye on developments and shortly thereafter informed his sister:

> The Catholics, I believe, are to allow their petition to remain on the table, if the ministers promise future support. Lord Moira, who goes between the

King and the Prince, wished to be advised of the arrival of their delegates in London. I know two of them Scully and Ryan, very honest and honourable men. I suppose their petition will be put off for the present.[39]

Drennan's prediction here was correct and two years later, in 1807, the Catholics agreed yet another petition which no party was willing to present to Parliament on their behalf. Drennan advised them to appeal to 'that power above King, above Lords and Commons – that is – public opinion'.[40] They accepted his advice and he drafted a long address for them, which he hoped they would use as an 'open and manly appeal to their fellow subjects of Great Britain and Ireland'.[41]

For as long as the *Belfast Monthly Magazine* lasted, Drennan advocated Catholic emancipation. In 1809, he was still vigorously condemning the oppression of Catholics. 'In every country in Europe [the Irish Catholic] was caressed and encouraged. To every country but his own, were his talents acceptable. In the career of science or of military honours, he met with no obstacle but at home. There he was an alien indeed: there he was treated as an enemy to God and to his king.'[42]

Ian McBride tells us that in 1813, when the emancipationists secured their first majority in the House of Commons, 'support for the Catholic cause in Belfast was directed by the Friends of Civil and Religious Liberty with William Drennan and Robert Tennant (1765–1837), at their head'.[43] In 1819, a year before his death, Drennan wrote a highly complimentary letter to Daniel O'Connell (1775–1847), predicting that O'Connell's 'manly spirit, his openness and candour, and his moral integrity, would ensure that his objective [Catholic Emancipation] would be obtained and his name be recorded in history'.[44]

McNally the informer, in his comprehensive report on the Catholic Committee told his masters in the Castle that Drennan hated his Catholic allies. Whether or not Drennan ever used the term hate, we know that, at least for a time, he was unsure of and harboured suspicions and resentments regarding Keogh, McCormack and their committee. These may or may not have been justified. His 'pigs and papist'[45] remarks in 1786 are unconscionable and can never be justified, particularly in one who claimed to be an enemy of religious sectarianism. In mitigation, however, his comments were made in private correspondence and were not a public statement of his position. They were made in the context of a politically engaged writer who felt isolated and stuck in a backwater who, after having enjoyed acclaim and admiration, was now deeply affected by ennui and conscious of his political irrelevance.

When looking at Drennan's political career in the round, however, the consensus which has emerged amongst modern historians that Drennan was an anti-Catholic bigot cannot be sustained. Had any of his contemporaries accused him of such he would, no doubt, have described the accusation as 'a cruel and ignoble calumny'.[46] In early 1798, when musing on his mortality and on the arrangements, he would like to be made for his funeral, Drennan wrote to Martha, 'Let me be buried in any of the country churchyards adjoining this city [Dublin], and let six poor Protestants and six poor Catholics get a guinea piece for carriage of me, and a [Catholic] priest and a dissenting clergyman attend with any other friends that choose.'[47]

In fact, many years later, when he was interred in Belfast, he was carried to his grave by six Protestant and six Catholics as he had wished.[48] Those who have branded him 'the Wretched Drennan' and as an anti-Catholic bigot must consider his funeral request to be very peculiar.

7

AMONGST THE DUBLIN DISSENTERS

In early August 1789, Irish newspapers carried accounts of the momentous events in France, including the fall of the Bastille. Drennan had no doubt that the news from France would please his sister. However, the French Revolution was alluded to only briefly in their correspondence which, at this time, was almost completely preoccupied with Martha's deteriorating health. She complained of ongoing problems with her stomach and bowel, an inability to sleep and a return of her old nervous problems. She pleaded with her brother to visit her. He found it difficult to get away from Newry as some of his regular patients were demanding his attention. He wrote to her Belfast doctors giving his advice on what he hoped might be suitable treatments. He was very distressed that notwithstanding his medical knowledge, he could not comfort his sister as he did not know the cause of her bodily ailments or mental distresses.[1] From August of that year and for a considerable time thereafter, their correspondence remained one-sided, as Martha seems to have been unable or disinclined to answer William's pleas for information on her condition. William, for his part, wrote regularly to Martha's husband, Sam.

When Drennan heard that Dr Moody, who had relocated to Dublin from Newry, was seriously ill and not expected to live, he began to conceive a plan to move to Dublin. He would attempt to establish a medical practice based on Moody's Dublin patient base, much as he had succeeded in doing in Newry. He was advised by his Dublin friends that this would be no easy task. They told him he would have many rivals in the city. The capital 'had men of great abilities, knowledge and address, with an education at Dublin College, and city connections'.[2] He replied that he knew it would be difficult for him at first but he never lacked courage and he was used to disappointments. He compared his venture into Dublin to the Prince of Orange landing at Brixham. 'Few came over to William on his first landing, but he conquered at last.'[3]

Just before Christmas 1789, Drennan arrived in Dublin and his 'die was cast'.[4] He wrote his first letter from the capital to Sam McTier, knowing that he would share his news with Martha. Drennan compared himself to a plant which had been transplanted. Initially, he felt himself wither a little, then at last he felt he had taken root, grown stronger and flourished better than ever.

About the time Drennan was moving south, his friend William Bruce was moving in the opposite direction. Bruce was taking leave of the Unitarian congregation at Strand Street, Dublin. He had been called to be headmaster at the new Belfast Academy and assistant minister to First Presbyterian Rosemary Lane, Belfast. As we have seen, Rosemary Lane was Drennan's birthplace and the scene of his father's first ministry. Bruce was already well known to the Belfast congregation and Sam McTier and Martha were amongst many of the members at Rosemary Lane with whom Bruce would have been well acquainted. The congregation that Bruce was leaving had moved from Wood Street to a new meeting house in Strand Street in 1763. Drennan senior had had connections to the Wood Street congregation from his time working with Francis Hutcheson at the Dublin Dissenter academy during the 1720s and in the following decade when he sometimes travelled from Belfast to preach at Wood Street. Travers Hartley (1723–1796), who was a member of Parliament for Dublin was also an elder at Strand Street. He welcomed the younger Drennan to the city with great civility, as he had known his father back in the Wood Street days.[5]

On his arrival in the city, Drennan affiliated to the Strand Street and Eustace Street congregations. He paid two guineas to each, perhaps in the hope of widening his circle of acquaintances and potential patients. Both congregations had strong republican associations, dating back to the Cromwellian regime of the mid-seventeenth century. The heterodox New Light Unitarian theology they espoused fostered close links, not just with Rosemary Lane but all the New Light Presbyterian congregations in Ulster. These Dublin Unitarians also had strong international links, many of which dated back from more than a century to the Laudian persecution of Protestant Dissenters in the reign of Charles I. A.T.Q. Stewart noted that 'Some special quality attaches to the Dublin ministers setting them apart from the rest of the Presbyterian body yet connecting them to obscure Dissenting congregations in the English Fenlands, to Rotterdam, Leyden, and to Roxbury and Boston Massachusetts.'[6]

When Drennan dined at the home of Reverend Philip Taylor (1747–1830) of Eustace Street, he met Isaac Weld (d. 1824) and his elderly mother. She was 'a fine old lady of eighty who remembered [Drennan senior] when he was resident in Dublin.[7] The old lady was the widow of Reverend Dr Isaac Weld (1710–1778) also of Eustace Street, whose father and grandfather had been dissenting ministers.

The founder of the Weld ministerial dynasty was the famous Puritan divine Thomas Weld (1595–1661). He had left England after having been deprived of his living by Archbishop Laud in 1631. He ministered for ten years in Roxbury, Massachusetts, and was, for a time, overseer at Harvard College. In 1641, he returned to England to support Parliament in the Civil War against the king. Thomas Weld's son Edmund, a Harvard graduate, was chaplain to Oliver Cromwell when he was Lord Protector and accompanied him to Ireland.[8] Edmund Weld's son, Nathanial (d. 1729) ministered at New Row Dublin and was a friend of Thomas Drennan and Francis Hutcheson. He was also a friend and confidant of Isaac Newton and he named his son Isaac after the great mathematician.

It was not just the Protestant Dissenters of Dublin who welcomed Drennan to the capital. His reputation as author of *Orellana* served to open the doors of political radicals also. Shortly after his arrival, he dined with James Napper Tandy (1740–1803) and several other city politicians. He regarded Tandy as a prime man in the city and he had no doubt that they would be friends.[9] He also dined with the old radical, the Chief State Physician, Dr Robert Emmet, at his home in Stephen's Green. The two men discussed Henry Grattan's lack of commitment to the reform of parliamentary representation. Drennan was pleased when, after dinner, a fine young boy of Emmet's recited one of the *Letters of Orellana* for the company. Drennan enjoyed the occasion but was not to know that Robert Emmet, the precocious twelve-year-old who entertained them, would be hanged and beheaded for high treason in Dublin in September 1803.

The young boy's talent for oratory, which he displayed that evening, stayed with him throughout his short life. When the notorious Judge John Toler sentenced him to be hanged, drawn and quartered for rebellion, after a trial lasting several hours, the then twenty-five-year-old Emmet addressed the court. With no time for preparation and no time to gather his thoughts, Robert Emmet made a speech from the dock which has long been recognised as one of the greatest trial speeches in the English language.

After the tedious and boring years of isolation in Newry, Dublin had, for Drennan, a very different and much more interesting and exciting aspect. The newspapers were full of news from Revolutionary France. Opposition papers such as the *Dublin Evening Post* were enthusiastic about the fall of the Bastille and the emergence of representative government in the form of the French

National Assembly. Pro-government organs such as the *Freeman's Journal* told of anarchy and lawlessness and the nefarious doings of French atheists.

Domestic politics were enlivened and invigorated because 1790 was a general election year. In May, Drennan had his first experience of how Dubliners relished the hustings. He described the carnival atmosphere to Sam:

> I have just seen Grattan and Fitzgerald[10] proceeding to the hustings at the head of more than 1,400 men, eighteen of the corporation's bands of music playing, etc., Grattan advancing on his light fantastic toe, hope elevating and joy brightening his crest, his eyes rolling with that fine enthusiasm without which it is impossible to be a great man. Fitzgerald a fine young fellow, bending to hear what Grattan is saying – both bare headed and at time bowing popularly low – each of them holding an arm of the aged and much respected Hartley;[11] while at some distance behind walks Napper Tandy in all the surliness of republicanism, grinning most ghastly smiles and as he lifts his hat from his head, the many headed monster[12] raises a shout that reverberates through every corner of the Castle.[13]

Despite the lively spectacle, he was a little disappointed that there were no slogans calling for a Bill to amend parliamentary representation. Lecky has left us a concise account of why the Irish House of Commons was in need of such a Bill. There were in all 300 members of the Commons. One hundred and fifty-four of them were nominated by fifty-two peers. Sixty-four members were nominated by thirty-six Commoners and thirteen owed their return in great measure to thirteen families.[14]

The nationwide general election was genuinely contested only in the few constituencies where freeholders had the franchise. Sam McTier was again very active in County Down on behalf of the Stewart interest. Robert Stewart, since losing his seat through his own ineptitude in the election of '82, had gone on to bigger and better things. Being a widower in 1775, he had married Frances Pratt, daughter of the Earl of Camden. The Earl was the leader of a powerful British Whig family. In eighteenth-century Britain and Ireland, such a marriage was a better and more certain route to achieving high political office than relying on elections, merit or talent. In 1786, Stewart became a Privy Councillor of Ireland. In 1789, he was raised to the Irish peerage as Baron Londonderry which entitled him to sit in the Irish House of Lords.

This meteoric rise of mediocrity was derided by establishment figures and political radicals alike. The Earl of Westmoreland said that Lord Londonderry was 'almost the only Irishman who received His Majesty's favour without rendering service'.[15] Reverend James Porter, Unitarian minister for Greyabbey, had been a supporter and friend of the Stewarts but satirised Londonderry's rise to the aristocracy and political apostasy. He lampooned his Lordship in a series of articles in the *Northern Star*, entitled 'Billy Bluff and the Squire'. Londonderry was not amused, and Reverend Porter paid a terrible price for the offence he had given. He was hanged in front of his Meeting House and congregation in 1798.[16]

In the general election of 1790, Londonderry's twenty-one-year-old son, Robert junior, stood for his father's former House of Commons seat. He was elected with the help of Sam McTier, Reverend Boyle Moody, Reverend James Porter and many other northern radicals who would soon be active in the United Irish Society. Drennan, now in Dublin, attended the House of Commons and was greatly impressed by what he saw and heard of the new MP. Young Stewart had been canvassing for a year before the election, at a time when he was underage, and Lord Hillsborough tried but failed to have him unseated as a result. Drennan told Sam McTier:

I saw Robert Stewart once in the House and once out of it. He is certainly a most promising young man, and one of the most handsomest [*sic*] in the House, perhaps one day to become the most able. Lord Hillsborough has petitioned against his minority and we hear he has the best legal opinion over the water in his favour.[17]

Hillsborough's petition failed but Drennan's optimistic predictions relating to young Stewart proved prophetic. He is known to posterity as Lord Castlereagh and went on to be one of the best known and ablest British statesmen of the late eighteenth and early nineteenth centuries. However, his road to political success involved the imprisonment, banishment and execution of many of his former supporters.

By early 1790, encouraged by the great events unfolding in France, Drennan had become a full-blooded revolutionary and Irish separatist and he began planning for a secret political club to forward his agenda. He wrote from Dublin to Bruce in Belfast:

It is my fixed opinion that no reform of parliament and consequently no freedom will ever be attainable by this country but by a total separation from Britain and I think this belief is making its way rapidly but silently amongst both Protestants and Catholics and I think that four quarters of the Kingdom are more unanimous in that opinion than they themselves imagine.

It is for the collection of this opinion the esoteric part, and nucleus of political doctrine that such a society or interior circle, might be formed whose opinions are still halting between, who are for temporizing expedients and patience and partial reform – I think this secrecy is as yet necessary to such an institution – and that the tyrant Britain must be assassinated. Why so soon? Why not let Caesar live his natural life? It is but a few years. Because in those few years the power of resisting oppression will be lost with the will. I think revolution not justifiable in England. I think it is in Ireland and that nothing short of convulsion will throw off the incumbency of our national political and civil grievances.

I think revolutions are not to be dreaded as such terrible extremes and it is the highest probability that it would be as peaceful here as in France, as in Poland as in Ireland in '79 provided the great and irresistible voice of the whole declares itself explicitly on the subject.

I believe a reform must lead rapidly to a separation and a separation to a reform. The Catholics in this country are much more enlightened and less under the trammels of a Priesthood as is imagined – it is improper to keep up religious controversy, when all should make common cause and it is said that you take up too much time speaking against Popery. I think the people can seldom if ever be mistaken in judgement. If the people are violent, it is because violence is necessary and all the doctrine of all the wise and guarded men in France was not half the consequence of the practical lesson of the people in storming the Bastille.[18]

In early 1791, things were looking up for Drennan. He found the weather in Dublin much better than Newry or Belfast. He was enjoying better health than he had before his arrival in Dublin. His weak chest and breathing had improved and the constant chest pain he had suffered previously had abated. He was making new acquaintances and his mantelpiece was covered with cards and invitations.[19] He struck up a friendship with Dr Emmet's son, Thomas Addis Emmet, who had studied medicine at Edinburgh a few years after Drennan but had recently qualified as a lawyer. Emmet was about to marry Jane Patten, the daughter of a Unitarian clergyman from Clonmel. Drennan heard a rumour to the effect that Jane Patten's dowry was £2,000, which he doubted, possibly because the family of a minister would not usually be so prosperous. However, the source of this generous dowry was William Colville, Jane Patten's unmarried uncle, a wealthy merchant and banker who became her guardian on the death of her father. William Colville was an elder at Strand Street for many years.

Jane Patten's mother's maiden name was Margaret Colville. She was of a well-known Northern Presbyterian family. Her grandfather, Reverend Alexander Colville, had been a controversial minister to a congregation at Dromore where he published pamphlets during the subscription crisis of the 1720s. Reverend Colville would have been well known to Thomas Drennan. Addis Emmet and Jane Patten were soon married at Strand Street and their children were baptised there over the next few years. Reverend John Moody officiated at the Emmet wedding ceremony and the baptisms. John Moody's career in Strand Street lasted more than fifty years He officiated at Drennan's wedding to Sarah Swanwick in 1801. In 1769, Reverend Moody had baptised Robert Stewart, who went on to be a member of the regime which was responsible for the imprisonment and death of his younger brother, Boyle Moody, in the aftermath of the 1798 Rebellion.

Massacre at Forkhill and Arming the Catholics

In late January 1791, at Forkhill in South Armagh, a few miles from Newry, Alexander Barclay, a Protestant school teacher, his wife and her fourteen-year-old brother were savagely attacked in the Barclays' home by a group of local men. The three were stabbed repeatedly, their tongues were cut out, the fingers on their right hands were hacked off. The young boy's leg was severed with a sword. It was immediately assumed that this was a sectarian attack by Catholics and the sole motive for the attack was that the victims were Protestants. Agrarian outrages involving the severing of tongues were not common in late eighteenth-century Ireland. However, it was an atrocity, when it did occur, which was sometimes visited on Catholic peasants by fellow Catholics. The victims, rather than being chosen for their religion, were usually people who were suspected of speaking to the authorities. In fact, the Barclay family were innocent victims of a gang which had originally set out to attack Barclay's brother-in-law, Captain James Dawson of the Orior Volunteers, who was held responsible for the conviction and execution of two Defenders at the Autumn Assizes in 1790.[20]

No account of the brutal affair at Forkhill mentions that the attackers had firearms or that their motive was to steal arms from the Barclay family.

Yet Sir Richard Musgrave had no doubt that the neighbouring papists, whom he described as 'a savage race', were responsible and went on to claim that they 'had great zeal to collect arms and that a large quantity had been imported into Newry for their use'.[21] Musgrave reported that the grand jury and high sheriff of Armagh at their next meeting resolved:

> That the rage amongst the Roman Catholics, for illegally arming themselves, has of late taken place, and is truly alarming: In order then to put a stop to such proceedings, and to restore tranquillity, we do pledge each other, as magistrates and individuals and to hereby offer a reward of five guineas, for the conviction of each of the first twenty persons, illegally armed and assembled as aforesaid.[22]

For Drennan, this brutal incident was a major setback and of course, he had supported and perhaps even helped in arming the Catholics of the Newry Volunteers. He knew that Lord Charlemont and Brownlow would hold a meeting to discuss the atrocity and would ask, 'why should we tolerate, why should we commit arms and rights to such savages as these Catholics?' For Drennan this was not the central question; rather, he would ask 'Why did you make them and keep them savages? For that they are such is without question. All this will put off the day of general freedom – the barbarians and Mr. Burke, and this island will be the last redeemed in all Europe.'[23]

It is not clear why Drennan mentions Edmund Burke in this context. Burke's son Richard had recently been engaged by the Catholic Committee as its agent. Richard's main advisor was, of course, his father. The elder Burke had always argued that the best way to bind Irish Catholics to the Empire was to extend toleration, including the acceptance of Catholics into the British armed forces. Burke was advocating a war against Revolutionary France and he believed that further toleration of the Catholics was unavoidable. He was pleased with the way the Irish Catholics had 'proceeded with deference and submission to the law, notwithstanding the endeavours of neighbouring countries suggesting to them to wrest [toleration] by force and violence'.[24] We cannot be sure what Burke meant by 'neighbouring countries' but he was already concerned that what he called the 'French disease' had altered the minds of the Irish Catholics that 'they will not in future bear the lash of Tyranny and oppression'.[25]

The law was changed to permit the recruitment of Catholics into the army and navy. Within a matter of months after the outbreak of the war with France in 1793, twenty-two new regiments were raised in Ireland.[26] By the following year, Irish Catholics made up one third of the strength of the British army. In one theatre of the war alone, the West Indies, 43,000 Irish soldiers perished between 1794 and 1801.[27] Had any Irish Catholics who had not been recruited into the army, or the militia, been found in possession of arms during those years, they faced imprisonment, transportation or execution. Both Drennan and Burke agreed that Catholics should have the right to bear arms but for different reasons. Drennan believed that Catholic and Protestant Irishmen should have the right to bear arms to defend their country and their civil and religious liberties. Burke believed that Irish Catholics should have the right to bear arms to defend the British Empire.

8

A BENEVOLENT CONSPIRACY

Drennan's negative views of the Whig Club hardened as he observed its activities in Dublin. He dismissed it as 'an eating and drinking aristocratical society without any fellow feeling with the commonality. When the people come forward these men draw back, and when they come forward, the People are lifeless and there is no strength in them'.[1]

Theobald Wolfe Tone also derided what he called 'the puny efforts of the Whig Club' and lamented that they had turned their faces against parliamentary reform.[2] In the winter of 1790, Tone invited Drennan, Joseph Pollock, Thomas Addis Emmet, Thomas Russell, John Stack and Whitley Stokes to form a political club which met in Trinity College. Stack and Stokes were Fellows of the College. However, there was a lethargy amongst the radicals at this point and the 'great things' which Tone hoped for from his club did not materialise.[3]

However, the unfolding dramas in France and reaction to those events in Ireland soon breathed life, energy and a new-found enthusiasm into the radicals. Tone tells us that when 'the French Revolution was "about twelve months in progress" [autumn of 1790] ... at length Mr. Burke's famous invective appeared; and this in due season produced Paine's reply which he called "*Rights of Man*". This controversy and the gigantic events which gave rise to it changed in an instance the politics of Ireland'.[4]

In May 1791, Drennan revived his plan for a club of conspiratorial radicals. He wrote to Sam McTier in the hope that Sam would discuss the idea with his friends in Belfast. Drennan told Sam that he much desired that a society be instituted having much of the secrecy and somewhat of the ceremony of freemasonry. He envisaged:

A benevolent conspiracy – a plot of the people – no Whig Cub. No party title – the Brotherhood, its name – the rights of man and the greatest happiness of the greatest number its end[5] – its general end real independence to Ireland and republicanism its particular purpose ... Communication with the leading men in France, in England and America so as to cement the shifting sand of republicanism into a body.[6]

Sam showed this letter in confidence to several gentlemen in Belfast, most of whom approved very much of it. The people with whom McTier consulted were not just a random group of friends or acquaintances. Nancy Curtin tells us McTier's discussions were with men of substance as they were 'a secret committee of Volunteers who constituted an advance democratic party in the radical town of Belfast. The leader of this group of eleven radical Dissenters was Samuel Neilson a prosperous linen merchant and also the son of a Presbyterian minister'.[7]

One person not associated with the secret committee, whom McTier brought into his confidence, was the newly arrived assistant Minister to Rosemary Lane, William Bruce. Bruce did not at all approve of the idea. He told Sam that he had argued against secrecy when Drennan first proposed the idea years earlier. Sam decided not to show the letter to Dr Haliday because he believed he would pass it on to Charlemont who most likely would not like the proposal. In Sam's view, Haliday merely 'wished to stand well with Charlemont and was greatly prejudiced against the Catholics'.[8]

In the same letter, Sam reported the rejoicing in Belfast at the news of the arrest of the King of France. Drennan felt that Martha, despite her illness, must be interested in this development. For his part, he was delighted to see 'the sovereign in the common sewer, and [as] Burke would say the fish woman in the sovereignty'.[9]

At about this time, preparations were underway in Belfast for a celebration of the second anniversary of the fall of the Bastille on 14 July 1791. The secret committee had asked Sam to draw up declarations or resolutions to be considered for what they hoped would be the most numerous gathering of Volunteers ever in Belfast. He knew that he had been asked only in the hope of getting something from his brother-in-law's pen. He begged Drennan to let him know if he would oblige and how soon they could expect it.[10] The last line in Sam's letter must have encouraged Drennan for it read, 'if your club, brotherhood takes place we will immediately follow your example'.[11]

Drennan replied with a draft resolution which he felt might be 'too spirited' for Sam and his group to assent to. However, he warned that he would not agree to any alteration to his draft. He was sorry that he had not room to express the necessity of conciliating the interests of Catholics and Protestants at present.

He told Sam that the aristocratic Catholics, led by Lords Kenmare and Fingal, were in a treaty with the government. They had been told that 'if they kept their fellow Catholics quiet that they would eventually get similar indulgences as the English Catholics had been given'. Drennan believed this was designed to divide the two great bodies, the Catholics and the Presbyterians, 'particularly at this time when Burke had foolishly licked up such a spirit and the "French disease" seemed so catching'.[12] If the government were to deliver on its promises Drennan suggested:

> 'In giving a sop to Cerberus[13] he will fall asleep'. If they do not, then the democratic part of the Catholics will have double energy and it is probably [sic] they will carry the whole body with them ... If therefore the Presbyterians come forward by drawing up some articles as a base, as it were, of amity and alliance between the two bodies in a common cause, this common agreement, this point of union, would shock government more than anything.[14]

He suggested that '14 July would be a good occasion for the northerners to show the Catholics that they were liberal enough to allow them their rights of entering the bar, of being justices of the peace and magistrates, their right to carry arms and also the right to the franchise.'[15] As he reminded Sam, 'when the Catholics were armed in the Newry Volunteers, they were at the mercy of any rogue or rascal who could have them subject to a fine of £50 or £100 and imprisonment for six months, if a firelock be found in their houses'.[16]

Drennan was not the only Dublin-based writer who was solicited to provide resolutions and a declaration for the Belfast celebration. Thomas Russell, a Cork-born army officer, had recently moved to Belfast and had so impressed the local radicals that he had been co-opted into Neilson's secret committee. He was asked to contact his friend Wolfe Tone to request draft resolutions. Tone was happy to oblige but he was careful when dealing with the question of Catholic rights.[17] Despite the hard work of Neilson's group, even this vapid resolution did not meet with the approval of most of the Volunteers. Tone was bitterly disappointed and within a short space of time began to work on his pamphlet, *An Argument on Behalf of the Catholics of Ireland*, which appeared in September 1791.

Sam McTier was so disappointed by the turn of events that he could not bring himself to write to Drennan with the bad news. However, the dark cloud had a silver lining in that Drennan received a short report from Martha, the first direct correspondence he had from her in more than two years. Martha informed him that though the Catholic question had gone badly for the radicals, Drennan's declaration to the French National Assembly had been adopted.

> Sam has neither the time or the temper to write at present, immediately after the grand procession and the reading [*sic*] the declaration where Harry Joy[18] has foiled him as he did in the committee last night. Your last paragraph in regard to the Catholics was lost by the previous question.[19] The declaration is adopted, and the Chairman Mr. Sharman is requested to transmit a copy to the National Assembly's president in French and English.[20]

Despite the failure of the resolutions regarding the Catholics, Drennan was not particularly discouraged. Over the next few weeks, he busied himself suggesting ways for the more progressive Volunteers to influence their conservative comrades. He advised that positive responses from Catholic Committees in various towns should not be published until 'the number was sufficient to form a goodly representation'. Otherwise he worried, if the aristocratic part of the Roman Catholics knew what was happening, they might try to 'damp down the proceedings'.[21]

In early October, Drennan, Tone, Russell and their Dublin network made plans to produce a twice weekly paper which they would call the *National Journal*. Russell was to be the editor. Tone was tasked with writing the prospectus which he produced on 4 October 1791:

> The great object of the paper shall be to unite and emancipate all the people, to abolish those unjust, invidious and ruinous distinctions which bigotry in religion and politics have raised amongst us, distinctions which, however they might once have appeared justifiable by necessity, cannot longer maintain their ground against truth and reason. To accomplish this purpose little more need be done than to make the great sects which divide this country, and by dividing, ruin and degrade it *know each other*; and what means as an honest unbiased Paper which shall ever be fully and freely open to the abilities of all parties.[22]

Drennan was, of course, prepared to contribute his writing skills to the new venture and felt that there was room for two new newspapers, one in Dublin and the other in Belfast. He was, however, anxious not to write anything that might injure Harry Joy who often published his work in the *Belfast Newsletter* and had always been civil to him as a gentleman and a friend.

Tone's pamphlet made a big impression on the Belfast radicals and resulted in him being invited to Belfast in early October. He arrived there on 11 October 1791 and, next day, he dined with Sam McTier, Thomas McCabe, Thomas Russell and other members of the Secret Committee. He found that the resolutions, which had not met with approval three months earlier, were now too tame and required revision and strengthening. Two days later, the Secret Committee met formally and opened their proceedings with a declaration of secrecy. Tone and Russell gave a report on the activities of the Catholic Committee in Dublin. It was agreed that the revised resolutions should be sent to Tandy in Dublin and he should be asked for his and his fellow citizens' co-operation. When Tone recorded this meeting in his diary, he suggested that the activities of the Secret Committee would reflect great credit on the United Irishmen of 'Belfescu'. Thus was the birth of the Society of United Irishmen and at last Drennan's concept of a secret society of radical reformers had become a reality. Tone and his friends had just created the first political organisation in the history of Ireland which was open alike to Catholic, Protestant and Dissenter. The new society was dedicated to non-sectarian democratic politics, parliamentary reform and civil liberty for all. Tone had been much impressed with the Secret Committee and found them all to be steady, sensible, clear men and extremely well adapted to serious business. This was indeed fortunate, for it was serious business they were embarked on and before it was over, many of them would suffer long terms of imprisonment and Tone and Russell would lose their lives.

On 9 November 1791, Drennan attended a meeting convened by Tandy at the Eagle Tavern, Eustace Street in Dublin, where eighteen men, Protestant and Catholic, formed a club. They called themselves the Society of United Irishmen of Dublin. They adopted the resolutions which Tone and Russell had brought from the Belfast United Irishmen. At the first meeting, a committee of six was established to draw up regulations for the new society. Tandy and Drennan were among the six appointed. Drennan proposed a solemn declaration or test, which was to be taken by every new member on admittance. We have noted already that Drennan was a great proponent of tests and that a decade earlier, he had proposed a test for the Volunteers. He had obviously come to this meeting with a well-prepared script for he succeeded in getting unanimous agreement to the following:

I, – AB in the presence of God, do pledge myself to my country, that I will use all my abilities and influence in the attainment of an impartial and adequate representation of the Irish nation in parliament: and as a means of absolute and immediate necessity in accomplishing this chief good of Ireland, I shall do whatever lies in my power to forward a brotherhood of affection, an identity of interests, a communion of rights, and a union of power among Irishmen of every religious persuasion, without which every reform must be partial, not national, inadequate to the wants, delusive to the wishes, and insufficient for the freedom and happiness of this country.[23]

Tone and Russell had not attended this first Dublin meeting but when they attended a later meeting, they both expressed their opposition to Drennan's test which they saw as too rhetorical and argumentative. When they pushed the question to a vote, they lost by a large margin.[24] Drennan felt that they were both imprudent and had made themselves unpopular and tended to treat the fellow members as instruments rather than partners. Neither Tone nor Russell was prepared to let the matter drop and they continued at a later meeting to argue against the test saying it was dangerous to exclude many who might, but for the test, wish to become members. Tandy vigorously defended the test and argued:

If the test kept them away we should do better without such men, and that it was better to have a society knit together and braced by a strong obligation, than to admit these scrupulous half-way men who would soon damp the zeal and spirit of the meeting and perhaps in some time, outvote the original members and defeat the purpose of the institution.[25]

However, Drennan was pleased that many of the Catholics were zealous to take the test which he thought was an indication of their sincerity, though he observed that 'the solemnity is a thing they like, perhaps from their religion'.[26] The membership of the Dublin Society grew quickly and by the end of December, it had grown from its original eighteen to ninety-six members.

9

THE FAITHFUL WOUNDS OF A FRIEND

In February 1792, after a hiatus of nearly two and a half years, Martha resumed her regular correspondence with her brother. She marked her epistolary comeback with a substantial letter to her 'beloved' Will. Unfortunately, the news she had was not encouraging. She began her missive in an urgent tone of near panic which continued throughout.

> You are attacked in the public paper, in your character, your religion, your head and worst of all your heart, and by whom, that man who by being for years cherished as your friend, ought to have known its value ... he knows, everyone here knows you were the author of the test – and it is with pain I add, that as such, I fear you are generally reprobated by those you most esteem here ... some who have gone so far when in their cups, as to wish to see the promoters of this work hanged – and at a time they knew you to be the chief one.[1]

William Bruce, probably Drennan's most valued friend and confidant of many years, attacked the United Irish test in a sermon at Rosemary Lane, from the very pulpit which Drennan's father had once occupied. The congregation at which Bruce's harangue was directed included Martha, Sam, Drennan's mother and many of the friends of his youth. Not content with confining his opinions to the Meeting House, Bruce also published his *Strictures on the Test taken by certain of the Societies of United Irishmen* in the *Belfast Newsletter*.[2]

Martha felt that Bruce had 'stepped out of his way into the pulpit and into a public paper to fix a stigma on a number of his townsman and his oldest friend'.[3] She also had no doubt that whoever had spread the report of Drennan, saying that the Catholics had acted with duplicity, was engaged 'in a wicked design to blast and damage' her brother. She worried that he 'might be hurt in his profession – be termed a fine writer but a dangerous and rebellious man'.[4]

Martha goes on to ask him how he intends to react to Bruce's attack? While claiming that she would not presume to advise him, she goes on to do precisely that. She suggests that Drennan should consider a public answer to Bruce which she hoped might do him and his cause honour.[5]

Drennan started writing straight away and within a few days sent a paper to Sam which he wished to be shown to Martha and Samuel Neilson before being sent to Joy's *Newsletter* and to Neilson's new paper the *Northern Star*.[6] He gave Sam permission to change any word or phrase that might be too sharp. He knew it was too long but he had not the time to make it shorter.[7] From early February 1792 to the end of March, the two old friends engaged in a bitter public paper war, with Bruce assailing the test and Drennan robustly defending it.

Bruce began his first paper by quoting the full text of the test. He then comprehensively deconstructs it. Firstly, he argues that those who pledge 'to use all their abilities' to achieve certain objects would have no time left for the ordinary business of life. He further suggests that pursuit of an impartial Representation of the Irish Nation implies that 'every man, adult or a minor, *nay every woman*, [emphasis added] in short every rational being shall have equal weight in electing representatives'. He points out that the test supports universal suffrage which goes beyond what then existed in America or France. His next point is that 'a communion of rights and a union of power would give the Roman Catholics who are ten times more numerous as Presbyterians ten times as much power'.[8]

Bruce then brings to his task what an Irish playwright of a later era described as 'all the added bitterness of an old friend'.[9] He suggests that the test 'is the composition of a Jesuitical, a rhetorical, or an enthusiastic mind: for either through craft, vanity, or precipitation, it is calculated to deceive'.[10] In any age it would be regarded as offensive to accuse a friend of calculated deceit. The term Jesuitical as used by Protestants in the eighteenth century is much more pejorative than the term is usually understood to be today. Today it might merely mean pedantic hair-splitting and answering a question in a way which conveys no information. In earlier centuries, it was understood to refer to religiously fanatical and professionally trained deceivers who felt a God-given entitlement to lie and to mislead even under oath.

Bruce went on to argue that the test was calculated to oblige men never to change their opinion which is inconsistent with 'the primary right of man', freedom of thought.[11] Of course, freedom of thought is a core value of the Unitarian world view which Bruce and Drennan shared. Martha was sure that Bruce was alluding to Sam, when he made the following point:

Such oaths entrap and imprison the mind, and someone thus sworn hates even his friend that would disturb his ignorant and bigoted repose. He accordingly associates only with his fellow jurors who foster his prejudices, influence his passions and throw dust in his eyes; so that when he issues from his club room and meets the old staunch and effectual friends of civil and religious liberty, he mistakes them for dotards, courtiers and sycophants.[12]

In Drennan's first answer to Bruce, he said that he read with extreme concern 'the ingenious though fretful strictures which he suggests betrays [in the author] pique and irritation'.[13] Drennan's main point is that when interpreting the meaning of words and phrases, Bruce defines them only in the loosest or narrowest sense. He keeps swinging between extremes instead of taking the words and phrases as they would be taken in common sense by common men. Drennan argues that the test is not an oath, as an oath is a promise to God whereas the United Irishmen's promise is to the public.

This gave ammunition to Bruce for his next attack. He seemed to enjoy himself when he revised the test to reflect how he interprets Drennan's clarifications and explanations.

I, A. B. *do* not swear, but merely, *in the presence of God pledge myself to my country, that,* till I think better of it, *I will use* as much of my *abilities and influence* as I can spare *in the attainment of* a partial, which I deem an *adequate representation of the Irish nation in Parliament: and as a means of absolute and* immediate *necessity, in the establishment of this chief good of Ireland I will,* unless I change my mind, *endeavour as much as lies in my inclination, to* forward progressively *a brotherhood of affection, an identity of interests. A communion of rights, and a common exertion among Irishmen of all religious persuasions; without which every reform in Parliament must be partial* – and anything herein contained to the contrary notwithstanding, I pledge myself in the presence of God, that no partial reform can be *national,* but must be *inadequate to the wants, delusive to the wishes, and insufficient for the happiness and freedom of this country.*[14]

Bruce then quotes at great length Drennan's fifth *Letter of Orellana* in which Drennan had asserted that, 'the Catholics of this day are absolutely incapable of making a good use of political liberty'. He claims to esteem this letter as '*the most exquisite morsel of genius and eloquence that this island can boast*'. He further claims, '*to esteem the author to be the most eminent ornamental and the ablest advocate of the Catholic cause*. It is difficult to be sure if this is Bruce's honestly held opinion. It might suggest the envy of one who had literary pretentions but never enjoyed the success that Drennan enjoyed from *Orellana*. Maybe it is an example of what Martha described as Bruce's forte for satire, in and out of the pulpit.[15]

In his second answer to the *Strictures*, Drennan refutes charges of inconsistency regarding Catholic rights between *Orellana* and the United Irish test. He invokes the Scottish Enlightenment idea that involvement in commercial society fits people for democratic government. His answer was:

> The circumstances of the times as well as the persons have changed, in the very manner wished for, and the mind must change along with them. – To commercial interest, a middle and a mediating rank had rapidly grown up in the Catholic community, and has produced that enlargement of mind, that energy of character, and that self-dependence, which men acquire whose interests do not hang at the mercy of this or that individual, but on general and necessary consumption.[16]

In his second answer, dated 20 March, Drennan finished by saying he was now done with the altercation. A week later, Bruce had the last word. He insisted that as to the emancipation of the Roman Catholics, his sentiments were not less liberal than those of the United Irishmen and that he never wished to impeach their intentions. He said that in commencing the controversy, he had sacrificed his feelings to a sense of duty. He finished with what he described as the words of a wise man:

> *Faithful are the wounds of a friend*
> *But the kisses of an enemy are deceitful.*[17]

When Bruce denounced his old friend's work publicly as *a Jesuitical composition calculated to deceive* or when he praised *Orellana* as *the most exquisite morsel of genius that this island can boast*, were both sentiments the faithful wounds of a friend or the deceitful kisses of an enemy? For his part, Drennan never felt much hurt from the attack and after he received a letter from Bruce which does not seem to have survived, he concluded that Bruce had acted from pure motives.

As Drennan and Bruce fought out their 'test' controversy in the Belfast newspapers, the Dublin Society was drawn into its first major crisis and confrontation with the government. The Solicitor General, John Toler (1745–

1831) attacked the United Irishmen in a speech to the House of Commons: 'I have seen papers signed by Tobias McKenna, with Simon Butler in the chair and Napper Tandy lending his countenance; I should have thought they could have put a better face on it. But sir such fellows are too despicable for notice; therefor[e] I shall not drag them from their obscurity.'[18]

Tandy, who was possessed of an extraordinarily ill-favoured visage, reacted to this matter personally. He demanded an explanation or apology which the Solicitor General refused. Toler let it be known that he was prepared to fight a duel and Drennan, who was not in possession of the full facts, mistakenly believed that Tandy declined to take the hint or the challenge. He felt that Tandy had mismanaged the business and lost ground in the affair. Firstly, he had dwindled down the general cause into a personal altercation. Secondly, when he made the affair personal and Toler stood his ground, Tandy should have taken up the challenge. Unknown to Drennan, Tandy had offered to fight Toler. His preference was to travel outside the jurisdiction to Holyhead, in Wales, where he might not be arrested.[19] Earlier, when the sergeant at arms attempted to arrest Tandy for his attack on parliamentary privilege, he made an undignified escape through a parlour window.[20] Tandy went into hiding and the government offered what Drennan described as a contemptuous reward of £50 for his apprehension. The Lord Lieutenant scornfully suggested the reward should be 50 pence.[21] Drennan thought it likely that Tandy would surrender shortly before the end of the parliamentary session. 'Tandy had two, or perhaps three, horrors about him – a horror of Newgate – a horror of the bar of the House.' Drennan may have been wrong in suggesting that Tandy had a horror of fighting.[22]

The Society held an emergency meeting to discuss the affair and Tone took on the role of secretary, in the absence of Tandy; Archibald Hamilton Rowan took the chair. Tone had talked to Rowan beforehand pointing out that, if the Society was not to sink lower in public opinion, it was necessary that some members should step forward and show that they would not be intimidated by the House of Commons. The meeting passed three resolutions which, according to Tone, 'were worded in a manner very offensive to the dignity of the House and in fact amounted to a challenge to their authority'.[23] These were inserted in the newspapers and 5,000 copies were printed under the names of Archibald Hamilton Rowan, chairman, and Theobald Wolfe Tone as secretary. Tone explained why he and Rowan had taken this 'bold step':

The least we expected ... was to be committed to Newgate for a breach of privilege, and perhaps exposed to personal discussions with some of the members of the House of Commons; for he [Rowan] proposed, and I agreed if any disrespectful language was applied to either of us in any debate which might arise on the business, we would attack the person, whoever he might be, immediately, and oblige him to recant his words or give battle.[24]

Tandy came out of hiding on 18 April, in the knowledge that he could not be detained once the parliamentary session had concluded the following day. He was sent to Newgate and he went there surrounded by supporters. A regiment took up positions around the gaol, 'in order to prevent or provoke a riot'.[25] Drennan did not go and he lamented that 'poor Tandy after eighteen years of struggle against his own interests in the public cause, has nearly lost his reputation in a quarter of an hour'.[26] Nonetheless when Tandy was released the next day, he marched home in triumph surrounded by his supporters.

Rowan and Tone attended the public gallery of the House the last day of the session, dressed in their gaudy Whig Club uniforms making sure that the members knew they were there. Their presence was obvious to all but their names were not mentioned, nor were they called before the next session of parliament to answer charges for their breach of privilege. Tone felt that perhaps the government was content with its victory over Tandy or had not thought himself and Rowan important enough to attract their notice or maybe 'they were reluctant to embroil themselves with a man of Rowan's firmness and courage'.[27] A further factor may also have been that, as Tone awaited his summons to the House, the building was destroyed by a fire which was apparently the result of an accident.

10

EDMUND BURKE

We have seen that William Drennan's first foray into literary propaganda was his open letter to Edmund Burke in 1781. At the time, Burke was fifty years old and already had a great reputation as a parliamentarian and statesman. Drennan was just twenty-six and completely unknown to the Irish or British public. For the rest of his life, Drennan took a great interest in what Burke had to say on Irish and international affairs. We have described in an earlier chapter the differing attitudes of Burke and Drennan to the Volunteer army of Ireland, free trade and the lifting of British commercial restrictions on Ireland. We have also seen that they held conflicting views on the circumstances in which Irish Catholics might have the right to bear arms.

We will now examine other issues that engaged their attention, the American war, the movement for parliamentary reform in Britain and Burke's attacks on the English Unitarians and the French Revolution. Drennan's and Burke's contrasting support for Catholic emancipation requires a chapter to itself and will be dealt with later.

During the American Revolution, both Burke and William Drennan sympathised with the colonists. However, their sympathies were of a very different order. Drennan was an enthusiastic supporter of the American drive for independence. He hailed the American victory at Saratoga as a victory for mankind and predicted, that 'future historians would date the fall of the British Empire from 16 October 1777'.[1]

Burke wanted the British government to make concessions to the colonists rather than wage a war against them, yet he was no supporter of American independence until the fortunes of war made it inevitable. Early on, he declared, 'I have always been and shall ever be earnest to preserve the Constitutional dependence of the Colonies on the Crown.'[2] He expressed his disdain for 'the mutinous spirit of America' and 'the colonies' poor behaviour'.[3] For Burke, 'the self-appointed champions of liberty' in America were subverting 'proper subordination' which he held to be 'an ineluctable maxim of the government of Empire'.[4] However, he did not believe that America could be conquered by 'naked force'. He accused Lord North's government of compromising 'public authority and inciting popular animosity in America'.[5]

Drennan's optimism that Saratoga might be the beginning of the end of the British Empire was misplaced, yet it was the beginning of the end of the American war. It was also a catalyst for the revival of a reform movement in Britain. Facing defeat in America in tandem with its problems in Ireland, the British government faced increasing pressure at home. The high taxation occasioned by the cost of the war was fuelling discontent. One objective of the reformers was to curb Court corruption by reducing crown contracts, offices, placemen and pensioners. This objective was very dear to Burke's heart. However, there were also demands for more frequent parliaments, fairer representation and a broadening of the franchise. Burke always dismissed these demands as dangerous speculative innovations.

Besides the notorious 'rotten boroughs' such as Dunwich, which had fallen into the sea, or Old Sarum, which belonged to the Pitt family with seven voters and two MPs, there was a massive imbalance in representation at Westminster:

> Seats were heavily weighted towards the south and south west ... Cornwall alone had forty-four Members of Parliament and its four neighbouring counties of Devon, Dorset, Somerset and Wiltshire contained roughly a quarter of the [English] seats. London, by contrast, had ten percent of the whole population but only ten seats. Nottingham and Newcastle then both large and important towns had just two seats each. Birmingham and Manchester had none.[6]

Some advanced reformers such as John Jebb and Major John Cartwright advocated equal representation and adult male suffrage.[7] Burke was emphatically opposed to any reform which would broaden the franchise and had distanced himself from what he described as Cartwright's 'speculative ideas for improvement of the constitution'.[8]

Burke tried to steer the reform campaign in England to concentrate solely on the question of Court corruption. He wanted parliament to be free of control by the Crown but he did not want parliamentarians to be answerable to citizens. In fact, any attempt to introduce fairer representation or broadening of the franchise was anathema to him.[9] He once declared that the idea that 'representation of the Commons should be chosen by the people to be absurd and dangerous' and that such 'a scheme of election had been at all times perfectly odious' to him.[10] He presented his so-called 'radical' reform package in his *Speech on Economical Reform*, published in March 1780. It contained nothing in relation to the franchise or reform of representation. John Jebb derided the speech as 'a raging tempest fit to do no better than drown a fly'.[11]

Another aspect of the reformers ongoing agitation was the campaigns for repeal of the Test and Corporation Acts which denied Protestant Dissenters access to public office. The existence of these Acts served to unite Dissenters in Ireland and Britain over the years in the agitations for reform. William Drennan had been raised in what was referred to in Ireland as the New Light Presbyterian faith. In Britain, this belief system was known as Rational Dissent. New Light Presbyterians and Rational Dissenters stood for private judgment in religious matters and held that no government or Church establishment had authority over an individual's conscience. They rejected the doctrine of the Trinity as unscriptural and were, in fact, Unitarians. They were often reluctant to publicly avow themselves as such, as it was illegal to deny the Trinity or to declare oneself as Unitarian until 1813. Drennan, who avowed his Unitarianism only in private correspondence, greatly admired the clergymen, Dr Richard Price (1723–1791), Dr Joseph Priestley (1733–1804) and Dr John Jebb (1736–1786), who were amongst the most radical of the British reformers. These clergymen had published extensively in favour of constitutional reform, the American cause and freedom of conscience for Dissenters

With the fall of the Bastille in July 1789, these same reformers hailed the National Assembly of France as the transfer of power from an arbitrary tyrant to an elected assembly of the French people. They enjoyed great popularity amongst liberals and Protestant Dissenters in Britain and Ireland. They also enjoyed friendships and admiration in America from the likes of Benjamin Franklin and Thomas Jefferson. Edmund Burke, however, was no admirer and certainly no friend. Although Price, Priestley and Jebb were ordained ministers of religion, Burke chose to regard them as atheists. He also described them as a dangerous political faction whose 'wicked principles and black hearts' needed to be exposed.[12]

When, in 1792, some Unitarians petitioned the British House of Commons for the repeal of those laws which forbade the expression of Unitarian views, they were viciously attacked by Edmund Burke. He had once dismissed Dr Price and his friends as, 'a half-dozen grasshoppers under a fern'. However, now he resorted to a more splenetic entomological metaphor:

These insect reptiles ... fill us with disgust; if they grow above their natural size, and increase the quantity, whilst they keep the quality of their venom, they become objects of the greatest terror. A spider in his natural size is only a spider, ugly and loathsome; and his flimsy net is only fit for catching flies. But good God! Suppose a spider as large as an ox, and that he spreads cable around us: all the wilds of Africa would not procure anything so dreadful.[13]

One reason for Burke's malice, which today would be regarded as 'hate speech', was that he was, at this time, strongly advocating that Britain should wage a war of annihilation against the French Revolution.[14] 'He argued that concerted [hostile] action with the continental powers against France should be accompanied by firm action against the radicals at home.'[15] As many Unitarians had welcomed the early stages of the Revolution, Burke denounced them as allies of the French Jacobins.

Burke's fervent desire was to convince the British government to go to war. Distinctions such as the difference between French Jacobins who were often Deists or Atheists and British Unitarians who regarded themselves as Christians, meant nothing to him. Dr Price and Dr Priestley were, of course, law-abiding citizens and not murderous traitors or incendiaries. This counted for little with Burke at this point. Better by far to paint the reformers as the enemy within, just waiting for the opportunity to murder their fellow citizens. Burke warned the Commons, without producing a shred of evidence, that the Unitarians sought to 'collect a multitude of sufficient force and violence to overturn the Church and State'. He urged the House not to wait until 'the conspirators, met to commemorate 14th July, shall seize on the Tower of London and the Magazines it contains, murder the Governor, and the Mayor of London, seize upon the King's person, drive out the House of Lords, occupy your gallery and thence, from as a high tribunal dictate to you'.[16]

Two years earlier, on 4 November 1789, just three months after the fall of the Bastille, Dr Price had given a sermon to the Revolution Society on the birthday of William III. This society existed, not to conspire at violent revolution but to commemorate the so-called Glorious Revolution of 1688. As far as British Whigs and Protestant Dissenters were concerned, the replacement of James II by William had delivered them from arbitrary power and brought about a limited monarchy and their much-vaunted British constitutional liberties.

In his sermon, Price covered the usual ground and grievances of the dissenters. The negative affect of the Test Act, the unequal representation of the people in Parliament and the continuing curbs on the freedom of conscience of

Dissenters. However, the sermon was delivered to an audience, who like many people in Britain at the time, were revelling in the recent fall of the Bastille and the absolutist monarchy in France.[17] Price was delighted that the Third Estate had transformed itself into a Constituent Assembly and made its Declaration of the Rights of Man. He finished his sermon on a high note and welcomed these developments with a flourish:

> Tremble all ye oppressors of the world! Take warning all ye supporters of slavish governments and slavish hierarchies! Call no more (absurdly and wickedly) reformation, innovation. You cannot now hold the world in darkness. Struggle no longer against increasing light and liberality. Restore to mankind their rights and consent to the correction of abuses, before they and you are destroyed together.[18]

When this sermon was published, Burke set about writing his famous *Reflections on the Revolution in France*, in which he poured torrents of abuse on Dr Price, the French Revolution and all those in England who wished the Revolution well. Burke's work was greeted with such enthusiasm that it shot through eleven editions in the first year.[19] The rancorous, heated tone of Burke's prose delighted conservatives but shocked reformers and Protestant Dissenters. One Dissenter observed that Burke lashed out, 'as if he was possessed by a daemon of the nether regions'. Yet even Burke's strongest critics recognised that despite the almost deranged tone, his pamphlet was, from his own point of view, a great success:

> The phantoms which his own disordered imagination had raised to alarm and inflame the members of the House of Commons, unhappily succeeded too well in misleading the more timid and lukewarm friends of liberty, and thus by detaching them from their more steady associates, served to encourage Ministers to a more open avowal of their hostility, and to the prosecution of measures which otherwise they never would have dared to impose.[20]

Burke's *Reflections* first appeared in November 1791. He said that the primary aim of his work was 'to awaken politically those who would not like to have their mansions pulled down and pillaged, their persons abused, insulted, and destroyed; their title deeds brought out and burnt before their faces'.[21]

There is a deep irony in this. We shall see presently that within a short time from the publication of *Reflections*, the mansions that were pulled down and pillaged belonged to Dr Priestley and his Unitarian friends. The rioters were aided, abetted and directed by men inspired by Burke's eloquence. The publication of *Reflections* signalled the beginning of a pamphlet war as many, including Mary Wollstonecraft, Thomas Paine and Dr Priestley, wrote to defend Dr Price and confute Burke.

The Unitarian society which had sponsored the petition to Parliament, which had attracted Burke's ire, had held its first meeting in February 1791. It was formed by a Unitarian network established the previous year which devised a plan for a correspondence with friends in every great town and district in the Kingdom. The organisers also hoped that 'Ireland and Scotland also by the by might come in.'[22] The new society defined its objective as 'To advance the interests of truth and virtue, to promote peace and liberty and good order in society; to accelerate the improvement of the species; and to exalt the character, and to secure the greatest happiness of individuals, by disseminating the right principles of religion, and by exciting the attention of men to the genuine doctrines of revelation.'[23]

Innocent as all this might seem, it was, in fact, illegal. The mere adoption of the label, Unitarian, was a breach of the law. The reference to the genuine doctrines of revelation suggests that they would deny that the doctrine of the Trinity was genuine revelation. This could have led to charges under the Blasphemy Act. Yet there is no mention of seizing the Tower or conspiracy to murder. William Godwin recorded that ten Dissenters, all of whom held anti-Trinitarian views, had been present at Dr Price's famous sermon but as Stuart Andrews has observed, 'this hardly amounts to a revolutionary army or indeed a fifth column.'[24]

Burke's strategy, posited as it was on a baseless, catastrophic fantasy, was completely successful. Theobald Wolfe Tone, William Drennan's fellow United Irishman, recorded in his memoirs that 'In England, Burke had the triumph completely to decide the public; fascinated by an eloquent publication, which flattered so many of their prejudices, and animated by their unconquerable hatred of France ... the whole English Nation ... retracted from the first decision in favour of the glorious and successful effort of the French people.'[25]

11

THE HOUNDING OF
PRIESTLEY AND PAINE

Even before war was declared, Burke's alarmism about the reformers' disloyalty, treachery and conspiracy had stoked fear and passions which led to mob violence against Dissenters. Burke was openly delighted[1] when a Church and King mob rioted for three days in Birmingham in July 1791. The mob demolished twenty-seven Dissenter homes, burnt four dissenter meeting houses including Dr Priestley's Unitarian chapel, his family home and his science laboratory. These events 'were undoubtedly fostered by local magistrates, Anglican clergy and local landlords'.[2] The *Times* noted that the rioters were 'almost to a man respectable housekeepers and manufacturers' and that the demolition workers laboured in a cool and orderly manner.[3] They were directed by two men on horseback (that is gentlemen) who suggested appropriate targets such as Priestley's new meeting house.[4] Dr Spencer, a Justice of the Peace, was said to be present, warning the rioters not to hurt each other.[5] On hearing of these events, King George said he 'could not be better pleased that Priestley was the sufferer for the doctrines he and his party have instilled'.[6]

There was great sympathy for Priestley amongst the United Irishmen and Samuel Neilson wrote an editorial which appeared in the *Northern Star* on 25 April 1792:

There is not perhaps an instance existing, of a more successful deception than that practiced on the people of Birmingham in exciting their indignation against Doctor Priestley. There is not a doubt that the very people who destroyed his house and its contents, and who would have gladly destroyed him in it, would be among the first to idolize him if they knew what his sentiments really are and what is the tendency of his meritorious labour. The great endeavour of his life is to soften and ease the condition of mankind: and as the condition of the lower orders of the people stand in most need of amendment ... they would consider his protection a debt of justice.[7]

There was little sympathy for Priestley in England, however, and Burke now stressed that the attack on Priestley, 'showed that all along he [Burke] had been supported by the nation whose sentiments he had undertaken to describe'. He believed he had succeeded in capturing British feeling.[8] Priestley left Birmingham for London but the Tory press continued to hound him and, by calling him 'Gunpowder Joe', cast him as a Guy Fawkes figure. A song entitled 'Old Mother Church' accused Priestley of wishing to kill his king:

Sedition is their creed
Feigned sheep but wolves indeed
How can we trust?
Gunpowder Joe would
Deluge the throne in blood
And lay the great and the good
Low in the dust
History thy page unfold
Did not their sires of old
Murder their king?
And they would overthrow
Kings, lords and bishops too.[9]

All of this had its effect and by February 1794, William Drennan was reporting that 'Dr. Priestley is about setting out for America. They say he cannot get a servant who will hire with him, he is so terrible an object.'[10]

Priestley had been in contact with the Dublin Society of United Irishmen almost from the formation of the Society and they had followed his case with great interest. A letter Priestley had written to the Catholic Committee had been read to an early meeting of the Society in December 1791, in which he welcomed 'the junction between the papists and the Presbyterians'. He suggested to the Catholics that they should 'seek a proportion (according to their numbers) of the tithes for the support of their own clergy'.[11] At one point, the United Irish Society discussed a proposal to confer honorary membership on Priestley.

In March 1794, William Drennan told his sister Martha:

Mr. Priestley's emigration will be a historical fact which will tell against England the longest day that it has to live, and I question if he could do no much service to the cause for which he suffers in any way by so much as by this action. Indeed, if there was to be an invasion of England he would probably be murdered, and it is therefore the highest prudence that he goes off in time.[12]

When news of his planned departure for America reached Dublin, Drennan was asked to draw up an address in his honour on behalf of the society. Stephen Small summarised the address as follows:

The United Irishmen noted with sadness that Priestley (a scientist and man of progress) had been driven out of his native land and would not be buried alongside his British reformer friends, Savile, Price, Jebb and Fothergill. They asked for Priestley's prayers for not only their own member Rowan but for the Scottish martyrs Muir, Palmer, Skirving, Margarot and Gerrald. The address is optimistic and visionary in that Priestley is going to a happier world not Heaven just yet but rather the world of WASHINGTON and FRANKLIN.[13]

When Drennan read this address to a poorly attended meeting of the Dublin United Irish Society, one member suggested that it should be postponed, as 'he had good reason to believe that Priestley was not going to America but rather was coming to Dublin to work for a Unitarian congregation who had offered £300 per annum for Priestley's services'.[14] Priestley did go to America where he settled in Pennsylvania and died in 1805. He had chosen Pennsylvania because it was free from the curse of slavery.

Many years later, in 1803, Drennan was disgusted when he heard rumours were being circulated in Dublin by some New Light Ministers, including Dr Bruce, that Priestley's son had tried to poison his father in America. Drennan did not believe these rumours and felt they were designed to poison Priestley's and his son's reputation. He was particularly shocked that men who had once boasted of being Priestley's faithful friends and followers were now telling these stories with an air of glee and satisfaction which might have been expected from Priestley's most trenchant loyalist enemies.[15]

The Persecution of Thomas Paine

The firm action which Burke had advocated against the radicals began even before the war commenced. Pitt's government used a combination of character assassination, official coercion and orchestrated mob violence to rid the country of Thomas Paine, whose *Rights of Man* was the most influential repost to Burke's *Reflections*.

Initially, William Pitt 'did not think *Rights of Man* or its horde of enthusiasts politically threatening but within a year came around to the Burkean position'.[16] Under the pseudonym Francis Oldys, a Scottish lawyer, George Chambers, was commissioned to write a scurrilous attack under the title, *The Life of Thomas Paine, Author of the Rights of Man*.[17] Paine thus became 'the first publicist in modern time to be savaged by a government muckraking campaign waged publicly through the press'.[18] Chambers claimed that Paine was a truant stay-maker, neglectful husband, lapsed Christian and atheist, failed shopkeeper and dishonest exciseman.[19] A counterfeit letter, supposedly from Paine's mother, complained of his debts, his terrible treatment of his wife and his undutiful treatment of his parents. 'Charles Harrington Elliot charged that Paine was known to engage in carnal relations with his "maiden wife" and a cat.'[20]

In May 1792, a royal proclamation was issued against 'wicked and seditious writings', targeting Paine.[21] That same month, the Dublin Society of United Irishmen debated a proposal to confer honorary membership on Paine and Dr Priestley.

According to the information supplied by Thomas Collins:

> The honourable Simon Butler moved that Thomas Paine from his singular exertions in the cause of freedom, deserves the upmost veneration of this Society and the same be published in the *Evening Star*. In the arguments in respect to the admission of Mr. Paine and Doctor Priestley every member present declared that they avowed every principle of both these gentlemen but from the critical situation of affairs at this crisis and being an inroad to admit other honorary members it would not be prudent.[22]

However, at the next meeting, honorary membership was conferred on Paine on a vote of thirty-one to six against. Dr John Burke, the then secretary of the Society, informed Paine accordingly.

The Pitt administration continued to pile the pressure on Paine. He was brought to court on 26 June with a trial date set for the following December. The purpose of this long adjournment was to tighten the screw slowly on Paine, 'in the hope that he would either buckle or emigrate'.[23] One of Paine's biographers had described the government's tactics in the run-up to the trial:

> Across England the government incited mass riots and demonstrations through a national society, the Association for Preserving Liberty and Property Against Republicans and Levellers. Cambridge University gave its support to local mobs and their violent assaults on political discussions at public meetings. Effigies of Paine were hanged and then incinerated along with copies of his book to shouts of 'God Save the King!' Local drinking songs included a new chorus: 'up with the cause of old England; And down with the tricks of Tom Paine'.[24]

Paine was trailed by spies everywhere he went. The original publisher of the *Rights of Man*, J.S. Jordan, was summoned to appear at the Court of King's Bench. Paine wrote to the Attorney General, Sir Arthur McDonald, accusing him of conniving with Edmund Burke to attack the innocent Jordan as a means of suppressing *Rights of Man*.[25] In this letter, Paine makes a serious accusation against Burke. He claimed that Burke was 'a masked pensioner at £1,500 per annum for about ten years'.[26] Paine is, of course, a hostile witness and he produces no evidence for his charge but does receive some support from other, albeit also hostile, sources. Wolfe Tone claimed that Burke was 'pensioned by the British government under a fictitious name to betray the cause of the people [the Irish Catholics who] had a most perfect trust in him'.[27] William Drennan was, of course, antagonistic to Burke's politics but recognised his talents as a writer. Whenever he had anything positive to say about him, he referred to him as the un-pensioned Burke. This suggests Burke was a one-time, but not lifelong, independent. If Burke had been, from an early stage, a paid agent of Pitt's government, he was good value for money. He split the Whig party and ensured that its leader, Charles J. Fox, was the best Prime Minister Britain never had. Thanks to Burke, William Pitt remained unassailable in office until he left of his own volition in 1801. One of Burke's recent defenders says that, 'as far as we can tell the allegation is entirely untrue'. However, the same writer concedes that if the accusation were true 'it cuts to the root not merely of Burke's achievement but of his moral authority. We may admire his technical facility, but we cannot respect him. He becomes not a great man but a little one'.[28]

Whether Burke was on Pitt's payroll or not, the relentless harassment was taking its toll on Paine. The proclamation against wicked and seditious writings was enforced rigorously and booksellers and printers were receiving severe sentences. The London *Times* suggested that, 'Mad Tom should embark for France and there be naturalized into the regular confusion of democracy.'[29] This was, of course, exactly what the government wanted. When William Blake told his friend, 'you must not go home, or you are a dead man',[30] it was the last straw. Paine headed for the coast. As he fled, Paine was harassed by officials who searched his papers and belongings. They wished to intimidate rather than detain him. Finally, as he boarded a ship bound for Calais, he was abused by a hostile mob.

Burke was usually not slow to respond to a challenge. *Rights of Man* was the most formidable and widely read public challenge to him. He decided not to respond to Paine as the law would probably do so. Once again, Burke's legendary power of prophecy was shown to be most perceptive. Paine's book was banned and he was convicted of sedition in his absence. Like Dr Priestley, Paine was to die in exile and never set foot in his native land again.

The war between Britain and France, which Burke worked so hard to bring about, lasted for twenty-two years, from 1793 until 1815, with a brief cessation in 1802–3. Gilbert Wakefield (1766–1801), a Unitarian minister, claimed that 'within [the first] twelve months, two hundred and fifty thousand lives had been lost in the field or on the scaffold'.[31] Wakefield's anti-war activity would soon land him in prison. He died from typhus shortly after his release in 1801. Drennan read Wakefield's autobiography which he thought 'a most singular book'. He observed that 'after a life of literary labour and afterwards confinement of two years in Dorchester Gaol for a pamphlet written against the war, he died of a fever got by excessive fatigue in walking in search of a house to lodge himself and his family'.[32]

The total number of casualties can never be known but six million people may have died in the conflict. For his part, William Drennan denounced Burke as 'the trumpet of war' and never wavered from his belief that the war was nothing more than a long-drawn-out pointless, wasteful folly.[33]

12

DRENNAN, BURKE AND
THE PENAL LAWS

William Drennan and Edmund Burke were both strongly opposed to the Penal Laws against Catholics in Ireland but for very different reasons. For Drennan, a more equal representation of the people in the Irish Parliament could not be achieved while political rights were denied to the majority population. He, therefore, was to make his life's work the forging of a brotherhood of affection between Catholic, Protestant and Dissenter in pursuit of radical democratic reform.

Burke had always been a trenchant critic of the Penal Laws which he once described as 'a machine of wise and elaborate contrivance, and as well fitted for the oppression, impoverishment and debasement in them of human nature itself, as ever proceeded from the perverted ingenuity of man'.[1]

However, Burke always strongly opposed any measure which might lead towards an equal representation of the people in Parliament and never supported any reform which might alter the status quo in Britain, Ireland or indeed anywhere else. He hated the idea that the Roman Catholics of Ireland might join forces with liberal Protestants and Dissenters with a view to achieving reform.

For most of his parliamentary career, Burke was in opposition and could not do much to the advantage of his Catholic fellow countrymen. However, in his pursuit of his ambition for a military intervention against France, he broke with his party leader and one-time friend, Charles J. Fox. He began to advise the British government to grant concessions to Irish Roman Catholics, in order 'to rally in defence of the established order and civilization, all men of sound principle'. For Burke, well-to-do Irish Catholics were, from 'their religious principles ... natural conservatives'.[2] His advice to government was to woo these well-to-do Catholics away from their dalliance with pro-reform Protestants and Dissenters. He suggested that 'the Irish Catholics', whether 'the old gentlemen who still retain their old religion and estates' or 'the new race of Catholics who have risen by their industry and their good fortune to considerable opulence' were clearly from 'their religious principles, church polity and habitual discipline, natural conservatives'.[3]

The end of 1791 and the beginning of the new year saw a major, if indirect, intervention by Burke into Irish affairs on behalf of the Catholics. With Burke's blessing and encouragement, his son Richard came to Ireland as agent for the Catholic Committee. Control of the Committee had been wrested from 'the aristocratical leadership' of Lord Kenmare and the leadership was now in the hands of John Keogh and Richard McCormack. McCormack and Keogh had joined the United Irish Society. Keogh devised a clever strategy to advance the Catholic cause. In December 1791, he appointed Richard to be an agent for the Catholic Committee in its dealings with the British ministry.[4]

Until his appointment by the Catholics, Richard Burke, with his father's encouragement, had been working with French émigrés to seek British support for a counter-revolutionary war against the French.[5] Burke junior, who held no government office, took it upon himself, in August 1791, to write to the King of France promising him that external assistance *'is coming'*.[6] This amateur diplomacy probably helped to seal Louis' fate. Perhaps it encouraged the beleaguered King to collaborate with a counter-revolutionary foreign invasion rather than come to terms with the Revolution.

John Keogh's hiring of Richard secured the support of the elder Burke who, since he had broken with Fox and the Whigs, had close ties with Pitt's government, particularly with Henry Dundas, the Home Secretary.[7] The elder Burke was, at this time, the darling of the British Tories and Dundas, 'since Burke's break with Fox had been eager to widen the split in the Whig party and took every occasion to conciliate or flatter Burke'.[8] By thus identifying with Britain's leading counter-revolutionary ideologue, now in close alliance with the British government, Keogh hoped to secure the Catholic Committee from charges of disloyalty.

In early December, there were rumours (emanating from Richard Burke) to the effect that the government was about to make concessions to the Catholics. Drennan heard they were to be admitted to the bar and the universities and shortly thereafter the army would be open to them. The Catholics would have to drop all thoughts of the elective franchise and all public meetings were to be discouraged by the Catholic leadership. When Drennan sat down to dinner with a very large party of Catholics and Protestants, he took the opportunity to ask the Catholics directly about how they would react to such an offer from government. All present replied that they would take anything on offer but would not settle for anything short of the elective franchise. They declared that they would rather die than come under any stipulation with regard to their future conduct. They also said that they believed that the bulk of their persuasion were of the same sentiment.[9]

In early January 1792, Richard Burke came to Dublin accompanied by John Keogh. Keogh called on Drennan to give him an account of how things had gone in London and to bring him up to date on developments within the Catholic Committee. Keogh reported that a person in high office in London had asked him whether, if concessions were promised to the Catholics in the event of them breaking off contact with the Presbyterians, they would be prepared to do so. He replied that they would not breach their promises and while they would be grateful for any concessions granted, they would not give pledges as to their conduct. Keogh and Burke were told by senior British officials that concessions would have to be negotiated with the authorities in Dublin rather than London.

Later that month, Drennan was shown a paper which he presumed to have been drafted by Richard Burke. The document was an address from the Catholic Committee to the general Catholic population. At that point, Drennan could not get his hands on a copy but attempted to summarise what he had read so that Sam could keep the Belfast United Irishmen informed:

First, they require the profession of the law in all departments. Second, the exercise of county magistries, sheriffs, coroners and justices of the peace with their inferior officers. Third, the right of serving and the right to be summoned to grand and petty juries in all cases whatsoever. Fourth, a participation in what they call our free constitution by obtaining the elective franchise.[10]

The paper, which had been dictated by Richard's father,[11] did not mention other Catholic grievances, such as the right to carry arms or the right to education and academical honours. Drennan was disappointed by the moderate tone and the lack of any mention of parliamentary reform. He also felt one aim of the paper was to dissociate the Catholics from the Dissenters and that the paper had a hatred of the Presbyterians. This assessment was apposite, as the elder Burke, at this time, was suggesting that the best way to disarm the United Irish threat, 'was to seduce the Catholic masses from all support for their enterprises'.[12]

Despite his disappointment, Drennan felt that if these concessions were granted to the Catholics, the Presbyterians should welcome the development.

For his part, he did not believe that the government would concede the franchise and the first three demands contained in the paper were only relevant to the Catholic aristocracy and not the people.[13]

At this point, a person, or persons unknown, were making mischief for Drennan amongst the Catholics. An extract from one of Drennan's letters to Sam was handed about in Dublin, which suggested that he had accused the Catholics of duplicity of conduct. He did not recollect ever having said this. He did believe 'that they [the Catholic Committee] had acted a double part as a body but he had never suggested that any individuals amongst them had acted with duplicity'. On the contrary, Drennan firmly believed that those he knew 'the most, acted with great zeal and sincerity'. Yet some damage was done to Drennan's reputation amongst the Catholics and John Keogh never called again, after their initial meeting in early January. Drennan mused that if the letter was not the reason for Keogh not visiting, perhaps it was because, while hoping the Burkes could deliver for the Catholics, Keogh might not want to be seen in the company of a known republican such as Drennan.[14]

Clever as John Keogh's strategy of employing Richard Burke was, it did not work. The younger Burke totally mishandled his brief and succeeded only in stirring up false hope amongst the Catholics, while annoying the majority in the Irish House of Commons. The Commons not only threw out the Catholics' petition, they spent the rest of the parliamentary session heaping vitriolic abuse on 'the Belfast Presbyterians, the United Irishmen and the personnel of the Catholic Committee'.[15]

John Keogh lost all confidence in Richard Burke and he and his Committee were greatly relieved when Burke decided to return to England in early April. Keogh was scathing in relation to how Richard Burke had performed his brief. He told how 'in the course of a few weeks Richard contrived to quarrel with the leading men of the Government while simultaneously giving great offence to the gentlemen of the opposition. Worst of all he treated ourselves with so little consideration he would not suffer our opinion to have any weight even in our own affairs, whenever it differed from his'.[16]

Shortly thereafter, Tone replaced Burke as agent for the Catholics. The Committee awarded Burke £2,000 for his efforts. On the night before his departure, nearly one hundred Catholics gathered for a dinner in his honour. Besides the guest of honour, only six other Protestants were in attendance. Simon Butler, Hamilton Rowan, Wolfe Tone, Samuel Neilson, William Drennan and Reverend Robert Black of the Synod of Ulster. Good and spirited toast and compliments were offered to the Protestant guests for their support for the

Catholic cause. Burke was so respectfully treated that he returned to England unaware that he was no longer wanted and had been ditched.[17]

In early September 1792, Richard Burke returned to Ireland much against the wishes of his former employers of the Catholic Committee. Wolfe Tone, his replacement as secretary to the Committee, had drafted a letter asking him to stay in England, which Burke ignored. He believed that only his continued presence in Ireland could prevent the Catholics uniting with the fractious part of the Dissenters.[18] Even when John Keogh met him to explain that his services were no longer required, he continued to style himself the agent of the Catholic Committee. Tone could not help expressing his admiration for Burke's 'consummate effrontery':

> He will be agent to the Catholics, whether they will or not, and absolutely commits a rape upon the Committee. His impudence is beyond what I could have imagined, and his vanity greater. He has the modesty to say that the existence of Ireland depends on his enjoyment of the confidence of the Catholics ... The Catholics astonished and angry at all this persevering insolence, resolved that Gog (John Keogh) shall write to him and tell him he is *not* the agent of the Catholics.[19]

Richard Burke called on Drennan several times in early September, perhaps because he was being shunned by his former employers and was anxious to talk to anyone who would listen to him. Burke assured Drennan that the British government was friendly to the Catholics regarding the elective franchise but it was the ascendancy in Ireland who were endeavouring to stimulate Irish Protestant opinion against concessions. Drennan listened to what Burke had to say but was conscious that all parties in Dublin had, by now, disowned him and he surmised that Burke was now acting merely as a spy for William Pitt. In early December, Burke bowed to the inevitable and returned to London to the great relief of all parties. Before he left, he asked Drennan to write to him. Drennan said it would be an honour, although he believed that any information he supplied would be used to brief Pitt. Drennan saw Burke as a friend to the Catholics and felt he might even be a Catholic, 'as his father is in grain'. He also felt that, were the Catholics not under some constraints, they would, in general, adore the father in all his opinions. However, Drennan's early negative impression had, by now, hardened into a conviction that young Burke 'hates the Presbyterians as he hates the devil'.[20]

In a flight of imagination introduced into a long, reflective letter that Drennan sent to Sam McTier in November 1792, he fancied how Edmund Burke had engaged with the King to break the Catholic Presbyterian alliance and help the Catholics of consequence to keep things in Ireland more or less as they always had been.

> Mr. Burke was called into the closet of the King who acknowledged his numerous obligations for benefits to himself, his family and his government, and asked Burke what return he could make for his abuse against France and his good service to the cause of monarchy? I do believe that Burke answered to this effect, nothing for myself, but much for three million of my loyal and suffering fellow countrymen, the friends and the victims of their attachment to monarchy. Sir, I warn you to do this immediately, an alliance which a little time will make more natural than it now appears, is about to take place between three million discontented Catholics and a half a million disaffected Presbyterian republicans, deeply intoxicated with French notions and French practices. Break this alliance or Ireland is lost to Your Majesty. The constitution will be changed even here and monarchy itself will be endangered. I do believe that the King said 'Burke, Burke let it be done, let the Catholics be emancipated immediately and let me get the credit before it is too late'. I do believe that to Mr. Burke's influence and the King's reasonable panic, all was accomplished without any communication with the Irish cabinet, and that the grand juries and the Chancellor and the council here were laughed at by the Catholics here who were well instructed what was going on in the back stairs conference.[21]

Of course, this fanciful dialogue between Burke and the king never took place. However, there is a lot of truth in what Drennan was suggesting in terms of why and how the Catholic relief question had been handled in England and Burke's influence and motives for becoming involved on their behalf. The major flaw in Drennan's analysis is that he failed to recognise that it was the grand juries and the Chancellor who had had the last laugh. In the event, Hobart had managed to steer the relief bill through the Houses of Parliament in such a way as to ensure that Catholic hopes were dashed rather than realised.

13

BELFAST: A NEST OF REPUBLICANS

In June 1792, Drennan was writing detailed advice through Sam to Neilson's Committee about how the third anniversary of the storming of the Bastille should be celebrated in Belfast. Since large crowds were expected, Drennan advised that plans should be made to carry off the business with as much ostentation and formality as possible. It was important to show such a day, 'can be celebrated in Ireland though they dare not in Britain'.[1] Due to the Birmingham riots on the previous Bastille Day and the subsequent intimidation activities of the Church and King mobs, the British reformers and radicals would make no public show of support for the French. Although a few of the Dublin United Irishmen, including Tone and Tandy, travelled to Belfast, there was little appetite for a Bastille Day celebration in the capital.

Tone went to Belfast to propose a resolution on politics at the request of Neilson's committee. Drennan had been informed that Tone's resolution would empathise adherence to the constitution and abhorrence of a republic. He accepted this was prudent and proper under the circumstances, for as he told Sam, 'these are just the sentiments of the Catholics'.[2]

To complement Tone's non-republican resolution Drennan composed an address to the French Assembly that was full of republican and revolutionary sentiment. It is a strange irony that Tone's moderate resolution ran into difficulty and caused a division between the radical and the more moderate reformers in Belfast, whereas Drennan's fiery and anti-monarchical hyperbole met with the universal approval of all, radicals and moderates alike. Drennan's resolution warrants being quoted in its entirety.

To the National Assembly of France

It is not from vanity or ostentation, that we, Citizens of Belfast, Citizen-Soldiers of that Town and Neighbourhood, take the liberty of addressing the Representative Majesty of the French people — We address you, with the rational respect due to a title elevated far above all servile and idolatrous adulation, and with that affectionate fraternity of heart which ought to unite man to man, in a mutual and inseparable union of interests, of duties and of rights; which ought to unite Nation with Nation, into one great republic of the World.

May you *Legislators* maintain by the indefatigable spirit of liberty, that constitution which has been planned by the wisdom of your predecessors, and never may you weary in the work you have undertaken, until you can proclaim with triumphant security, it is finished! Manifest to an attentive and progressive world, that it is not the phrensy of philosophy, nor the fever of wild or precarious liberty, which could produce such continued agitation, but the imperishable spirit of freedom alone, which always exists in the hearts of man, and which now animated the heart of Europe, and which in the event will communicate its energy throughout the world, invincible and immortal.

We rejoice in the sincerity of our souls, that this creature spirit animates the whole mass of mind in France. We auspicate happiness and glory to the human race from every great event which calls into activity the whole vigour of the whole community; amplifies so largely, the field of enterprise and improvement and gives free scope to the universal souls of the Empire. We trust that you will never submit the liberties of France to any other guarantees than God, and the right hands of the People.

The Power that presumes to modify or to arbitrate with respect to a constitution adopted by the people, is a Usurper and a Despot, whether it be the meanest of the mob, or the ruler of Empires, and if you condescend to negotiate the alteration of a comma in your Constitutional Code, France from that moment is a slave. Impudent Despots of Europe! Is it not enough to crush human nature beneath your feet at home, that you thus come abroad to disturb the domestic settlement of the nations around you, and put in motion those armies, those enormous masses of human machinery, to beat down every attempt that man makes for his own happiness? It is high time to turn those dreadful engines against their inventors, and organized as they have hitherto been, for the misery of mankind, to make them now the instruments of its glory and renovation.

Success therefore, attend the Armies of France!

May your soldiers, with whom war is not a trade but a duty, remember that they do not fight merely for themselves, but they are the advanced guard of the world; nor let them imagine that the event of the war is uncertain. A single battle may be precarious, but not so a few campaigns – There is an Omnipotence in a righteous cause, which masters the pretended mutability of human affairs, and fixes the supposed inconsistency of fortune. If you will be free you must ...

We conclude with this fervent prayer. That as the Almighty is dispersing the political clouds which have hitherto darkened our hemisphere, all the nations may use the Light of Heaven: that, as in this latter age, the Creator is unfolding in his creatures, powers which have long lain latent – they may exert them in the establishment of universal freedom, harmony and peace: may those who are free, never be slaves: may those who are slaves be speedily free.[3]

This strong resolution is more remarkable when we take account of how events were playing out in France as Drennan was composing it. In June 1792, pike wielding sans-culottes had stormed the Tuileries Palace in Paris and confronted the King in his private chambers. The Duke of Brunswick had invaded France at the head of Austrian and Prussian forces whose objective was to capture Paris and rescue the King. The mob in the palace warned the King, 'in the bluntest terms not to look for salvation from France's enemies.'[4]

Tone and Tandy travelled to Belfast for the big occasion while Drennan was unable to leave Dublin due to his medical responsibilities. On the night of 12 July, the various corps from the surrounding towns and districts converged on Belfast. There was a carnival atmosphere as the town's citizens entertained the visiting Volunteers in their own homes. Drennan had strongly advised Sam that this should not be yet another review of the usual kind. He suggested that the celebration should be spread over two days, with a procession as well as a review. There should be a role for the ladies, the lower people and with handsome youths carrying the flags of France, America, Poland and Ireland. Sam and Drennan also exchanged ideas regarding suitable toasts for the occasion. To judge by the report of the festivities in the *Northern Star*, the events were carried off very much according to Drennan's plan.

At nine o'clock this morning the different corps paraded on High-street and were there formed into brigades of three battalions, from whence, at ten, they marched off to the Review Ground, distant about a mile, the discharge of cannon told of the approach of the General, John Crawford ... attended by the Belfast Troop of Light Dragoons.

Immediately after the Review, the Brigade returned to Town to hold a Grand Procession

Grand Procession
Which was arranged in the following manner
Reviewing General
(Preceded by two Troopers)
Belfast Troop of Light Dragoons
Commanding-Officer, and his Aide-de-Camps
Train of Belfast Volunteer Company
Standards of the *Five Free Nations*, with their respective mottos, vis
Ireland – Unite and be free
America – the Asylum of liberty
France – The Nation, the law and the King
Poland – We will support it
Great Britain – Wisdom, Spirit and Liberality to the People

These were the national Flags, elegantly executed, for the different nations for whom they were a carried, borne by boys dressed in the

National Uniform of Ireland
With blue sashes.[5]

The aspect of Tone's intentionally moderate *Address to the People of Ireland*, which caused the problem, was the question of whether the Catholics should attain their political rights immediately or gradually. On the night before the review, Neilson was passing a room in an inn where some of the Country Corps were lodging. He came across Waddell Cunningham, one of Belfast's wealthiest citizens and a leading Volunteer, haranguing some of the visitors, denouncing Tone's resolution. Neilson confronted Cunningham and defended the resolution and though the meeting broke up without a decision, he warned Tone that they would have hot work in the morning.

The next day, Tone attended 'a council of war' in a potato field, where a small group of radicals discussed whether they might be better not to move the resolution rather than see it defeated. Tandy was frightened out of his wits. Tone summarised the waverers' panic in his diary:

> We are undone, shall be defeated; all the Country corps decidedly against us, from the report of some seditious paper (the old story) better to adopt something *moderate* that shall include all parties; danger of disunion; risk of credit if we should succeed even with a small majority which is the best that can be hoped for. The country folks afraid.[6]

In the event, Tone succeeded in steadying their nerves and when, a few hours later, the motion was moved, at an 'astonishingly full' Linen Hall,[7] an attempt by Cunningham to amend it to make Catholic emancipation gradual, was heavily defeated. Tone's original motion was passed by a large majority. When the business in the hall was finished, the company adjourned to a dinner in the Donegall Arms where the *Northern Star* assures us that the greatest harmony and good humour prevailed.[8] However, there was no disguising the fact that liberal Presbyterianism in Belfast was irrevocably split and from then on, the United Irishmen and the moderates went their separate ways.

It is strange that this small but influential minority, which included William Bruce and Henry Joy, were so exercised by Tone's resolution but seemed to have gone along with Drennan's, which was far more extreme and seditious. By unanimously adopting a republican position which supported the French armies in their efforts to defeat foreign intervention, the town of Belfast was marking itself out as 'a nest of republicans'.[9] Edmund Burke's high-profile efforts to drag Britain to war had their effect and nobody could have been surprised that six months later, following the execution of the King, Britain joined the counter-revolutionary coalition and went to war against France.

In 1794, Bruce and Joy published a book entitled *Belfast Politics*, which gave an account of the fateful discussions in Belfast in 1792. The book contained the documents relating to both sides of the Bruce vs. Drennan test and strictures debate. The authors lamented the fact that, as they saw it, Belfast 'having been subject to martial law; the emporium of commerce become a military station, the inhabitants insulted and put to the sword in the streets, and the whole kingdom looking on with acquiescence. Do our demagogues ever ask themselves how it came to pass?'[10]

They suggest three reasons why this had happened. They held the 'demagogues' of the United Irishmen entirely responsible. According to Bruce and Joy, the first aspect of the United Irishmen's activity which prompted government oppression was 'the affectation of secrecy and mystery' which the authors describe as unconstitutional and unmanly. Secondly, the imitation of republican principles and language, accompanied by extravagant demands and menaces, were published with a view to intimidation. Thirdly, the ill-conceived demand for immediate Catholic emancipation which would have 'drowned the few good voters in a deluge of the meanest class of Catholics'.[11]

Bruce and Joy ignore the main change of circumstance which made the dragooning of Belfast possible. Britain had joined in the counter-revolutionary war against France. Thanks to Drennan's resolution, the armed and organised citizenry of Belfast had declared publicly in favour of the French. Belfast had declared that by going to war against the Revolution, King George and his government were placing themselves alongside 'the Impudent Despots of Europe'. Once Britain entered the war democrats, reformers and radicals throughout Britain and Ireland became the target for increased oppression. In England and Scotland, democrats who had always worked openly and publicly, who had never used the language of intimidation and who had said nothing about Catholic rights, found themselves facing charges of treason for seeking democratic reform, for wishing the French Revolution well and opposing Britain's entry into the war.

There is no reason to believe that, had Waddell Cunningham's amendment to Tone's Bastille Day resolution been carried, or if the United Irishmen had accepted Bruce's stricture on their test, Belfast might have been spared martial law or the tender mercies of his Majesty's dragoons. Neither was it Drennan's and his friends' affectation of secrecy which brought on the oppression but rather their open and public support for the French Revolution and their opposition to British intervention on the side of counter-revolution.

By early August 1792, the political world in Dublin was, in Drennan's words, 'at peace or watching in silence the grand scenes that are now acting on the theatre of France'.[12] Grand and dramatic scenes there were aplenty, particularly in Paris. The Duke of Brunswick, at the head of an army of Prussian and Austrian veterans, had invaded France, declaring that if any harm came to the Royal Family, Paris would pay the ultimate penalty.[13] Drennan observed that 'there is no boy's play there'. He mused that if Brunswick reached Paris 'the carnage must be dreadful indeed'.[14] The city was in the grip of panic and on 10 August, enraged sans-culottes once more attacked the Tuileries palace where the

King was being held and slaughtered hundreds of his Swiss Guards. Brunswick's proclamation proved counterproductive for, rather than help the Royal Family, it precipitated the fall of the monarchy.

Rumours that the Jacobins were working in the counter-revolutionary interest by driving the people to madness were dismissed by Drennan as 'a mere Burkeism, an ingenious subtlety without truth'.[15] He was contemptuous of some former friends of the Revolution who were going about snivelling, 'all is lost, the mob, the mob'. He had no doubt that the slaughter at the Tuileries was justified. He had long held the opinion that:

> there never was an insurrection of the people, call them a mob, sans-culottes etc., or what you please which was not justified by the necessity of the case, except perhaps a religious mob. It appears to me a second Bastille business rendered necessary by the treachery of the king, the corruption of the officers, and the gold of Coblenz and all of the confederate kings finding its way not only into the palace, but even into the National Assembly itself. There was no time to be lost in debating and adjourning debate and society rose once more into the seat of government and decided the question.[16]

On 29 August, Brunswick's troops captured Verdun and the last fortress on the road to Paris. This news increased the panic in the city and precipitated a second massacre on a much larger scale. On 2 September, armed bands entered the prisons of Paris and murdered up to 1,400 prisoners over the next few days. Political prisoners and priests were executed along with common law offenders such as thieves, prostitutes, forgers and vagrants.[17] When Drennan heard the 'melancholy accounts'[18] of the slaughter, he did not know what to say. Jean Marie Roland (1734–1792) had written a letter condemning the atrocities, which Drennan hoped Neilson would translate and publish in the *Northern Star* as 'it says all that is right and proper on the subject'.[19] Drennan feared that Brunswick would reach Paris which would be defended by men without arms and the slaughter would be great. However, if the fight for Paris was made a bayonet and pike business and fought in the ancient style of man near man, then he believed the French ardour would prevail.[20]

In this time of existential crisis for the Revolution, Drennan had no qualms about the violence and massacres which had taken place:

> The murder of the prisoners is one of those things which must be openly condemned and perhaps tacitly approved. We would in the same way

condemn the assassination of the king and the emperor. If a boat which escapes from a wreck be sinking with the weight of men, some of them ought to be thrown into the sea. It is no time to weigh nice points of morality, much less of legal forms. Suspicion is a shrewd sign of guilt. Brissot was suspected but instantly gave up all his papers and manifested his innocence. I doubt much if a single man lost his life that was not guilty of *lèse-nation*[21] – and executed by a summary martial law. When the extreme danger ceases the amenability to law will resume its former place. Law is precedent which really cannot anticipate the circumstances which occur in revolution periods, and therefore all that is to be referred to is the instinctive decisions of the people and were not the aristocrats and intriguers of Paris kept down by such vehement procedure, in such a city of 600,000 there would be a plot in every section. The approach of the enemy would increase their strength and if the federates etc. had left Paris in such a situation, there might have been an enemy within worse than the one without. I fear the French armies are by no means a match for the enemy even in numbers and I should imagine a battle would be dangerous for their case even to save Paris. The time for hope is in the retreat, but then the taking of Paris may subdue the whole kingdom. I should hope not – particularly the south would rather divide the whole kingdom than yield.[22]

Two days after Drennan wrote these words, on 20 September, 'the soldiers of the Revolution won a dazzling victory over the forces of Brunswick at the Battle of Valmy'.[23] The army that had threatened Paris with fire and slaughter went into ignominious retreat.[24] On 22 September, France was declared a Republic.

Illuminations, that is lights, were placed in windows in Dublin and Belfast to celebrate the French victory. Support in Dublin was not general, possibly because the Lord Mayor had issued a proclamation forbidding it and had sent horse and foot into the streets in great force.[25] In Belfast, every window was lit up, with the exception of that of Reverend Bristow, the town vicar. The townsfolk of Belfast testified to their politics with great ingenuity by using transparencies, which shone over the dark streets with slogans such as 'Vive la République', 'Vive la Nation', 'Church and State separated' and 'Union amongst Irishmen'.[26]

Martha, who felt the renewal of her wonted spirits, rejoiced with ardour at the downfall of tyranny and hoped that 'Kings will now stay at home for it is there only the gaudy puppet is of any consequence.' She found herself singing 'Over the Hills and Far away' with Prussia and Brunswick skipping before her eyes.[27] She urged her brother to compose a song to 'the jolly tune the Pretender had danced to'. Her good spirits were enhanced by her enjoyment of reading Thomas Paine. Martha had never liked kings and Paine said of them what she had always suspected. She imagined his writings would have a most important effect on the public mind.[28]

Upwards of eighty members were present at a meeting of the Dublin United Society on 2 November 1792, when Drennan was elected President for the ensuing three months and Archibald Hamilton Rowan was elected Secretary. Their term of office would prove exciting, eventful and dangerous for them and their Society. Rowan was not present at the meeting, as he had travelled to Belfast to attend a dinner hosted by the Northern Whig Club and to meet the Belfast reformers. He was armed with letters of introduction from Drennan addressed to William Sinclaire and Samuel Neilson. Drennan had previously recommended Rowan to his brother-in-law, Sam, as 'a true patriot, excellent in head and heart, zealous and actively zealous in the cause of his country'.[29] However, Rowan was not a stranger to some of the Northerners. When the Belfast Whig Club was founded in 1790, Rowan's father, Gawen Hamilton, was its first chairman, and Dr Haliday, the secretary, had written to Rowan as follows:

When we first thought of establishing a Northern Whig Club you naturally occurred to our thoughts; your excellent principles were too well known, and your exertions on behalf of liberty and justice, not to excite a general wish that we might have you to boast of as one of our members. I write now with the pleasing expectation that I shall be empowered to add your name to our respectable list of original members, and in the hope that we might sometime have the satisfaction of seeing you amongst us.[30]

The Whigs gathered on 5 November at the Donegall Arms. It is clear, from Martha's brief report to her brother, that the meeting went very well from Rowan's point of view. Haliday introduced Rowan to the meeting and he was given the honour of taking the chair. Martha reported Sinclaire, as secretary, moved resolutions 'which went decidedly into the Catholic question' and which, according to Martha, all were carried with a 'solitary, feeble no from Dr. Haliday'. Tone recorded the precise terms of the resolutions in his diary. The first resolution was as follows:

With the greatest satisfaction we embrace this opportunity to congratulate our Country on the late ignominious flight of the Enemies to Liberty from the territory of the French Republic and to express our hopes that the present disturbances in that Country may speedily terminate in the stable tranquillity of a good Government founded on the principles of equal liberty and the inalienable Rights of Man.[31]

This resolution was passed unanimously. It was the second resolution which Haliday opposed:

That as an early acquiescence in the just demand of the People is the surest pledge of peace and tranquillity in any Country, we trust we shall see the wishes of this Nation complied with by an honest and effectual Reform in the Representation of the People on a broad principle of equal Justice and equal Liberty to all sects and denominations of Irishmen, satisfied as we are that a sincere union amongst ourselves and a total oblivion of past dissentions from whatever cause arising can alone secure to this Country Freedom, Happiness and Prosperity.[32]

Haliday was a long-term friend and mentor to Drennan but was now seen as Lord Charlemont's man and was clearly in the moderate camp. He did not oppose a third resolution which welcomed 'the rapid decay of Prejudice and Bigotry' in the country. It seems a little harsh that Martha was now describing Haliday as 'the most open aristocrat' and lamenting how much he had fallen.[33]

On the day following the Whig Club meeting, Martha and Sam invited Rowan to dinner. After dinner, when Rowan offered to carry anything to Dublin for Martha, she was greatly tempted to ask him to bring herself. Martha mentioned that she intended to visit her brother in Dublin soon. Rowan politely requested her to accompany him in his chaise as he would be glad of the company. Not having time to think about it, she too hastily refused, which she later regretted.

Martha informed her brother that many of his old acquaintances in Belfast, who had formally been on the moderate side, were now coming round to the view that the friends of the Catholics had the best of the argument. Haliday would not yield on the question and did not attend the next meeting of the Club. When Sam tried to encourage him back, by asking him to chair a meeting, 'he sulkily refused'.[34] This was a most humiliating fall from grace for the founder

of the Whig Club who, for a long time, had been looked up to as the leader of
Belfast Whiggery. Rowan, whom Haliday had invited and introduced into the
Club, returned to Dublin, circulated the resolutions and let it be known that he
was vastly pleased with his reception in Belfast and talked much of his friends
there.[35]

14

CITIZEN SOLDIERS TO ARMS!

Martha congratulated her brother on his elevation to the presidency of the Dublin Society, although she believed he might make some enemies and suffer professionally by it. However, she thought that of small importance when measured against the need to be consistent to the honest principles of the United Irishmen. She believed their principles were daily gaining credit. Her strong advice was that he be guarded but honourable in his public utterances and that any political matter he might publish should be checked by lawyers in advance.[1] It is not clear how much attention Drennan gave to this advice but at least two significant addresses Drennan published during his presidency led to charges of sedition against himself and others.

Early on, he wrote a fraternal address to the Friends of the People Convention in Edinburgh which was held on 11 December 1792. When Drennan introduced the address to the Dublin Society, it was received with 'great acclamation and Tandy bedaubed him with praises'.[2] The address was signed by Drennan as chairman and Rowan as secretary. Thomas Collins, a member of the Dublin Society and a government informer, told his employer that the language in this address far exceeded 'anything as yet produced by our Jacobins for style, art and boldness'.[3] In fact, such was the boldness of the language that the soon to be famous Scottish radical, Thomas Muir (1765–1799), was forced to withdraw the address from the Edinburgh Convention. Although 'there was much in the address which was attractive to the delegates', many objected to the 'intemperate and dangerous nationalistic language'.[4] When Muir was convicted and sentenced to fourteen years transportation to Botany Bay at his show trial in August 1793, the most damning evidence against him that the prosecution could produce was this address and letters which linked Muir to Rowan and Drennan.

Rowan and Tandy, at the urging of the leading Catholic United Irishmen, made plans to raise a new company of Volunteers with a national uniform, consisting of ten companies of one hundred men each. Collins, the informer, reported that 200 select men had already been enrolled and described the uniform as resembling that of the sans-culottes. Collins identified the leaders of the new corps as Hamilton Rowan, Tandy, Henry Jackson and Oliver Bond and 'some others very contemptable'. He suggested that Keogh and Drennan were 'the grand movers in the scheme'[5] For his own part, Drennan told Martha she need not worry as he had not 'the smallest design of entering amongst them'.[6]

When this new Corps adopted the French style uniform and title of the National Guard, the Castle clearly decided to act. War was on the horizon and, within days, recruiting drums would be beating in Dublin.[7] The French had driven the armies of the Prussian, Dutch and Austrian coalition out of France and were now threatening Brussels. Their armies 'seemed irresistible'.[8] At home, the Catholics were gathering for a major convention and their demands seemed 'so insistent that refusal might lead to an armed revolt'.[9] Drennan told Martha:

> Dumouriez is only at Brussels and the Catholic cause is making only as much progress in the public mind as he is doing in the Pay Bas. He is without his knowledge, fighting hard against the Protestant Ascendency in Ireland and the fortunate event of the French revolution has the effect of adding daily numerous converts to our national union. The political rats are beginning to make their appearance and to indicate the tottering situation of the mansion. I really think the government here are panic struck.[10]

If Drennan was right, the pro-French sentiments being openly espoused in Dublin and Belfast would have been driving that panic. The Castle was determined to suppress support for the French before the formal hostilities with France commenced.

At the end of November, Drennan was approached at his doorstep again by the intimidating John Pollock. Pollock began by saying, 'Drennan I am your friend and whenever you wish to befriend yourself and get some good from your abilities, apply to me.' Drennan took this to be an offer to change sides and work as a government hack. He asked Pollock into his lodging, as he wanted to draw him into a more explicit offer, so that he could have the 'glory of refusing it'. Pollock entered the house but was too wary to be drawn on his offer. He warned Drennan that if he persisted in his political activities, he would ruin his medical practice. Their tête-à-tête was interrupted when Thomas Addis Emmet called. Pollock left saying he would leave the pair to hatch rebellion.[11]

A few days later, Pollock called again and asked for a private discussion, this time hopefully without interruption from any caller. He spoke pretty much in the same terms as he had in the earlier discussion. Drennan began to feel that he was being unfair, pretending to be interested in a deal he had no intention of accepting. When he decided to drop the pretence and be straight with Pollock, he became inordinately emotional:

> I said that I had early formed my principles in politics and that my father to his last hour had desired me never to forsake them, and here on, recollecting that best of men and thinking that I saw his meek and venerable face bending over me with a placid and approving smile, I burst into tears and remained for some time much affected.[12]

Pollock now realised that he would make no further headway in suborning Drennan. However, he kept the conversation going, presumably to get as much information as he could for his employers. He asked about Drennan's views in relation to granting the elective franchise to Catholics, on the constitution and on a republican frame of government. Pollock 'inveighed bitterly' against the establishment of these new Volunteers, called National Guards, suggesting that they would be guilty of overt treason and be treated by government as such.[13] Having heard Drennan's candid opinions, Pollock declared that no one with such views could benefit under the present government. He insisted that all that had passed between them must remain confidential and that he was acting on his own behalf and without authority from any person whatever. Drennan was, it seems, quite happy to give an honest exposition of his views to a man he knew to be in the pay of the Castle. For his own part, Drennan was now satisfied that he had been given an offer, albeit an indefinite one.

On 3 December 1792, the trial of the King of France began in Paris. That same day in Dublin, the Catholic Convention convened in the Tailors' Guild Hall, Back Lane. There were 244 delegates, representing every county in Ireland and over forty towns.[14] At the same time, Dublin was agitated by so many rumours and lies that, Drennan suggested, there 'might be an office from whence they issued ready made for the day'.[15] Some of the false stories concerned alleged scuffles between Volunteers and the military at Belfast and Arklow. Perhaps to intimidate the delegates to the Convention, the artillery corps marched through Dublin from their base at Chapelizod to the Castle.

The Belfast and Dublin United Irish Societies wanted to publicly support the Convention but Drennan felt that many of the Catholic delegates did not wish to have communication with people whom they regarded as sinners and republicans. The Belfast resolution was received but not publicised by the

Convention. When Drennan asked Tone about the paper, he 'almost had his nose snapped off'.[16] The Dublin Society adopted a supportive resolution which Rowan, Butler, Rice, Tandy and Chambers, all Protestants, were deputed to bring to the Convention. However, the deputation was not admitted instead being confined to the ante chamber.

Many of the leading Catholics were themselves United Irishmen, as, of course, was Wolfe Tone, the secretary of their Committee. However, they needed to keep their more moderate and even conservative members united in their fragile coalition. Drennan, although annoyed, seems to have understood what the Catholics were about but Rowan and Butler were hurt by the distant manner in which their deputation was treated.[17]

Rowan and Tandy were pushing ahead with their National Guard plans which Drennan claimed the Catholics had originally moved. While the Convention was meeting, between 3 and 8 December, the Catholics did not want to be seen to be 'trying the military instrument'.[18] After five days of deliberation, the Convention agreed a programme in which they would send a five-person delegation, including Keogh and Tone, to London to appeal directly to the King over the heads of the Castle administration. Having decided on this approach, the last thing the Catholics would have wanted was to be associated with the Irish supporters of those who were about to execute the King of France.

On 8 December, as the Convention concluded its deliberations, Rowan and Tandy were about to hold the first muster of the National Battalion. The Castle issued a proclamation against seditious meetings, threatening to disperse the new corps if it assembled.[19] Even before the proclamation was issued, the Catholics' enthusiasm for Volunteering had been waning and now Drennan believed they were regretting putting the Volunteers in motion in the first place.[20] By damping the Volunteers, the Catholics were, in his view, 'leaving Rowan and Tandy etc. in the lurch. The National Battalion did meet, to the number of about thirty [Protestants] and agreed to a deputation to the other corps on the following Sunday.'[21] Drennan drafted an address to the Volunteers of Ireland which was accepted by the Dublin Society and was to be distributed throughout Ireland.

The Castle was given early warning of the content and nature of this address by Thomas Collins. He reported that, at a meeting of the Dublin Society held on 8 December,

> Doctor Bourke introduced a letter addressed to the Volunteers inviting them to arm *immediately* as they are called on by the late proclamation to preserve the internal peace of the country, and to prevent the necessity of

a *terrible militia*, the times are such in both England and here as to require every man to *arm*, this letter by far exceeds any other publication of the society for violence not to say wickedness, the whole drift of it being the express purpose of inflaming the nation particularly the north of Ireland and bringing about an *immediate national Protestant convention*, ordered that the said letter be directly published so as to be ready for delivery against the meeting of the Volunteers.[22]

There were three reasons this address incensed the Castle government. Firstly, it called out the Volunteers at a time when the government wished to suppress Volunteering. Secondly, the government was preparing to prohibit representative assemblies and the address called for a Protestant convention. The first step towards assembling this convention was to be an Ulster gathering at Dungannon on 15 February, 'a day ever memorable in the annals of this country'.[23] Finally, as the trial of the French King was proceeding and war with France looming, the address used a language 'style that was dangerously French' with its slogan, 'Citizen Soldiers to arms!'[24]

Drennan summarised the government proclamation for Sam and described Rowan's reaction to it:

It is signed by twenty-three, a grand, grand jury – it recites seditious meetings, corps to be raised with devices and intentions against the constitution etc., and empowers magistrates to disperse all such meetings of people who act under the colour of the Volunteer institution which had done service, striving in this to make a schism between the new and the old Volunteers. In short it is levelled at the first National Battalion, nicknamed the national guards.

It did not prevent H[amilton] Rowan and one or two other Protestants from walking in the streets with a green uniform and side arms. The mob surrounded them and huzza'd much. They spoke to them requesting peace and quietness and begging of them particularly to have respect and proper behaviour towards the soldierly.[25]

The government proclamation brought the crisis to a head. Besides his *Address to the Volunteers*, Drennan's habitually active pen became even more diligent. In the two weeks following the proclamation, he wrote six long letters, totalling almost 4,500 words, to Sam in Belfast. He reported all the significant developments in Dublin. He advised and, on occasion, appeared to instruct the Northerners on how they should respond. He knew that the government's tactics were to split the old Volunteers from the new corps and to isolate the National Battalion and Belfast from the rest. In his letter of 10 December, he expressed a sense of urgency which was repeated in his subsequent correspondence when he told Sam 'the proclamation aims really at the North, though it hopes to strike the first panic into the capital. God direct you all for the best but if you do not act with spirit and determination, the Protestant cause is lost'.[26]

The Catholics had completed their deliberations at the Convention and had agreed the strategy of their delegation to the King. Drennan reported that the Catholics did not want any meeting of Volunteers to oppose the Castle proclamation. 'Rowan deemed it his duty to stand forth as a Protestant Volunteer leaving the Catholics to act as their wisdom and prudence should suggest.' The Dublin Merchants corps took fright and baulked at a meeting, leaving 'Rowan as mad as a Russian bear'.[27] While Drennan reported all this to Sam, he did not want it to become known even to Neilson in Belfast.

By 15 December, Drennan was reporting that the panic occasioned by the proclamation was wearing off. However, he stressed that the, 'North must bestir itself as the influence exerting in Dublin on all persons is astonishing.' He enclosed his *Address to the Volunteers*, which was to be distributed to a meeting of Volunteers in Dublin the next day. He was more in fear than hope about the reception it would receive as, 'Lord Charlemont has all his officers busy countermanding.'[28]

The meeting the following day, Sunday 16, was held in Pardon's fencing academy in Cope Street. There were more than 150 armed Volunteers present in uniform and with side arms. The Address was well received at the meeting with all the Dublin corps, except the Merchants, thanking the United Irishmen for their support. The public were admitted to the gallery at Pardon's and at least two men, who claimed to have been present, would later testify at Rowan's trial that he had played a leading role in the proceedings. Within days, Rowan was arrested at his home and charged with distributing a seditious libel. A warrant was issued for Tandy who left for the countryside. Rowan was released on bail. Fourteen months later, in January 1794, Rowan would be sentenced to two years in Newgate for his part in distributing this address. After Rowan absconded from Newgate in May of that year, the government targeted Drennan as the author of the *Address* and he was tried, but acquitted, of sedition in July 1794.

The Dublin Society held several well attended meetings throughout December to discuss the proclamation and the arrest of Rowan. Collins, the informer, reported that some of the Protestants present were annoyed that there appeared to be 'a great backwardness' on the part of the 'papists'.[29] Tone and the Catholic delegation had left for London shortly after the Convention had completed its work.

In his letter of 19 December, Drennan enclosed an account written by Rowan of the National Battalion but it was for Sam's, 'and Neilson's eyes only and no other'. Presumably he did not want the Catholics' reluctance to publicly oppose the government proclamation to be generally known in Belfast. Just a week earlier, Tone and the Catholic deputation had passed through Belfast on their circuitous route to London. They were given a tumultuous welcome by crowds who chanted, 'Success attend you! Union equal laws and down with the Ascendency.'[30]

Drennan advised his Belfast friends that 'the cry of revolution and republicanism is raised against us. No king etc'. He told them to take great care to obviate this. They should stick to 'an equal representation of the people and let posterity go on to republicanism if they choose'.[31] The charges of government would be hard to parry and a Dungannon meeting was an absolute necessity. He urged Sam to take immediate action to prevent the isolation of Belfast and he pleaded for help for Rowan's beleaguered National Battalion:

> You ought to have a town meeting immediately to prevent Belfast from being forced asunder from the rest of the North by its enemies. Your resolutions should be plain but decided on reform as our sole business. Let your new regiment be green, I beseech you it will serve the National Battalion amazingly. We want your help – If not ready now the counties will be made so before 15th February [the Dungannon Volunteer Convention] for every week will bring changes.[32]

Drennan clearly had significant influence in Belfast either on his own account, or perhaps, because of his position as president of the Dublin Society of United Irishmen. His suggestions were acted on. Just one week later, on 26 December, a Belfast town meeting was held at Reverend Vance's Second Presbyterian Church, Rosemary Lane. The usual venue for such meetings, the Town House, was deemed too small for the expected attendance. A committee of twenty-one was appointed to consult with other opinion formers and to prepare for the forthcoming Dungannon convention.[33] Neilson, acting as secretary, recorded several resolutions which Drennan greatly admired. He said, 'I hope your committee of twenty-one will not be summoned to Dublin for I swear they speak more treason by half than we venture here.'[34] Within a month, Neilson led 360 members of the First Belfast Regiment of National Guards, clad in green uniforms in a church parade to the same Rosemary Lane Meeting House.[35]

Throughout December, Drennan's letters to Sam focused mostly on the crisis in Dublin and his advice on how the Belfast radicals should respond. He repeatedly stressed the importance of a good turnout at Dungannon. However, he still clearly had an eye to French affairs. When he heard of rumoured French reverses, he knew that Britain would soon be joining the war. He told Sam, 'they should execute the King immediately for the sake of the union – if not there will be terrible work'.[36]

Throughout December and into the new year, Drennan continued to direct Sam in the planning for Dungannon. He sent some drafts of a likely summons to the convention and advised that the resolutions should demand an adequate and impartial representation of the whole nation in parliament. 'Let it be simple but solemn. Let it deprecate all revolution, all republicanism, yet stick to its principle and never desert it.'[37] Drennan was not abandoning his own views but attempting to preserve the unity of the Volunteers. On Christmas Eve, he ended his missive with a clear statement of his own political position. 'For my part I am in heart a real republican and if we must conform to others for a time, it is prudential and to make them serve us. Adieu – *Vive la Republique.* WD.'[38]

15

THE MERITS OF PERSONAL COURAGE

As the new year dawned, Drennan observed that the government had a plan 'to blacken and calumniate the people and to put down their friends by all the terrors of legal torture'.[1] When the *Northern Star* failed to arrive in Dublin at the end of the month, Drennan thought perhaps Neilson, the editor, had already been arrested. He suggested that the Dublin printers were frightened, some in panic and others in the pay of government. It was proving very difficult for the Dublin Society to get its resolutions printed. Drennan continued to demand urgent action from the North:

> If the North does not go on we are lost, for the Catholics all now act as if they were cowed and we are scarcely able to keep them from altering the very character and spirit of our society. The two who are at their head or affect to be so in the society are exerting all their power in and out of the society to infuse a milk and water spirit or to water down every resolution.[2]

At the time that Drennan was reporting this, Tone, Keogh and the Catholic delegation were in London, consulting with Henry Dundas, the Home Secretary, and awaiting their audience with the King. All their business was being kept secret and they were telling their Protestant United Irish allies nothing. Drennan was disappointed with the lack of a reaction by the Catholics to the proclamation against the Volunteers and the arrest of Rowan but he was naive to think the Catholics should jeopardise their prospects of achieving reform by joining publicly in support of alleged conveners of 'seditious meetings' or organisers of National Guard battalions. It was not, however, that Drennan thought that the Catholics were not entitled to pursue their own interests, but it was their attempts to dampen the Protestant reaction to the attacks by government which most concerned him. He admitted to Sam that 'there is evidently a misunderstanding taking place between the parties here and both are perhaps in fault; but it is certainly proper all circumstances considered that the Protestants should not be damped, quieted and restrained but acting at first for the union let them now act for the reform which was their object from the first'.[3]

Tone, Keogh and the Catholic deputation eventually presented their petition to the King on 2 January.[4] Their efforts had a positive effect, as the King's speech to the Irish Parliament of 10 January was altered in London to commit the Castle government to further Catholic relief. The Irish Commissioner of Revenue, John Beresford, Chief Secretary Robert Hobart and, indeed, many members of the Irish House of Commons were dismayed that they had not been consulted about having to support something they had always opposed.[5]

In the House of Lords, the Chancellor John Fitzgibbon launched into a vociferous attack on the Catholic deputation and their petition, saying that the petition was a lie and a libel and accusing the deputation of misleading the King.[6] He said that if the Catholics got political power in Ireland there was an end to peace and that there would be war in Ireland in a short time. Drennan heard it said that such was the Chancellor's disgruntlement that he, Lord Westmoreland and the Beresfords might resign.[7] He wondered who would replace them.[8] However, he underestimated the determination and temerity of the Castle clique. Hobart engaged in a horse-trading exercise with the Catholics, designed to ensure that the favour be 'shorn of its beams' and, instead of 'considering any longer how much might be accorded with graciousness, the minister only calculated what might be withheld in safety'.[9] After protracted wrangling which continued from mid-January until early April, the franchise was extended to Catholic forty shilling freeholders but they were still to be barred from the Parliament, the Bench and the corporations.[10] As the negotiations continued, the Castle carried on a campaign of vilification against the Catholic Committee, the United Irishmen, the National Guard and the republican levellers in the North. The Catholic Committee was therefore caught in a bind. They needed to keep the negotiations going and therefore, could not afford to publicly respond even to government-inspired malicious attacks on themselves and their community.

Throughout January, Sam and Martha kept Drennan informed of the preparations and the various local meetings around Ulster passing resolutions and appointing delegates to the Dungannon meeting. The Down meeting went well from the United Irish point of view. It became fractious when Lord Hillsborough claimed that there were 'French emissaries to his knowledge in Ireland to sow such and such seeds', his remarks were greeted with 'a lie, a lie, from fifty different voices'.[11] When he went on to say that the French were planning to invade Ireland, the meeting reacted with 'a long loud laugh'. At the end of the month, Sam reassured Drennan by telling him 'you need not fear a Dungannon meeting. Every county in this province have now chosen delegates or appointed meetings for that purpose, except Armagh, and we are told that in a few days a call of that county also'.[12]

The preparations for Dungannon were going well but the tide was running against the United Irishmen in many other ways. Neilson and the proprietors of the *Northern Star* were summoned to Dublin and charged with sedition. They were granted bail immediately by Lord Clonmell. In a show of unity, a Catholic and a Protestant acted as bailsmen.[13] The Belfast men were given a lavish dinner at the Star and Garter in Essex Street, with Archibald Hamilton Rowan in the chair. Drennan could not attend because of his medical duties but he was glad to have saved the guinea admission fee.

Meanwhile, the cry of insurrection was being kept up and more artillery was being sent to Belfast to keep that town in order. In Dublin, on 27 January, a major stand-off occurred when the old Volunteer Liberty and Goldsmiths' corps mustered at Ship Street Square, outside the rear gate of Dublin Castle. Aldermen Warren and James told the Volunteers that if they marched out the military would disperse them. The aldermen had the backing of a strong detachment of soldiers and two field pieces. They also threatened to take the volunteer officers into custody.[14] Matthew Dowling, a Volunteer Captain, interrupted a committee meeting of the Dublin Society, at which Drennan was presiding, to tell them what was happening. Dowling, who was himself a lawyer, was advised by the other lawyers present[15] to tell the aldermen that this was no illegal gathering and that they would march out and only disperse after the Riot Act was read and not before. Dowling went back to Ship Street, accompanied by three lawyers and Tandy. Drennan carried on with the committee meeting. He tells us that two hours later:

> McNally of the lawyers and Tandy returned, when McNally declared the dispersion was made of their own accord and by Tandy's advice. Tandy said that he had advised it to avoid confusion, that several of the Volunteers had sworn that they would not give up their arms (which bye the bye was not demanded) and that a full meeting of the Volunteers should be called ... to deliberate on what was to be done. That is after being spit in the face, you are to say, I shall consider in a week how to resent it and in the meantime put it in my pocket.[16]

Drennan described Tandy as 'a great coward and the curse of Ireland'. Rowan did all he could to get a meeting of the Volunteers to respond, while 'the Catholics were in motion to give up the pass'.[17] When Rowan succeeded in getting the meeting, he proposed that the Volunteers should march out as soon as possible and disperse after the Riot Act was read. As he could get only two others to support him, he resigned from the Volunteers and 'was glad to get out of a set of men who had neither the spirit nor the manners of gentlemen'. Drennan thought that Rowan might burn his uniform in front of the faces of his erstwhile comrades. Rowan got no support from Tone, Russell and Emmet, who were 'so entwined with Catholic trammels [they] cannot act as their hearts lead them'.[18] All of this caused Drennan to reflect on the merits of personal courage:

> I believe personal courage is the best quality almost a man can possess – not merely for serving him on this or that emergency but for the effect it has on every word, every gesture, every action. The one is to be waked to action – the other is ever vigilant. There is as Mr. Burke says some difference in blood ... Tandy and Dowling are not gentlemen – Rowan is every inch of him body and soul.[19]

We know that the Catholics were anxious to avoid a clash with the Castle as they were negotiating the terms of their Relief Bill. Perhaps it was the increased military activity in the streets which produced the timidity in the Dublin Volunteers or it might have been the momentous events in Paris. Less than a week before the stand-off in Ship Street, the execution, which Drennan had long believed necessary and desirable, had at last taken place. Louis Capet had been beheaded on the guillotine on 21 January. Drennan knew that 'the cause would be hurt in these countries by the shock of the execution' but it was necessary to save the French Republic. However, he also realised that the execution would serve Britain by making the war against France popular.[20] It was inevitable that these circumstances would leave many Volunteers conflicted. Some of the veteran Volunteers had joined initially to resist a French invasion but now the more radical elements in Dublin and Belfast were cheering on the French and even forming National Guard Battalions. The Belfast radicals' annual celebration, each 30 January, of the beheading of Charles I went ahead as usual. However, Martha did not wonder when just nine days after the execution of Louis, the attendance at the Washington tavern was a 'bit thin'.[21]

On the same day as the revellers in the Washington were toasting regicide, the Dublin House of Commons warmly supported the ban on the Volunteers. Even the opposition supported the government. Henry Grattan 'denounced the insolence, disaffection and seditious tendency of the counter proclamation issued by the United Irishmen'. Drennan observed that, 'Ponsonby too [was] as violent as the Attorney General.'[22] This appeared as an attempt to influence the jury that would eventually hear the case against Rowan. However, pandemonium broke out when Lord Edward Fitzgerald intervened in the debate to tell the House majority and the Lord Lieutenant that they were the king's worst subjects.

Fitzgerald had arrived in Dublin with his new French wife, Pamela Egalité, a few days earlier. He held his parliamentary seat compliments of his brother, the Duke of Leinster. He had been a career soldier and had recently been cashiered out of the British Army without charge, trial or hearing. The previous November in Paris, at a large social gathering in company which included his dear friend Thomas Paine at White's Hotel, Fitzgerald had toasted 'the armies of France: may the example of its citizen soldiers be followed by all enslaved countries till tyrants and tyranny be extinct'.[23] One of Fitzgerald's most recent biographers tells us what happened next:

> Then Lord Edward and Sir Robert Smith renounced their titles. As they swilled the wine around their glasses and drank to 'the speedy abolition of all hereditary titles and feudal distinctions', Lord Edward Fitzgerald, fifth son of Ireland's premier peer, nephew of the Duke of Richmond and great grandson of Charles II became as he told his mother 'le citoyen Edouard Fitzgerald'.[24]

All of this was public knowledge as it had been reported in the British and Irish newspapers. His outburst in the House of Commons was greeted with outrage. Members shouted 'to the Bar! to the Bar!' 'Take down his words.' The public gallery was cleared, and the House went into private session. Drennan told Sam:

> The House was cleared on Fitzgerald's expression, and it is said he refused to ask pardon. The House was in a flame – and it is not known today if he is to do it this evening or not. His brother the Duke and the opposition will, it is likely, prevail on him. Tandy says he is an honest hearted fine fellow and not easily moved, greatly irritated as he must be having been deprived of his commission. It is not unlikely that he and his elegant wife will lead the fashion of politics in a short time if he stays here.[25]

There followed three hours of browbeating as both the majority and the opposition tried to wrangle an apology from Fitzgerald. The best they could get was delectable sarcasm when he said, 'I am accused of having declared that I think that the Lord Lieutenant and the majority of this House are the worst subjects the King has. I said so, tis true and I am sorry for it.' This was deemed unsatisfactory and insufficient by the enraged members and Fitzgerald was brought in custody to the Bar the next morning. Whatever he said on this occasion was enough for most MPs to readmit him to his seat in the House. However, fifty-five voted against accepting his 'apology'.[26]

Drennan and Rowan's three-month term as President and Secretary of the Dublin Society ended and, on 1 February, they were replaced by Simon Butler and Oliver Bond respectively. The Society passed a complimentary resolution thanking Drennan and Rowan for their services. When Rowan heard of Fitzgerald's exploits in the House of Commons, he called around to Leinster House where Fitzgerald and his wife were lodging. A few days later, when Drennan visited Rowan at home, Fitzgerald was there and Rowan was very anxious to introduce Drennan to his new friend. Their conversation lasted an hour and Drennan was very impressed by what he heard. All Fitzgerald's 'thoughts bend to France' and Drennan deemed him an honest, zealous, republican. He said that war with France was coming; the French minister, the Marquise de Chauvelin (1762–1832), had assured him that in that event there would be a French landing in Ireland. Fitzgerald also said that his friend, Tom Paine, had 'nearly a desire to come over' to Ireland. However, they agreed that, given the present situation, such a visit would do more harm than good. Fitzgerald was a little concerned at the constitutional resolutions involving King, Lords and Commons going forward to Dungannon but Drennan explained that the majority would be for constitutional reform. Fitzgerald talked with enthusiasm of the proposed Protestant Convention. Drennan left the meeting convinced that Fitzgerald was 'a noble emissary from France – but an incautious one and I fear that he might be entrapped by some of our state inquisitors'.[27]

There was little enthusiasm for a Protestant Convention in the House of Commons. Robert Stewart, the member for Down, railed against the idea of the Convention and lashed himself into a passion. Here again the Opposition supported the government and Grattan said that if such a convention met, it would be the end of all established government. The government would shortly thereafter bring in an Act banning conventions and the Protestant convention which Drennan and the United Irishmen had been calling for never took place.

16

THE SECRET COMMITTEE

In early January 1793, the House of Lords established a Secret Committee 'to enquire into the state of the country and especially into these troubles in the North'.[1] Its purpose was not to identify grievances, which might be remedied to reduce discontent. Rather, it was to identify those who were alleged to be promoting discontent to put a stop to their activities. The Committee had the power to order the apprehension of anyone they wished to interview. They interrogated people daily about their views on Tom Paine, the National Battalion and the state of discontent in the North. The Committee was very keen to find out who had instigated the Defenders. When they questioned Henry Jackson, he told them he believed the government must be responsible for creating the Defenders.[2]

The informer Collins helpfully provided the Committee with a list of eleven United Irishmen to question. Among the names suggested were Thomas Warren and Richard McCormack whom Collins described as hard mouthed; he said he was convinced the pair had contact with the Defenders. Another person Collins recommended for interrogation was Hamilton Rowan. Perhaps Drennan might have been flattered had he known how the informer concluded his report that 'it will be losing time to examine Butler, Drennan, Keogh, Tone, Bond or Tandy, for I don't think anything will be got from them, though the present alarming situation in this country has been entirely caused by Keogh, Tandy, Drennan and Butler, yet you know them too well to suppose that they will ever confess equity'.[3]

The Secret Committee made strenuous efforts to link the Defenders to the Catholic Committee and for this purpose, they were prepared to use innuendo as evidence. After two months of persistent inquisition and vain attempts at blackmail and entrapment of leading Catholics,[4] the Secret Committee said this of the Defenders:

> The people at this time called Defenders are very different from those who originally assumed that appellation, and as far as the committee could

discover of the Roman Catholic persuasion; in general poor, ignorant labouring men sworn to secrecy and impressed with an opinion that they are assisting the Catholic cause. At first, they took nothing but arms; but afterwards they plundered the houses of everything they could find. Their measures seem to have been concerned and conducted with the utmost secrecy and a degree of regularity and system not usual in people in such a mean condition, and as if directed by men of superior rank.[5]

When Sam read Rowan's report, he was disappointed that the Volunteers in Dublin had allowed themselves to be intimidated and he felt the behaviour of the Goldsmiths' corps was a disgrace. He assured Drennan that if a scuffle were to happen between the Volunteers and the military who were now occupying Belfast, 'we could have in this town in less than forty-eight hours not less than ten thousand men armed with such weapons as they can get. A great many of them would be very well armed.'[6] Within a few days he gave a comprehensive report to Drennan:

Our Volunteers have been out this day in uniform and side arms, the Regiment Green march to church to hear Bryson, their number above two hundred though a very bad day, and the Blue Battalion went to hear Vance, they were not quite a hundred though it is very lately they determined their uniform. There has not been any attempt yet to seize our cannon, but it is expected every day and also a search for gunpowder etc. When they make it I don't believe they will be much gratified for I fancy they will not find any cannon and but little military stores. We are perfectly quiet here and on very good terms with the military, from General White down to the privates.[7]

Sam went on to say that General White told him he could summon eight regiments and suitable artillery to Belfast at short notice if they were needed. Sam observed that triple or twice that number would not suffice if the people were inclined to insurrection. He observed that 'all the towns near Belfast were now, to some measure, under military government due to the troops that are quartered in them'.[8]

The government was keeping the pressure up on the radicals on several fronts. Attempts were being made to further entrap Rowan while he was on bail. This took the form of soldiers coming to him pretending disaffection but Rowan refused to listen to them. Drennan supposed they were being sent by some higher men, perhaps even Jack Pollock. Liberty of the press was being gagged more than ever, not only in Ireland but in Scotland. Drennan observed to Sam that 'in Scotland, there are sixty indictments out for publications as innocent as the Lord's Prayer – and they are under courts that would force a jury (who are packed by the sheriff) to bring in Abel guilty of the murder of Cain, and Jesus Christ of that of Pontius Pilate'.[9]

In early February, the government brought in an Arms and Gunpowder Act to prevent the importation or movement of arms from place to place. Lord Edward was the only voice in parliament against the measure,[10] Drennan knew this was intended to bear hard on the Volunteers. He believed that the government and opposition together intended to put down the Volunteers and the people. He told Sam:

> I declare it to you once for all that government and opposition mean to put down the Volunteers and the people – that the Volunteers here and that the city is completely put down – that another meeting cannot be held: that every man is watched as by an inquisition – that the nation is gone if Dungannon does not facilitate a national convention – and remember I say it Friday the 8th of January 1793.[11]

The Convention went ahead at Dungannon on 15 February. The Unitarian minister and leading United Irishman, Reverend William Steele Dickson, attracted great applause for his many contributions and set the tone for the day's deliberations. Sam reported to Drennan that while the meeting was rather led by the aristocracy, the people's spirit was infused in the resolutions which were adopted. The first two concerned the attachment and loyalty to the current form of government. The third resolution was along the lines that Drennan had suggested, objecting to republican principles applied to Ireland. A resolution in favour of Catholic emancipation and several approving reform of parliament and of never giving up on reform, were also adopted. The Convention condemned government plans for a militia, thanked the Volunteers and vowed that the Volunteers should never dissolve.[12] All of this came as good news to Drennan and he liked them 'pretty well'. However, there were two aspects of the proceedings that disappointed him. Rather than name the day for a National Protestant Convention, it was agreed merely to consult the other provinces on the desirability of such a convention. The war against France was condemned but only when the formal business of the day was over.[13]

Despite the relative success of Dungannon, Drennan was despondent and felt that the public mind had received a shock and 'had fallen in for a time to the cry of government'. This had been brought about by calumnies invented by government concerning republicanism, rioters, revolution, Defenders, arms, the North, etc. He warned Sam that troops would be poured into the North and opposition would be silenced by force, as it had been in Dublin. He felt that Dublin had been cowed and complained that 'this city I look upon as completely put down, and I question much if there not be more liberty of speech in Venice and even at Constantinople than there is here at present. The liberty of the press is put down and the liberty of speech almost as much so.'[14]

In Dublin, on 24 February, ten armed Volunteers in uniform went out into the country to breakfast with their Major John Ashenhurst who was also a leading United Irishman. On their way through the city, they were confronted in the street by police constable Oliver Carleton and commissioner William James. The proper procedure, if the policemen wished to disperse the group, would have been for them to read the Riot Act. Instead they tried to confiscate a firelock belonging to one of the Volunteers. This man, whose name was Black, knocked James to the ground and 'nearly left him in the gutter'. The two policemen ran away to the Castle where they gathered a military force of 200 horse and foot and they went after the Volunteers into the country. The Volunteers ate their breakfast as planned at tea rooms in Drumcondra. The military passed the tea rooms without realising the Volunteers were there.[15] The Volunteers watched through the windows as the military marched past, 'with Carleton and James at their head both pale as death on a black horse'.[16] As the soldiers marched further out into the country, the Volunteers marched quietly back to the city. Black declared his intention to bring an action for assault against Carleton. Drennan saw this incident not only as illustrative of the tensions in Dublin but as a warning to the Northerners. He told Sam:

> Nothing was done which could make them be deemed a riotous or tumultuous assembly, but an unlawful one they are made, and even papers distributed to this unlawful combination or conspiracy will be deemed libellous and perhaps felonious by a packed jury, from the terms of the Riot Act though that act was made particularly directed to the Whiteboys,[17] etc., under which class the Volunteers will now be ranked. Therefore, be prepared for the consequences – as I cannot suppose that they will attempt to do here what they will not do to you when they have gotten sufficient force.[18]

On the same day that Volunteer Black threw commissioner James in the gutter, the Dublin Society issued a report attacking the Secret Committee. Drennan was fortunate that his term of office had finished and the address was signed by Simon Butler and Oliver Bond. Drennan thought the address legal and sensible but he knew it would vex the Committee. He could see an impending storm and felt 'somewhat of panic before the battle' which he feared was about to begin. He signed off his letter with, 'God save the right. Yours ever, but in the meantime, I go to a ball.'[19]

Butler and Bond were summoned before the Lords on 1 March. Drennan was amongst the large group of citizens who accompanied them marching in file. After a most vehement debate, masquerading as a trial, the pair were fined £500 and sentenced to six months in Newgate. The Lords considered issuing a proclamation banning the Society but John Fitzgibbon, the Chancellor, said that the punishment of Butler and Bond was enough to put it down. He passed sentence with harsh words aimed particularly at Butler:

> Simon Butler and Oliver Bond, you are called to the bar [of the House] to answer for a libel on this high court of parliament. You have confessed that such a libel, which for its presumption, ignorance and mischievous tendency is unprecedented, was printed by your authority. You, Simon Butler, cannot plead ignorance in extenuation; your noble birth, your education, the noble profession to which you belong, his Majesty's gown which you wear, and to which you now stand a disgrace, gave you the advantage of knowledge, and are strong circumstances of aggravation of your guilt. It remains for me to pronounce the judgement of the House, which is that you Simon Butler and Oliver Bond, be imprisoned six months in the gaol of Newgate, and that each of you pay a fine to the King of £500 and you not be discharged from confinement until such fine is paid.[20]

Butler was a lawyer and the brother of Lord Mountgarret who would have been regarded by Fitzgibbon as a fellow aristocrat. He did not take kindly to being publicly branded a disgrace. The following October, after he had completed his sentence, Butler requested Rowan to call on the Chancellor to extract an apology and to offer challenge if no suitable apology was forthcoming.[21]

There was a general opinion that the sentence imposed on Butler and Bond 'was beyond example severe' and Drennan believed there would be petitions from the city for mitigation. The Castle probably hoped to receive a petition from the prisoners themselves but Drennan was confident that would not happen. Next day he led a delegation to Newgate, where he read a resolution from the Society commending their behaviour. The prisoners responded with firm and determined language.[22]

During the second week of confinement Drennan reported that the prisoners were in good spirits and that the Society was doing everything in their power to alleviate their suffering:

> Seventy-one members subscribe a guinea a piece for wine and articles of accommodation, and each in turn gives a dinner to eight in their rooms at the gaol which costs a second guinea. Last night the motion was made in the Society to pay the fine, and I believe nearly £350 was collected from those present, I set down £3 8s 3d which was as much or more than I ought give but I believe that most of those present did the same.[23]

A few days later, a bench warrant was issued for Tandy for distributing what Drennan considered a very foolish paper entitled, *Common Sense*. Tandy set off for Dundalk to answer the charges. However, Butler and other United Irish lawyers, after serious consultation, advised Tandy to skip bail as he would be punished severely if convicted and because they suspected the authorities were holding more serious charges in reserve. Drennan believed Tandy would take this advice because 'two years imprisonment would kill him, and less it is supposed, would not be inflicted'.[24]

The Secret Committee issued its report on 7 March consisting of what Drennan described as 'a whole tide of calumnies' against the Catholic Committee, the United Irish Societies and the town of Belfast.[25] The main thrust of the report suggested that Defenders' outrages were being organised by well-to-do Catholics connected to the Catholic Committee. The report went on to suggest that the Defenders' actions were countenanced and encouraged by seditious and inflammatory papers published in Dublin. This accusation was clearly aimed at the United Irishmen but the Secret Committee did not quote any example of a paper in which the United Irishmen had countenanced Defenders' activity.

The report suggested that an unusual ferment had been disturbing many parts of the North, encouraged by cheap papers published in Dublin and Belfast. 'The conduct of the French was being shamefully extolled and hope and expectation have been held up for hopes for their [French] assistance by a descent upon this kingdom. The report also suggested that prayers were being offered up at Belfast from the pulpit for the success of French arms.'[26]

Drennan noted that with all its talk of 'the instigators of riots, conspiracies etc., not a single person is named'. However, what alarmed him most about the report was:

> a powerful recommendation not to let any armed men appear except under the authority constituted by law, and next week will probably see a bill brought in for actually disarming the North. So again take my warning. The Militia Bill is passing rapidly and there must be personal service, or a substitute found or £10 paid. Perhaps it might be proper for the Volunteers to turn into militia and not appoint substitutes. I confess in all this your town seems very inactive as a town; the whole country seems stunned, a perfect inquisition reigns here in companies, in the street, in the shops.[27]

Drennan remarked to Sam in early March that 'they are hanging Defenders in Trim at a great rate'.[28] Sir John Meredith had been bringing in prisoners he had rounded up in the Kells area and had delivered twenty-five alleged Defenders to Trim assizes.[29] Proclamations printed in the newspapers offered a £100 reward for giving information against any Defender. As a result, more than 300 men had fled their homes in Meath due to the number of approvers coming forward for this easy money. In his letter to the Earl of Fitzwilliam the following year, Drennan described these bribes as serving 'to breath up the bloodhounds impelling the poor to hunt after their own'.[30]

17

'THERE NEVER WAS A BELFAST MOB'[1]

Within days of the report issuing from the Secret Committee, the military aggression that Drennan had long predicted was unleashed on Belfast. A troop of Light Dragoons, lately arrived in the town from Dundalk, rioted and 'attacked in a reckless manner several inhabitants'[2] and certain business premises including the offices of the *Northern Star*, public houses and inns, some of which, such as the Franklin and Dumouriez, bore the names of French and American heroes. The dragoons smashed the windows of the well-known United Irishman Thomas McCabe. Miss Mills' milliners' shop in High Street was attacked because she had Volunteer hats and cockades displayed in her window.[3] Martha, who witnessed the events, believed that the dragoons had hoped to engage the Volunteers or provoke a mob reaction to justify further excesses and violence. In fact, she believed that they hoped to fabricate an excuse for the butchery of the inhabitants of the town.[4] She described the event for her brother:

> I could myself produce a credible witness, who in Dundalk heard one of their officers, and would <u>name</u> him, desire them when they came to Belfast not to spare leg, arm or life. They served to this trade with remarkable success in the American war and, to prevent rust, have kept it up with the wretched Defenders, since which they are denominated the Speaker's Bloodhounds. The Belfast troop [of Volunteers] was their object but they got a hint of their danger. Disappointed in this plan for a tumult, they sallied forth with a ladder, which reached Dumouriez, but Franklin could not be got down even by these heroes. These were signs [for inns] I never heard of, and had passed unnoticed but to the two or three incendiaries amongst us. One of Lord Hillsborough's humble friends pointed out the fit places to attack which were marked on paper. This same man Sam knows voted for that noble man seven times at the last election and perjured himself each time.

You will see that the Volunteers have come on some terms with General White. On Sunday and Monday they certainly triumphed. The town was full of country men, above 1,000 armed met in the new erection, [Third Presbyterian Meeting House, Rosemary Lane] and though Mr. Bristow and Captain Hill Wallace lately justice of the peace went to them and used every argument they could suggest, they were treated with scorn and denial till they heard the agreement made by the Volunteers for these men were not of that body – forty recruits joined the regiment yesterday – the committee sat yesterday examining like their betters, and to say the truth I think with equal wisdom. Now the criminals are gone they departed in triumph with General Dumouriez' wooden head, and while there was a huzza of women and children at their departure, one of these sign-slaying heroes slashed his sword on a lad near him, cut him desperately and rode off unmolested. In any other town they would have been stoned to death, but there never was a Belfast mob – happy for us at present, for I do believe it was ardently sought for.[5]

Drennan was expecting to be called before the Secret Committee and he had told Martha that if he was, he would tell them all he knew. Martha warned him that while the truth is delightful, he needed to be well advised about how far he could go in safety before a bitter enemy with undefined power and no fear of exerting it. She did not believe what she referred to as 'the old wives in Dublin' were interested in the truth. Had they wished to know the truth about Belfast they could have commissioned 'the Londonderry Lordling [Robert Stewart]' to make inquiries among the respectable inhabitants of the town. It was misinformation the Committee wanted.[6] Misinformation became plentiful.

The prevailing 'universal lie' in circulation that most concerned Martha was put about by Bristow, the vicar of Belfast.[7] The vicar told several people that Sam had received a letter from France offering the country 10,000 men. At first, Sam laughed and left it as a story to amuse the old women of Belfast and the Secret Committee in Dublin. However, he felt he had to take it more seriously when men he respected asked him if it were true and these same people confirmed that Bristow was the source of the rumour. Sam brought two friends with him to confront Bristow with his lie. Martha reported that 'Bristow frittered it away the best he could' but that 'his complexion bore testimony against him'.[8]

Drennan also was trying to keep his spirits up while 'feeling the poison wind of calumny blow so pestilentially'. He had been advised once 'that when the sirocco blows in the desert the best response is to fall flat on your face, and don't open your mouth till the blast has gone over'.[9] The Secret Committee was continuing its examinations and had called Dr James Reynolds before it. Reynolds was a United Irishman from Cookstown, County Tyrone, who had recently settled in Dublin. Drennan thought Reynolds' strategy for challenging the committee might stop them.

> He has resisted all their arts and threats to answer, until they tell him the nature of their authority, whether they ask him questions as a legislative or as a judicial body. If the first he denies that they have any such right by the constitution, the principles of which he values as much as any of them; if in their judicial capacity he protests against all secrecy as equally unconstitutional. They committed him to the Black Rod, reported him to the House, and when at the bar he still persisted in his refusal to answer, was remanded into the same custody, from a view that in the interim he might alter his resolution.[10]

While in custody, Reynolds sent a note to Drennan asking him to call by for a few minutes. Although Drennan did not know Reynolds very well, he came immediately. Reynolds wanted his advice, for though he had resolved not to answer, he was getting so much contrary advice he did not know what to do. Drennan's only advice was that consistency of conduct was always desirable. This appeared to settle Reynolds' nerve and he assured Drennan that he would 'persevere from honour and from duty'.[11]

While Drennan was talking to Reynolds, two Catholics came in to show their support for the prisoner and Drennan went away. He observed acidly, 'the Catholics hang upon everyone who comes up from the North and have no objection to them running risks but seem determined, for the present, to put themselves in no danger'.[12] This was perhaps unfair for, as we have seen, the Catholics were in a bind. The legislation which was supposed to give them the reliefs was going through parliament. They could not afford to be seen to be too close to those whom the Chancellor was describing as 'a nest of conspirators who were conspiring to separate these countries which God and nature has joined'.[13] However, it must have been galling for Drennan when he heard Lord Clonmell abusing the United Irishmen in a most scurrilous manner and, at the same time, complimenting the Catholics in not joining in any of their schemes. Drennan believed the real independence of Ireland was what was nearest to the hearts of the Catholics and that is why he adhered to them notwithstanding his dislike of many of them and their mode of conduct.[14]

The Secret Committee kept Reynolds in custody for some time without calling him before it. This was an attempt to increase the pressure on him. When next questioned, he was asked if Drennan had advised him to persist in his refusal to answer. He said that Dr Drennan had not advised him one way or another. Reynolds behaved most obstinately yet respectfully before the Secret Committee. They invited him four times to take the oath, when at last he replied that 'he knew he was injuring all his interests but though he were on the rack he would keep silent'. Drennan observed that when 'Dean Swift in a similar case took the book and swore by it that he would not answer them a word. They think they will terrify this very young man, they are mistaken. The Chancellor said to him as Jefferies said to Sidney – you are mad Sir!'[15]

When the secret committee consigned Reynolds to prison, they did not send him to Newgate. From 'poor and contemptable spite' he was ordered to Kilmainham, the county jail, to separate him from Butler and Bond. The Society made similar arrangements for his comfort as they had for his fellows at Newgate. Drennan led a deputation to Kilmainham to read a supportive resolution to the prisoner. He was much better off than Butler and Bond, having a very large room and being able to walk in the garden. Drennan sent him books and offered him £10 which he did not accept.[16] Drennan never mentioned at the time that when he called to see Reynolds, the Reverend J. Horner, a Presbyterian, was present. Years later, he suggested that Horner had made himself useful to government by suggesting to Lord Clare that Drennan had encouraged the prisoner to persist in refusing to answer.[17]

Lord Edward called by Drennan's. He seemed very subdued and expressed great fear for the French. The French armies had suffered their first defeat at the battle of Neerwindin on 18 March and Dumouriez had defected to the Austrians on 5 April. Drennan suggested that gold was being used to raise a civil war to help the external powers. Britain was now participating in the war and the French had suffered two setbacks. Although Drennan was not unduly concerned by the defeat at Neerwindin, he was however disgusted by the delight some were taking in the carnage:

Many more must be received before France is conquered. The more they are repressed like air, the more elasticity will they acquire, and the greater will be their resistance the nearer the enemy approaches Paris – great joy and laughing here at the destruction of perhaps 20,000 human beings. God in his power, defend the just side, and in his mercy, forgive those men who hear with such gout the carnage of humanity, but shudder at the death of a treacherous despot.[18]

In the wake of the Secret Committee's report of 7 March, Thomas Collins, the informer, was reporting with glee the most extraordinary falling off of attendance at the meetings of the Dublin Society. On 15 March, just one week on from the proclamation, the Society could not muster more than forty members. Collins told the Castle that 'the spirit of Jacobinism was totally broken down'.[19] The meeting of the following week 'was remarkable [sic] thin' with only forty-four in attendance. In Collins' view, 'among that number [there was] scarce a person worth naming' and 'all the leaders of sedition absent except Drennan, Dowling, Burke, Chambers and Jackson'.[20] Drennan was elected president in the absence of the imprisoned Butler, while Dowling replaced Bond as secretary. Collins reported that Drennan told the meeting he was accepting the honour, contrary to the advice of his friends, his interests and his personal safety.[21] Drennan gave a similar account to Sam of why he had agreed to take on this dangerous role at a time when others were clearly keeping their heads down:

> I took the chair because I never will desert the wreck, at such a time when cowards flinch I was asked would I go into the chair in place of Butler and I said I would not give any answer about it. I was unanimously balloted in, and I accepted of it, contrary as I told them to my interests personal and professional but dragged to it by a sense of splendid duty, and fidelity to one certain tenor of conduct.[22]

In April, Collins was reporting that the Dublin Society, which continued to be presided over by Drennan, was in such disarray that 'the serpent's teeth are nearly drawn' and that 'this nursery of rebellion is totally blasted'. The finance committee reported that while between £1,500 and £2,000 was required to discharge the fines of Butler and Bond and to keep their daily table at Newgate, only £300 had been subscribed and of that figure, only £100 had been collected. However, Collins' reports also show something of a recovery in attendance figures, in that by the end of the month he recorded eighty members present.[23]

The pressure on the Dublin Society was intense at this point. Butler, Bond and Reynolds were in prison. Rowan was expecting his trial for sedition to begin at any time.[24] Tandy was in hiding accused of distributing *Common Sense*. On 10 April, a Mr Byrne from Dundalk was sentenced to two years for distributing the same pamphlet. Peter Carey, the printer who had published Drennan's *Address to the Volunteers*, was facing prosecution and appeared before a meeting of the Society pleading in vain for money to escape abroad.[25] This would not be the last time Carey would appeal for and be refused help from the Society. In early May 1794, Carey again appealed for help and Drennan proposed appointing a committee to consider the application. Collins suggested that this was a change of stance by Drennan and a proof that he was very much alarmed. Drennan's proposal was defeated and Collins advised his handlers that he thought Carey might be *had* on very easy terms.[26] Collins' advice may have been acted upon, for in June 1794, Carey appeared as the main prosecution against William Drennan at his trial for publishing a seditious libel.

In early 1793, Drennan had been expecting a summons to appear before the Secret Committee. He was not called but the Castle decided to increase the pressure on him indirectly. John Pollock again called on him asking for an interview. When they met, Pollock told Drennan, 'with a very terror inspiring countenance': 'that he was just come from the assizes, and that he thought it a piece of friendship to inform me as soon as possible, that he had reason to apprehend I was in danger – and in the course of the conversation, insinuated that he had it on the authority of the Attorney General'.[27]

Drennan replied with 'gay assurance' that he was not conscious of having said, written or done anything from which he apprehended any danger and he would appear before any tribunal 'and challenge his accusers to the proof'. He told Pollock that when he had been advised by friends to conceal his papers, he had laughed at the idea and said he did not care if the whole Secret Committee read them at their leisure. He told Sam how the conversation continued:

> [I told him] that I was obliged to him for telling me I was in danger but that I had heard so in every company I was in these two months. He told me not to mistake or misreport his words which were that he had reason only to apprehend I was in danger. We talked a good deal about the times, and he, inveighed most outrageously against the publications, particularly *Common Sense*, in which I agreed with him as I thought it a scurrilous, personal, mean production ... He talked of the blood of the Defenders being on the head of certain people and I said, God forgive those who utter such things without proof. I again said I thanked him for his information, but I did not say what good it would do me, for what I had done, I had done, and not being conscious of anything ill done, or at least with a *malus animus*, I could not alter or correct my plan of conduct. I took my leave and he said, God bless you, my dear Doctor. I think if on our former conference

he meant to seduce me, his aim at this was to terrify, or to find out whether there was really any ground for terrifying me.[28]

Along with the pressure and threats, Drennan was convinced his enemies were trying to ruin him in his profession as a doctor. He believed that they 'carry revenge so far' as to try to damage him in the eyes of his patients, many of whom 'were of that party'. Mrs Grierson, one of his former patients who had deserted him, met him in the street and asked him with a sneer, how all his patients were. Although he found the remark 'pretty cutting' he answered without the least acrimony – if things go on so, all I can do is think of America. However, when Pollock told him in their recent conversation that his brother-in-law, William Sinclaire, a United Irishman was emigrating to America, Drennan told him that for his own part, he would be 'clinging to the ship till it went to pieces'.[29]

The Catholic Relief Act finally passed in April but while Catholics were granted the franchise, they did not achieve the full emancipation they had demanded and anticipated. Catholics were not granted the right to sit in parliament. In order to benefit from the relief, a voter was required 'to deny papal infallibility and the power of the confessional to absolve all sins, to vow recognition of the country's landed establishment and do nothing to weaken its Protestant religion and government'.[30] Such was the disappointment that 'the Catholic Committee tore itself apart in mutual recrimination'.[31] Tone was disgusted and blamed Keogh for letting it be known during the negotiations that the Catholics would settle for less than full emancipation. Drennan obviously got wind of this, for he told Sam, 'Keogh has been complained of for negotiating on this side of the water underhand and with the undersecretary Nepean in England and for having been the cause of obstructing total emancipation. There is however a division among them, but I imagine the most of them are satisfied.'[32]

The Catholic Committee dissolved, but before doing so they formally thanked Hobart, the man who had thwarted their hopes. They voted £2,000 for a statue of the King and the substantial sum of £1,500 to Tone for his efforts on their behalf.[33] Drennan thought the sum awarded to Tone was 'very handsome and well deserved'.[34] The Catholic Committee also thanked the Northerners for their support but Drennan was disappointed that they made no reference to the need for reform of parliament, much less any commitment to work with the Northerners in the future.

18

EARTHQUAKE IN THE
MERCANTILE WORLD

Martha travelled to Dublin to visit her brother arriving at his Dame Street lodgings on 16 April. She found him looking better than she had ever seen him. He was pleased that she too was looking well and had put on weight. Her journey down had been slowed by snow, which had been falling until they got to Newry. They were delayed after Dundalk 'for want of chaises owing to judges and lawyers, etc., from Dundalk assizes'.[1]

She told Sam that he could see from the papers how things had gone there. What Martha meant by this is that the 'Speaker's Bloodhounds',[2] the light dragoons, had been active and the assizes were enthusiastically dealing with alleged Defenders by sending them to the gallows or for transportation to the penal colonies in numbers. The *Freeman's Journal* named twenty men who were hanged, another eighteen transported for life and one man who was sentenced to be whipped through the streets at Carlingford. However, *the Journal* assured its readers that 'all the prosecutions were carried on by the Crown in which the Attorney and Solicitor General were indefatigable and their conduct distinguished with great humanity'.[3]

Shortly after Martha's arrival in Dublin, Hamilton Rowan and his wife Sarah called to Dame Street and spent some hours with her and later invited her to dinner. Martha found Sarah Rowan to be 'a clever sensible woman'.[4] Rowan told Martha that he hoped that his trial would begin soon as he could depend on the goodness of Hutton, the present sheriff, and rather feared the man who would be the next sheriff. There were very good grounds for Rowan to prefer Sheriff Henry Hutton (1754–1808) to his successor, the future Orangeman John Giffard.[5] The person who held the office of sheriff could have a major influence on empanelling a jury and on the procurement of witnesses for the prosecution.

Hutton was a very successful coach builder from Eccles Street in Dublin.[6] The Hutton family were pre-eminent Dublin Unitarians whose ancestor had come to Ireland as a cavalry officer with Oliver Cromwell's army in the mid-seventeenth century. Henry Hutton's brother, Reverend Joseph Hutton, was associated with Great Strand Street Unitarian congregation. The Rowans and Drennan were members of that same congregation. Reverend Hutton was married to Mary Swanwick, from Wem in Shropshire, and in 1800, William Drennan married Mary's sister, Sarah Swanwick. Henry Hutton was not a United Irishman but as sheriff, he had presided over a meeting demanding reform in 1793.[7]

Rowan felt he had some chance of a fair trial if Hutton was still in office. On the other hand, he knew that Giffard was a government agent and the editor of a pro-government paper, *Faulkner's Dublin Journal*. What perhaps Rowan did not know was that Giffard was also something of a spy master, in that he was Thomas Collins' handler. When Rowan's trial came on in January 1794, Giffard packed the jury and procured, amongst other witnesses, his nephew, William Morton, to give evidence against Rowan. He even coached his nephew from the body of the court when he was having difficulty with his memory. At one point in the trial, John Philpot Curran, Rowan's defence council compared Giffard's rise in office to 'a corpse floating to the surface from putrefaction'.[8] Later that year, after Drennan's trial, Giffard led an armed attack on the crowd in Dublin celebrating the acquittal. Probably the most heinous act of Giffard's long and disreputable career was during the 1798 Rebellion when he participated in the mass murder of 350–500 unarmed rebels who had surrendered at Gibbet Rath, near Kildare town. He later boasted that 'the Curragh was strewn with the vile carcasses of popish rebels and the accursed town of Kildare is reduced to ashes'.[9] Curran has left us a prescient summary of Giffard's career and character. He told the world that Giffard was 'the hired traducer of his country – the excommunicated of his fellow citizens – the regal rebel – the unpunished ruffian – the bigoted agitator, in the city a firebrand, in the court a liar, in the streets a bully – in the field a coward'.[10]

Sam had hoped to join Martha in Dublin but he could not leave Belfast as his duties as a notary public kept him busy dealing with the 'serious and alarming; number of bankruptcies and business failures that were occurring'. He 'thanked his stars that he had no concern in trade'. In his letters, he conveyed to Martha a sense of the worsening tensions between the military and the Belfast townsfolk and he gave an account of a near riot which had taken place on 22 April.[11]

Henry Haslett (1758–1806), one of the proprietors of the *Northern Star*, heard a rumour that the military were again about to attack the offices of the paper. He approached Bristow, the town sovereign, seeking a letter asking Captain Lucius Barber of the Royal Artillery to be particularly careful about the behaviour of his men that evening. Barber promised to keep his men in order. However, some drunken soldiers got into a row with local people and an officer's servant made several sword strokes at the crowd. When the servant was knocked down, the officer drew his sword and Captain Barber was about to do the same when Henry Joy McCracken (1767–1798) stepped forward. McCracken told Barber not to draw. Barber accused McCracken of being the ringleader of the mob and called him a rascal. McCracken said he was Barber's equal and would have satisfaction. Barber said this was not the proper place and anyway he did not know McCracken. McCracken introduced himself and told Barber that Bristow could tell him who he was and that he would meet the Captain anywhere. The following day, Bristow called McCracken to an interview to discuss what had transpired. He asked McCracken to apologise to Barber which he refused to do. Colonel French, who was present, then lost his temper and burst into a rant. He said he was not prepared to have his soldiers continually insulted and he would order them not to suffer it. He warned that if one gun was fired at any of his men, he would immediately burn Belfast to the ground. He threatened that he had ordered three new regiments into the town and would bring back the dragoons.

Sam and the Reverend Vance collected a great deal of signatures requesting that Bristow call a town meeting to discuss these threats and intimidation. Bristow was reluctant to call the meeting and suggested that Sam and Vance meet Henry Joy who had drawn up a paper on behalf of an association to preserve the peace and to prosecute offenders. Sam thought the paper a good one but was not sure it precluded a town meeting. He was worried that 'a parcel of little blackguard boys' were gathering in the streets at night taunting the soldiers and inviting them to 'smell gunpowder'.[12]

Drennan was very disappointed that Sam could not leave Belfast but he understood as things were as bad in Dublin in terms of 'political and mercantile fears operating in every breast'. While visiting a bookshop, a lawyer whispered into Drennan's ear asking after the imprisoned Reynolds. Drennan was furious:

I answered him loudly that he was very well, saying why the devil do you speak in a whisper to me as if it were treason to ask about a friend's health. If things be come to such a pass, let us lock up ourselves in our closets. The shop was divided into three or four whispering *tête-à-têtes* at the time, one in each corner.[13]

The Catholic Committee was in the process of winding-up and as well as granting the generous awards to Tone, they had also granted £500 to the imprisoned Simon Butler. Drennan was pleased that they had proposed a resolution supporting parliamentary reform and promising to join with their fellow Protestant citizens in every constitutional measure for gaining this great national objective. He believed that whether this would be carried depended on John Keogh who was still the Catholic leader in spite of being generally suspected of having bargained away the demand for full emancipation. Keogh might also have agreed to break with the Northerners, 'not suddenly but gradually so as to save appearances'.[14] However, Drennan's doubts were banished a few days later when he heard the final outcome of the Catholic Committee's deliberations:

> The Catholics have come to a resolution pretty strongly expressive of their attachment to a reform sanctioned as it has been by the House of Commons in its principle, and after doing so this committee has dissolved itself resigning their trust and considering their duty as preformed. How they will act in consequence of this resolution is not easy to say, but it certainly is as explicit a document of their political beliefs as a body, as any Dungannon resolution on the part of the Protestants, and therefore they are in this business as least abreast with the other part of the nation – and indeed considering the declared enmity of the English minister to this reform and the supposed aversion of their royal benefactor to the same measure, I think their resolution indicates a decided and honest public mind.[15]

At the next meeting of the Dublin Society, Drennan produced a paper which attempted to use what he saw as the positive resolutions passed at the final meeting of the Catholic Committee to tie the general Catholic body closer to the campaign for parliamentary reform. Collins, who was often dismissive of Drennan's efforts, seemed to think that this paper had the potential to do mischief. He warned Giffard:

> Doctor Drennan produced an address to the Catholics of Ireland, in which he recapitulates the resolution of their committee relative to reform, it is rather long but very strong, dangerous and captivating and particularly flattering if not fulsome to that body, it met with the most unbounded

approbation and several were for having it immediately printed but it was at length referred to a committee of correspondence for their consideration against next Friday, and an extraordinary meeting of the society is to be advertised previous to that day.

I think if it goes forward it will do a great deal of mischief at this time, and though the meetings are poorly attended at present, there are a lot of men now in the society (if they are allowed to proceed without interruption) that are perfectly equal to the task of setting the country in a flame.[16]

The paper was hotly debated over several meetings of the Society as some members believed that it might injure the Catholic body to whom it was addressed. 'Mr. Sheares junior opposed the address as not speaking sufficiently to the calamity of the times.'[17] Four weeks after he had first introduced it, after several apparently tedious debates long into the night and after many adjournments Drennan's paper was adopted by twenty-eight votes for, twenty-three against. However, Collins was happy to report to Giffard:

The address to the Roman Catholics has undergone many alterations by Drennan since he first read it and now appears as to be a very dull, fulsome poor production greatly inferior to what might be expected of him, its appearing in public cannot be expected to do any sort of injury.[18]

Despite her separation from Sam, Martha enjoyed her month-long stay in Dublin, catching up with old friends such as old Mrs Bruce, Fanny Mussenden[19] and Mrs Orr.[20] She had the opportunity to see a performance by Fanny Abington (1737–1815), the Drury Lane actress, and spent an enjoyable evening in the Gentlemen's theatre which had opened its doors for the first time the previous month. She thought Trinity College library 'a noble room' and she saw much to admire in the Museum building. A painting in the newly open Shakespeare gallery of paintings inspired by the play *King John* almost moved Martha to tears.[21]

One Sunday she heard Reverend John Moody preach to her father's old friends at Strand Street and later, she also heard a sermon given by Walter Blake Kirwan (1754–1805) the famous charity campaigner. Kirwan was, she thought, a wonderful man who will do great service by his preaching. She found herself giving a donation of a half-crown but 'he made her tremble at the smallness of the sum'. Friday 18 February being a fast day, she went to Christ Church cathedral where she saw the Lord Lieutenant, the Lord Mayor and heard Robert Fowler, the Archbishop of Dublin, preach. She was not impressed by the Bishop, particularly when he recommended that 'every person should serve his country by being good and virtuous – here at least', said he, 'we may all be United Irishmen'.[22]

Many of Will's Dublin friends, who were strangers to Martha, called by to meet her and treated her with great civility. Amongst these was Richard Kirwan (1733–1812) the chemist and natural philosopher. He sat with her for an hour and she found his company agreeable. Mrs Elizabeth Emmet, her daughter, Mary Anne, and daughter-in-law, Jane Addis Emmet née Patten, called to introduce themselves. Although they had never met Martha, she knew that Jane Patten's late father had been a Unitarian minister at Clonmel and was well known to her own father. Drennan was very anxious for Martha to meet all the Emmet family and she therefore reluctantly agreed to go to their house for dinner on a Sunday evening after a long day's activity. She predicted that when she got there she would 'be a witch'.[23]

Martha heard a rumour that McDonnell, the printer who produced the *Address to the Volunteers* that led to the arrest of Rowan, 'had given proof against Counsellor Emmet', Jane Patten's husband. Some of Will's friends feared that he might be in danger but 'he remained un-attacked and in good spirits'. Given all the pressure that Drennan was under both politically and professionally, Martha was amazed at how well he was bearing up:

> I have never seen Will in such spirits. He is the life of every company we have been in, and though there is little reason for this in the business way, yet I plainly perceive his character as a man and as an author are respected, nor do we ever walk the street without my perceiving some token of it.[24]

Martha was particularly pleased to hear how happy her brother was that she had come to visit him. Mrs Emmet told her that her son had said 'he did not believe there was a happier man in Dublin, than Drennan the night his sister arrived'. Martha observed that he was 'greatly improved in his general conversation, particularly among women, is in excellent spirits and says many good things'. What seemed to give Martha the most pleasure was the public recognition that her brother enjoyed in the city. She told Sam:

> As we passed Lady Fitzgibbon's seat, Isaac Corry called out to him by his name so loud that I could not but believe it was done to point him

out to the rest of the party who instantly turned their eyes on him, and I never walk out with him that I do not hear someone say, that is Dr. D[rennan].[25]

The economic recession and the multiple business failures which were detaining Sam in Belfast were being replicated all over Ireland. Within a few short weeks of Britain going to war, many workers and their families in Dublin were starving. Writing to Sam in early May, Martha said she felt that 'the whole world was going to destruction' as she saw the starving tradesmen of the Liberty going through the streets and the shop keepers closing up.[26] Drennan added some details to the end of Martha's letter.

> The Liberty weavers in the silk, worsted and cotton lines are in great ferment and the women are in a rage. Some of them this morning attacked the bakers' shops, and where there was bacon to be sold, and in a panic most of the shops in the city were shut for half an hour, but the guards were ordered, and I believe still are parading through the Liberty. More danger is apprehended on Saturday night or Sunday when they will become sensible to the extent of the evil.[27]

The Dublin Society placed a notice in the *Dublin Evening Post* recommending the non-importation of British goods and suggesting that purchasing Irish goods was, 'the only means of diffusing comfort and independence in the place of idleness and indigence through the great manufacturing classes of our fellow citizens'.[28] This notice was signed by Drennan and Rowan and received a warm address of gratitude from the Broad Cloth Weavers of Dublin. Usually the Dublin Society would be pleased to publicly answer such an address but not so on this occasion. The correspondence committee of the Society drafted a response but it was withdrawn because some felt that their enemies would say they were 'reduced to corresponding with the mob'.[29] Francis Higgins (1745–1802), also known as the Sham Squire,[30] the editor of the government-sponsored *Freeman's Journal*, poured scorn on the non-importation policy which he said would 'take profits from the fair traders of Dublin and transfer it to the smugglers in the north'.[31]

Tone published a short paper addressed to the manufacturers of Dublin, signing himself 'A Liberty Weaver'. He warned that the war with France would 'drive our most industrious people to idleness, want and beggary'. He asked the questions:

What quarrel have *we* with France? What did she ever do to us, or we to her? *Why the French cut off the king's head.* That to be sure is shocking and barbarous, and I for one am heartily sorry for it; but will our going to war put it on again? Or what right have we, to meddle in their disputes, while they let us alone? I remember to have read that the English cut off King Charles's head just as the French did with their king, but I do not find that any nation in Europe was so foolish as to go to war with them on that score.[32]

Tone predicted that England would lose its best markets in France, Holland and Germany and they would throw all their surplus goods into Ireland and he alleged that 'English riders are already swarming amongst us for that purpose.' Maintaining his fictional persona, he bemoaned, 'for my part, when we are all turned out of work, and ragged and hungry, I do not see how we are to feed and clothe ourselves and our little families'.[33]

In early May, as Drennan walked down by the River Liffey, he passed knots of manufacturers on the quays begging for relief. He hoped that the parochial meetings which would have to be called to discuss the crisis would be an opportunity for expressing detestation of the war which had brought on this national calamity. Rather than the war being the sole cause of the disaster however, Drennan claimed that many were suggesting that the war had merely accelerated or ripened the [existing] evil:

They date the origins of the calamity from the period of the Protestant ascendency resolutions ... At that time the Catholics were driven to great despair and were resolved to go to extremities rather than again be driven from the door of the constitution – a contest was expected – both parties had joined issue – the prospect was black, and a storm apprehended. At that time merchants and houses particularly in the south, began to draw in, and we are now feeling the consequences of the panic which has been for a year past influencing the credit of the country.

Government has all along done what it could to create and spread this panic, and in my opinion are to be denounced for being accessory to the ruin of the credit and character of the country. They sanctioned every calumny as soon as invented: they instituted a secret committee to generate and hatch libels on the land; to foster reports of plots and desperate designs, to create and keep up mutual distrust and to agitate the mercantile interest with alarms kept up from day to day, or when report died, to give birth to another; for this [purpose] men were successively summoned up from the country and affidavits, the most absurd, sworn against them, merely to carry on the plan which was professedly against French principles, but which were really to divert the country from reform, and like which all cunning schemes has ended in the ruin of public and private credit and consequently in the deficiency of that revenue which has supported these monopolists in their power, in their patronage and in their pensionary system of government. Our Society has been a useful target for their arrows, and they have really and truly stabbed the nation through our sides, and the nation has been so blinded by a thousand falsities as to give them credit for destroying the only sincere, disinterested association of men that ever sat for so long [and ruining] the capital of this country.[34]

What Drennan described as 'the dreadful earthquake in the mercantile world' continued unabated and many of the wealthiest merchants in the cotton and silk lines were ruined. Every person concerned with cotton manufacture was said to be close to bankruptcy. In a species of black humour, Drennan suggested that all the business failures in Ireland and England, the retreat of Dumouriez, and for aught he knew, the partition of Poland would be attributed to the United Irishmen.[35] His jest may have been laboured but it proved prophetic. Through the pages of the *Freeman's Journal*, the Sham Squire rubbished the idea that the collapse of Irish manufacturing had anything to do with the war. If the workers wanted to know the source of their miseries, he told them, they 'will find it in the rebellious manifestos of their worthy friends the United Irishmen and the Levellers in the North'. They might also blame 'Tom Paine's productions and the activities of the National Guard and the Defenders'.[36]

Three months had passed but Butler and Bond were still in Newgate. The high life they were enjoying there was becoming a major embarrassment, not to mention a significant cost to the Society. Estimates as to the bill for their wine consumption differ. Harold Nicolson's claim that the prisoners imbibed £500 worth of wine in two months is probably an understatement.[37] Maura Maher, a hagiographer of Bond, claims the £500 sum was in respect of their full six-month detention.[38] Thomas Collins reported in August that after their release, '£2,000 was owed to young Tandy for their wine'. Drennan tells us that three months into the sentence, the Society read a resolution of economy to the prisoners, showing them a statement of accounts showing £12 for fruit and £100 for wine.[39] Drennan, whose total earnings for the previous year was £170,[40]

143

swore he would not subscribe another farthing more while so many thousands of manufacturers were out of employment.

Martha was scandalised and not only on account of the copious consumption of wine. She told her husband:

> Butler is behaving very ill in Newgate and Bond, a virtuous Presbyterian with a rigid wife and father-in-law, is likely to be corrupted there. A Mrs. Blosset, wife of a counsellor of that name and mistress of Butler, goes there frequently, the only woman among a dozen men, sometimes with her husband sometimes not, joins in the devouring fruit etc., and all the rarities of the season and her servants follow her out with a loaded basket. 'Will' has declared his resolution of not subscribing another guinea, but as he thinks the Society pledged to support them he does not care to damp it by bringing forth a resolution, but I suppose Rowan will, who is much displeased.[41]

If the friends of the prisoners were embarrassed about this excess at a time when workers and their families were starving, their enemies were not slow to highlight what they regarded as their blatant hypocrisy. The Sham Squire was scathing when he jeered at the United Irishmen's alleged concern for the destitute. 'Most benevolent society' he mocked 'why not check the vagrancy of your table? If your subsidies to the carousals at Green Street [Newgate] Saturnalia have left you anything besides words for the cause of benevolence, devote a little cash for the relief of the miseries you effect to pity. Words my masters are a windy diet.'[42]

19

LOVE AND MATTERS OF HONOUR

In July, the government brought in an unlawful assembly Act outlawing meetings and Conventions. This spelt the end of Drennan's hopes for a Protestant Convention in support of reform. It also prevented any re-establishment of the Catholic Committee. The Chancellor continued to abuse the town of Belfast and Drennan was astonished that the town was prepared to submit to such 'calumnies without saying a word for itself'. He could not understand why every man in Belfast had not put his name or his mark to a petition to his majesty to remove John Lord Fitzgibbon, Lord High Chancellor of Ireland from the King's counsels forever. He adopted a harsh and accusatory tone and said to Sam:

> The fact is, you are all <u>cowed</u> by this bouncing bully of the law, and I much doubt whether it can be your duty at such a time to persevere in pettish silence, when every remaining right is thus insolently torn from you and your miserable countrymen every day murdered before your eyes. If you do not meet and declare your sentiments of this bill and its author, why – you deserve all you have got and more.[1]

When the government bill passed with a majority of over one hundred, Drennan's idea for a convention was no longer tenable. He next suggested that a national petition to the King might be a way forward. It need not be organised by the Society of United Irishmen nor any individual marked with opprobrium. He suggested to Sam that if it was started in Belfast that the Catholic leaders would concur and co-operate. He had already suggested the idea to people in Newry who seemed to relish the idea.[2]

Butler and Bond were finally released in August, and on Friday 16, they were received back into Dublin Society with 'the loudest acclamations at a meeting in the Tailors Hall'. There were no more than fifty members present to salute 'the virtue and fortitude of the martyrs'.[3] Collins described Drennan's address

145

of welcome as more violent and alarming than any of his previous productions. Yet despite his determination to appear steadfast and determined, Drennan could not disguise his disenchantment. He was careful not to mention that of the total fines of £1,000 all but £30 to £40 had been paid by the Society. Nor did he make any reference to his belief that the Catholics had only remained in the Society because they thought 'it might be deemed disgraceful to quit while these gentlemen were in prison'.[4] Where his disappointment showed through was in his lamenting 'the torpor of the people in their submitting to their few remaining liberties being frittered away'. He finished his address suggesting that if the people are not prepared to act, that brave gentlemen should consider 'emigrating from a land where they were compelled to wear the most ignominious chains'.[5]

According to Collins, Butler and Bond responded pretty much in kind but the *sufferers* advised their friends not to despond:

> Though the people are at present silent, their spirit and energy only want a proper time and cause to rally them round the standard of freedom, they then assign as causes for the present submission of the people, the general depression of trade, the alarms of the timid, the aristocracy of the landed interest, and the desertion of those mock patriots heretofore distinguished by the name *opposition*. They assured the Society and the people at large that the persecution they had suffered in their cause shall not deter them from persevering in the same line of conduct until their emancipation is completed, and that not only are they willing to risk their *future* liberty but their *lives* in the *cause of freedom*.[6]

Such was the enthusiasm for Drennan's address and Butler and Bond's reply that the Society decided to have them published. However, they knew that in the current climate, none of the Dublin newspapers would dare to print anything from the Society, so it was agreed to publish a handbill and judiciously disperse it among the populace. Drennan sent the scripts to Sam telling him that Neilson should publish them in the *Northern Star* and charge it to the Society. He signed off this letter by telling Sam, 'I am heartily sick of politics'.[7]

Drennan's next letter to Sam, dated 1 September 1793, is long, thoughtful and reflective. Most people who knew him were expecting him to be imprisoned at any time. In the letter, he speaks frankly about how his political profile and activity has affected him in his profession, his fear of running into debt and how he was being shunned and vilified as a Jacobin. He discusses how his personality is not suited to his chosen career and complains that the Catholics he has suffered for have not befriended him professionally. It was in this letter that he inserted the imagined dialogue between Edmund Burke and the King regarding Catholic relief referred to in Chapter 9. Towards the end of the letter, he justifies the terrible things that are happening in France and finishes by saying that, despite everything, he will not leave Dublin 'until farther trial' for reasons he cannot even share with Sam.[8]

He began by saying the sky, or at least his horizons, had for some months been a good deal clouded. Most people who knew him had expected him to be arrested at any moment and this fact led to a diminution of income from his medical business. This had led to an exhaustion of his capital and a horror of running into debt. He had initially thought he might gain professional advantage by his public spirit but the fortunes of war had dictated otherwise. His speculations into politics had been made partly to get himself known in Dublin but the change of men's minds had led to him being shunned. Perhaps he was genuinely self-deprecating when he described himself as being democratic without being popular, social in mind yet repulsive in manner. So why, with this view of himself, had he chosen to profess obstetrics his branch of medicine? Because, he said, 'it was impossible to make a living without it, for he complained no man could like this work'.[9]

The Mayo grand jury had passed a resolution not to associate with anyone who was for innovating on 'our excellent constitution'. Drennan observed that 'what they are not ashamed to profess, others, particularly in Dublin, are not ashamed to practice'. Women make it their business to vilify and calumniate persons as incendiaries and Jacobins and atheists.[10] The lack of support from his Catholic acquaintances was particularly discouraging:

> Even those [I] have endeavoured to oblige, and to have suffered very considerably in that endeavour, have never shown the least disposition to befriend me in my profession: I have never received more than a single guinea from a Catholic in my life – and I believe they have given credit to stories of my republicanism and violence, and imprudence and enthusiasm, and poetry thrown artfully in at times by one or two such in confidence, by which they could never prove by anything I have said, written or done.[11]

He expressed the opinion that Siberia was better fitted to be a republic than Ireland. Drennan went on to suggest that the reason why his address on the subject of the Catholic resolutions in support of reform was obstinately opposed within the Dublin Society was because some amongst the Catholics wished to turn their own resolution in favour of reform into waste paper. Usually Drennan's letters were composed with a view to having them read to his family and friends. The opinions he was now forming would not be expressed publicly:

> I do believe our Society is detested by some among them, detested by government, detested by opposition, detested by the aristocratic Catholics, detested by the Protestant aristocracy, and all for being friends of reformation of the constitution. Such is my present belief in the politics of this time, into which I have wandered without designing it, and which I would not want to be disclosed as my sentiments.[12]

'Too suspicious a temper is often a sign of a disposition to madness, yet he vowed he would never go that far.' He believed though that he saw into the Catholic mind as much as others and did not like it. 'It is churlish soil, yet it is the soil of Ireland and must be cultivated or we must emigrate.'[13]

When he considered international politics, he felt that the present was the most awful moment the world had ever seen:

> – all hangs on France. I declare to you it is my firmest conviction that not a thing has been done there which ought not to have been done. It is true many terrible things have happened and much ferocity has been displayed, but ferocity on the one part must meet ferocity on the other. It is a lion attacked by tigers – providence has ordained that the nation that is to make the old world new should be France – and every trait in the character of that ardent, impetuous, ferocious, great nation fits it the better for the mighty task she has to perform. Her ferocity is her virtue, and were she less so, she were lost – and the world, the world that watches so many dogs on this noble suffering animal, without sympathy and without even selfishness, would be lost along with her.[14]

Following the letter of 1 September, there was an uncharacteristic hiatus in Drennan's correspondence. He did not write again until 25th of the month, maybe because he had 'become squeamish and was not paying the least attention to Irish politics'. It might have been that his medical practice had finally began to improve and in August and September he had been busier in those months than he had been in the 'former part of the year'. However, he may have taken time and care preparing this letter for he had momentous news for Martha, Nancy and his mother. William Drennan, in his thirty-ninth year, for the first time in his life, had fallen in love.[15]

The object of his affections was Sarah Swanwick (1770–1870) from Wem, in Shropshire. She had recently come to Dublin to visit her two sisters, Susan and Mary, who were married and had settled in the city. Susan (1769–1849) was the wife of William Hincks (1770–1848) merchant and United Irishman, and Mary (1767–1864) was married to Reverend Joseph Hutton (1765–1856). Sarah stayed in Dublin for six weeks and Drennan met her frequently. When she had returned to Wem the pair kept up a regular correspondence. He confided in Martha that his heart was engaged and he was determined to marry Sarah.

Sarah and her family were Unitarians. Her father ran a boarding school at which her brother, John Swanwick, was a pupil. John Swanwick's closest friend at the school was William Hazlitt (1778–1830) who went on to be the famous essayist. Hazlitt's father, also William, was Minister to the Wem Unitarian congregation. Reverend Hazlitt was an Irish-born, radical republican, who had been a student of Adam Smith at Glasgow and through Smith's influence, had become a disciple of Francis Hutcheson. He had spent his entire adult life in Ireland, America and England embroiled in controversy due to his uncompromising, unorthodox religious opinions and his militant support for the American revolution. Amongst his close friends were Richard Price and Joseph Priestley and he corresponded with Benjamin Franklin. Hazlitt senior was also a supporter of the United Irishmen.

Thomas Muir was finally brought to trial at Edinburgh in October 1793. He had been charged with treason in January of that year, just one month after he had circulated Drennan's address to the Scottish Friends of the People. When he was granted bail, he travelled to London and then on to Paris in a vain attempt to convince the French not to execute their king. Robert Dundas the Lord Advocate of Scotland (1758–1819) brought forward Muir's trial by a few months knowing that the accused could not return in time. Although Muir issued a statement that he would return as soon as possible to answer the charges against him, he was declared an outlaw in his native Scotland.

In July, on his way back to Scotland, Muir called at Dublin and visited Rathcoffey, where he was entertained by Rowan who was still waiting for his own trial to come on. On Saturday 21 July, Muir had dinner with Drennan who reported to Sam that his guest intended to go to Belfast in a day or two on his way to Scotland, where he would stand his ground. Drennan thought Muir 'a very honest, intelligent man' and gave him a letter of introduction to Sam and Samuel Neilson.[16] There is no record of how Muir fared in Belfast but when he landed in Scotland he was immediately arrested. After a scandalous mock trial, he was convicted and given the savage sentence of fourteen years transportation.[17] E.P. Thompson tells us that, 'Braxford the Lord Justice-Clerk, was more virulent in his conduct than the prosecution' and said to a member of the jury 'Come awa' Master Horner, come awa' and help us hang ane o' thae damned scoundrels, he whispered to a juror who passed behind the bench.'[18]

Muir's papers had been seized and correspondence he had received from Drennan and Rowan were read to the court. When Drennan saw his own work as reported in the papers he was very pleased and 'could not help thinking that it was an elegant piece of rational declamation'.[19] This was of course before he heard the savage sentence. However, Rowan was furious when one of his letters was produced:

> The Lord Advocate described it as having been written by a most ferocious person, and said it was sealed with the emblem of a human heart transfixed by a spear and that the United Irishmen's address was composed by one of those wretches who had fled from justice in their country. The seal was the cap of liberty on a pole supported by two hands that of a Protestant and a Catholic united in the grasp of friendship. [20]

Muir openly admitted his contacts with Drennan and Rowan whom he described as gentlemen of distinguished qualities and though he agreed that Rowan had been indicted, he denied that he had fled. Rowan was not happy for Muir to defend his reputation and on 11 October, he wrote the first of two letters to Dundas asking if the obnoxious expression the Lord Advocate had used applied to him? [21]

On the same day that Rowan wrote his first letter to Dundas, Simon Butler wrote a like missive to John Fitzgibbon the Chancellor, regarding what he considered their unfinished business of the previous March. He told the Chancellor that he wished to communicate with him through a third party. The Chancellor agreed and on the following day at 12 o'clock, Rowan arrived at Fitzgibbon's home at Ely Place. Rowan introduced himself, but the Chancellor said he knew well who he was and invited him to sit down.

There then followed a conversation where Rowan accused the Chancellor of using expressions towards Butler which would be offensive to the feelings of any gentlemen. The suggestion was, of course, that Fitzgibbon should apologise or face Butler in a duel. Drennan was aware of Rowan's plans to confront the Chancellor and had expressed the view that, 'if ever a duel was called for it is here for the sentence was all from personal vengeance and can only be met by the same'.[22] Fitzgibbon responded to Rowan that he never spoke in his public capacity without consideration and that he had been much concerned to see Mr Butler had been playing the fool, as he belonged to a profession to which the Chancellor was much attached.[23]

The meeting was unsatisfactory from Rowan's point of view and so he wrote a minute of the interview which he passed to Butler. He sent a copy to the Chancellor informing him that Butler intended to publish the document. The Chancellor responded by saying it was not for him to advise Mr Butler how he should act. Butler published his version of the affair in a handbill and there the matter apparently ended.

Well might Butler have felt an obligation to his friend. Rowan, who was on bail awaiting trial on a very serious charge, had called to the home of the highest law officer in the kingdom on a mission that could easily have been construed as intimidation. Early the following month, Butler honoured that obligation when he accompanied Rowan to Edinburgh on a mission to seek a retraction or satisfaction from Robert Dundas for the remarks he had made at Muir's trial.

Rowan's second letter to Dundas was ignored and on 31 October, accompanied by Simon Butler, he set off from Dublin by way of Donaghdee and Portpatrick heading for Edinburgh. They had a tempestuous crossing to Scotland in a small sloop but they reached Edinburgh on 4 November. They went immediately to the Tollbooth, that dark, medieval dungeon, in which Muir was being held awaiting his transportation to the penal colonies. In Muir's cell, Rowan was placed under arrest by the Messenger at Arms.

Sarah Rowan, back in Dublin, was distraught as she believed that Dundas' provocation was an attempt to lure Rowan to Scotland 'in the hope that he could be implicated in Thomas Muir's seditious activities, convicted by an amenable Scottish jury, and sent off from there to Botany Bay'.[24] On 8 November, Drennan called to Sarah Rowan at Dominick Street who had just received a letter from her husband telling her that he had been bailed by Norman Macleod (1754–1801). Macleod, who was a Member of Parliament for Inverness and a prominent advocate of reform, put up 3,000 scots marks, approximately £165, bail.[25]

For the next few days, Rowan and Butler were feted 'by some of the most eminent of the Scottish reformers'.[26] At a celebration dinner given by Macleod at the Hunters' Tavern, Rowan and Butler met William Skirving, Thomas Fyshe Palmer,[27] Joseph Gerald and Maurice Margarot, all of whom would shortly be convicted of treason and would accompany Muir in chains to Botany Bay.

Margarot was the only one who would see his native land again. They have become known to history as 'the Scottish Martyrs' and are commemorated by a ninety-foot obelisk erected on Calton Hill, Edinburgh. Along with their names, the monument is inscribed with a quote from Muir: 'I have devoted myself to the cause of The People. It is a good cause – it shall ultimately prevail – it shall finally triumph.'

The matter of honour between Rowan and Dundas was dealt with by what looks, to the modern observer, to be a pantomime-like exchange of notes reminiscent of, oh yes you did! oh no I didn't! To be precise, Dundas' answer echoed Fitzgibbon's and amounted to: 'what I did and said, I am not prepared to retract, but all was done or said in my official capacity and therefore I am not answerable for it as a personal matter'. Perhaps because this amounted to a refusal to fight, it was taken by Rowan and his partisans as a triumph for their side. Drennan felt that Rowan had shown that the age of chivalry had not passed away.[28]

When Rowan and Butler arrived in Belfast on the return journey, they were given a heroes' welcome. They spent the first evening in Belfast relatively quietly in the company of Martha and Sam. The next night, they were invited to spend in the company of the United Irishmen which was likely to be a boisterous affair and which Martha predicted would be an event which there would 'be no reason to term respectable'.[29]

By this time, Belfast had been several months under military occupation having been interdicted by the Secret Committee. Citizens had been attacked and threatened by a hostile soldiery. The town's Volunteer corps, of which it was so proud, could not assemble in public. The Edinburgh affair was regarded as a sorely needed boost for the radicals and they were determined to savour the victory.

The chairman of the revelries was none other than Rowan's father, Gawen Hamilton, of Killyleagh. There were 200 in attendance and they congratulated the recently released Butler 'on his safety after the pains and penalties inflicted on him by the satellites of tyranny'. The assembly assured their guests of honour that 'though Belfast remained quiet under the unmerited abuse and calumniation of the enemies of freedom still it was ready to act in obtaining what must very speedily prevail namely liberty, justice and truth'.[30] Butler thanked them and said that before their great object could be achieved many must bleed. Despite this determined talk, Drummond tells us that 'the evening was spent with that conviviality and heartfelt pleasure which the patriotic and the virtuous alone experience'. Among the many toasts in favour of the returning 'heroes' was, 'May the friends of liberty be ever found virtuous and brave.'[31]

Martha gave Drennan a graphic account of the post-party carousing. The formal proceedings over, the revellers departed to their homes. Some, including Thomas Russell and Thomas McCabe, proceeded to the inn for more wine. As a party of drunken militia men were parading the streets, Mr Dawson, a shoemaker, shouted a cheer for the United Irish Society. This was heard and objected to and the militia men called out the guard. Several scuffles took place. One handsome Captain Gore mistook Dawson for a gentleman and challenged him to a duel. The news that a friend of the United Irishmen had been insulted reached the Inn and McCabe thought it best to try to get a very inebriated Russell home. Unfortunately, on their way out they found themselves amongst the drunken militia. Martha relates what happened next:

> Russell went up close to them, did not speak one word, but it seems surveyed them with such a countenance, that after McCabe had got him passed them, they pursued and coming up with Russell, demanded the reason for that look of insolence. Here also, there was great danger – several on two – a young man wanted to fight Russell and always cried out <u>he</u> was Lord Cole,[32] which he repeated so often that one of the mob cried out, you are very fond of that title, take care or it may not be long till you lose it. Another officer however would not allow his Lordship to fight but told Russell <u>he</u> was his man. However, on being reminded that they were but two unarmed men and at their mercy if they chose to bayonet them, a practice now familiar to us, they also had the goodness to put off the affair till the next day. It brought reflection and atonement from the officers in the fullest and most gentlemanly manner. They sought out Russell and apologized to him.[33]

McCabe did all in his power to get Russell to apologise as he believed the look that Russell had given the militia officers had been the cause of the row. Russell wrote out an apology which the officers accepted and after Mr Dawson met the officers, all agreed that the incident had been merely a drunken frolic. Drunken frolic or not, Belfast was by this time clearly a tinderbox of tension that could explode at any time into serious violence. Martha had obviously become quite fond of Russell whom she regarded as somewhat unfortunate. She said of him 'he seems very poor, is very agreeable, very handsome and well informed, and possessed of most insinuating graceful manners. His dress betrays poverty and he associates with men every way below himself, on some of whom I fear he mostly lives.'[34]

20

A HEART AS DANGEROUS AS HIS PEN

On 2 December, the Dublin Society and their friends held a dinner at the Druid's Head tavern to celebrate the release of Butler, Bond and Reynolds. The dinner was 'uncommonly splendid, whatever the season afforded being served in profusion'. The toast included: 'the people', 'the rights of man', 'the double rights of citizens, to be armed and represented', 'the Catholic convention', 'The British convention of delegates of the people, associated to obtain universal suffrage and annual parliaments and now assembled at Edinburgh' and 'Thomas Muir the suffering friend and advocate of the people'. There were many other toasts, including one of 'peace to the bleeding patriots of France and the starving manufactures of Great Britain and Ireland'.[1]

Drennan did not attend this dinner, perhaps because he found the idea of toasting starving workers at a sumptuous drunken banquet to be distasteful. Or maybe he stayed away because he had made only £164 in fees for the entire year; he could not afford the £3 entry fee. Instead, he went to see Mrs Siddons perform in *The Grecian Daughter*, where he admired and wept for two shillings.[2]

The only political writing that Drennan was engaged in at this point was an address from the Society to Thomas Muir, who was by now incarcerated on a prison hulk at Portsmouth, awaiting transportation to Botany Bay. As there was no prospect of having the address published in any newspaper, other than the *Northern Star*, the Society had now the practice of printing many thousands of hand bills for distribution by its members.

Thomas Collins warned his handler that a more dangerous production never issued from that body and that the purpose of Drennan's address was not to console or compliment 'the delinquent' Mr Muir but rather, 'to alarm the minds of the populace for whom it is wrote'. Collins was an unusual informer, in that he did not confine himself to providing information but often presumed to advise his masters as to how they should act. His advice on this occasion had the potential to be very dangerous for Drennan.

By my informing you at this time, so that steps might be taken (if you think it prudent) to prevent the dissemination or to punish the parties I do my duty, and at the same time beg leave to assure you that the author of this address is more likely to injure the peace of this country than almost all the rest of that body and whether it would not be well done to silence him, as his heart is fully as dangerous as his pen is for your consideration.[3]

As the year 1793 drew to a close, Drennan was much pre-occupied with his personal affairs particularly his long-distance courtship with Sarah, who had returned to her family at Wem. He had toyed with the idea of travelling to England to further pursue his connection with her. However, he was reluctant to pursue the matter as far as proposing an early marriage, given his poor financial situation. At the end of the year, after paying his rent and bills, he had five guineas in his pocket. As he felt he was in no position to marry, he suspended his affair with Sarah, with what he felt was honour on his part.

As the new year opened, Drennan was convinced that the government would go on with additional severity. It was now more than a year since Rowan's arrest and Drennan felt his trial would soon come on and that he would be convicted and punished severely. On 16 January, Joseph Corbally, a tailor for the Naul in County Dublin and a Defender, was convicted of perjury. He had accused Justice Graham of suborning him and others, as witnesses against Rowan and Tandy, by promises of rewards, etc. Rowan claims in his memoir that Corbally had called by his house offering to teach his manservant how to make artillery ammunition. Assuming Corbally to be yet another of several government agents, who were sent to further entrap him prior to his trial, Rowan sent him away.

Justice Graham then attempted, unsuccessfully, to bribe Corbally and having failed, had him arrested on charges of high treason. He was told that the only way to save his life was to give evidence against Rowan. He was kept in prison for five months, as every effort was made to get him to turn state's evidence. Another prisoner, named Maguire, was also pressured by Graham to swear against Rowan. Corbally and Maguire brought charges against Graham. Graham released Maguire on bail and he disappeared. Corbally then had no corroborating witness and was found guilty of perjury and sentenced to two years in prison.[4] Corbally's trial took place just two weeks before Rowan's. Drennan was convinced that Corbally's trial was a touchstone for what was about to happen to Rowan.[5]

Following Rowan's confrontation with the Chancellor, as part of the Simon Butler affair in the previous October, Captain Murray, an old friend, called on

Rowan warning him against a repeat of his imprudent behaviour. When Murray reported that Rowan had suggested that he was thinking of leaving the country, the Chancellor used him to open a negotiation designed to facilitate Rowan's departure from Ireland. However, these negotiations broke down due to a government insistence that Rowan publicly resign from the United Irish Society.

When Drennan called round to Dominick Street to see the Rowans on 17 January, he found his friend in very low spirits. Sarah was insisting that her husband do some deal with the Castle to save himself and the family from destruction. The couple's disputes had become, in Drennan's words, 'outrageously violent' and, in fact, he felt they might be on the brink of separation. Dr Reynolds had been living with the Rowans since his release from Kilmainham, which Drennan thought just as well for domestic harmony. Reynolds was a 'staunch fellow' and Sarah found it harder to deal with 'his mild firmness' than 'the ferocious obstinacy' of her husband. Drennan felt himself to be on the best footing with Mrs Rowan, 'as the case would admit', but he had no doubt she often wished all her husband's United Irish friends 'to the devil'.[6]

He may have been right about Sarah's attitude to her husband's associates. However, there was never any possibility of a marital separation. Sarah Rowan might have been exasperated by her husband's obstinacy but once she knew he was not for turning, she supported him courageously in all his vicissitudes. When Rowan was sent to Newgate and when he escaped to live the life of an exiled outlaw, leaving Sarah alone to rear their large family, she never faltered in her support or her great affection for her flamboyant husband. The loving couple finally separated more than forty years later and then only at Sarah's death, aged seventy, in February 1834.[7]

Throughout January 1794, the attacks on the United Irishmen continued and not only from the Secret Committee, the Houses of Lords and Commons or the opposition but now, the clergy of the Established Church were joining in. Drennan told how the pulpits of the Established Church of Dublin every Sunday, 'ring against some society which they say has been established for abolishing the Christian religion'.[8] He believed they were trying to put atheism on the French and find the United Irishmen guilty by association. He was furious that he was being 'whispered as one of this club':

> I! the son of a dissenting minister who have all my life been rigid rather than loose in that persuasion, who was about being made an elder in Newry for my punctual attendance on public worship – I! who pay my four guineas a year to Moody and Taylor[9] will perhaps be obliged to depend on them to

say I have any religion. But take notice, a Unitarian and a Deist here rank as the self-same character, and if you deny the Trinity, you will be set down to deny that there is a God.[10]

Even the Lord Lieutenant was raising the cry of religion in his speeches. The government was trying to bring religious rancour into the war with France with a view to encouraging 'all the men of property to join as a man against French principles', which Drennan suggested, was 'the declaration of rights'. He believed that even, what he referred to as, the 'warm Belfast patriots' would 'ere long join with the rest'. For some time past, he claimed he had judged many in Belfast, 'to be no better than a Brissotine faction'. A few trials like those which had been visited on Muir and his comrades in Scotland would, in Drennan's view, 'settle them all'.[11]

Jacques Pierre Brissot de Warville (1754–1793) was a leader of a moderate faction of French revolutionaries, known as the Girondists. The previous October he and many of his faction, including Manon Roland, had gone to the guillotine after losing out in a power struggle to Robespierre and the Jacobins. One of the central issues in their dispute was the Girondist wish to prevent the execution of the king. It is unlikely that Drennan's apparently anti-Girondist position would have been shared by many of his fellow radicals in Ireland and England at this time.[12] However, we have seen that from very early on, Drennan believed, and never wavered from the belief, that the execution of the king was essential if the Revolution was to survive.

In the same letter, Drennan went on to complain that Henry Grattan, the leader of the opposition, was supporting the government in all matters pertaining to the war. He felt that if the war continued, it was almost certain that a French invasion of Ireland would take place; he mused that, 'in that case the Belfast people will have a curious card to play'. He then went on to lament that despite the efforts of such as Samuel Neilson, the Presbyterian, and John Keogh, the Catholic, there was ongoing disunity between Presbyterians and Catholics, which he attributed to differing attitudes to the French Revolution, religion and politics:

The true cause which really disunites the Presbyterians and Catholics is that the former love the French openly and the Catholics almost to a man hate them secretly – and why? Because they have overturned the Catholic religion in that country and threaten to do it throughout the world. Now the Catholics are, still more religionist than politicians and the Presbyterians are more politicians than religionists. The one still cherish their creed as the first object: the creed of the other is general liberty and equality, but then they are far from that conviction which makes practice.[13]

Rowan finally came to trial on 29 January 1794, almost fourteen months after his arrest. A few days earlier, Drennan sent a note to John Philpot Curran, Rowan's defence council, which he hoped might help.

> Sir, I beg leave to say a few words to you. Mr. Rowan is I hear to be tried on Wednesday for the distribution of an address to the Volunteers of Ireland, and you are to be his advocate. If the paper be not itself seditious, the distribution of it I imagine cannot be seditious, and as the intention with which it was written is the pith of criminality and the ground of decision, who can declare that intention so well as he who wrote it, and were I asked as exculpatory evidence whether I had any design of stirring up revolt, or of exciting resistance to existing laws, I could answer no – before God and my country – no. My single design was to endeavour to revive the Volunteer army of Ireland, and I wrote it as if I had felt the departed spirit of 30,000 of my countrymen stirring in my breast. I speak in the sincerity of my heart in the presence of him who is its judge and were I to get into the pulpit, the only place where it is now safe to talk politics, I do not think I could read a lecture more exhortatory to peace and tranquillity than this very paper, and if the jury do find it malicious, scandalous, and seditious libel, the public might suspect they are wrong, but I know it. I am with the respect due to great abilities yours etc., WD[14]

Drennan thought it odd that Curran did not respond. A very eminent lawyer, writing at the end of the twentieth century, dismissed Drennan's note as pooterish and a bizarre communication from which no benefit could have flowed to the defendant. He described Drennan's efforts as self-justifying and legally irrelevant.

This dismissive conceit and sense of superiority which seems so common-place amongst many lawyers down the centuries may be innate or may result from their training in the law. It would be very strange for any witness who chose to explain his motives to a jury in a criminal case not to be self-justifying. Rowan was about to be tried by highly politicised judges who were determined to get a conviction. He and Drennan knew that the sheriff and prosecution had stooped to every dishonest stratagem to deny Rowan a fair trial. Drennan could have stood by and made no effort to help. He did not do so because of his sense

Overview of Clifton House, formerly the Belfast Poor House, from where William Drennan ran a smallpox inoculation scheme. Courtesy of Kevin Cooper.

Belfast Academical Institute today. Courtesy of Kevin Cooper.

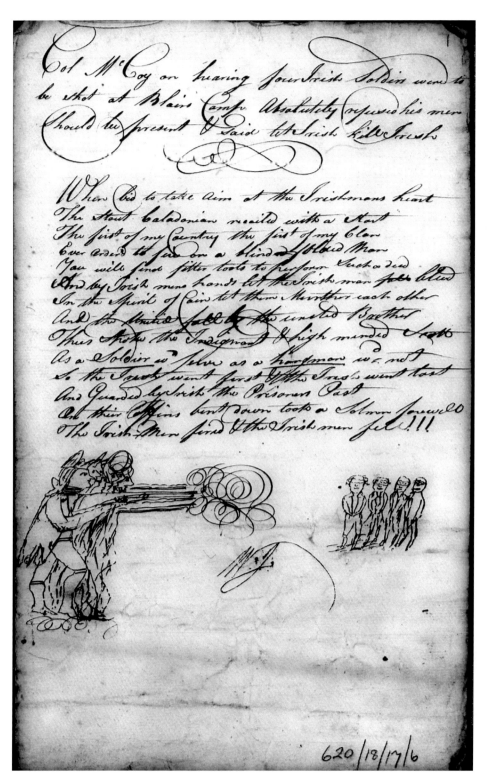

Col McCoy on hearing four Irish Soldiers were to
be shot at Blairs Camp. Absolutely refused his men
should be present & said let Irish kill Irish

When bid to take aim at the Irishmans heart
The stout Caledonian recoiled with a start
The first of my Country the first of my Clan
Ever order'd to fire on a blind folded Man
You will find fitter tools to perform such a deed
And by Irish mens hands let the Irishman bleed
In the spirit of Cain let them Murther each other
And the United fall by the united Brother
Thus spoke the Indignant & high minded Scot
As a Soldier he felt as a hangman we not
So the Scots went first & the Irish went last
And Guarded by Irish the Prisoners past
On their Coffins bent down took a solemn farewell
The Irish Men fire & the Irish men fell !!!

620/18/17/6

William Drennan's sketch of Blaris executions. Courtesy of the National Archive of
Ireland.

Rev. William Bruce. Courtesy of Dublin Unitarian Church.

Rev. John Abernethy. Courtesy of Dublin Unitarian Church.

Martha McTier by Eileen Ayrton. Courtesy of National Museums Northern Ireland.

William Drennan (*c.*1790) by
Robert Home, 1752–1834.
Courtesy of National Museums
Northern Ireland.

William Drennan mural, New Lodge Road, Belfast. Courtesy of Kevin Cooper.

Author, Fergus Whelan, at William Drennan's grave. Courtesy of Kevin Cooper.

William Drennan's grave. Courtesy of Kevin Cooper.

Eulogy by William Drennan to his father, inscribed on the back of his father's image. Courtesy of First Presbyterian Church, Rosemary St, Belfast. Photo courtesy of Kevin Cooper.

The late REV.ᴰ WILLIAM JACKSON,
Convicted of High Treason.

In the Court of Kings Bench, Dublin, 23. April 1795.

Rev. William Jackson. Courtesy of the National Library of Ireland.

MAY—EVENING SPORTS; or, ROWAN lost in the SMOKE.

Archibald Hamilton Rowan's escape from Newgate prison, as pictured in *Faulkner's Weekly*, May 1794. Courtesy of the National Library of Ireland.

Rev. Thomas Drennan. Courtesy of First Presbyterian Church, Rosemary St, Belfast.
Photo courtesy of Kevin Cooper.

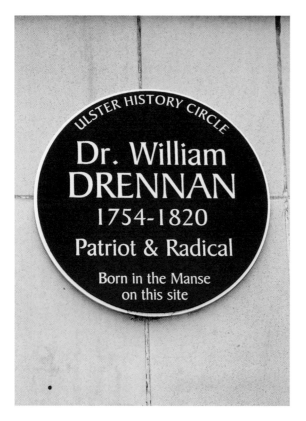

Plaque at William Drennan's birthplace. Courtesy of Kevin Cooper.

of duty to advert the punishment of a friend. His note was designed to appeal to the jury, many of whom may have had fond and proud memories of the Volunteer army of Ireland. Drennan showed courage in his willingness to admit his authorship of the address and to be prepared to state in open court that the only safe place to discuss politics in Ireland in 1794 was the pulpit. Drennan had no legal training and was not possessed of a great legal mind but what he clearly possessed, in great measure, was personal loyalty and physical courage.

On the morning of Wednesday 29 January 1794, Drennan hurried to Green Street Court House to witness the start of Rowan's long-awaited trial. John Scott (1739–1798) Lord Clonmell, otherwise known as Copper Face Jack, presided, with Justices William Downes (1752–1826) and Robert Boyd (d. 1814) also on the bench. Rowan attempted, in his own small way, to set the scene by presenting the United Irishmen as a respectable non-sectarian society of gentlemen. He sat in the court flanked by Hampden Evans and John Byrne, both wealthy United Irishmen. Evans was a Protestant and Byrne was a Catholic.

Giffard the sheriff was determined to set the scene in his own way with an intimidating show of military strength. He appeared in uniform and stationed an armed platoon of soldiers at key points in the public gallery. Curran, of course, objected to the presence of the soldiers and asked, 'if this was the sort of atmosphere where a jury should decide the fate of a fellow citizen?'[15] However, his objections were ignored, as were his and Rowan's objections to the make-up of the jury. Rowan offered to produce proof that two jury members had declared 'Ireland will never be quiet until Hamilton Rowan and Napper Tandy are hanged.'[16] Drennan observed that half the jury were aristocrats. He did not mean by this that they were titled nobility (though at least one, Sir Francis Hutchinson, c.1726–1807, was a baronet), but rather that some of them were known enemies of the United Irishmen who were known as democrats.

Arthur Wolfe (1739–1803), the Attorney General, began the proceedings by accusing Rowan and the United Irishmen of using the Volunteers to terrorise the administration. He then read Drennan's address, commenting now and then on the seditious nature of the document. Perhaps Drennan should have been worried when he heard his address being described as seditious and designed to promote tumult and anarchy. His main concern seems to have been the miserable manner in which Wolfe had read the prose of which Drennan was so proud.

Drennan thought much of the evidence poor and it was clear to him that Giffard had made at least one witness perjure himself. This probably refers to the incident where Giffard had to shout from the body of the court to help his nephew, Morton, remember what he was supposed to say. Curran's speech in defence of Rowan was described by Drennan as 'a finished piece of eloquence'.[17] It has long been regarded as one of the best of Curran's long and illustrious career. Drummond said of it, nearly a half a century later:

> Mr. Curran pronounced a speech which will forever associate his name with that of Rowan. So splendid an exhibition of eloquence had never before been witnessed in an Irish court, nor perhaps in any other court of law. While it dazzled and electrified by its brilliant coruscations, it drew forth reiterated applauses, which no power of self-control or respect for the Bench found it possible to suppress; but it produced no conviction on the mind of the jury.[18]

Lord Clonmell's direction to the jury was, in Drennan's view, 'the most bare-faced piece of partiality ever heard in a court'.[19] The jury retired for just ten minutes and when the guilty verdict was announced, Rowan was taken under heavy military guard of foot and horse to Newgate to await sentence. Clonmell had decided that the accused would have to wait four days to hear what punishment he was to receive. Curran was carried home by a cheering mob who had taken the horses from his carriage and pulled it through the streets.

Early next morning, Drennan and Simon Butler called to Newgate to visit their friend. On their way in, they met Sarah Rowan, who was just leaving, and they saw her to her carriage. She did not seem at all crestfallen but was very angry at Lord Clonmell. Rowan was in good spirits and he let it be known he was not going to emulate the high living of Butler and Bond. He would have no wine and would be served with food from his own house, which he would share with family members and fellow prisoners of lesser means.[20] While his friends speculated as to the possible severity of the sentence, Rowan busied himself preparing an application for a retrial. He believed he could prove that Giffard had packed the jury with some who were known to be biased against Rowan and that the prosecution witnesses could be shown to be less than trustworthy.

On Sunday morning, Drennan went to a religious service at the Unitarian Meeting House at Great Strand Street. Sarah Rowan was there with her son, who Drennan thought one of the handsomest boys in the city. He described how 'the congregation ogled Sarah and old Mrs Bruce praised her much; old Mrs Dunn told her she was sorry for her husband's imprudence'.[21] The two old ladies were widows of ministers. It is possible that Sarah carried out some financial transactions on her husband's behalf. The minister's ledger records more than £100 donated by A.H. Rowan, during February 1794, while he was incarcerated at Newgate.[22]

On Monday, Curran made an unsuccessful application for a retrial and, on Tuesday, Rowan was sentenced to two years in prison, a fine of £500 and sureties of £4,000 to be of good behaviour for seven years. Drennan went to Newgate immediately and found Rowan in excellent spirits. 'He was soon in a crowd of sympathising friends, without affecting smiles or forcing sorrow, distressed but not dispirited.'[23]

In early February, Drennan became aware that Jack Pollock was visiting various printers in Dublin, to see if he could get one of them to name the author of the *Address to the Volunteers of Ireland*. Pollock sent a note to the wife of Randal McAllister, a printer and United Irishman, who had gone bankrupt the previous year.

> The gentleman who wishes to see Mrs. McA. Begs she will not leave town this day. Most important business has prevented him from seeing her yet, but he will certainly be with her as soon as possible – perhaps in the course of one hour. As the business he has with her is of the upmost consequence he hope she will not disappoint him by leaving town, or if she does she will leave her address.[24]

Pollock asked Mrs McAllister why her husband had not been seen in public and suggested it might be on account of the prosecutions commenced against him by government. The wife replied that the government could do her husband no more harm, as they had already ruined him in his business. She said that he was in hiding from his creditors. Pollock said he knew McAllister had not written the address but if he came forward to disclose the name of the author, her husband would no longer be molested by government and his debts would be paid. Mrs McAllister said she would have nothing to do with carrying such a message. The pair parted somewhat less than amicably but Pollock suggested that if she could find a sensible man to represent her, he would discuss the matter more fully with him.

It was Simon Butler who told Drennan about Pollock's approach to Mrs McAllister and he also informed him that McAllister had applied to the Society for money to allow him to leave the country. Drennan had not the patience to copy the letter, dated 2 February, which McAllister sent to the Society but he briefly summarised it for Sam:

> He [McAllister] requested aid to go to London at least, if he cannot procure what is necessary to go to America, for to stay here to be tried, convicted and pine in prison would he says be folly. He says that if the Society suspects him, they have saddled the wrong horse. He says that he had hidden himself up and down for five months, often wanting the necessities of life, robbed, imprisoned, calumniated, exiled in order to force him to be a tool of government. There have been offers made him, but he has fortitude he says to resist all, and will shortly lay before the public particulars which will show a system of villainy to shock every honest man.[25]

Drennan's reaction to this was rather strange. He seems to have developed some suspicions of Butler and believed he was part of an effort to alarm him. He felt Butler wanted to involve him in some deal with McAllister. For his part, Drennan said he 'was determined not to contribute the smallest donation whether he [McAllister] may have the original address or not and I believe he has it not'.[26] He felt to make any kind of donation would be an admission of guilt. Despite the decision of the judges and jury in Rowan's case, Drennan was clearly clinging to the illusion that his address was not seditious. Butler endeavoured to get Drennan along to a consultation in Newgate on the matter, presumably to take place in Rowan's cell. Drennan refused to go. It may not have been Drennan's illusions of his innocence alone which determined his attitude to this affair. It may have had something to do with his recent decision to end his engagement to Sarah Swanwick. He had little or no money.

Drennan was not the only one who seemed to harbour suspicions regarding Simon Butler. At the quarterly meeting, Butler was not re-nominated to the correspondence or constitution committees of the Society. He was, however, nominated for the finance committee, which should have been a cause of embarrassment to him. He was obliged to furnish a set of accounts which would show that most of the Society's debt was incurred on his account.

It is not clear what the origins of the suspicions against Butler were but there may have been two contributory factors involved. The first was that, in conversation, he often expressed a contempt he had developed for the people and felt, 'that it is ridiculous in any man to run further risk for them'.[27] Perhaps of more importance was the way in which his challenge to the Chancellor played out. Drennan recounted this version of the affair to Sam:

> The Chancellor on being asked by several lords to bring on the affair of the challenge before the House, said that he should never trouble the House

with personal disputes. Butler said in the courts on hearing this, 'that it was manly conduct; let him let me alone and I will let him alone'. This has raised the cry of desertion, and it is fostered by those who do not like Butler, such as Rowan, Emmet, Reynolds etc.[28]

If Rowan did not like Butler, his wife Sarah Rowan hated him. She believed that Butler had sent word to the Chancellor putting the blame on Rowan for publishing the account of the conversation between himself and the Chancellor. If Sarah Rowan was right in her suspicions, it seems Butler's behaviour was cowardly and he was guilty of the gross betrayal of a friend. We shall see presently that Drennan eventually concluded that Butler was no coward.

21

SPIES, ENTRAPMENT AND GAOL BREAK

Throughout the month of February, Drennan heard ever more details of Jack Pollock's efforts to get information from printers to the effect that Drennan was the author of the *Address to the Volunteers*. Pollock had approached one Lewis, McAllister's foreman, and now the employer and employee had quarrelled, each accusing the other of selling the pass. Drennan did not believe either had anything to sell.[1]

Far from being panicked by Pollock's efforts, Drennan began to conceive a plan to let Pollock know that he knew what he was up to. He could threaten to expose him as a hypocrite who, while he had declared his friendship to Drennan, was intriguing with potential informers to destroy him. He felt he could not publicly challenge Pollock with duplicity because the information he was given 'had been couched in general terms'. However, he suggested either Sam or Martha could write to Pollock 'appealing to his conscience to justify either the integrity or manliness of his conduct'.[2] In such a letter, they could remind him of his meetings and offers of advice and friendship and let him know that they and Drennan knew all about his other activities.

At the end of the month Drennan said to Sam:

Nothing, I join with you, is to be said to Pollock, yet a little, but the more I think of it, if all be true as reported, it appears we have his character as a gentleman a good deal in our hands, although it would not be possible to legally entrap him. I think he might be put by proper proceeding on our part into a fright, and I don't know but a threat, a serious threat of laying the simple facts before the public would not be a good way. Turn it in your mind what should be done, for the concurring stories proves sufficiently his conduct.[3]

Drennan had no idea of the peril he was in or just how dangerous and unscrupulous a character he was dealing with in John Pollock. As he had had no dealings with these printers, Drennan naively assumed that Pollock would not be able to secure the evidence he was seeking. This was a major miscalculation, as was Drennan's idea of appealing to Pollock's conscience. For Pollock did not possess a conscience and was a skilled spymaster, a venal seducer and an adapt suborner, who was as happy to procure perjury as truth in his relentless pursuit of victims and reward. However, the full details of Pollock's nefarious activities emerged many years later, when both he and Drennan were long dead.

Drennan may have flattered himself that Pollock had failed in his attempts to buy him off. However, Pollock had had much more success seducing other leading United Irishmen including the lawyers Leonard McNally and James McGucken. Francis Joseph Bigger tells us that, in the *Book of Secret Service Money*:

> We find vast sums of money set down opposite the name of John Pollock for himself and other 'managed' parties, and especially 'John Pollock for M.G., £60,' 'for M'Gucken, £100' and then again £100 – also 'M'Gucken, Belfast per post, by direction of Cooke, £50,' 'M'Gucken, per Marsden, £50'and so on hundred after hundred *ad nauseam*.[4]

In 1797, William Orr was the first United Irishman to be hanged. His execution followed a stage-managed trial involving perjured witnesses and a drunken jury. Drennan took a very keen interest in this affair and it was the inspiration for one of his best-known poems *The Wake of William Orr*. William Orr was convicted of administering the United Irish oath to Hugh Wheatley and John Lindsay, members of the Fifeshire Fencibles. Joseph Bigger doubted very much if the pair were *bona-fide* fencibles at all. However, he had no doubt whatever 'that John Pollock had managed these "fencibles" just as he had managed other noted informers'.[5] McGucken was William Orr's attorney but it is not clear that he had been seduced by Pollock before or after Orr's trial and execution.

Had Drennan known the true nature of Pollock's character, he would not have assumed that his reputation as a gentleman counted for much with him. However, Martha was only too happy, when the time came, to write to Pollock reminding him of the details of his interviews with Drennan the previous year, when he had proclaimed his friendship and offered to help him in his career. Martha dated her letter 7 March 1794. She told Pollock she had a note of what transpired between himself and Mrs McAllister and she accused him of pressing Lewis, the printer, to name Dr Drennan as 'the author of that paper denounced by government'. She threatened to make public all his underhand methods.[6]

Pollock's reply has been justly described by John Larkin as 'a masterpiece of vulpine elegance'.[7] Martha knew that she had met her match and been given 'a smart, not ill-humoured dressing'. Pollock obviously took great time and care in his reply and his mocking tone is palpable when he thanks Martha for her advice:

> As to the advice you have done the honour to give me, I receive with all due consideration. It is particularly kind in a lady to whom I have the misfortune of being wholly unknown, to take so much trouble on my account – yet looking as I do, on the great superior talent, to the gentleness, the feminine expression and to the beautiful and amiable insinuation, and the manners, that mark every line of the performance you have bestowed on me, allow me to assure you that whenever I venture to solicit your advice, I shall most thankfully receive and attend to it.[8]

Martha had no doubt that Pollock chuckled as he wrote his reply but she was determined not to let him have the last word. In her own opinion, the second letter she sent was the best she had ever written. However, she believed, and Drennan agreed with her, that while there was some satisfaction in letting Pollock know they were on to him, nothing they could do or say would stop him seeking information to put Drennan in the dock.

Pollock's sarcastic masterpiece is mostly designed to obfuscate and deceive but it contains one sentence which is an honest statement of his motives and is fully borne out by what we now know of his subsequent behaviour. He told Martha that the only ambition he had was to be permitted quietly to enjoy the fruits of a very industrious and laborious life, to take care of his family, to fix them in a reasonable state of competency, to fear God and honour the King.[9]

Besides the many very large sums of secret service monies paid to Pollock which W.J. Fitzpatrick found 'too tedious to enumerate',[10] Castlereagh saw to it that Pollock was rewarded with the enormous sinecure of the Clerk of the Pleas of Exchequer. He carried out the duties of this office 'indolently, inefficiently and often fraudulently'.[11] *The Evening Post* described it as the most lucrative and unnecessary post in the country. When eventually Pollock's activities in office were investigated, 'a more monstrous labyrinth of abuses were never before' discovered. Chief Baron O'Grady passed judgment on Pollock: 'We are obliged to declare from the acts lately for the first time come to our knowledge, that he has abused his duty – abused his discretion – he has done acts without authority – by accepting gratuities he has degraded the court and permitted fictitious charges.'[12]

Pollock finally lost his reputation as a gentleman, only in 1817, after a very successful career recruiting informers, suborning perjurers and amassing a corrupt fortune in public office. He had played an important, if covert, part in the judicial murder of William Orr. He received several payments from the secret service fund in August 1803, about the time his toady Leonard McNally was basely betraying the life of his young client, Robert Emmet. It was perhaps as well for Drennan that he was not fully aware of Pollock's malevolent perfidy. Drennan's naïve belief in his own innocence enabled him to declare to Sam, 'they have nothing against me, even though they want to make terror the order of the day. I don't think even though they had any paper in my writing they could swear to my hand – I neither brave nor flinch'.[13] He might indeed have flinched if he had appreciated the magnitude of the evil he was up against. It would be six years later that Drennan learned that Pollock's pursuit of him was at the behest of Robert Hobart, the Chief Secretary.[14] In other words, the orders to suborn or entrap Drennan had come from the very top.

Throughout March and April, as Rowan remained in confinement, the Dublin Society held its regular meetings and spent time discussing routine issues. They spent several hours discussing what should and should not be included in an address being drafted by Drennan for presentation to Rowan. They argued about whether the Society's plan for reform of the House of Commons should be addressed to the House or the people at large. Emmet acted as editor for an account of Rowan's trial including Curran's great defence to be printed. However, Collins told his handlers that 'either from fear or policy nothing of consequence would be agitated in the Society at large' and that any mischief intended was being planned in private.[15]

On 24 March, Drennan read a reply from Thomas Muir to the Dublin Society, dated 10 March, from the prison ship *Surprise Transport*, then at anchor in Portsmouth but about to set sail for Botany Bay. Collins summarised Muir's letter:

> Muir told the Society that the greatest happiness of his life is the reflection that he presented the address of the Society to the Scotch convention which was handed to him by that suffering patriot *Archibald Hamilton Rowan*. He assured the Society in the strongest terms that the great majority of the Scottish people are firmly attached to the great cause of freedom and that they impatiently wait a favourable opportunity of obtaining that grand object.[16]

At the same meeting, Drennan proposed that the Society should award a very handsome medal to any member who could produce the best and simplest treatise on the rights of man to be calculated for the purpose of enlightening the minds of the lowest orders of the people. It appears from Collins' reports that Drennan was very active in the Society throughout March and April. He drafted an address to Dr Priestley on the occasion of his emigration to America. On 11 April, he asked the Society for more time to complete a plan for parliamentary reform.

A message was sent to the meeting by Carey the printer to the effect that unless his bail was exonerated and he was paid £200, he would inform against Drennan, Rowan and some others. At the same meeting, six stewards including Drennan, Bond, Reynolds, Henry Jackson, Matt Dowling and Robert Dillon, were selected to organise a birthday celebration for Rowan which Collins mis-records as falling on 22 May. Rowan's birthday fell on 12 May. This mistake is of little consequence since no party took place on either day due to the absence of the guest of honour who had fled Newgate and the kingdom before the big day.

From the beginning of Rowan's confinement, Drennan paid a daily visit to his cell at Newgate. On 2 May, he was taking Moses Dawson, a friend of his from Belfast, on just such a visit. However, on the way to the prison they heard the astonishing news that Rowan had absconded from the jail the previous day. They rushed around to Rowan's house in Dominick Street to see Sarah Rowan. A short time later, Gregg the jailer arrived with orders to search the house. Sarah handed over all the keys but no Rowan was found. By mid-morning, the whole of Dublin was in a state of high excitement:

> The town talk this morning [is] great – most reproach him – the hacks for want of honour and involving the sheriff, others on other accounts. Most think he will not effectuate his escape and will be stopped at any of the out-ports. Some say he has implicated himself with Jackson the man who is closely imprisoned in Newgate on a charge of high treason. This man, though I call at Newgate to see Rowan daily, I never saw and know nothing about. Others say Rowan has turned mad and was evidently so for some time. The council I find have offered £1,000 reward for apprehending him.[17]

This Jackson facing treason charges was Reverend William Jackson (1737?–1795) who had arrived in Dublin four weeks earlier. He was on a mission from the French government to assess how a French invasion force would be received in Ireland. The reason for Rowan's sudden departure was indeed because he had become implicated with Jackson. The first part of Jackson's mission was to democrats and reformers in England, most of whom told him that a French invasion of England would be a big mistake. When in England, he made his mission known to a lawyer friend, John Cockayne, who tipped off William Pitt and then, on Pitt's instructions, accompanied Jackson to Ireland.

Although Jackson did not realise it, his mission had now become a British government plot to entrap the United Irish leadership. Jackson and his friend based themselves at Hyde's coffee house in Dame Street. The authorities could rely on more than Cockayne to keep them fully informed. The pair's first social gathering with United Irishmen in Dublin was a dinner hosted by Leonard McNally. Most of the those present at McNally's did not trust Jackson and Simon Butler laughed when the question of a French invasion was raised. Jackson only began to make progress when he called to Newgate for the first of several meetings with Rowan.

It was not long before the other informer, Collins, was telling his handlers to watch Hyde's and suggesting that John Keogh and some of his fellow Catholic Committee members were 'deeply concerned with Messrs Rowan & Jackson'.[18] Rowan prevailed on a reluctant Wolfe Tone to draw up a paper on the likely reaction of the Irish people to a French expeditionary force. The final paragraph of this paper is more than enough to illustrate the danger it might prove to anyone found with it in their possession:

> The force necessary may not be more than 20,000 men nor less than 10,000. Supposing them 10,000 – 7,000 should land in the west, and having secured and fortified a landing space, should advance into the middle of the country, at the same time 3,000 should land immediately at the capital and seize all the stores and persons that might be troublesome. In that event, the North would rise to a man, and so having possession of three fourths of the country and the capital, the remaining part were it so inclined, could make no resistance.[19]

A few days before he made off, Rowan and Drennan met for breakfast at Newgate. Rowan was in high spirits and was making a copy of the paper which Tone had prepared. He read it to Drennan and asked for his opinion. Drennan thought the paper very well drawn up but very dangerous to keep and much more to copy. Rowan then gave Drennan an option:

> He asked me if I wanted to stay and be in the cabinet, or to be in the parlour or in the hall. I immediately understood that someone was to be with him in confidence and that as I had not apprised him of my intention of staying

to breakfast, I said laughingly I should not wish to be in the cabinet and in about a minute after went away. He took me at my word, for I believe the fellow now imprisoned for high treason. Tone and Reynolds have had conferences together, and Cockayne a man who came over with Jackson, has been examined before the council and it is said reported their conversations etc., and it is said here today that Tone and Reynolds are not to be seen.[20]

Thanks to Cockayne, the Castle now had Tone's paper in Rowan's handwriting. Rowan had no option but to escape to avoid the death penalty on charges of high treason. Reynolds clearly thought the Castle had evidence on him, so he absconded to America. Tone had been careful not to allow Cockayne to hear any of his conversation and though the authorities knew he was author of the paper, they might have had difficulty in sustaining charges. Tone had some influential friends and through them commenced a negotiation with government.

For Drennan and the other Society members not directly caught up in the business, Rowan's flight was a disastrous set back. Martha predicted that it would bring disgrace, suspicion and ignominy on the Society. She may have alarmed her brother when she wondered who would fill the vacated seat in Newgate. When Drennan went to the next scheduled meeting on Friday 3 May, he was disgusted to find the room in darkness. A woman came to the door and said that Leonard McNally and Nicolas Butler had come to tell her there would be no meeting of the Society that night. Drennan and Moses Dawson entered the room and asked the woman to light all the candles. The members began to drift in in ones and twos until finally they had a considerable number and the meeting went on until a late hour.[21] Drennan moved a motion of censure against those who had behaved improperly by taking it on themselves to try to postpone the meeting.

It was vital for the Society to hold this meeting as normal for, had it failed to do so, they would all have appeared panic struck and they would all have been implicated with Rowan, Tone and Reynolds. Drennan felt this might be the case particularly in relation to himself. He knew that some action would be taken against the Society and was disappointed that his friend Emmet had not appeared. Simon Butler was there and whatever cloud of suspicion had been hanging over him appears to have lifted for Drennan praised his manly spirit and observed: he is a man. The fact that this meeting had taken place was a small victory in the midst of a terrible crisis for which Drennan claimed total credit.

And were it not for me and me alone, there would not have been a meeting last night. I gave myself credit for having saved the Society from an acknowledgement with having implicated itself with Rowan and treason etc., and my appearing and Butler's exculpates us in the eye of the world about us – as we are in reality, for I know nothing of it, nor ever saw this Jackson in my life.[22]

In his letters to Sam and Martha, Drennan is very anxious to disclaim any knowledge of what was going on between Rowan and Jackson or of any advanced notice of Rowan's plans to flee. While he may not have 'been in the cabinet' he was very close to the action. He was aware of the content of Tone's document and would have known it was drafted to encourage a French invasion of Ireland. He had clearly also surmised that the document had been prepared for Jackson to transmit to Paris. When Cockayne was being questioned by the authorities, he was asked specifically if Drennan had been present at any of the meetings with Jackson. His answer was that 'he had never seen such a person'.[23]

The Lord Lieutenant Westmoreland wrote to the British Home Secretary Henry Dundas on 12 May,[24] suggesting that Drennan had indeed been involved with Jackson and the Irish government had considered, but ultimately rejected, the idea of doing a deal with Jackson to implicate Drennan and Tone:

> The Attorney General is afraid if Drennan is caught that we have not a tittle of evidence against him, and as little against Tone, for you observe Cockayne ... will not speak positively to the different conversations with these persons, but only caught the substance by hints and accidental words. I cannot agree in thinking it wise to save Jackson and punish the other two. With how bad an appearance of evidence (Cockayne and Jackson, hardly a corroborating circumstance) we should go into court. Not a person in court but would attribute the whole to a snare and the government would be sadly disgraced.[25]

Three days before Rowan's flight, Drennan had found him in a state of great agitation. In fact, Drennan described him as having been 'in a state of great perturbation and what one would call madness'. By this time, Rowan was aware that Jackson had been arrested at Hyde's with a copy of Tone's document in Rowan's handwriting in his possession. Drennan describes a man who was deeply disturbed by his situation:

> He bade me say he was a baby and a fool and was led into ruin by his own unguardedness and by some inaccuracy of Tone's. The case is, he has no

doubt implicated himself with this Jackson, but I believe or rather I suspect, he has a scheme getting if possible to France and returning as a guide and that there is some army ready for invasion. You see this letter is to be burned immediately and don't mention a syllable to one soul but Matty.[26]

Faulkner's Weekly carried a cartoon captioned 'May-day Sports, Rowan Lost in the Smoke' with some amusing but completely fictitious depictions of the escape. In one scene, Rowan is galloping away from the prison on a white horse through the smoke of a May Day bonfire shouting 'liberty or death'.[27] In another, he is seen getting into Sarah Rowan's coach dressed as a servant. Another shows the jailer asleep in bed, the door of the prison wide open with the guards and the sentry in a drunken sleep outside.

Drennan knew exactly how the escape had been affected. Rowan had bribed the under-jailer to allow him to spend the night of his wedding anniversary with his wife at home. The armed under-jailer had accompanied Rowan to Dominick Street. At twelve o'clock, Rowan was let down from his bedroom window on a rope ladder. Drennan had heard that the authorities 'had promised every retribution to the under-jailer which they would probably perform' if Rowan managed to get off safe.[28]

The editor of the *Freeman's Journal*, the Sham Squire, had long been very hostile to Rowan and the United Irishmen. He carried the story of the escape with his usual flair for telling a good story with complete disregard for the truth. The Sham treated his readers to a droll and creative fiction. 'The business of the escape was a concerted one. The post-chaise on which he travelled to Rush changed horses at "The Man of War" and he reached Rush at three in the morning, where everything was prepared for his reception and conveyance on an American vessel *The Hope* which lay at anchor to receive him and instantly set sail.'[29]

Unfortunately, from Rowan's point of view, no such elaborate arrangements had been made for him and it was not going to be a simple matter for him to avoid capture. When he climbed down from his window, he met up with Matthew Dowling who had horses at the ready. Both men rode through the night to Sutton, a small seaside village on the north side of Dublin. There they were given refuge by John Sweetman, a wealthy Roman Catholic United Irishman. Drennan thought Rowan might try to leave Ireland through Rush, another seaside village a few miles north of Sutton. Rush had long been notorious for its entrepreneurial smugglers who, in war time, were inclined to go privateering. Drennan thought that if Rowan did try to leave from Rush, the revenue cruisers would take him.

In fact, Sweetman did go to Rush to try to procure a passage abroad for Rowan but by the time he got there, the military were searching house by house, paying particular attention to the houses of some recently released smugglers who had dined with Rowan at Newgate. On 4 May, Rowan sailed for France in a small pleasure vessel belonging to Sweetman, crewed by three smugglers. Christopher and Denis Sheridan and the other crew man named Murray knew that there was a reward of more than £1,000 for Rowan's capture. One of the Sheridans said to Rowan as they set sail, 'Our boat is small, but God looks after those like you who have the blessing of the poor.'[30] Toward the end of the month, Drennan was reporting with remarkable accuracy the detail of how Rowan had managed to escape to France. On 28 May he told Sam:

> It is said that he made his escape on Thursday night from this to a house in Howth from whence he set sail on Sunday night with three men in a wherry well provided, and that two of the men were to have £500 between them. What the third was to get is not said though they showed him the proclamation. The report said that Baldoyle a village within a half mile of Howth was searched but they overlooked the house where he remained.[31]

Howth, Baldoyle and Sutton are within a mile of each other so Drennan knew not only Rowan's point of embarkation but also knew something of the vessel and crew. Drennan also told Sam that Rowan had taken a red nightcap with him which he said he would put on the mast head if he reached his destination. In Rowan's memoir, published in 1840, he described how he reacted on reaching France when their small vessel was saluted by a shore battery from the French coast. 'I borrowed Sheridan's night cap which by chance was red, filled it with straw stuck it to the boat hook and lashed it to the helm as a *bonnet de Liberté* and thus sailed into the mouth of a small bay near Roscoff.'[32]

Drennan also had it right when he reported that Rowan had landed in Roscoff and had been released after one night in custody. However, he was wrong when he said that Rowan had probably proceeded to Paris. In fact, Rowan was treated as a suspected spy and disappeared into the wartime French prison system from which he did not emerge for some time. He eventually escaped to America and finally returned to Ireland to be pardoned in 1805.

22

THE END OF THE DUBLIN SOCIETY

Gawen Hamilton, Rowan's father, came to Dublin to support Sarah at this very difficult time for her. Drennan called to see Sarah each day and was a little taken aback when, on his departure on one occasion, she said, 'May God preserve you.'[1] The Sham Squire was trying to unnerve Drennan and his associates. He wrote in the *Journal* that 'on the morning on which Mr. Rowan escaped his room was crowded with his cronies, Dr R[eynol]ds, Dr D[rennan], Councillors McN[even], E[mme]t and S[imon Butler] and three engineers from Rush recently tried for abetting the Defenders'.[2]

Drennan was disappointed in his friend Emmet, who appeared panic struck and talked of his mother and wife, and seemed to be on the verge of quitting the Society. For his own part, Drennan seemed to have no fear for himself but felt that Rowan's departure, like Tandy's before him, would adversely affect the Society though he hoped the damage would be short-term.

Carey the printer had written to the *Dublin Evening Post* complaining of his treatment by the Society. When at a meeting on Friday 9 May, Drennan proposed setting up a committee to examine his complaint. Collins believed this to be 'clear proof that he is very much in alarm'. And when Drennan's proposal was lost, Collins advised that Carey could be *had* on very easy terms.[3] However, Drennan's proposal had nothing to do with him being alarmed. This is Drennan's version:

> On Friday last I got up and said I had read Carey's second publication addressed to the Society, that from the dates and style it had an air of probability which might have [made an] impression on the public, that it was little disgraceful for a society as for an individual to retract if it had done anything wrong, that therefore I threw it out whether it would not be proper to appoint a committee of review to look over the whole transaction and if complete justice had not been done to report to the Society.[4]

Perhaps Drennan should have been alarmed, for at 8.30 p.m. on the following Monday, Grant and Logan, two police messengers, arrived at his lodging with a warrant requiring him to appear before Lord Clonmell. They had information that he published and caused to have published in a certain newspaper, the *National Evening Star*, a seditious libel tending to disturb the public peace. He accompanied them at once, stopping by Emmet's on the way, but he was not at home. Clonmell met him in his Lordship's hall and advised him to go and find bailsmen. The policemen accompanied him as he visited several friends and acquaintances, many of whom were not at home and some who were at home but declined.

Drennan appears to have been very cool under pressure, for as he walked under guard down Jervis Street, he could not 'refrain from the temptation' of knocking on John Pollock's door requesting him to go bail:

> [Pollock] was just coming up the steps. I said I was arrested on a warrant from Lord Clonmell and had got one bail and was in search of another – would he be one? No Sir says he very stiffly. Good night says I familiarly. Now he may puzzle himself if he will about my reasons and laugh at me as a new instance of my simplicity but the true cause I leave to himself at some future time to know.[5]

Eventually he got Dr Burke, a Protestant, and Simon Maguire, a Catholic United Irishmen, to go bail for him. When they got back to Clonmell at a quarter past eleven, it was too late to do the paper work. Drennan believed he had Clonmell's assent to spend the night in custody in his lodgings but Alderman Warren instructed the policemen to bring him to Newgate. He 'cheerfully accompanied them and slept pretty well considering the time and place etc., with a large Bible by way of a pillow and the gaoler very civil in little accommodations'.[6]

Unfortunately, both of his bailsmen had to withdraw next morning for family reasons and Drennan assured them that he understood and that they should not be troubled about it. It was not until 5 p.m. that he could go back to Clonmell seeking his release. His eventual bailsmen were Beauchamp Bagenal Harvey (1762–1798) and John Chambers with Emmet, Bond, Butler and several others in reserve. Harvey was hanged and beheaded in 1798, Bond died in prison and Chambers and Emmet were imprisoned and banished in the aftermath of the Rebellion. Simon Butler had died of natural causes in 1797 at the age of forty.

Drennan's bail was set at two sureties of £500 and his own reconnaissance of £1,000 and he 'was soon as well and as hearty as ever at home'.[7] He seemed to be very easy in himself that the charge was merely sedition, and not treason, for which no bail is granted. In fact, the first warrant handed to him was for high treason but it was in the name of Dr Reynolds. The policeman who made the mistake blushed and asked Drennan not to mention it, which he did not. It soon became clear that it was the old matter of the *Address to the Volunteers* and not Rowan's more recent and far more dangerous dalliance with treason which was the subject of the indictment. Drennan appeared to regard it as a sort of victory that none of the authorities' more recent attempts to entrap him had yielded anything. They were therefore forced to dig up a charge from one and a half years before to move against him.[8]

Alexander Stewart (1752–1825), an attorney and an old friend from their Belfast days, called to see him a few times shortly after his arrest. Drennan presumed he was on a mission from John Pollock whom, Drennan was now convinced, was 'if not the cause at least the helper on of this whole business'. Stewart pretended to give him advice as to whom he should choose as his defence counsel. However, his central message was that if Drennan would agree 'not to take any part against government in future he did not doubt that the whole thing would be dropped'.[9] This was a compact which Drennan could not, in conscience, agree to.

In the week following his arrest, Drennan wrote three letters to keep Sam, Martha and the family fully informed. He was determinedly upbeat and once even suggested that his arrest 'might turn more to his advantage than to his ruin'. He was very anxious to hear from Martha, but he wanted a cheery letter for he said any sign of panic amongst his family or friends would discourage him.[10]

As usual, Martha obliged and her letters read almost like an offering of congratulations rather than condolences. She said his arrest was not unexpected and she was neither surprised nor depressed by it. She believed if he was found guilty, he would not be sent to Botany Bay and his life was not at risk. The most that could happen would be a fine or imprisonment which she believed he would be able to bear. She assured him that as long as he was debased by no crime, she would not even be crestfallen. Country people were flocking in to Martha to ask after her brother and went away relieved when they were told the charge was not high treason.

The only downbeat note from Martha was when she told of a chilling letter in red ink which had been addressed to her:

It began by saying the writer who had the <u>pleasure</u> of informing me that my ferocious brother was in Newgate, that the two Sheares brothers were taken up and that the whole nest of U[nited] I[rishmen] would soon atone for their crimes, bade me write no more high-flown letters to my b[rother] but to pray for him if in our conventicles if the name of God is admitted, and promised me a place as matron to a mad-house in Botany Bay – of such a letter I would not even guess an author. My mother behaves with spirit.[11]

Drennan told his sister she should 'laugh at this letter and that John Chambers said the wove paper used is chiefly used in public offices and therefore it was most likely the work of some of the under clerks'.[12] The jibe regarding the admittance of the name of God is clearly directed at Martha and Drennan's Unitarianism. It was a constant trope of anti-Unitarian polemic that Unitarians were not really Christians but infidels, deists and atheists.

Drennan thought long and hard about whom he should employ as his defence counsel. His friend Emmet, while promising every helpful assistance, at first declined to act for him. He said that he believed if he acted it would have the effect of turning the bench and the jury box against Drennan. He also felt that as he had gone with Butler and Rowan to the printers with the *Address to the Volunteers*, that he was under government power if they chose to exert it. As Drennan had hoped to employ Emmet and Butler, he was now at a loss. His main concern was 'to preserve the line between professional advice respecting process and etiquette of the court, and my regard to any little capital of public character I may have attained which is all my fortune, and which may be lost and with it my future peace of mind by subservience to their advice'.[13]

It appears therefore that it was not the question of conviction or acquittal which was uppermost in his mind at this point. He clearly wished to come away from this case not merely having been found not guilty but also with his public character maintained if not enhanced. This is perhaps why, when he finally settled on engaging John Philpot Curran as his counsel, he embarked upon writing a detailed address which he intended for the jury which was not so much a legal defence as a vindication of his character.

Drennan went to the scheduled meeting of the Dublin Society on Friday 23 May in the Tailors' Hall. He did not want to miss two successive meetings in case, as he said, 'it was supposed I have been knocked under'.[14] He did not intend to stay long or to play an active role in the meeting. In the event, the decision was taken out of his hands. Shortly after the proceedings began with Dr Burke in the chair and John Collis acting as secretary, the meeting was raided. 'Alderman Warren, the chief commissioner of the Dublin police, accompanied by the high sheriffs (Meredith, Jenkin and John Giffard), Mr. Carleton, the high constable, and a number of police dissolved the gathering and seized the books of the society and a number of addresses to the people of Ireland.'[15]

Martha would later congratulate Drennan for being at the first and last meetings of the Dublin Society of United Irishmen. There were between thirty-five and forty men present when the Dublin police suppressed the city's first democratic political club which welcomed Catholic, Protestant and Dissenter to work together for religious freedom and reform of parliament. The Dublin Society had existed for only thirty-two months and had less than a hundred members at any meeting during that time. All the Society had ever done was to correspond with like-minded reformers or issue political tracts. As far as the British and Irish governments were concerned, this could not be tolerated. To try and heal the religious divisions in Ireland or to wish the French people well in their attempts to shake off royal absolutism was the mark of a traitor.

Within a few short years, Theobald Wolfe Tone, Thomas Russell, Beauchamp Bagenal Harvey, John and Henry Sheares, Oliver Cromwell Bond and Thomas Bacon would suffer traitors' deaths. Matt Dowling, John Chambers, Thomas Addis Emmet and John Sweetman would be imprisoned in Fort George in Scotland and afterwards banished from Ireland. Archibald Hamilton Rowan, James Napper Tandy, Henry Jackson and Dr James Reynolds all fled their native land into long-term political exile. William Drennan might be described as by far the most fortunate of the prominent early members of the Dublin Society, for his only time in custody was the night of his arrest.

23

'MY HEART DOES NOT TREMBLE'[1]

Nearly six weeks elapsed between the arrest of Drennan and the case coming to trial. During that time, although he fully expected to be convicted, he was in no way dispirited. He was prepared to wait out the time with 'equanimity' and had determined that whatever else, he was not going to fly his country. If he did so, he felt he would lose at one stroke any little capital of credit he had with his fellow countrymen. He advised his family in Belfast that they should get used to the idea that he would be convicted. Martha thought he might get sentenced to a year in prison which she felt he would be well able to bear. Drennan also believed that the worst that could happen is that he would be imprisoned for a year which he believed could be borne by his 'temper and disposition'.[2]

He thought long and hard about which lawyers he should use. However, even before he had settled that question, he was working on his own idea of an appropriate defence. He did not intend to go into the merits of the *Address*, which he felt had already being 'prejudged and condemned'. Presumably he was referring here to the outcome of Rowan's trial. He began working on a paper which was to be, in his own words, 'a sincere, simple, succinct account of the context of my life and political conduct which in comparison with one act, the subject of accusation, may counter balance in the minds of the jury and operate by way of mitigation on the discretion of the court'.[3]

When he had completed the draft of his defence statement, he showed it to Emmet who informed him that if he retained lawyers he would not be allowed to address the court until after the verdict. He was disappointed to learn this as he felt that making his own defence would make more of an impression on the jury than 'ingenious cross examining the witnesses which I believe will be to little purpose, or speaking as they call it to evidence which will have as little effect'.[4] This seems to suggest that he felt the prosecution would have little difficulty in proving its case and that his priority was to vindicate his character rather than prove his innocence.

The *Freeman's Journal* of 3 June announced that Drennan's trial had been set for 25 June and gratuitously included an item for which they provided no evidence.

> Private letters were received in town by the last packet from high authority which assert that discoveries of concerted preparation for insurrection and rebellion in England, Scotland and Ireland through the machinations of those nests of conspirators styling themselves Constitutional Societies – Friends of the People – Committees of Correspondence etc. etc. must make any friend of public tranquillity shudder in horror.

> These conspirators are followed in all points exactly on the Parisian principle, barbers, cork-cutters, smiths, publicans and such fellows are the Secretaries and Presidents of these assemblies of republican fanatics and profligate desperadoes are the scribes and spokesmen and an inveterate enmity to all social order, all legal authority, all distinction of meum and tuum from the leading principles of action and their teeth water with an eagerness for plunder, while their hearts pant with a desperate thirst for blood.[5]

This was an obvious piece of black propaganda directed at Drennan who was well known to have corresponded with the Constitutional Societies and the Friends of the People on behalf of the Dublin Society.

Two days before the trial began Sam arrived from Belfast. Drennan was glad to see him as he hoped Sam could be of assistance to him. At least one thing Sam did was to accompany John Chambers to a negotiation with Francis Lestrange, the Stamp Officer, who was a crown witness. He also had meetings with Chambers, Oliver Bond and other confidential friends.

On the strong advice of his bailsman Bagenal Harvey and Emmet, Drennan engaged John Philpot Curran as his lead counsel with Emmet and William Fletcher (1750–1823) assisting. His solicitor was Matthew Dowling, the man who had helped in Rowan's escape. Drennan never could bring himself to like Curran. He had seen him act in a case in Dundalk in 1788 and he afterwards described how his ears still tingled 'with the wild hubbub and dissonance of the lawyers, particularly with the yell of Curran the fiercest imp in the pandemonium and whose currency, or rather currency of eloquence is singularly keen and malignant'.[6]

The trial began at ten o'clock on Wednesday 25 June 1794, with Lord Clonmell and John Toler on the bench. The main prosecution witness was

William Carey who swore that Drennan had read the *Address to the Volunteers of Ireland* at a meeting of the Dublin Society in December 1792. He further swore that Drennan had proposed that the *Address* be published in the *Dublin Evening Post*, the *National Evening Star* and the *Hibernian Journal*. Carey was the editor of the *National Evening Star* and he claimed that Drennan had asked him to print the address in his paper.

This might have been enough to convict had not John Philpot Curran, in his long and severe cross-examination, destroyed Carey's credibility. Curran attacked Carey's character and memory and destroyed any prosecution value in his evidence.[7] Sam McTier said afterwards that Curran displayed abilities greater than he had ever witnessed and he forced Carey to perjure himself three or four times. He added 'to be sure there never was any man made such a devil of as Curran made of Carey'.[8]

The trial ran for twelve hours and the jury retired for an hour before bringing in a 'not guilty' verdict on all nine counts of the indictment. Only when the jury retired did Drennan begin to entertain some hope that he might be acquitted due to the opinion of some of his lawyers, who felt they had done enough to destroy any evidential value of Carey's testimony.

Nearly eight hours into the trial, at a point when he was 'in composed certainty of an unfavourable verdict', he wrote a short note to Martha with an unsteady hand.

> I am perfectly easy about the event which will probably be what you fear. It is now half after five. We have been here since ten this morning. Carey's evidence appears to all to be very impeachable, but the judge will I suppose charge and the jury find as usual in these cases. Farewell ... I write this on my knee, but my heart does not tremble though my hand does.[9]

Many historians have not taken these words at face value. One commentator has implied that Drennan's post-trial conduct suggests that both his hand and heart had been affected.[10] Another claimed that 'shortly thereafter he was standing aloof from the radicals and dropped out of the [United Irish] society'.[11] Yet another suggests that the experience of his trial 'seems to have given him a distaste for the more extreme views in politics and thereafter, while still a keen observer and supporter of that party, he seems to have taken no active part in its projects'.[12]

A literary critic, who is an admirer of Drennan's prose, lamented the fact that, 'after his arrest and departure from public writing life his "impassioned

181

eloquence" fell by the wayside'.[13] This admirer goes further and claims, contrary to a great deal of evidence: 'This trial was the defining, critical moment of his [Drennan's] life, the borderline between Before and After ... it spelled the end of Drennan's public literary career and of the fame he had legitimately enjoyed, it also spelled the end of what had supported his career ... the audience he wrote for'.[14]

This does not accord with what we know. We shall see presently that Drennan never shied away from public writing and publishing on the issues which he felt were important. Sometimes he did not put his name to his work and, on occasion, he used pseudonyms.[15] For the most part, he was prepared to sign and publish trenchant criticism of the Dublin Castle administration, the Irish aristocracy and William Pitt's regime.

When the clerk of the court announced 'not guilty' to the first of the nine counts, there was prolonged cheering both inside and outside the court room. This vexed Drennan as the second and eight counts were the ones upon which he felt certain he would be convicted. However, when order was finally restored he heard he had been acquitted on all charges. Drennan described the jubilation:

> The applause was very great both in and out of the court and I was liked to be smothered with congratulations on all sides and the difficulty was now to get safe from the mob about the courts, which was at length done by stealing through a back-door, and being carried by two friends through bye alleys to Dame Street where with great difficulty we got into the house or rather were carried, Sam and I both out of breath and I but with one shoe on and the mob shouting and huzzaining at a tremendous rate.[16]

As soon as Sam got in the door at Dame Street, he wrote a long letter to his wife relating the news of the acquittal and the detail of how the trial had been conducted and the delight of the Dublin crowd at the result. The next morning, Drennan himself wrote to his mother along similar lines. Martha had spent a gloomy evening with many of her friends in Belfast waiting for news. When the mail coach arrived with Sam's joyful letter, it went into the post office before being delivered to Martha. Almost instantly, Mrs Bruce came in to congratulate Martha on the acquittal of her brother. A Miss Rainey, who had travelled up on the mail coach, had supped with Drennan himself the previous night. Thomas Russell, the *Star* people and many others flocked into the house to share their delight at the good news. Martha was overcome with unexpected joy and that night treated herself to 2d of porter, fearing a sleepless night.[17]

One consequence of the acquittal was that it denied Drennan the opportunity to read the vindication of his character he had so scrupulously prepared. However, even if he had been convicted, he may not have used it as he had been advised that it might do harm where it could do no good. After the trial, Sam, knowing Drennan's 'itch for publication', took this manuscript back to Belfast to show it to his friends and to keep it from the printers,[18] Drennan never lost that itch and twenty-one years later, he published his proposed defence in his book entitled *Fugitive Pieces*.[19]

Drennan wanted the jury to know that his political radicalism did not arise from a sympathy with French Jacobinism but rather was grounded in Irish and English Protestant Dissent. He was also anxious to refute the rumours of deism, atheism as well as republicanism which were being circulated about him. He declared:

> I am the son of an honest man, a Minister of that gospel which breathes peace and goodwill amongst men, a Protestant Dissenting Minister in the town of Belfast ... He was a friend and associate of good and may I say great men. Of Abernethy, of Bruce, of Duchal, and Hutcheson; and his character of mild benevolence is still remembered by many in the North of Ireland and by not a few in this city.

> I may be imprudent in mentioning that he was, and I glory to be, a Protestant Dissenter, obnoxious as that appellation is at present in both countries.[20]

A.T.Q. Stewart has described this statement as a slender clue and suggests that it is the key to a door which leads us from a drear churchyard into a well-lit room in the early eighteenth century.[21] It is certainly a clue and a key to understanding Drennan's political outlook and what had informed his civil and religious principles. Drennan's father and his four friends were eminent intellectual leaders of New Light Presbyterianism. For Drennan to cite their names without qualification in a statement directed at a jury of Dublin Protestants in the 1790s suggests that these men had reputations which had endured long after their own lifetimes. It is hard to believe that he thought invoking the names of these well-known religious radicals would appeal to a jury composed of members of the Established Church.

Perhaps, however, he was not appealing to them but defying them. He knew that glorying at being a Protestant Dissenter would not play well with such a jury. Edmund Burke had made his onslaughts on Dr Price and the Unitarians.

The Church and King mob had savagely attacked the Dissenters at Birmingham and Dr Priestley had been forced to flee to America. The Secret Committee had claimed that the Belfast Dissenting ministers had prayed for the victory of French arms. All of this had served to make the appellation of Protestant Dissenter obnoxious in both countries. When Drennan wrote his intended defence, he seems to have been convinced that he would be convicted. He may have wished to honestly express his political position regardless of the consequences.

If he had been convicted, the severity or otherwise of the sentence would have been in the hands of the judges. The reasons he gave for being a Protestant Dissenter could not have been designed to win the favour of the bench. He said his reasons were 'Early drawn from a book named *The Dissenting Gentleman's Answer to Mr. White* and afterwards from Blackburne, Furneaux, Priestley and Price; so, my prime authority in politics is Locke's *Essay on Government*'.[22]

The *Dissenting Gentleman's Answer* was written and published in England by Maiah Towgood (1700–1792), in 1745, and republished by the General Synod of Ulster in 1766. It is likely therefore that Thomas Drennan was involved in the Ulster edition. Had the judges who were members of the Established Church read this work, they would have known it to be a provoking, vigorous, sustained and comprehensive attack on their church and nearly all it stood for. For example, Towgood argues that the Church of England is really a parliamentary church; that it is not properly an ally but a mere creature of the state.[23] He goes on to assert that 'the guilt of separation lies wholly' on the Established Church, because 'it insists on unchristian and unscriptural terms of communication'.[24] There is nothing in Towgood's work to spare the feelings of a loyal, believing member of the Established Church. His critique of the hierarchical nature of Anglicanism is devastating:

> In the scriptural church of Christ there are no such officers ever heard of as archbishops, deans, deacons, archdeacons, prebendaries, canons, chancellors etc – But there is another church, you know Sir where these are officers of great influence, of high importance and rank. But whence came this pompous train! From the apostolic fountain at Jerusalem or from the corrupt source at Rome.[25]

Whatever Drennan was at in mentioning Towgood's book, he could not have been trying to curry favour with the judges and jury. His defence may have been for the benefit of his fellow Dissenters in Dublin, the North of Ireland and England who perhaps might have been familiar with and approved of Towgood's work. However, it may also have been to convince himself that whatever the judges and jury thought of his character that he was acting in a way which would have been approved of by a long dead and much venerated father.

Drennan was very proud of his defence and many years later, when the political temperature had cooled following the death of William Pitt in 1806, he considered publishing it. He suspected that Emmet had shown the defence to the trial judges and that it had wrought his acquittal.[26] This is very hard to accept. He gave no explanation for how or why he came to suspect that Emmet had disclosed his defence and it was the jury who acquitted him not the judges.

24

CRUEL AND IGNOBLE CALUMNIES

When the euphoria occasioned by his acquittal had subsided, Drennan and his associates in the Society were in a dilemma about what to do next. He believed the government to be 'exceeding mortified' that he had escaped 'the fangs of the wolf'.[1] He had been warned that it was seeking other grounds on which to prosecute him.[2] He was determined, despite the risks involved, that the Society should continue in some form. Martha was also anxious that the Society should continue its work: 'I do earnestly wish the society may still exist and if they dare not do much at present in reality – alarm government by supposition. Nor let its friends boast of its strength in this instance – it being destroyed now would indicate much to its disadvantage to all parties.'[3]

In August 1794, Wolfe Tone and Thomas Russell[4] met Drennan for breakfast to discuss the unfolding situation. The regeneration of the Society was proceeding slowly, as there were suspicions of informers in the ranks. Drennan spoke in favour of Leonard McNally, whom he did not believe had been treacherous. He eventually regretted that McNally had been re-admitted. Years later, McNally was exposed as a government agent. McNally's treachery reached its apogee when, acting as counsel for the defence, he betrayed Robert Emmet, who was executed in 1803.[5] Ironically, a statement by McNally to the effect that 'Drennan declares his hatred of the Catholics' has been used as evidence for charges of bigotry and prejudice against Drennan, which have stood unchallenged to this day.[6]

In late August 1794, Drennan attended a United Irish society meeting at Henry Jackson's[7] house on Church Street, with fifty others. One of the Sheares brothers proposed a plan of organising the society into sections of no more than fifteen in number which would meet in different parts of the city.[8] Drennan did not like the plan much and decided he 'would not attend these petty private plotting meetings, which while they might multiply numbers will not add real power and will annihilate and disorganize ... the society'.[9]

The lawyer, Simon Butler (1757–1797),[10] favoured a more open approach to re-organisation. He argued that the dispersal of the society, in the wake of the escape of Archibald Hamilton Rowan from Newgate, was illegal. He proposed that they should advertise a meeting in the Tailors' Hall. Drennan favoured this approach but believed that even if such a meeting was allowed, the society would soon be dispersed again. He knew that any such meeting would be watched and had no doubt that there were 'spies still among us to report all our proceedings'.[11]

He felt that he had to be careful about putting himself at further risk. He believed his presence or absence from an advertised meeting was of little importance.[12] He told Martha, 'my conduct is nice at present but I shall not risk myself where I do not see it as absolutely necessary'.[13] Martha supported the idea of a legal challenge to the dispersal and suggested that he 'keep clear of trifles which without serving your cause may be just sufficient to hurt you'.[14]

Thomas Russell visited Belfast in October and gave Martha an account of some of the Dublin Society's proceedings and he assured her that her brother was 'gaining friends daily on the basis of unimpeached integrity'.[15] However, Drennan saw things differently:

> I have gotten nothing ... but hard knocks, and suspicion and calumny to boot, which nothing I can do or say is likely to remove. As I know myself to have acted dis-interestedly, this abuse of my motives must originate chiefly from the characters of the political companions I was obliged to keep ... Hence if I ever write again ... if I ever attempt politics again, I will do it for myself and in my own name – at present I am really damped, discouraged and disgusted.[16]

His morale improved somewhat when he heard that Thomas Hardy (1752–1832), a shoemaker and member of the London Corresponding Society, had been acquitted of charges of High Treason in London.[17] Hardy's pregnant wife had died from rough handling she received during his arrest. Drennan observed that 'Hardy's visit to the grave of his wife whom he had not seen since his arrest is very pathetic.'[18] He wished that the society would send an address to Hardy. 'Were our society alive, it would address the poor shoemaker in whose cause the ladies were much interested until Erskine [the defence counsel] unluckily blundered out his occupation. Our society is asleep if not dead and I don't think I am the proper person to rouse it.'[19]

The Society may have been asleep but it was not dead and despite Drennan's petulant claims of discouragement, he was, by this time, hard at work on a new pamphlet. The Earl of Fitzwilliam (1748–1833) was about to come into office as Lord Lieutenant and Drennan was determined to put his radical analysis of Ireland's problems before both the new Lord Lieutenant and the public. In late December, he promised his brother-in-law Sam, a new year gift of his 'epistle' and said he was neither 'afraid nor ashamed' to put his name to such a thing.[20]

Drennan's *Letter to Fitzwilliam*, January 1795

A more prudent man might have been reluctant to put his name to the document which John Chambers (1754–1837), the printer and United Irishman, delivered to the newly arrived Lord Lieutenant at Dublin Castle on 12 January 1795.[21] Just a few months earlier, Drennan had been acquitted because the jury were not prepared to convict him of being the author of a paper the judges had declared a libel. Now he signed and published a document which, it is almost certain, these same judges would declare a libel, had charges been brought.

Drennan began by telling Fitzwilliam, 'you come, at a time when general society is in much internal agitation'. He warned Fitzwilliam that he might not remain long in office and suggested that there was 'a general improbability in any very able or active man remaining long in the government of Ireland: unless by striking out a new line of conduct equally honourable to himself and useful to his country'.[22]

The pamphlet runs to fifty-six pages. Drennan used it to display his writing skills. In the opening pages, Drennan calls on Fitzwilliam to direct his immediate attention to a reform, which was to be a recurring theme in much of Drennan's future writing. He urged Fitzwilliam to introduce a system of universal education in Ireland.

> The common people need to be educated, as the people are daily becoming more sensible to their physical power education is vital to stop them roaming in the savagery of nature ... The most pernicious error that has ever poisoned the happiness of mankind, has been the prejudice that there is one sort of knowledge fit for the learned and another adapted to the vulgar.[23]

Drennan deplored, 'the doctrine which suggests the utter incapacity of the multitude ... to enjoy the rights of man'.[24] Mentioning 'the multitude' and 'the rights of man' in a letter to a member of William Pitt's administration was audacious. A few years earlier, Thomas Paine had been run out of England and convicted of sedition in his absence for suggesting that the common people were entitled to the rights of man.[25] In August 1793, the Scots radical Thomas Muir had been transported to Botany Bay. The prosecution had used an address drafted by Drennan as evidence of Muir's sedition.[26]

In his letter to Fitzwilliam, Drennan goes on to deplore the doctrine that 'vilifies and abuses the human race with systematic scurrility as a swinish multitude and a beggary of no value or estimation'. 'The swinish multitude' is, of course, the term used by Fitzwilliam's friend and mentor Edmund Burke for the common people. 'A beggary of no value or estimation' is a quote from the notorious government informant, Francis Higgins, known colloquially as the 'Sham Squire' who, through the pages of his *Freeman's Journal*, poured vile abuse on the common people of Ireland in the run-up to Drennan's trial. Drennan probably had Higgins' invective in mind also when he bemoaned the fact that, 'whoever ventures to talk to the populace, is looked upon as holding correspondence with the enemy'.[27]

Drennan next turns his attention to the current political crisis and suggests that the Lord Lieutenant's main duty is to mediate between the two classes of society to avert a 'rude and revolutionary collision'.[28] He deplores the fact that the 'property interest', 'for sinister reasons represent [Ireland] as peopled by untameable savages'.[29] Fitzwilliam would have been well aware that a considerable number of Defender[30] outrages were being reported in Louth and Meath and that large rewards were being offered in the *Freeman's Journal* for information. Drennan described these bribes as serving 'to breath up the bloodhounds impelling the poor to hunt after their own'.[31]

He declared that accusations by the Secret Committee of the House of Lords, that Catholics of higher social rank were helping the Defenders and the alleged links with money from France to finance Defender outrages, were 'cruel and ignoble calumnies'.[32] He also described as fiction the suggestion that the Presbyterians were Jacobins engaged in 'a reformer, republican and regicide plot'. Nor was there a Catholic Defender plot. There was a real plot, however, which involved representing 'the Catholic Committee, Defenders, United Irishmen and the National Guard as French emissaries [as] stitched together to hold up a scarecrow ... calling a small town [Belfast] a little nest of republicans, and the arrest of decent industrious men in the street and at their doors ... this is the plot of the Protestant Ascendancy'.[33]

Drennan went on to say that he believed Catholic Emancipation, which he seemed to think was about to be granted, was a 'great and glorious measure'. But if emancipation were granted without 'taking the axe to the root of corruption, it would only be making a bad situation worse'. However, he warned that 'if nothing is done the people will be in despair'.[34]

Throughout his letter, Drennan denounced the propertied classes and the Protestant Ascendency for their treatment of the common people of Ireland. He finished by professing himself a United Irishman, a Protestant Dissenter and an advocate of universal suffrage. To put his name to this document, which he circulated widely, in the tense atmosphere which existed in Ireland in January 1795, was an act of considerable courage.

Drennan had promised Martha that he would not risk himself unless absolutely necessary. For her part, she thought the letter more than answered her expectations; she told him: 'It contains much and good matter, little declamation, just satire and manly boldness – perhaps rather in that extreme, but it was far the best [sic]. I rejoice that you own yourself a U[United] I[Irishman]. May you never do what you dare not avow. It will give the [united] societies great pleasure and you owe it to them.'[35]

Drennan sent a parcel of copies of the letter to Belfast because he hoped that it would be 'generally liked in the North for which it was chiefly designed'.[36] It did sell well and proved popular in Belfast where it sold more than any other pamphlet except Paine's *Rights of Man*.[37] It also sold well and was well received in Dublin where 'Emmet,[38] and several others, said it was well written and well timed' and Henry Grattan, admired its style.[39] Lord Edward Fitzgerald[40] came to breakfast one morning and with an air of great friendship congratulated Drennan on the letter.[41]

Drennan's assumption that Catholic emancipation was about to be granted proved to be incorrect. However, his warning that Fitzwilliam might not remain long in office was borne out by events as was his warning that if nothing was done, the people would be in despair. Fitzwilliam was abruptly recalled in February and the high hopes and expectations of the Catholics were frustrated. Drennan told Sam:

> The Catholics are in dudgeon – all their hopes are dashed down – some of them may turn desperate. It is incumbent on me to be on my guard, for some of them may think that I am ready at all time to be the instrument of a plot – No – I deplore deeply that there is so little open acting and so much mole work. It goes against my nature.[42]

There appears to have been mole work aplenty underway. Francis Higgins informed Dublin Castle that the Catholic Committee was going around central

Dublin soliciting the inhabitants to close their shops in protest at the recall of Fitzwilliam.[43] When they succeeded in this, they set about organising a similar protest, as 'the most marked insult and disrespect to [Camden][44] the new viceroy', Fitzwilliam's replacement.[45] Higgins also reported that different persons were being sent amongst the clubs of journeymen, artificers and tradesmen. He warned that:

> those who appear like a mob are an infatuated number of low working artisans, restless, drunken and riotous capable of any mischief ... They're something also above the common rabble who by readings newspapers, Paine's politics of *Liberty and Equality* and now by way making them truly desperate – religious emancipation and a union with England[46] = occasions them to quit their advocations and associate in numbers.[47]

Higgins warned that it was openly and publicly being declared that 'the coming of the French would save their cause and give freedom to Ireland and that people were cursing Great Britain, the Earl of Camden, the King and the Prince of Wales'.[48]

It was not alone the lower orders and the Catholic Committee that were discontented. The Protestant Dissenters of Dublin, in their different congregations, agreed to discontinue the custom of addressing the new Lord Lieutenant on arrival.[49] Drennan was present at the Strand Street meeting where the decision was unanimous.[50] Lord Londonderry had been a member of the congregation at Strand Street but did not attend the meeting, perhaps because he was married to a sister of the new viceroy Camden.[51] Londonderry's son, Robert Stewart later to become Viscount Castlereagh, would work closely with Camden in the years that followed. He had been elected MP for Down in 1790 and at that time, Drennan thought him 'the most promising young man in the House'.[52] Now, however, the young MP was 'assuming the airs of the future secretary'.[53]

On 8 April, Drennan attended a meeting with two or three thousand people present in Francis Street Chapel.[54] He was greatly pleased with the speeches and felt it was a proud day for the Irish people. He was particularly pleased that the meeting reprobated 'all idea of a union even though total emancipation were the price of the boon'.[55] According to Francis Higgins, Thomas Moore (1779– 1852)[56] attended this meeting and declared on behalf of the Trinity students that they were ready to join in any act with the Catholics and he 'damned the current administration'.[57] Drennan believed that this was a very important meeting. It has been said 'that for many present these proceedings announced the long-awaited merger of the Catholics with the United Irishmen'.[58] The discontent generated by the recall of Fitzwilliam and the rejection of the Catholics claims are considered crucial turning points in the drift towards rebellion.[59] Three years later, in 1798, when the country was on the precipice of that cataclysm, Drennan gave his verdict on the Fitzwilliam affair:

> Lord Fitzwilliam you see has accepted an office under the administration which recalled him. He was the most insidious viceroy that ever came to Ireland; he came to break the unity of Catholic and Protestant and had he been suffered to remain, he and Grattan and Ponsonby would have effected this plan, but his recall has consolidated internal union, and now opposition and the people are also uniting.[60]

25

DEATH IN THE HIGHLANDS

At the end of April 1795, Reverend William Jackson stood trial for high treason and was convicted. As the trial proceeded, Drennan felt that the affair was very damaging to the United Irishmen and that they would be 'completely extinguished in the general opinion' in Dublin. He felt he was being looked at in the streets rather more than usual by people who wanted him to be arrested or thought he should abscond. William Sampson, a friend of Drennan and a fellow United Irishman, made a transcript of the trial with a view to publication. Drennan was very anxious that the public should be aware that his name was at no time mentioned during the trial. However, Tone's name was mentioned several times. Drennan told Sam that 'Tone walks the streets I find, and therefore I suppose has secured himself by some negotiation of which I know nothing, but which I doubt not is honorable on his part, for I believe he would have suffered himself rather than be evidence against any poor unfortunate man, and as he stays here notwithstanding he has certainly triumphed.'[1]

In preparation for the execution of Jackson, a gallows was erected in front of the Parliament House. Jonah Barrington, a lawyer who was present at the sentencing hearing, has left us a graphic account of what transpired when Jackson was brought before Lord Clonmell:

> He was conducted to the usual place where prisoners stand to receive sentence. He was obviously much affected as he entered; his limbs seemed to totter and drops of perspiration rolled down his face. He was supposed to fear death, and to be in great terror. The judge began the usual admonition before he pronounced sentence: the prisoner seemed to regard it but little, appearing abstracted by internal agony. This was still attributed to apprehension: he covered his face, and seemed sinking; the judge paused, the crowd evinced surprise, and the sheriff on examination,

declared the prisoner too ill to hear his sentence. Meanwhile the wretched culprit continued to droop, and at length his limbs giving way, he fell! A visitation so unexampled created a sensation in the court; a physician was immediately summoned, but too late: Jackson had eluded his denouncers, and was no more.[2]

Jackson had taken arsenic before coming to court. Drennan had been told that Jackson had expressed his perfect ease of mind about what he was facing and had intended to reply 'smartly to the stupid and swaggering solemnity of Clonmell'. Perhaps by his suicide he had spoken 'to his lordship in a more emphatic manner'. In Drennan's opinion, Jackson 'had acted like a Roman or perhaps he would wish us to say, like a Frenchman'.[3]

Jackson was a stranger in Dublin and Drennan tells us that 'his exit was talked of with disgust' by most he had heard mention it.[4] Yet, according to Jonah Barrington, Jackson was given a splendid funeral, which, to the astonishment of Dublin, was attended by several members of parliament and barristers. The Attorney General had been solicited to take harsh measures against those barristers who had attended the funeral but out of a sense of his and their profession he refused to do so.

Rowan, Tone and Reynolds, all known to be close associates of Drennan, were named at the trial. The fact that his name did not come up he put down to his own cautious resolution. He felt he had saved himself from the gossip of 'this most malicious city which would convert [any slight association] into real connection'.[5] He was being naïve to think that just because his name was not mentioned the malicious gossips were not convinced he was up to his neck in the affair. Many months later, Martha told her brother that 'a lady of much penetration and opportunity of knowing general opinion' had said that ninety-nine in a hundred believed that Drennan was 'one (nay chief) in Rowan's plot to bring the French into this country' and that he had contrived well from all appearances of taking part though he had instigated the others.[6]

In May 1795, Martha and Sam went on a visit to Scotland and Drennan asked his sister to call on his old friend Dougal Stewart at Edinburgh and to present him with one of his *Letters* and to give him an account of Irish politics. Instead of reunions with old friends and a tranquil jaunt around the Western Highlands, this trip turned into a horrifying experience for Martha and a fatal one for Sam. Hamilton Young, a cousin of the Drennans, had accompanied Martha and Sam on their trip. Young had made a fortune in New York and when he returned, he let it be known that the Drennans would be his heirs. Young frequently lapsed into insanity and Martha and Sam would occasionally bring him on journeys to help improve his mental state.

Sam was suddenly taken ill as their carriage approached Carrickdool near Inveraray. When Martha tried to get him into the carriage to move him to Glasgow and proper medical care, he fell at her feet. She had no option but to bring him to an inn where for several nights she felt she was watching by the bed of a dying husband. Hamilton Young made this terrible situation worse by begging Martha not to leave him and making a number of attempts to get out of an upper window. The weather, that had been delightful before their troubles began, broke and the torrential rain only added to the horror of their journey. Sam passed away and Martha then faced the arduous task of bringing his body back to Belfast.

Her distress became even more acute when she realised Sam had made no will. Instead of a life interest in her husband's property which she expected, she was only to get one third, as Sam's daughter Margaret from a previous marriage was also a beneficiary. Instead of the financial independence she had expected, she had to think long and hard about how much she would have to live on and where she could afford to live. Drennan was in no position to help her financially and Mrs Drennan was not prepared to help other than to offer that Martha should come and live with her. However, it appears that Martha did not like her mother much and thought her conduct towards her in her time of trouble was unkind, indelicate and hard-hearted.[7] She did not immediately accept or reject her mother's offer but confided in her brother:

> I have lived in a calm (at least of temper) for one and twenty years, and never, never will while health and my mind is spared, subject myself to the coarse, vulgar storms, which yet and ever will rent her dwelling. T'was but a few nights ago, she turned out a young and pretty little girl for staying out about a half an hour longer than was allowed ...

> To sit from morning till night listening to such and more effecting scenes, to be a porter to her door, to be subjected to entertain drunken Jimmy Orr, his wife, daughters and two or three old gossips, to give up a respectable acquaintance and live in solitude in this town, to part with the only place I have any stake in – a stake which while I live will be my own – to sell off all my share of the furniture, and a fourth time having to gather up new, to go into a house only for <u>her life</u> and after that again embark on a new scheme, certainly another habitation, these and fifty more too touching

to give, are reasons which must make me if possible decline accepting my mother's offer.[8]

Eventually Martha decided to live with Margaret McTier and, with the help of a £20 annual remittance from Hamilton Young's sister, she carried on, augmenting her income by providing a home for Grace Gordon an orphaned young woman of good family to whom she acted as companion and chaperone.[9]

In a letter to Martha in late July or early August, Drennan enclosed two notes, one written to him by Mary Anne Emmet and the other his reply to her. Mary Anne was a sister of his friend Thomas Addis Emmet. The exchange of notes arose from an incident which had happened some six weeks previously. A party of friends went for a ramble from Emmet's house in the country across the fields late on a Sunday evening. A very heavy shower came and forced the party to scatter in different directions for shelter. Drennan found himself sheltering for at least an hour under a shed alone with a pretty young lady (presumably Mary Anne). He told Martha that he had then 'done what most men would do in the situation and what would have been the subject of her ridicule had he not done so'. He 'saluted [kissed] her twice or thrice without rudeness or need of great violence'.[10] We do not know what Miss Emmet said in her note but she had clearly objected to Drennan's behavior. Drennan asked Martha what she thought of the matter.

Martha had no doubt that his behaviour was highly improper:

If the lady was giddy you acted foolishly for yourself. If she was respectable you insulted her. Miss E[mmet']s notes were delicate and even to you good natured. You put yourself in her power, even to your ruin as a professional man. If I mistake not you got into a scrape of this kind in Belfast with a married woman, but it was when you were young. Nothing could be more unfounded than your observation that you would have been the subject of ridicule had you in that situation acted otherwise. The situation was the very one that should have protected a girl of character from insult unless her companion was a libertine and such, or those who are ignorant of the world, only judge as you did. The last note you think intimates regret at having made so much of the matter, I wish it may prove so.[11]

Drennan, who knew his sister very well, could hardly have been surprised that she would condemn his behaviour in taking advantage of a young woman without her consent. He had earlier acknowledged that, in this instance, he could have spared himself a dressing down by not disclosing anything about the event. However, he knew that his bereaved sister was preoccupied with financial and other worries and that she felt herself in an awkward, embarrassing and distressing situation. Sharing the details of this mini scandal with her was his way of diverting her. He was inviting her to do what she most enjoyed, advising her younger brother on the propriety or otherwise of his feelings and behaviour.

By late August, Drennan heard a rumour that Rowan had managed to get to Philadelphia and he asked Martha if she had heard anything in Belfast that might verify this. She was able to assure him that Rowan was in Philadelphia as Dr Reynolds had written to his Belfast friends to that effect. Drennan described himself as being at the bottom of the coal pit with regard to information but said that people looked at him as if he knew everything whereas in fact he knew nothing, nor did he desire to know.

Martha wanted her brother to resume writing in order that the people might not forget him, for she was sure its enemies, if they triumphed, would remember and mark him down as an early sower of their trouble. For his part, he was in no mood for writing and was clearly smarting from the remarks of the well-informed lady who said most people believed he had been the chief instigator of the Jackson affair. He complained: 'I am to be concluded it seems not only seditious, but a traitor, a hypocrite, a coward and many who wished to see him convicted were now disappointed that he had not exposed himself to be hanged.' From indolence, he did not feel like writing again but he had lately read over all he had written and would not retract one sentence. However, he concluded these musings with enigmatic petulance:

> I am a hypocrite, but God knows not in politics and so blind in this world, that of all my actions I believe those in the political line least sinful or most innocent. I do sincerely nauseate many things in this life and I fear it will grow on me. I shall endeavor to keep it off as well as I can, but whenever I can procure, by others even, what I can make in my own mind a competence, I shall then act in the manner I think most conducive to my own happiness and that perhaps against your opinion.[12]

Martha seems to have understood what he meant but she thought his letter most disagreeable and was disgusted by it. On this occasion, she was even harder on him than when she took him to task over his behaviour with Mary Anne Emmet. She did not hurry to answer him perhaps because she did not want to be too heated but nonetheless, when she finally put pen to paper she was clearly still annoyed.

> I hate croakers, and above all affected ones, and if the picture you draw of your own mind be just, you have had better fortune than you deserve. You panted for fame, you got it – you were read, praised, admired, prosecuted, cleared and abused, what would you have more? Could you suppose that in this career you would not make enemies, that you would not be painted in dirty colors – even here I think you have escaped wonderfully.[13]

Martha took grave offence at her brother's remarks about acting in a manner conducive to his happiness and perhaps against her opinion. She took this to mean that he was thinking of marrying and that she had somehow thwarted him in this regard in the past. This she rejected and said that when he made a choice she had always taken pleasure in it, rather than put obstacles in his way. She had often suggested that an amiable companion would be good for him and that even if his fortune was small at present it would eventually improve. She knew that her response might anger him but she said that she could not always send soothing letters and never get one.

26

THE SMELL OF A GREAT GAOL

Drennan was not at all impressed in March 1796 when he read Edmund Burke's *Letter to a Noble Lord*. This was to be Burke's penultimate publication to attack the friends of the French Revolution. His son Richard had died from tuberculosis a few days after inheriting his father's House of Commons seat in July 1794. The King and William Pitt were anxious to reward Burke for his anti-Jacobin efforts and his role in damaging Charles J. Fox and the Whig party. He might have been elevated to the peerage but with no son to inherit the earldom, he was given a pension of £3,700 per annum instead.[1]

Burke had, for many years, denounced such pensions as corruption and a device for increasing undue Court influence over parliament. He and his pension were attacked by the Duke of Bedford and the Earl of Lauderdale in the Lords. His *Letter* was a justification of himself and an attack on his critics. It has been described as 'the most brilliant specimen of withering sarcasm and dignified resentment the English language ever exhibited'.[2] Yet it is full of his usual splenetic abuse towards those of whose opinions he disapproved. Burke often expressed a particular aversion for females involved in politics, which on this occasion he expressed in this nightmarish allegory:

> The Revolution harpies of France, sprung from the Night and Hell, or from the chaotic Anarchy which generate equivocally 'all monstrous all prodigious things' cuckoo-like, adulterously lay their eggs, and brood over, and hatch them in the nest of every neighboring state. These obscene harpies, who deck themselves in I know not what divine attributes, but who in reality are foul and ravenous birds of prey (both mothers and daughters,) flutter over and sous down on our tables, and leave nothing unrent, unrifled, unravaged, or unpolluted with the slime of their filthy offal.[3]

Drennan was scornful of this scabrous prose and felt that such a repository of abuse was never printed before even by this skimmer[4] of a statesman himself.[5] He suggested the *Letter* had been written in the very dotage of Burke's wit. Burke's 'invective was as coarse and vulgar as one of Robespierre's hirelings'. He wished 'the world to think he knows all the arts and sciences from the mysteries of rat-catching to those of religion'. Drennan also felt that it was most unseemly for Burke to be lamenting 'his son on the public stage before the whole world, rather than the deep retired distress which becomes the occasion and the subject'. At the same time as he was professing to mourning like Israel's king over his son, he was hosting elegant dinners for the emigrants from France. Drennan felt that Burke was motivated by a venal self-interest:

> With a mixture of insanity, he joins the wiliness of a crafty politician. From the day that he steeled his heart against the tears of C. Fox and the intercession of common friends, he has in my mind stood upon the tack of self-interest and has gladly taken the opportunity of the French Revolution, as many thousands in both countries have done after him, to varnish over his venality.[6]

At one point, Drennan had attempted to write a satirical poem in the style of the Roman poet Juvenal, about how elevation to the peerage and titles can be used to change and cleanse a name that might otherwise be in disgrace. He never finished it but copied out the lines on Burke for Martha's entertainment:

> But how can wash of heraldry efface
> The name of Burke and dignify disgrace?
> Can peerage blazon over the pensioned page
> And give gloss to ignominious age?
> Himself the prime corrupter of his laws
> Himself, the grievance that, incensed he draws
> Not to be blam'd, but in a tender tone
> Not to be prais'd, but with a heart-felt groan
> He lives – a lesson for all future time
> Pathetically great, and painfully sublime.
> Oh why is genius cursed with length of days?
> The head still flourishing – the heart decays
> Protracted life makes virtue less secure
> The death of wits is seldom premature
> Quenched too by years, gigantic Johnson's zeal
> Th' unwieldly elephant was taught to kneel

Bore his strong tower to please a servile court
And wreathed his lithe proboscis for their sport
Of Burke and Johnson fly th'opprobrious fame
And if you seek their glory – dread their shame.[7]

In the same letter in which he had enclosed his lines on Burke, he told Martha that Dublin, 'with all the talk of Defenders, plots, discoveries, arrests and executions' had for him 'the smell of a great jail'.[8] People were accosting him in the streets, wondering why he had not fled and asking him 'Are you here yet?' This had the effect of making him more determined to stand his ground.

> If I ever do leave this place, I will not steal away even in the day time. I will exalt my insignificance so far as to give fair warning either publicly or privately to those who are my political enemies, and have, I know it, when they could not terrify me, have endeavored by indirect means to ruin me in my profession and may probably succeed. I will in substance say. I am going. Have you or any man anything to bring forward against me? Here I am and here until – I shall remain.[9]

In February 1796, an Indemnity Act was introduced to give magistrates more powers to deal with disturbances and an Insurrection Act making the administering of oaths a capital offence and the taking of them punishable by transportation.[10] In Dublin, what Drennan described 'a scenery of plots' was beginning again with a view to creating public terror. Alleged Defenders were being rounded up and in one letter, he described how 'about sixteen lads, apprentices to workmen in this city, were taken out of their beds and escorted to Newgate (all handcuffed) by a strong guard – their crime said to be taking some treasonable oath to be true to the French, in a society they had established here'.[11]

Drennan feared that 'wretches' were being offered pardons to denounce 'people they never saw' and he told how a social war was under way, with 'one description of people running to despotism for salvation and another to anarchy'. He was reminded of how, as a boy, he went skating on the river Clyde within a foot of the channel that ran in the middle. Now he felt himself 'a desert island said to be surrounded by quick sands and sunken rocks and to contain nothing but what kisses and stings'.[12]

In March, seventeen-year-old Patrick Hart was sentenced to death for being a Defender and plotting to kill an informer. The Attorney General had promised the youth that if he pleaded guilty he would be transported and avoid the death penalty. Drennan told how Hart replied that 'he would die a thousand deaths rather than do so'. This 'wretched boy' was put to death in front of the Parliament House in what Drennan described as 'circumstances too horrid and disgusting for a female's ear though the eyes of several thousand of that sex were directed to the reality'. One Church of Ireland clergyman had used his influence with the sheriff to get a good seat for the spectacle.[13]

It was rumoured that one of Hart's co-accused, Thomas Kennedy, had become an informer and Drennan heard he was promising 'great discoveries'. Usually Drennan refused to be concerned by such stories but this time, he thought 'there might be occasion for alarm'. There seemed 'great rancorous vexation' on the part of the authorities at not being able to find 'any trace of connection from these infatuated desperadoes to some of higher life'.[14] There is evidence to suggest that Matthew Dowling, Drennan's defence solicitor, had established the Telegraph or Telegraphic club, the revolutionary cell to which Hart and Kennedy had belonged.[15]

In early April, Lord Edward Fitzgerald called by Drennan's house and told him he was going to England with his wife. What he may not have told him was that his purpose was to meet with Arthur O'Connor and both would try to get to France to negotiate an alliance between the United Irish Society and the French.[16] That same month, the government enacted a bill designed to disarm the whole country. Under the terms of this Insurrection Act, Hayter Hames tells us:

> A death sentence could be imposed for administering and transportation for life for taking a seditious oath. All arms had to be registered. If a district was proclaimed as disturbed under the Act, a curfew began at dusk until dawn. During curfew, JPs could go through houses to check on the whereabouts of inhabitants and search for arms. JPs could demand the surrender of even registered arms. There were clauses against 'tumultuous assemblies', nighttime meetings in public houses and against seditious papers. JPs could send men untried to the fleets.[17]

Drennan felt that the Act would leave Catholics who were not prepared to perjure themselves, 'liable to any low informer'. He believed he knew what the government intended and how the Northerners should react. 'Hide and go seek must become the play of the northern Protestants if they do not register their arms before the first of May; after that the country is thus at peace ..., the country will be more easily dragooned into a union as Scotland was.'[18]

In September 1796, there were rumours, which Drennan believed had originated in England, that a French invasion of Ireland was imminent. The militia were being transformed into regulars before being sent abroad. The 'gentlemen of property' were busy raising yeomanry corps.[19] Drennan felt that the invasion rumours provided an excellent pretext for 'putting the country into a sort of barracks, garrisoning it with Englishmen preparatory perhaps to a forced union'.[20]

The *Belfast News Letter* carried reports of loyalist mobilisations and Drennan feared that 'the parties were rallying under the standard of war' and that it would lead to a civil war or a rebellion. He felt that the contending powers were too equally balanced to hope for a speedy termination, or a happy one.[21] He told his sister:

> In 1641 the English puritans, the Irish government and the Presbyterians in the North, were all against the Irish natives. At present the puritans are turned into infidels, the Catholics verge to republicanism, they unite together against the orthodox, and the Established Churchmen who alone seem anxious in support of Christianity. The disaffection of the Catholics is openly said to be great and to include eleven out of twelve of the whole number.[22]

In late September, the military oppression of Belfast was increased significantly and several prominent United Irish leaders, including Samuel Neilson and Thomas Russell, were arrested. Martha wrote:

> They are taken for high-treason. I hope there will be no irons. Neilson will be easily killed though he looks bluff. Russell, I feel for as if a younger brasher brother ... I hope you will get to see them. If you do remember me to Russell and Neilson and tell them if there is anything I can do here it will give me great pleasure.[23]

Drennan learned of the arrests on Sunday morning as he made his way to the Strand Street meeting. He then received Martha's letter and a copy of the *Northern Star*, where he got 'an account of the business'.[24] He went to Newgate and the under-gaoler showed him a list of those confined there. As some of the prisoners had been sent to Kilmainham, Russell was the only one at Newgate whom Drennan knew. He was refused permission to see him.[25] Drennan believed that if the government had good evidence, the trials would come on speedily but if not, their confinement would be protracted and their trial put off. The prisoners were refused visitors, pen ink and paper and Drennan, for his part, saw it all as a piece of ministerial terrorism. He tried to help as far as he could and Francis Higgins informed Dublin Castle that 'Doctor Drennan, and four other United Irishmen, met at Counsellor McNally's and gave him a retainer of 50 guineas... [and] the next day waited on Counsellor Curran.'[26]

As time went on, the terms of confinement were less restrictive and in October, some of the prisoners' wives who had come from Belfast were given free access and allowed to stay overnight at the prison with their husbands. Mrs Neilson and Mrs Hazlitt, when they were not staying at the prison, stayed in the home of James Dixon (d. 1809) of Kilmainham, a rich Catholic tanner. Dixon was a senior United Irishman and was to feature frequently in Francis Higgins' reports to Dublin Castle. Amongst the allegations Higgins made were that Dixon was Baronial treasurer of the United Irishmen, that he was of violent principles and had sheltered Father James Quigley, later hanged at Maidstone in Kent in May 1798. Higgins also alleged that Dixon had stored a cart load of pikes which Samuel Neilson intended to use for an attack on Kilmainham Gaol during the 1798 Rebellion.

Drennan had breakfast with Dixon and Mrs Neilson and Hazlitt and thought both women acquitted themselves well. He found Mrs Neilson to be very conversable and a very good kind of woman and Mrs Hazlitt to be comely and complaisant. He invited them, on the following day, to view the procession of the Lord Lieutenant to Parliament which passed under the window of his Dame Street lodgings.[27]

The following month, as Drennan went with some ladies to see the town sights, they crossed Dublin Castle yard and there they met Colonel Lucius Barber. Barber's sister was one of the party and he invited them to view the armoury. 'It contained 25,000 stand of arms beautifully displayed with artillery etc., etc. in busy preparation.' When Baron George's[28] wife heard that Drennan had been one of the visitors, she wished with all her heart that they had put him in one of the seven pounders and shot him off by way of trial.[29]

In mid-November, Drennan was hearing that Belfast had been consigned to destruction and that a battery was to be erected in the town to keep good order. He warned Martha that 'it is said also that all those who registered their arms in these districts warned by proclamation, will be immediately required to deliver them up, and that a search will be made where they shall be supposed to be concealed. More of the military are to be sent down for that purpose'.[30]

Martha encouraged her brother to write again in what she deemed 'this most important period'.[31] She wanted him to prove his patriotic consistency but also write in a so wise, moderate, honourable fashion as not to throw himself into danger. Drennan, however, knew that in times such as these, anything he said or wrote would be dangerous. He told her:

> I cannot write without harm to myself or my former friends – I am of late no association nor shall I, because it brings on a responsibility moral as well as political for what has been done, for what is doing or for what may be done, which may be more than I choose to bear, even as an individual without lead or importance, I suppose many men will be taken up, of whom or of whose designs I know nothing, and I don't choose to say or show in public, whether I am or am not in habits of association even with those who are so unfortunate as to be arrested without being conscious of any crime.[32]

At this time also, John Chambers, Drennan's printer, was called before the Secret Committee and Drennan was expecting to be called at any time. Thus, he was 'not in humour to write petitions'.[33] More importantly he was anxious that Martha and any prying eye with access to his correspondence should be convinced that he was, to use his own phrase 'of no late association' with his United Irish friends. He also provides a very credible rationale for this, which absolves him of any taint of timidity. He did not choose to bear the moral or political responsibility for the awful things that were happening and about to happen.

He may not have been directly involved in the armed conspiracy which was being prepared by his old associates Tone, Russell, Bond, Jackson, Neilson and Fitzgerald. Yet he was in close association with those of his friends who were still in Ireland, whether at liberty or in prison. Francis Higgins' report accuses Drennan of procuring legal aid for the *Northern Star* prisoners. We know from Drennan himself that he tried but failed to get access to Russell at Newgate and that he associated with the spouses of Neilson and Hazlitt. When the visiting restrictions were lifted, he managed to visit two of the prisoners but was not suffered to remain long in their company. He does not name those he met, but it was Neilson and Russell.[34] Both Hazlitt and Russell were key conspirators with Neilson at the heart and centre of the conspiracy. Drennan was one of the last people whom Edward Fitzgerald spoke with before Fitzgerald left on his dangerous and treasonable mission to France. We shall see presently that he was, at this time, also writing at least one song, *Erin*, which was to play a part in United Irish literary propaganda. His claim of 'no late association' is hardly credible.[35]

27

'FRIGID NEUTRALIST'[1]

In early December 1796, Tone embarked from Brest with a French fleet of fifteen ships of the line and ten frigates bound for Ireland. General Lazare Hoche was in command. Although some of the ships were scattered and separated on the journey, sixteen ships including Tone's vessel reached Bantry Bay. After being buffeted at anchor for a few days in fierce weather, much to Tone's disappointment and annoyance, no landing was attempted and the fleet returned to France having accomplished nothing. Drennan hoped the dispersal of the French Fleet might give the administration a pause to conciliate with the people but, in fact, a very different approach was adopted.[2]

The government decided that its best hope for survival was to increase its savage coercion of the disaffected. The objective now was to goad the people into rebellion which could be crushed by overwhelming military force before the French returned. However, the arrival of the French and the expectation of their return had stimulated a huge surge in membership of the now militarised United Irish Society. All over Ireland, thousands were taking a new oath rather than Drennan's test which required 'a pledge not to discover directly or indirectly, upon anything said or done collectively or individually, in pursuance of the spirit of the foregoing association'.[3]

In February 1797, Drennan was in a dilemma and complained bitterly to Martha while also seeking her advice:

> Is it not curious my dear Matty, that I who was one of the patriarchs of the present popular societies should be at present civilly shoved out of their company, and I, who of my own accord wrote the test upon which the new associates are still in chief founded, should in pursuance of the spirit of the same test be excluded and treated like a frigid neutralist, until I take it again in their form, and all this without the smallest change in my political principles or practice, except in not writing so as to throw myself, as other

patriot suicides, into the gulf of a prison which, whatever it may do to them, would soon close upon me in dark oblivion. On the other hand, this state of exile from the confidence of all parties is not only painful in itself, but perhaps not prudent in anyone gifted with the least political prophecy.[4]

He believed his nearest friends had taken the new test and were thereby, 'under a degree of restraint in the conversation and contact' with him.[5] He also believed that 'a hundred thousand of all ranks had taken the new solemn league and covenant'. He was anxious to vindicate his 'uniformity and courage' and he wondered, should he conform to the will of the vast majority? He wondered also whether he should do it now, or wait until everyone, great and small, must take a side, 'which time is perhaps at no great distance'.[6] There was at least one other early member of the United Irishman who had doubts about this oath. Jemmy Hope was a Presbyterian weaver who was to fight at the Battle of Antrim in 1798 and worked with Thomas Russell to raise support for Robert Emmet in Ulster in 1803. Hope argued that oath-taking was pointless as 'an honest man is bound by his word, but no oath can bind a knave'.[7]

Martha appears to have given no direct response but she must have known that one could face transportation if convicted of taking such an oath. However, in her next letter, she may have been hinting her advice by telling him his friend, Dr William Bruce and others, had taken an oath to carry arms for the other side.[8]

If we can believe the evidence of an informer who signed himself 'Left Hand', Drennan may indeed have taken the oath, for Left Hand told Dublin Castle in May 1797 that:

> Almost every night, Pat Ewing ... a violent republican, Dr. Drennan, O[Oliver] C[Cromwell] Bond, Henry Jackson and some more of the same description meet at the house of John Chambers of Abbey Street, who was lately examined by the Committee of Secrecy ... for what purpose such meetings are held t'is easy to guess.[9]

About the time Drennan was agonising about whether he should take the new oath, Francis Higgins named him as the author of a letter from the 'King Killers of Pill Lane'[10] to their friends in the North urging them to remain firm in the cause. The letter stated that the claims of the government that the people were loyally attached was a trick. 'If Hoche had made a landing the government would have soon found the difference of the boasted attachment of the people.' The letter went on to claim that the government intended to further coerce the inhabitants of Belfast by not allowing them to carry on their trade or business if they were not prepared to take an oath of loyalty or enrol in the yeomanry. Higgins claimed that Drennan was not in attendance at the Pill Lane meeting where his letter was discussed and approved.[11] If Drennan ever did take the test, he had not done so by January 1797, the date of Higgins' report and, therefore, he would not have been admitted to their meetings. However, if the Pill Lane group wanted someone to compose a letter addressed to the North they could have chosen no one better qualified for the task than William Drennan.

Edward Fitzgerald's mission with Arthur O'Conner to seek French aid had gone well. The French refused to allow Fitzgerald to enter their territory because of his association with Philip Égalité who had gone to the guillotine three years earlier.[12] However, O'Connor had crossed into France and met with Hoche and made an agreement with him. One aspect of their agreement was that Hoche would bring an invasion fleet to Bantry. Their plan had been that Hoche would rendezvous at Bantry but disembark at Galway. It was hoped the British would march their forces out of Dublin to meet the French and that O'Connor would lead an army of 30,000 Northern Presbyterian Volunteer veterans to capture Dublin and then advance to the Shannon.[13] O'Connor perhaps was over-estimating his chances when he outlined his plan:

> Everything was arranged for all the old Volunteers marching on Dublin the instant the English troops should be marched off to the western coast, when everyone was to provide himself with the best arms he could until we got to Dublin, and I could find all the means for a perfect organisation and equipment of my army and then march to the Shannon putting the English army between us and our allies.[14]

In November 1796, O'Connor had travelled to Belfast ostensibly to fight for a parliamentary seat for Antrim. However, his real purpose was fulfilling his promise to Hoche. O'Connor was expecting the French fleet in late January or early February 1797 and when they came more than a month early, it was a disastrous set-back[15] but the election gave him the opportunity to address public meetings and publish an election address. Drennan was, therefore, partially right when he supposed that O'Connor did not have much idea of being returned for Antrim but wished to see the North. When Edward Fitzgerald came to Belfast and he and O'Connor, Simms and William Sampson were keeping 'a set', Martha began to see the election 'as a mere blind'. The more she observed, the greater reason she had for fearing the event with which Ireland was threatened.[16]

When news of the French arrival at Bantry reached Belfast, the High Sheriff called a town meeting to press the townspeople to swear that they would resist the invasion. O'Connor pushed forward and told the Sheriff that he was not a recruiting sergeant and continued: 'The people had already been disarmed by law. Now rather than being defended by 100,000 Volunteers they had 20,000 English mercenaries who instead of defending the Irish disarmed us like slaves. Let them do the fighting while we await the issue.'[17]

On 2 January, O'Connor called a town meeting and the numbers attending were so great that the Exchange could not hold them, yet they were refused the use of the Linen Hall. The town vicar, Bristow, who usually chaired town meetings 'skulked' and could not be found so a chair was brought into the street and William Sampson placed on it. Martha did not give her brother a detailed account of these events because she did not want to give extra work to the inspectors who were opening her letters at a time when they already had 'their hands full'.[18] She knew that he would get all the information he needed from the *Northern Star*. Drennan admired Sampson's audacity:

> If I be the quietest man in Ireland, Sampson is certainly the most active, that can leap upon a joint-stool and harangue the populace, at such a time and on such a topic, with such temper, and near such a body of military who were in the town; and I hear that had they waited another quarter of an hour Barber would have broken up the meeting.[19]

Great pressure was being exerted on the different professions to enlist on the side of government and Drennan heard that the Lawyer corps were meditating taking some action against Sampson. Besides Sampson, Emmet and Curran were the only lawyers that Drennan knew of who had declined taking up arms for the government side. Drennan was never going to bow to any such pressure but neither was he prepared to let himself be used as a tool of political friends who had treated him with neglect and indifference. He had not lost his sense of humour; he told Martha, 'I should not like to be classed with the two fat-headed Jesuits of whom when a lady expressed her surprise to the father of the order that such men could have been admitted to so able a community – Oh Madam said he with a meaning smile, they will serve us excellently well – as martyrs in China.'[20]

Drennan would, however, stick to his United Irish test and if he felt that called him to write now, he would do it regardless of the risk to his person or profession. However, little or no regard was being paid to writers of more ability, so for now he would 'turn and take another nap'. Yet he lamented the fact that so many of his acquaintances and friends had bound themselves or suffered themselves to be bound to government service. He described the government as acting like the highwayman who points a gun at a man's conscience and cries 'Deliver – why a man must do it as he would deliver his purse.'[21]

Drennan had been very quiet for a considerable time but if he hoped that this would help him to avoid public attention, he was being naïve. He was still talked about both by friends and enemies alike. Martha told him that Lord Edward Fitzgerald in Belfast was toasting Dr Drennan as 'a particular friend of his' but she pointed out that this was 'an honor that would not gain much credit here but rather suspicion'.[22] Perhaps more worrying was the outburst of the Chancellor in the House of Lords following the departure of the French fleet. A friend of Drennan who was in the House told him how the Chancellor railed against:

The United Irishmen – their resolutions fabricated by a Mr. Tone, Dr Drennan, Rowan the fugitive traitor, etc., etc. He then came to French alliances – Hoche his orders to massacre all but those of one description etc., etc. Why he might as well have talked of my grandmother as me, and I had some idea of writing him a note, about throwing a stick at such a harmless animal as me at this time but repented. I should have merely said – My lord, for misspending a single moment so much as your lordship has done by mentioning my name in a speech on the present state of Ireland, I have the most perfect sense of your lordship's condescension and humanity, but I declare to God, I can scarcely forbear smiling at your want of information. But this you may suppose I should never venture to send to this implacable and never forgiving man.[23]

Much as he apparently did not want his name bandied about, he wrote an attack on the Chancellor's speech which he sent to Martha to insert in the *Northern Star* with his name attached if she thought it good enough. He did not intend to send it to the Dublin papers because he thought them cowed and he did not want to risk a refusal from any of them. He had mixed feelings about the Chancellor's speech. On the one hand, he thought it an honour to be calumniated by such men but on the other, the speech indicated the future tone of government which suggested that there would be no conciliation.[24]

In fact, the *Dublin Post* did print his paper as an advertisement and charged him a guinea. Most people thought it 'a Rowland for his Oliver', including William Sampson who called on Drennan having newly arrived in Dublin from Belfast. Sampson talked a great deal and mentioned his intention to start a newspaper in Dublin. When Drennan told Martha about the new newspaper, he also said he was thinking about writing a letter on conciliation to Lord Camden.[25]

O'Connor's *Address to the electors of Co. Antrim* appeared in the *Northern Star* in late January 1797. It was so portentous that Martha was afraid to send it to her brother by post as she believed it would be stopped at the Post Office. She sent it to him by the hand of an acquaintance. The Address is a cutting attack on the Castle administration and the nature of the British connection to Ireland. O'Connor seemed to delight in treason:

Abandoned Administration! Who have trampled on the liberties of my country, do you presume to accuse me of dissuading my countrymen from arming to oppose an invasion, which *your's and your accomplice's crimes have provoked?* Is it that the inalienable rights of free-born men to make their laws by delegates of their choice, should be bartered and sold by usurpers and traitors, that I should persuade them to arm? Is it that our markets, our manufacturers and commerce, should be sold to that nation which appoints our Government, and distributes our patronage, that I should persuade them to arm? Is it to support the Gunpowder Bill, which deprives them of arms, or the Convention Bill which aims at perpetuating the usurpation of rights, by proscribing the only obvious and orderly means to regain them, that I should persuade them to arm? Is it to support the suspension of Habeas Corpus Bill, which has destroyed the bulwark of liberty by with-holding the Trial by Jury, that I should persuade them to arm? Is it to rivet the bolts or to guard the dungeons of their fellow citizens who, torn from their homes and their families by Administration, vainly demand that trial by Jury, which is proving *their* innocence must establish *its* guilt that I should persuade them to arm?[26]

To print this material in wartime, within weeks of an attempted enemy invasion, seemed like a deliberate effort to court arrest on charges of treason. Martha considered that O'Connor might have written the paper from a desire to be taken up and others thought O'Connor had gone mad. Having thought about it, she soon concluded that there was too much method in it. She displayed an uncanny level of insight when she suggested to her brother that the *Address* reflected an impatience to bring on some work which the disappointment of the French retarded. And that was indeed O'Connor's motive.

O'Conner's biographer, Hayter Hames, explains that he needed to get an urgent message to Hoche that another invasion should be attempted and his usual lines of communication were too slow for his current purposes. The quickest and surest way to get a message to Hoche was to send it publicly through the Press and Hayter Hames suggests that was the main purpose of having this material published in the *Northern Star*. Not for the first time, Martha displayed a talent of perception in discerning the truth in a situation where there was more to a circumstance than meets the eye.

In March 1797, Belfast and many parts of the North were proclaimed and Martha's letters tell of prisoners taken up, house searches, arms seizures and men daily being brought on board tenders to be sent as prisoners to the Fleet. On one occasion she related, 'On the quay a decent man who was seeing others shipped off, was asked what that man now going had done? – nothing replied the other but lived in peace and union with his neighbor. I have the honour of being his father.' She regretted having foolishly registered Sam's gun now that the authorities had called in all registered arms. She vowed they would not get Sam McTier's.[27]

Drennan apparently had other sources of news from Belfast, for in an undated letter (probably April or May) he told his sister:

> I hear Dr. Crawford and Mr. Kelburn are arrested and on their way to Dublin, and that a man with a mask points to those whom he thinks likely to disturb the public peace and who are taken indiscriminately. This is really an improvement on the Black Art. Hundreds in the North are said to be under the net, are to be taken out when room is found to lodge them in.[28]

When Crawford and Kelburn arrived in Dublin, there were three or four more coach loads of prisoners with them and they were sent immediately to Kilmainham which Drennan described as 'a mile out of town, in a fine air and the prison quite new'.[29] This was where Neilson and Hazlitt were being held and Drennan felt their situation would be as well as such a situation could be. He promised he would make an effort to visit the prisoners.[30]

Martha had long expected another attack on the offices of the *Northern Star* and it finally happened on 22 May when a party of Monaghan Militia gutted the offices and destroyed the books, types, paper, etc. The *Star* had refused to print an advertisement proclaiming the loyalty of the militia which described Belfast as a seditious town. No magistrate or officer intervened. Martha was terrified and believed the town would be attacked and the inhabitants driven into the fields. She made plans to hire a chaise to get her aged mother and her ill relation, Miss Young, out of town and hope to escape herself on foot.

The attack on the *Star* office took place just a week after four soldiers of the Monaghan Militia had been executed at Blaris camp outside Lisburn. The Belfast radicals had been hard at work with no little success recruiting within the ranks of the militia and the four executed men were regarded as ring leaders in this conspiracy. General Lake lamented that he could not bring charges against Cunningham Greg (1762–1830) and Francis Jordan, Belfast businessmen whom he suspected of having suborned the militia men. The prisoners had been held in custody in Belfast and were conveyed to Blaris and their deaths on two carts in a great military procession which included detachments of 22nd Dragoons, the Royal Artillery, the 64th Regiment of Foot, the 3rd Battalion of Light Infantry, the Monaghan and Carlow Militia and Breadalbane and Argyle Fencibles.[31] The four men were shot as they knelt on their coffins.

Drennan wished his sister had given him the details of the procession to the camp which he felt had probably made a deep impression on the spectators. He had heard a rumour that was widely believed that Colonel McCoy of the Highlanders had refused to let his men carry out the executions saying, 'Let the Irish kill the Irish.'[32] He composed this verse:

> When bid to take aim at the Irishman's heart
> The stout Caledonian recoil'd with a start
> 'The first of my country – the first o' my clan
> E'er ordered to fire on a blindfolded man!
> You'll find fitter tools to perform sic o' deed
> And by Irish hands, let the Irish bleed
> In the spirit of Cain, let them murder each other
> And the United fall-by his United brither'
> So spoke the indignant and high minded Scot
> As a soldier he'd serve as a hangman would not
> But the Irish went first, and the Irish went last

And guarded by Irish the prisoners pass'd
On their coffins knelt down – took a silent farewell
The United fired and the United fell![33]

He learnt some time later that it was English troops who had made up the firing squad. There is a copy of this epigram in Drennan's handwriting with a sketch of the four blindfolded men being shot, amongst the Rebellion Papers held in the Irish National Archive.[34] It is signed W.J. and it is located alongside Francis Higgins' letters to Under-Secretary Edward Cooke at Dublin Castle. This suggests that the sketch had fallen into Cooke's hands at some point. We shall see presently that when the United Irish paper the *Press* was suppressed in early 1798, Drennan had retrieved some papers from William Sampson the editor, lest the Castle would acquire a sample of his handwriting. Perhaps he had not been completely successful.

Martha heard that Cunningham Greg had been warned by a magistrate friend, who had been informed by 'someone in high office', that his sister Jenny, who was in England, was in correspondence with Martha and Francis Jordan in Belfast.[35] Martha had, a few weeks previously, copied correspondence from Jenny to Drennan, the contents of which she asked him to keep secret. Jenny now wrote a spirited note to the magistrate saying she would not allow threats to deter her from writing and she enclosed two letters that herself and Martha had exchanged to show the innocence of the correspondence.[36] However, she also told the magistrate that she was, in principle, a United Irish woman.

Martha was not best pleased that her letter was now in the hands of the Secretary of State. She told her brother:

> Let me here however declare that I know of no society of United Irishwomen, that I never heard it said that there was one in this place, that I never even subscribed as thousands did to the charity for relief of the prisoners, that private transactions are my abhorrence, that I was never engaged in any act I should care was known either to the public or secret committee and the chief wish of my heart is to pass through my life without giving offence or (strange as the wish appear it is now mine) of not receiving insult.[37]

When Martha made this declaration, it was not for her brother's benefit. She believed her letter would be opened and she put it into the post office the night before to give the post master time to read it. Her next letter was hand delivered by Francis Jordan who had come down to Dublin from

Belfast. Jordan's life and property were being threatened and Gregg's house had been attacked and wrecked. Martha, who knew nothing of their suspected involvement in the Blaris camp affair, believed the men were being persecuted because Jordan had advised the *Star* not to publish the Monaghan Militia advertisement because they refused to join the yeomanry and because they had taken up a subscription for legal aid for a servant who had been sent aboard the tender.

28

REMEMBER ORR!

By July 1797, several friends of Drennan were in prison in Kilmainham and Newgate including Russell, Neilson, Robert and William Simms, Reverend Kelburn and Dr Alexander Crawford. Drennan thought it would not be prudent to visit them weekly and he went four or five times in six months. Martha urged him to call and see Russell and Neilson more often 'to help cheer them through their long captivity'.[1] Arthur O'Connor had been arrested in February and was being held in solitary confinement in the Tower of Dublin Castle. When the authorities were advised that they could not get a conviction for high treason because the *Address* did not attack the King, they reduced the charge to sedition, which meant he was eligible for bail. He was released at the end of July.

Drennan went almost immediately to the hotel where O'Connor was staying and found him in good spirits and tolerably healthy: 'His paleness was pathetic from the idea of confinement. Treason it seems has come down to sedition, having been bailed which cannot be done for the former crime. He certainly is a singular looking man as Grattan is, but the ladies might, and I believe many do think O'Connor singularly handsome.'[2]

In October, Drennan and another Dr Plunket visited Neilson who was now in his fifteenth month of confinement at Kilmainham. His health was declining rapidly and the doctors certified to the Castle that he should be released on health grounds. No notice was taken and Neilson was not released until February of the following year.

On 15 September 1796, William Orr, a prosperous young farmer from Farranshane near Antrim town, had been arrested and charged with administering the United Irish oath to two soldiers of the Fifeshire Fencibles. Orr was a New Light Presbyterian and had been an occasional contributor to the *Northern Star*. He was held in custody for more than a year before being brought to trial in October 1797. Shortly before the trial began, Drennan enclosed a note to his lawyer friend Robert Orr who was on circuit in Belfast:

To Counsellor Orr

Look at the Insurrection Act and at the last section where you will find that the continuance is to 1st January 1797 and the next session of parliament. Observe the important word omitted, the omission of which is made the Act itself expire and the judges act under a statute which really has no existence. It is the word <u>Then.</u> The legal and literal meaning is that the Act was to expire the next session of parliament from the enactment of the Act, and the judges may I think shake on the judgement seat for their misinterpretation. The flaw is found out by the sagacity of Emmet. Many lawyers have this day been to Grierson's to look at the Act. If it saves the life of Orr and others it will be a great thing. I am not certain whether the judges are to be addressed in print on the subject, but something will be done. I suppose you ought not to mention it, though I suppose that Curran and the rest will get knowledge of it.[3]

Curran and Sampson were Orr's defence team and his attorney was James McGucken. We saw earlier that McGucken was an informer handled by John Pollock but it is not clear if he had been turned before or after Orr's trial. Curran used the argument contained in Drennan's note but could not save his client. Although the jury was packed, they could not agree their verdict and were locked away from seven at night until six o'clock in the morning. During the night, they were plied with bottles of whiskey and the chairman of the jury afterwards claimed he had been intimidated into bringing in a verdict that was contrary to his opinion.[4] Sampson was a very experienced court reporter and by the time of the trial, he had managed, in collaboration with Arthur O'Connor, to establish his new paper in Dublin calling it the *Press*. The *Press* reported the shocking details of the trial and the execution. It also published a very moving dying declaration of William Orr. Sampson may have had a hand in drafting the declaration. The last paragraph reads:

I trust that all my virtuous countrymen will bear me in their kind remembrance, and continue true and faithful to each other, as I have been to them. With this last wish of my heart, not doubting of the success of that cause for which I suffer and hoping for God's merciful forgiveness of such offences as my frail nature may have at anytime betrayed me into, I die in peace and charity with all of mankind.[5]

William Orr went to the scaffold on 14 October 1797 on an open common one mile from Carrickfergus. The streets of the town were deserted as 'the townsfolk showed their contempt for an act of shameful injustice'.[6] As the rope was placed round his neck, he exclaimed, 'I am no traitor. I die for a persecuted country. Great Jehovah receive my soul. I die in the true faith of a Presbyterian.'[7]

The case had a major impact on Drennan. He was disgusted when he heard that Barry Yelverton (1736–1805), the judge who sentenced Orr, had buried his head in his hands and burst into tears. He told Martha:

> There are tears – those of the wife about to be a widow in a prison, her four children close by her, a fifth stirring within her, her husband in the condemnation of a vindictive Draconian statute, striving to comfort her – he does not shed tears. I hate these Yelverton tears. The angel of mercy will not waft them to heaven nor will God look kindly on the man.[8]

He was also disgusted when he heard that social harmony was undisturbed in Belfast. 'Shame on the town, Dancing at coteries and suppering with General Lake in such a season is very disgraceful.' If the more genteel people had no kindred feeling with ordinary people Drennan felt, 'they could at least pretend to have'.[9] Such was the impact of the execution of William Orr that it brought forth from Drennan the poem entitled *The Wake of William Orr* which many regard as his best work. He did not put his name to it and never mentioned it in his correspondence to Martha. This is not to be wondered at. The poem was composed in late 1797 and published in William Sampson's short-lived *Press* in early 1798. Later that year, when the long persecuted and oppressed Northern United Irishmen rose in rebellion, their battle cry was 'Remember Orr'.[10]

In December 1797, Peter Finnerty (1766–1822), a printer, was prosecuted for publishing 'a false, scandalous, malicious and seditious libel' against the Earl of Camden in the *Press*.[11] A few months earlier, Francis Higgins had warned Dublin Castle that the Dublin United Irishmen were planning to set up a replacement newspaper for the *Northern Star*; according to Higgins: 'M. Dowling, Sweetman, McCormick, Bond and Dr. Drennan are appointed a committee for procuring a printer, type etc. to set up a newspaper which for treasonable and seditious publications is to exceed the *Northern Star*. Stockdale is to be acting manager provided they can procure a nominal printer to enter his name and make application to the Stamp Office.'[12]

Shortly thereafter, Higgins reported that 'a man of straw, one Finnerty, had sworn himself proprietor' and that Drennan and his committee were to wait until October before their paper would appear.[13] We cannot know whether there was truth in Higgins' reports regarding Drennan but we do know that the *Press* appeared in September and proved as treasonable and seditious as Higgins had predicted.

The letter which led to Finnerty's arrest appeared in the *Press* on 26 October 1797. The author, styling himself 'Marcus', excoriated Camden and his administration over the execution of William Orr.[14] Marcus alleged that Camden's regime had brought only massacre, rape, desolation and terror to the people of Ireland.[15] He described the execution of Orr as one of the most sanguinary and savage acts that had disgraced the laws.[16] He told Camden that 'beastly criminal drunkenness was used to procure the murder of a man better than any that now surround you'.[17]

The oath Orr was alleged to have taken was described by Marcus as one of charity, union, humanity and peace.[18] It should be borne in mind that Drennan was inordinately proud of the original United Irish test which he had composed. He had gone so far as to set it down word for word in his letter to Fitzwilliam.[19] He was still claiming credit for it in 1806 when he wrote to Charles J. Fox. Marcus finished by rising to a crescendo of passion in which he appears to threaten the administration: 'It will not do! though your guards and your soldiers your thousands and tens of thousands should conduct innocence to death. It will not do! A voice has cried in the wilderness; and let the deserted street of Carrickfergus proclaim to all the world that good men will not be intimidated and they are more numerous than you.'[20]

Peter Finnerty was convicted and sentenced to two years in gaol. He was also sent to the pillory at Green Street.[21] There, surrounded by leading United Irishmen, he made a speech about press freedom. Amongst those who stood at the pillory with Finnerty were Edward Fitzgerald, Arthur O'Connor, Oliver Bond, Henry Jackson, the Sheares brothers, Leonard McNally and William Sampson.[22] When the crowd applauded the prisoner's speech, they were attacked by the Armagh militia.[23] The authorities put great pressure on Finnerty to give up Marcus, which he refused to do.[24] He was threatened with a species of punishment he was 'too proud to name'.[25]

Arthur O'Connor told R.R. Madden in 1842 that one Mr Deane Swift was the author of the Marcus letters while claiming that Swift and Drennan had been the chief penmen of the Dublin leaders at the time.[26] O'Connor was eighty-two years old and was recalling events after forty-five years. Madden did manage to track down the 'Dust of Drumcondra', as Swift was sometimes known, to Gravesend where he was still living as late as 1843. Madden asked Swift's brother who neither confirmed nor denied the accuracy of O'Connor's account. Madden did not, it appears, discuss the matter with Swift himself.

There are several reasons to believe O'Connor was mistaken and that William Drennan was the author of the Marcus letters. Not least of these is that the letter had much of the characteristic mixture of 'highbrow eloquence and colloquial forcefulness' attributed to Drennan by a literary critic who has evaluated his work.[27] We know Drennan delighted in writing open letters to well-known individuals. The previous January, he told Martha he was thinking of writing a letter to Camden but that he was 'so much a pismire as to be only able to sting the great-man mountain'.[28] In much of his writing, Drennan took great satisfaction in displaying his education in the classics and his familiarity with the works of Shakespeare. In his letter to Camden, Marcus referred to Domitian, the Persian tyrant, and Lady Macbeth. Moreover, it is clear from Drennan's correspondence that he was deeply troubled by the murder of William Orr and he had followed the trial, conviction and various futile appeals for clemency with great interest.[29]

Drennan had often used the pseudonym 'Brutus', whom Ian McBride tells us was one of Drennan's 'ancestral ghosts'.[30] In 1813, he had suggested that a bust of Marcus Brutus should be placed around a model printing press as one of the great emancipators of mankind.[31] In his *Fugitives Pieces*, published in 1815, Drennan includes a translation of a letter form Marcus Brutus to Marcus Tullius Cicero in which Marcus Brutus upbraids Cicero for his 'cringing adulation of Octavius Caesar' saying that 'the rank and station of a republican recoils at the idea'. Brutus finishes with the sort of flourish at which Drennan excelled and with a sentiment with which he could identify: 'The people may, the people must be free, if the leaders of the people be ready, with head and heart and hand, to write, to speak, to act to suffer in their cause.'[32] When writing to William Bruce dismissing the Whig Club and suggesting that a more serious club was required, he said, 'I would sign such a Confederation of Compatriots with my Blood. Oh, I think I see Marcus Cato looking down from Heaven, and austerely smiling while he calls us prattlers-mere prattlers.'[33]

Drennan admired the *Press* when it first appeared but warned that it was too good. 'It will be put down and perhaps this is the great reason for putting it up.'[34] He held his own writing skills in the highest regard and could not resist his self-declared itch for publication.[35] When Martha heard that Arthur O'Connor was 'standing forth as the publisher' she believed that the demand for the *Press* 'would be trebled and its cowardly opposers baffled'. She urged her brother to support O'Connor in everything good, for in her view O'Connor was 'a clever spirited fellow and perfectly fitted for his present post'. We can be certain that

Drennan contributed his poems *Erin* and *The Wake of William Orr* to the *Press* but never mentioned this in his correspondence at the time.

On Saturday 14 October, Marcus had written to the *Press* on the question of press freedom. His main point was that without a free press the people are held in ignorance. Drennan had always written in favour of a free press and stressed the need for the common people to be given the necessary knowledge 'to know their duty as members of the state'.[36]

On Tuesday 2 January 1798, Marcus wrote again, calling on the people not to react to the provocations they were enduring but to await the right moment to resist:

> I beseech you a continuance of the patience you have shewn. A patience beyond all example, under the calamities you have endured, be steady my friends for without steadiness resistance is a weak virtue[37] ... In proportion as you have elevated your minds to liberty a flowing benevolence, mutual kindness and undivided union of affection have banished the grosser passions from your breast and bound you to one great prevailing interest.[38]

The phrase 'a union of affection' echoes a key element in Drennan's test. Martha, who took the *Press*, 'under sentence of house wrecking', thought 'the letter for which the printer was taken up a very cutting one, perhaps too much so' and asked Drennan if *he* could explain why the late Camden's daughter's name was included in the letter.[39] Martha was hurt by this reference to Lady Londonderry, as gratuitously mentioning her in such a letter might appear as a threat or identify her as a target for revenge. It was well known that Lady Londonderry had interceded, vainly, on William Orr's behalf.

In his reply, Drennan denies knowledge of why the lady's name was used and suggests that 'the conductors offend in that particular very greatly'. He said that 'if it had meaning it was a cruel and unmanly one and it was particularly ill-directed'.[40] Why did Martha feel that her brother ought to be able to reassure her about this matter if she did not suspect that he might be Marcus? After implying his innocence to Martha, Drennan goes on to compare himself to Junius, the anonymous author of many letters in the *Public Advertiser* in 1769–72.[41] He told her:

> It makes me smile in a sort of way, to hear anyone compare me to Junius ... In purity of motive I am perhaps his superior, perhaps too in the lambent light of enthusiasm which plays around unexpectedly on a political topic.

He covers himself with the majesty of darkness ... Yet his great merits have been overrated and my small merit has not received its due credit.[42]

On Saturday 13 January 1798, *The Wake of William Orr*, was published in issue no. 46 of the *Press*. Although Drennan's name did not appear, it is now widely regarded as his most popular work.[43] The last verse is a call to rebellion very consistent with the rhetoric of Marcus:

Conquer fortune – persevere! –
Lo! it breaks the morning clear
The cheerful cock awakes the skies
The day is come – arise –arise

If Drennan was indeed Marcus, then he had reason to be grateful to Finnerty for his loyalty, for the consequences of betrayal would have been severe. Years later, in 1811, Peter Finnerty was once more in gaol for libel; this time it was Camden's nephew, Lord Castlereagh, who had sent Finnerty to prison in Lincoln. Drennan was by then editor of the *Belfast Monthly Magazine* (*BMM*) and he organised a campaign in support of Finnerty.[44] Francis Burdett held a public meeting at the Crown and Anchor tavern in London to support Finnerty while a little known poet, Percy Bysshe Shelley, sold some poems to raise money on Finnerty's behalf.[45] Although Drennan and his Natural Leader associates all contributed, the *BMM* campaign was a failure as a total of only thirty-six readers were prepared to publicly identify with a prisoner with United Irish connections who was in a public dispute with Lord Castlereagh.

The Wake of William Orr was a call to rebellion published by the most radical faction of the United Irish Society in a newspaper that Drennan believed was about to be suppressed. On a Wednesday evening in early March, Drennan saw what he described as

the quiet interment of the *Press*, I met twenty soldiers and five or six journeymen apprentices with a car and a white sheet thrown over it I took for some body laid upon it, but which was *the soul of the Dublin public* [italics added] and they conveyed it without the least disturbance to the Castle, leaving a pretty strong guard at Stockdale's.[46]

Drennan made his way to William Sampson's who lived a few doors from Stockdale and begged for the return of a paper. He felt 'it was safe in my own hands. It is not yet the time for history.'[47] Within days, Sampson, who was facing charges of high treason, finally absconded to England on 16 April 1798.[48] Sampson, in his memoir, gives us a graphic account of the atrocities in Dublin which precipitated his flight:

> I remained in Dublin until 16 April when the terror became so atrocious that humanith could no longer endure it. In every quarter of the metropolis, the shrieks and groans of the torture were to be heard, and that through all hours of the day and night. Men were taken at random without process or accusation and tortured at the pleasure of the lowest dregs of the community. Bloody theatres were opened by these self-constituted inquisitors and new and unheard-of machines were invented for their diabolical purposes.[49]

In the same letter in which Drennan recounted the demise of the *Press*, he told his sister that Arthur O'Connor had been arrested with four others at Margate in Kent. O'Connor and his companions had been trying to procure a passage to France. Drennan felt that O'Connor may have been betrayed by some Judas.

On 12 March 1798, several leading United Irishmen were arrested in Oliver Bond's house in Bridge Street in Dublin. Others were taken in follow-up swoops. Seven people Drennan considered to be close friends were now in prison. Lord Edward, Sampson, Chambers, McCormick and Dixon had absconded.[50] Drennan hoped his absconding friends would escape. He and his sister had long agreed that there was something dishonourable in flight. However, he had now changed his mind and told her:

> You seem to think it disgraceful to fly, and so did I, but under the present circumstances where a man is taken merely to keep in a cage of stone (as the habeas corpus is suspended, that is hanged for the good of the people) in such case, I do not think it disgraceful for those who have consulted their health, without injuring their honour, by escaping, and all that I wish is that they may be successful. The Chancellor may imagine he has taken off the heads of the union, but it is a perfect asparagus bed and bears cutting.[51]

He was glad to have retrieved some papers from Sampson's desk for, while they were of little importance, he did not want the authorities to have a sample of his handwriting.[52]

People were now regarding Drennan as 'a solitary nine-pin standing by chance when the other eight are bowled down'.[53] Old ladies would shake him by the hand in the street and say they were glad to see him. He was in reflective mood:

> I have done my country some service, though they don't know it. I have helped ... to elevate and give a certain turn of public enthusiasm to the national mind. I have been the inventor of some things that have grown into great good or great evil, but I can answer to my conscience for the intention. ... the man who invented the balloon had not the courage to ascend in it. These are different talents. Yet still I think I am at my post and here I shall remain.[54]

On the last day of March, Francis Higgins sent a songbook to Dublin Castle. This was almost certainly *Paddy's Resource* or *The Harp of Erin Attuned to Freedom. Being a collection of songs for Paddy's amusement* (Dublin, 1798). Higgins reported that the songbook was being 'used in taverns, clubs and ale houses where United Traitors frequent'. He claimed that many of the parodies were the work of Dr Drennan.[55] He also identified William Sampson as a contributor. Higgins was well informed. The first song in the collection was Drennan's 'When Erin First Rose', which had been published anonymously in the *Press* of 5 October 1797.[56] Drennan had circulated it a few months earlier, at least amongst his friends. Martha reported the previous July: 'Erin rises to notice here. The tune it was set to in Dublin did not imply the man of taste and the fair Miss Rainey sings and plays it to an old one of Carolan's which commands the attention of even the servants of the family – she turns face to Britain and back to the West.'[57]

Drennan was not happy with the efforts of a music master in Dublin to set a tune to *Erin* but Reverend Taylor of Eustace Street 'did well to come up with a tune that was less tedious in the singing'.[58]

One literary critic suggests that by this point Drennan was steadfast against physical force and violence and had rejected armed rebellion.[59] Yet she believes that Drennan may have had some connection with the publication of this 1798 version of *Paddy's Resource* and a later edition which appeared in 1803.[60]

The same critic acknowledges that the six months of the *Press'* existence marked the United Irish movement's acceptance of armed rebellion.[61] However, she seems to want to distance Drennan from his collaborators in the *Press* and *Paddy's Resource* when she says of *Erin*: 'The poem's message is a call to unity and forgiveness rather than violent revolution, underscoring Drennan's growing disaffection with the United Irish movement as armed revolution supplanted literary propaganda as their means of political reform in 1797 and 1798.'[62]

It could be argued that the unity and forgiveness *Erin* advocates are the same that the United Irish movement had always called for, that is, reconciliation between Irishmen of every creed. The third-last verse reads:

> Arm of Erin prove strong; but be gentle as brave
> And uplifted to strike, still be ready to save
> Nor one feeling of vengeance presume to defile
> The cause or the men of the EMERALD ISLE.

There is nothing here to suggest any disaffection from the United movement or indeed from armed rebellion. Rather it expresses the hope that the Rebellion, which Drennan and his United comrades now knew was certain, should not lead to sectarian slaughter. The 1798 edition of *Paddy's Resource* contained sixty-four songs, twelve of which had appeared in the recently suppressed *Press*.[63] Many of these songs are calls to arms and rebellion. If Drennan was disaffected from the United movement, why would he have been connected with this songbook or indeed the later edition of 1803?

29

Martial Law

The Chancellor held a visitation to Trinity College from 19 to 21 April 1798 on account of 'rumours too well founded that principles of a treasonable nature have made their way within these walls'.[1] Drennan informed Martha that nineteen students had been expelled and Stokes, the fellow, suspended for three years. He felt that those who were suspected as United Irishmen chose not to appear 'for fear of farther prosecution'. In fact, the first person called before the Chancellor was Robert Emmet. He was not present and was expelled. The Chancellor carried on his inquisition over three days and Drennan thought his lectures on morality and religion ironic, in the light of his conversation that was 'a tissue of obscenity and blasphemy'.[2]

John Browne (1779–1808), a native of Belfast and a firm friend of Robert Emmet, was also expelled.[3] Browne carried messages for Drennan which he dared not trust to the postal system.[4] When Drennan told his sister that she could get more details of the visitation from Browne, he prudently omitted that Browne himself had been expelled. Drennan thought that Robert Emmet might accompany Browne to Belfast and told his sister that the young man was a wonderful orator, though modest and diffident in company.[5] Within a week, a warrant was out for Emmet. When Drennan heard the news, he called around to visit Emmet's father but there was nobody home.[6]

The Castle now regarded Dublin as the headquarters of treason and the military were patrolling the streets. Drennan joked that if he met one of these patrols at night:

> I could safely say it was not Cinna the conspirator but the poet, though they might treat me to the touch of the bayonet for my bad verses. I should not like to be put to death yet a little, and therefore will keep myself as I have done the most politically innocent man in my conscience I do believe in this city, as yet the one most generally suspected.[7]

On 24 April, Drennan arrived back at his Dame Street lodgings where he found a Mr Wilkinson waiting on him with a letter which read as follows:

> Dear Drennan
>
> You most probably have heard of my being in custody under a charge of high treason for which I am to be tried on 30th of this month, at Maidstone in the county of Kent. My life being at stake, I trust no other apology for me entreating you to accompany the bearer of this letter to England, for the purposes of giving your evidence which my counsel are of opinion will be very material on my behalf. Yours ever most sincerely A. O'Connor
>
> Maidstone 19th [17]98.[8]

It was most inconvenient for Drennan to go at that time and he knew that professionally the journey would be very considerably injurious to him. He also doubted his evidence would be of any use. Yet he immediately agreed to travel. He was compelled by a sense of duty to risk any injury to himself to do anything he could to help a man with whom he was very little acquainted. He was determined that the slightest omission on his part should be of any disservice to the life of a man. He hoped his family in Belfast would agree with his decision. Martha assured him that while they were surprised, the family were not at all dissatisfied that he had put the call of duty or humanity first. His mother let it be known that she would pay the expenses of the journey.

However, when he reached London, he was advised by Thomas Erskine (1750–1823), the famous lawyer, that if he called Drennan to give evidence it could do more harm than good. In the event, O'Connor was acquitted but his co-accused, James Coigly (1761–1798), was hanged. Drennan's journey to England was a waste of time except that he got to see the English countryside and enjoy a very short period in London. When he reached Liverpool late on Sunday, the smell of the docks reminded him of the slave trade. But he enjoyed his coach journey across England.

> How many beautiful country seats did we pass, built for the pleasure of the traveler rather than the possessor. How many comfortable cottages did we see, more certainly filled with happiness, such lovely verdure in the fields, such neatness, and even elegance in their little gardens, in their houses, and in the kitchens of their inns, in the dress of their servant maids who

in general officiate as waiters, such excellent roads, such exact time keeping drivers, such hearty, and seemingly happy horses, such a smooth celerity of pleasant conveyance is not to be found but in England, and who that sees such a charming country in such a season, will not exclaim what a pity it should ever chance to be discoloured with blood, or laid waste by the horror of war.[9]

His travelling companion was Henry Grattan who, throughout the journey, was civil, kind, courteous and accommodating. When they reached London, they spent a lot of time together dining at the White Hart, Holborn, and visiting the opera and Drury Lane. George Smith, one of O'Connor's legal team, gave Drennan a seat in his carriage and they visited the famous British radical, John Horne Tooke, at Wimbledon. Drennan was impressed by Horne Tooke whom he felt 'to be a person of superior mind'.[10]

Drennan returned to Dublin on 7 May. A few days later, he learnt that the authorities were offering a reward of £1,000 for the discovery of Lord Edward Fitzgerald. Hearing that Lord Edward's wife was anxious to know about his visit to England, he called on her and chatted with her for some time.[11] Given the reward for her husband, Drennan must have known that Pamela Fitzgerald (1776–1831) was being closely watched by spies and informers. He believed that the administration was using talk of informers of high degree and low 'to infuse distrust and complete division'.[12] He told Martha:

> Domiciliary visits are to be paid here every night as well as day, in search of strangers from the country who have taken refuge in town or for concealed arms. I suppose three or four people will be set as spies of each division or sub-division of the city. The County of Dublin including part of the city will be proclaimed during the next week ... I marvel much, standing untouched as I do that they have not raised the cry against me of an informer ...[13]

Just as Drennan had predicted, martial law was formally declared in Dublin city and county on 18 May. Edward Fitzgerald was wounded during his capture on 19 May and died in great agony a few days later. Ruán O'Donnell describes the measures taken by the authorities when Dublin was proclaimed:

> From that day the constant patrolling of the yeomanry and the posting of sentries on the Liffey and canal bridges brought an air of menace to daily life in the capital. Preparations were made to fit iron gates, in storage for

229

over a month, to all the main bridges. This was intended to increase the efficiency of the curfew and impede illegal traffic.[14]

After the city was proclaimed, Drennan wrote just one short note to his sister dated 2 June merely assuring her he was well and had nothing to fear. That was his only communication with her for nearly two months until the end of August, by which time the Rebellion had been mercilessly crushed. We have no details of how Drennan behaved in late May and June as the Rebellion raged in Wicklow, Wexford, Kildare, Antrim and Down and as a reign of absolute terror was unleashed in Dublin city. He presumably obeyed the 9 p.m. to 5 a.m. curfew. We may never know whether he saw the body of his old friend Francis Bacon[15] along with dozens of others hanging from Carlyle bridge or the hundreds of rebel corpses thrown into the rubbish pit outside the Royal Barracks.[16] Many of the homes of suspected rebels were torched in the city and the home of Drennan's friend James Dixon at Kilmainham was occupied by the military. Drennan was fortunate that he was not among those caught up in the 'vicious circle' in Dublin who, 'fearing courts martial and flogging were driven from their homes with little option other than joining the rebels gathering in the woods, bogs and mountains of south Leinster'.[17]

Martha wrote three letters to her brother between late May and the end of June. She admonished him severely for not keeping in touch; she knew little of what was happening in the Northern countryside except what she read in the papers. She did get a first-hand account of the battle of Antrim from a woman who had taken the wounded Lord O'Neill from the street in the town. He died from his wounds on 18 June. She took some comfort from the fact that Belfast was being guarded by a yeomanry corps which included old friends of the Drennan family such as Dr Bruce, Reverend Vance and James Kennedy Trail. This should not be taken to mean that she was supporting the yeomanry and opposing the rebels. She had long feared that the Armagh Orangemen who were welcomed into the yeomanry by General Lake might burn the town of Belfast if they got the opportunity. Better to be guarded by New light Presbyterian ministers of her own congregation[18] and a prosperous citizen with loyalty to the town than by its sworn bitter enemies.

Martha reported that many respectable citizens of Belfast had been arrested but she hoped this was as a preventative measure rather than there being evidence against them. She was forced to give free quarter to eight soldiers who had been fighting all day at Newtownards and she pitied them much as two of them had been wounded. When the soldiers left she bolted her door and made everything ready for flight.

James Crombie (b.1775), a close friend of Drennan, was arrested for his part in the revolt in the North. Crombie often stayed with Drennan on his many visits to Dublin. In fact, he was at Drennan's the night of Drennan's arrest and mistook the arresting officers for patients. Martha wrote a petition on Crombie's behalf to General Nugent asking that he be allowed to emigrate rather than face courts martial. However, Crombie was convicted and afterwards interrogated by Martha's old protagonist, the egregious John Pollock. He told Crombie that his only chance was to give information and he seemed particularly interested in getting information against Martha. She told her brother that the prisoner was asked:

> Did he know me, had he seen me, what was the conversation and what did I give him? Yes, was the answer to the two first, 'the officer on guard will tell you' to the third, and to the last 'her purse'. It was also asked where I was now, replied believed in Dublin. Tis supposed this man will affront me – I have not a fear of any such.[19]

Crombie escaped, or was allowed to escape, when on his way with other prisoners to Donaghadee. He got away to America.[20]

Martha spent most of the month of August and September in Dublin with her brother. She was there when they heard that the French had landed in Killala with a force of 1,500 men on 23 August and was still there when General Humbert was defeated at Ballinamuck in County Longford on 8 September. During that time, Dublin remained 'perfectly quite [sic] and was not so near the great agitation or appearance of disorder, as in the time of the rebellion.'[21]

William Sampson had been arrested in England and brought back to Dublin where he was held in custody until October. He was then released under the Banishment Act, which obliged him to go into exile with the prospect of execution if he returned to Ireland. Drennan reported that Sampson had set sail for Portugal but had to return after becoming ill on board and vomiting blood.[22] At about this time, Drennan began to hear rumours that William Pitt was going to attempt what Drennan had feared was always his objective, to abolish the Irish parliament and institute an Act of Union between the United Kingdom and Ireland.

Both Drennan and Martha heard of a naval battle off Tory Island on 15 October, after which three captured French frigates were brought into Lough

Swilly. Wolfe Tone was taken prisoner in this engagement. On 8 November, Drennan reported that he had heard 'that Tone came into the city this day under a strong military guard, dressed in rich French regimentals and the carriage passed the Four Courts just as the lawyers were coming out. It is said he looked well and unembarrassed'.[23]

The authorities claimed that on 11 November Tone cut his own throat. He died in custody one week later. When Drennan heard the news, he told Martha, 'Tone is liberated'.[24]

30

MAN OF LETTERS

By early January 1799, Drennan was hurriedly composing an open letter to William Pitt, opposing his plans for a Union between Great Britain and Ireland. The previous year had been a dreadful one. Wolfe Tone, Edward Fitzgerald, Oliver Bond, Henry Joy McCracken, Bagenal Harvey and the Sheares brothers were dead. Reverend Boyle Moody would soon die from the effects of his harsh imprisonment. Thomas Addis Emmet, Thomas Russell, Arthur O'Connor, William Tennent and Samuel Neilson were in prison in Fort George in Scotland. William Sampson and Archibald Hamilton Rowan were in exile.

Drennan was about to add his own pamphlet to the shoal that had already been circulating 'like a sudden influx of herring'.[1] However, he complained that, 'the North was as silent as the Catholics', whom he believed to be, 'resolved never more to speak as a distinct body'.[2] This silence is hardly surprising given the atmosphere of instability and oppression. The Rebellion was over but the threat of a French invasion had not receded, at least in peoples' minds. Government reprisals and revenge atrocities continued[3] and A.T.Q. Stewart tells us that 'it would be difficult to compile a comprehensive list of all of those who were hanged' and that 'for the most part the hammer of justice fell on the men of no property and the poor'.[4]

In a speech to the Irish House of Commons in early 1799, Francis Dobbs said he considered Ireland 'as a vast slaughter house, in which 40,000 men of different descriptions were already dead and some hundred thousands are devoted to future immolation'.[5] Martha told her brother of authenticated murders and crimes against women committed by crown forces in Antrim. She gave a detailed account of one example of what she believed would be 'the ground work of many barbarous deeds':

One of the men condemned by court martial to be hanged was taken for that purpose to Ballymena where on the market day he was brought out, he was near seventy years of age, two men taken up on suspicion of being concerned in whipping an informer who died of it were ordered to hang the old one. Both refused, and in consequence were struck and cut in a most inhumane manner, with the old man beseeching them to put the rope about his neck to save themselves, since it was impossible he could escape. One of them appearing to consent, his father burst from the surrounding crowd, and commanded his son to meet death at the foot of the gallows first. He was then struck and sent to prison and the affair concluded that day – by the condemned putting the rope round his own neck, knotted so as by getting a pull his thread of life was broken forever.[6]

Even Francis Higgins who had always been an advocate of the sternest measures was shocked by the behaviour of government forces in 1799:

> Regardless of the protections granted these misguided people who were concerned in the late rebellion but who have endeavoured to make some atonement by a peaceable demeanour, many of them are dreadfully harassed, taken from their homes at a dead hour of night, tied on horses and sent before a court martial who on the solitary word of an approver (interested to save his own life) are condemned or either hanged or sent to Botany Bay.[7]

The Government continued to believe that 'unless the strongest measures were used the country was lost' and that 'there was a rebel directory which was waiting for its good friends the French to rise in general insurrection'.[8] In his correspondence, which Drennan knew was being monitored, he thanked God that if such a plot existed he was unacquainted with it.[9] He believed that there would soon be a general arrest of those suspected of treason. He claimed that he was not expecting to be arrested himself as he believed that would show a total want of true intelligence on the part of the authorities.[10] He told Martha:

> They once talked of me as a deep conspirator, but there is not a man on either side of the question that has acted from the first more openly and above board ... When I was in the Back Lane society, everything was carried out as it were in the open day, and I have never had any share nor confidence placed in me, since the society has been forced – for forced it surely was – into a dark and desperate policy.[11]

When one considers that letters which Drennan sent by post were frequently opened and read by government agents, it is not surprising that he makes no mention of his contributions or involvement with the *Press* or *Paddy's Resource*.[12]

Drennan's first *Letter to William Pitt* appeared on 23 January and 300 copies were sold on the first morning.[13] He had long believed that Pitt wanted to force a union on Ireland. He began by telling Pitt he was, 'but (and nothing but) the convenient tool of a regulated faction' going on to tell him that he 'was ever the passive puppet of sessional expediency'.[14] He declared that the Union was a military measure designed to keep the war out of England. Drennan said there was reason to fear that Ireland 'might form the field of final conflict between the two hostile powers' and 'this Union would make certain [that] which was but probable'.[15]

Ireland is about to become a 'buckler for Britain', on which the heaviest strokes will fall. Drennan, then, uses the first of many tortured medical metaphors which spoiled the letter for Martha. He told Pitt that realising that the Irish Parliament had lost control, 'it is become in your mind necessary for the support of religion, good government, and social order, to brace up with an iron collar the *distorted* spine of a body politic, become already too weak to support itself, and grown decrepit even in infancy'.[16]

Drennan suggests that the Union was a scheme 'to hold fast these kingdoms, like keys, by a metal ring of British manufacture'. However, his next sentence may refer to ongoing United Irish diplomacy with the French. For he advises Pitt: 'take care! One of them, [keys] at least, has been mislaid, and may have been falsified'.[17]

Drennan went on to accuse Pitt of starting the unnecessary war with France and instead of commanding the affections of the French people, frightening them by his aggression into fighting like 'a lioness robbed of her young'. Once the war had started, Pitt had drifted into interminable war by necessity.[18]

Drennan suggested that when the Union was achieved, 'the business of the state will be transacted by aide-de-camps and the whole country will be converted into a great barracks'. He then employed a metaphor which Martha disapproved of so much that it made her feel sick.[19] He said that 'Irish representatives would be what the Scotch were, the wretched semblance of their castrated country.'[20]

Not only was Pitt responsible for the war but his policy in Ireland had alienated what Drennan describes as 'a habitually royalist people' and turned them towards an 'undisguised hostility'. He accused Pitt of creating the United Irish society and causing the Rebellion: 'This same Jehu of Jacobinism after having sown the seed of internal Union, and forced the society of United Irishmen (of which he himself was the founder) from the despair of reform to the desperation of revolution, after having hastened forward a rebellion, which he himself helped to create.'[21]

For Drennan, the Union, was a question of honour and he claimed that the nation that does not feel the debasement of the very proposition, deserves to suffer the prostitution. Warming to his theme of castration, he says that Irishmen could not be prevailed upon 'to make a capon of our country – a Eunuch of Ireland'. He warned that Pitt's policy might lead to the creation of a union against the Union in opposition to the proposed annihilation of Ireland 'for the good of the Empire'. If Ireland is faced with 'the cruel alternative of uniting forever with England, or separate forever', Drennan would say *separate, in the name of God and nature'.*[22]

He concluded by comparing Pitt's plan for Union to the cruelties which had been meted out to his countrymen over the previous years and months:

> as we have seen smaller triangles erected in our public places, and stained with the blood of our countrymen, you are going to construct one great triangle from these three kingdoms, [but] – I will pursue you through the measure ... if the dying words of a single Irishman shall be able to revive your remembrance, or awaken your conscience either as man or as minister, what is to be expected from the last cry of an expiring nation?[23]

He signed off with a characteristic flourish with 'I am your humble servant but not yet your slave, William Drennan.'[24]

Martha, who usually enjoyed Drennan's pamphlets, was not pleased with his performance on this occasion. One of his metaphors, 'which might not have been too coarse to a male friend in private', should never have been printed and it made her sick.[25] She thought him 'too fond of <u>professional</u> images'. She advised him that, 'if Dr. Drennan makes use of terms such as – scrofula, spinal marrow, capon, virility [and] rape on the same page, his style will be justly caviled'.[26]

However, Drennan was quite pleased with the reception and the sales of his pamphlet in Dublin and he responded to Martha:

> Five hundred copies more (in all 1,500) are now striking off, which I suppose will be more than sufficient to supply the present and future demands in country and town. I have had several cordial shakes of the hand for it and if you don't like it you go against the general sentiment here ... I hear again

in the street as I pass – 'There goes Dr. D' but I hope to have some profit as well as praise.[27]

Perhaps it was the positive public reception of his first letter or perhaps he was trying to make amends with Martha, for he published a second letter to Pitt a month later, on 28 February. This time he dispensed with his castration metaphors and declared that 'It will not be *now*, that we will submit this country to the Right Honourable William Pitt.' He told Pitt that Ireland 'had survived the thunder of the Tudors and the exterminating sword of Cromwell'. The country, for 'so many hundred years, has been separated, alienated and disowned by England'. Whenever Ireland resisted oppression, Britain would express its 'horror at the perfidy of an odious race'.[28]

He did not mention the fact that many of his comrades had recently been executed but he did not scruple to identify himself as a former prisoner and salute those who were now in prison. 'Many more [of my Volunteer comrades] are at this moment silent sufferers in the living grave of the prison where I have spent twenty-four hours (the prisoner counts by hours) and some of these men have spent as many thousands. Dear and gallant souls! Whom fifteen years ago, I addressed and whom I now respectfully salute.'[29]

It was courageous of Drennan to publicly 'salute these dear and gallant souls' who were being generally referred to in the Houses of Lords and Commons as bloodthirsty, Jacobin traitors. Why Drennan seems not to have feared arrest and charges of seditious libel is hard to understand. For as one writer has observed, 'attacks on writing and publishing is everywhere a defining feature of Pitt's reign'.[30] Cobbett's ... *Collection of State Trials ... for High Treason and other Crimes ..., 1790–1800* gives details of 118 persons who were brought before the courts. Forty-six of these were charged with sedition (including seditious libel and words).[31] To accuse Pitt in print of provoking the war with France and of responsibility for the Irish Rebellion could easily have been construed as a seditious libel. To salute the leaders of the Rebellion as 'dear and gallant souls' is provocative to say the least. Perhaps Pitt and his administration were concerned with stamping out the remaining embers of rebellion, teaching the common people a lesson they would never forget, avoiding a French invasion of England and pushing through the Union. Perhaps they had no interest in confronting provocative, personal and political insults which could not harm them or divert them from their objectives.

In early 1800, when it was clear that Pitt's plan for a Union was going to succeed, Drennan published yet another short pamphlet on the subject entitled

A Protest on behalf of One of the People of Ireland against a Union with Great Britain. He wondered exceedingly: 'that men of superior talents and approved patriotism, who raised their hearts, their voices, and their arms, and their Country to the elevated prospects of the year 1782, should close the century so ingloriously, and not lift at least a naked hand against a blow that must annihilate Ireland'.[32]

He questioned the right of the Irish Parliament to vote for its own demise and stated that 'there is not upon this earth a rightful Power competent to such a measure – not even the People *themselves*, who have not a right to chaffer for their Country or to barter away their birthdom'. 'The Briton,' says Drennan, 'by birth, breeding and bigotry fears that the Irish infant of [17]82 might come to maturity and he would stifle it in the cradle.'[33] Usually Drennan's polemics attempted to influence events. He knew by now that this Union could not be written away and though he felt that people would laugh at his efforts on this occasion, he did not fear ridicule.[34] He declared that 'men become slaves by not being able to pronounce the mono syllable no!' 'I do therefore protest against a measure which turns Ireland into a headless, and heartless trunk, annihilates its rights and wither its capacities and its prospects ... If men do not learn to say no – then adieu to Ireland – to the mercy and justice of God is she left and to the hearts and hands of Posterity.'[35]

Not all good writers can be on form all the time. Drennan's first letter to Pitt, which so disappointed Martha, must stand for Drennan's off-form day. It was written in what were probably the darkest days of eighteenth-century Ireland. The Rebellion crushed, his friends dead, in prison or in exile, the common people dreadfully harassed, some condemned to be hanged or sent to Botany Bay. It is not surprising that his usual eloquence seems to have given way to personal invective and abuse. However, it may have been in tune with the public mood for it proved popular with the Dublin public.

31

A PERSONAL UNION WITH ENGLAND

In early 1797, Drennan told his sister he wished he was married. By this time, he was forty-three years old. Martha suggested that he should renew his contact with Sarah Swanwick but he did not follow this up. A year later he met Sally Scott, a young widow from Derry. She was in Dublin visiting her brother-in-law John Galloway, a friend of Drennan, living in 152 Abbey Street. Drennan took Martha into his confidence and asked her to find out what she could of Sally's family and fortune from Martha's contacts in Derry. However, when he finally asked Sally to marry him in February 1798, she rejected his suit. Drennan must have been disappointed at this rejection. However, had she accepted his proposal they would not have enjoyed a long and happy life for by June of the following year, Sally's death was recorded in the newspapers.[1]

In late 1798, Drennan borrowed money from his mother and bought a house at 33 Marlborough Street. He spent the next few months renovating the house and Martha helped with advice and shipped various items of furniture and furnishing from Belfast. In May, Martha again suggested that he should contact Sarah Swanwick and gave him some information which suggested it might be worth his while to do so. Sarah was still teaching at her family's boarding school in Wem in Shropshire. Wem is a long way from Dublin and a far greater distance from Belfast so how is it that Martha could receive useful information at such a distance? The answer lies in their shared Unitarian heritage which involved strong family connections. The source of Martha's information was Bethia Hincks.

Bethia was a member of a distinguished Dublin-based Unitarian family. She was a sister of Reverend Thomas Dix Hincks (1767–1857) Unitarian minister at Cork. Her other brother William (1770–1848) was married to his own cousin Susan Swanwick, an older sister of Sarah's. Sarah had another sister, Mary (1767–1864), who was married to Reverend Joseph Hutton who was a minister at Eustace Street. When Bethia was visiting Belfast in May 1799, she called to see Mrs Drennan and Martha took her out for a walk to probe her for information about Sarah. She found out quite an amount.

The whole Swanwick and Hincks family had known about William and Sarah's engagement and that the ending of it had made a deep impression on her. So much so that no one ever mentioned Drennan's name in her presence. Bethia had been given so many instructions on it that she was very guarded when she was in England. However, once in her presence, a male visitor mentioned having been in the company of Drennan and Grattan and drew a comparison of their characters in Drennan's favour. Sarah cast a look of surprise and enquiry at Bethia who explained that the pair had been summoned for Arthur O'Connor's trial and were in England for a few days only. Later that evening, Sarah asked how Drennan was getting on in his profession and if his politics were leading him into danger. She wished him well in both.[2]

Shortly thereafter, Drennan wrote to his mother to tell her that if Sarah was agreeable, he would marry her, although she did not have much by way of money and his own earnings were only £200 per year. However, he quipped:

> It is certainly a kind of fortune in the English lady that she is liberal in her mind and well educated, without I think being too finely fineered. She is a dissenter and, with her friends, of a democratical turn of politics ... On the whole therefore I am to become the advocate of a union with England, but personal not political and I wait chiefly to know the mind of the other party on the subject.[3]

He travelled to England in September and was delighted that Sarah agreed to marry but she needed time to put her affairs in order and would not be able to come to Dublin until the early new year. Sarah arrived in Dublin on 29 January 1800 and Drennan met her at Lurgan Street in the home of her sister Mary, the wife of Reverend John Hutton. They travelled from there by coach to the home of her brother-in-law Joseph Hutton, the highly successful coach builder. This was the same man whom Hamilton Rowan had hoped would be in office as sheriff at the time of his trial.

William and Sarah were married at Summerhill on 3 February by Reverend John Moody, a brother of Drennan's recently deceased friend Reverend Boyle Moody. Robert Orr, William Hincks and John Hutton were the witnesses.[4] Drennan thought his new wife the loveliest and most amiable of women and he was the happiest of men. All went off well on the day. Sarah liked her new home at Marlborough Street but Drennan was in no doubt that it would benefit from her improving hand. They spent the next few weeks visiting friends and well-wishers. 'There was cake and wine handed about freely'[5] and Sarah was welcomed in a very friendly way by many families of Drennan's acquaintance. The couple repaid this hospitality by inviting their friends to dine at Marlborough Street.

One social evening enjoyed by the newlyweds must have been tinged with sadness and must also have served for Sarah as a stark introduction to the fearful reality of life in post-Rebellion Ireland. One Saturday evening was spent in the company of Eleanor Bond, the widow of Oliver Cromwell Bond. Her husband had been arrested along with many other United Irish leaders at a meeting in his house on 12 March the previous year. He was held in custody until 23 July when he was tried and convicted of high treason. He was sentenced to be hanged, drawn and quartered. However, a deal was done involving the State prisoners disclosing their involvement in the planning of the Rebellion in return for an end to the executions. Bond's death sentence was commuted but this did not prolong his life. Drennan, around this time, had heard rumours that Bond had collared a jailer and was being kept in irons as a consequence.[6] James Davock, a friend of Bond, saw him one evening in the prison yard where he seemed to be in perfect health. The next day the *Dublin Journal* announced: 'On Thursday evening last Oliver Bond died suddenly in Newgate.'[7]

When the Drennans met Eleanor Bond, she was in the eighth month of her widowhood and raising four children, two boys and two girls, the eldest of whom could not have been more than eleven years old.[8]

One visit which Drennan made at this time, where he was not accompanied by Sarah, was when he went to Newgate to visit his dear friend the barrister Robert Holmes (1765–1857). It is possible that Holmes might have been a witness at Drennan's wedding had he not just about then commenced serving a six-month sentence for sending a challenge to one Counsellor Hamilton of the Northeast Bar Association.

As part of the post-Rebellion persecution of United Irish sympathisers, the Bar decided their members would not meet with any barrister who had not carried arms for the government side in the late Rebellion. This, of course, was designed to cast pro-United Irish barristers out of their livelihood and the profession. The two main targets of this witch hunt were close friends of Drennan, Holmes and Robert Orr. Orr pleaded poor eyesight and escaped sanction but Holmes refused to plead any excuse and instead challenged Hamilton to a dual. Hamilton had Holmes arrested and he was told if he did not withdraw and apologise for the challenge he would stand trial.[9] In order to keep the affair hanging over Holmes' head, the authorities put off his trial until February 1800. He was eventually sent to Newgate for six months and though there was no fine, he was given a heavy lecture from the bench.[10]

In the previous September, Holmes secretly married Mary Anne Emmet, she from whom Drennan had stolen an inappropriate kiss back in 1795. Her brother Thomas Addis Emmet could not attend the wedding as he was in prison in Fort George in Scotland. At the time, an arrest warrant was out for her younger brother Robert. Holmes knew if he was publicly associated with this notorious republican family the courts might give him a more severe sentence for the challenge offence. Robert Emmet attended the wedding ceremony and signed the marriage certificate as a witness. This would not have been possible if the wedding had been public knowledge. Reverend Moody who, six months later, united William and Sarah, presided at the ceremony. The marriage took place on 21 September 1799 and almost four years later to the day, on 20 September 1803, young Robert Emmet was hanged and beheaded in Thomas Street for high treason.

Drennan sat with Holmes for an hour in his cell and observed that he had a good room and was in good spirits. He was determined to give whatever help was in his power to his incarcerated friend. After Holmes was sentenced, his marriage became public knowledge and his wife would stay with her husband for a week at the prison and stay at her father's home on alternate weeks. In March 1800, Drennan and Sarah waited on the Holmes couple at the prison and Drennan was a frequent visitor through the six months. On one occasion, he met old Dr Emmet at the prison and they chatted over public and private matters as cordially as they ever did. Drennan thought the Emmets 'the suffering family of the time'.[11]

In April, the Drennans visited Belfast where Sarah met her new mother-in-law, Martha and Nancy and she made a very favourable impression on the family and all their friends and acquaintances. Drennan mused that 'his lovely and beloved Sarah' had been so well-received in Belfast that Dublin might be dull for her after it.[12] Martha assured her brother that he 'would hardly believe how much Sarah was admired in Belfast', and that:

> pleasing this was to us all, and however just as to <u>looks,</u> it was the charm of mind which captivated your mother and sisters, and to that which mutual happiness I hope may be built, and I think it a <u>mind</u> more indebted to nature, than formed by education, though here no deficiency appears ... In short, she in every way pleased and delighted me and did so to all, while <u>you</u> appear to possess her whole soul.[13]

Happy as the newlyweds were, it was not long before Sarah realised that the couple were in a precarious financial position. Her friends, who had been economical housekeepers in Dublin for years, persuaded her that with the heavy rent[14] they were paying and in order to keep up appearances they could not manage on less than £300 a year.[15] Drennan was anxious to have children and when and if such happened, their financial difficulties would increase. However, it was important that appearances be maintained and to that end, the Drennans entertained many of their friends in July by which time Sarah was not feeling at her best and her husband suspected correctly that she was pregnant.

Amongst those families and friends who enjoyed the Drennans' hospitality were Dr Bruce and his wife; Reverend Philip Taylor and his wife; the Welds; John Hutton and his wife; Eleanor Bond[16] and her daughter; Mr and Mrs Hincks; Reverend Hincks of Cork and Mrs Stapleton;[17] Bruce's sister Elizabeth; and Miss Jane Rainey, also related to Dr Bruce. It would appear from this that the Drennans favoured the company of these Unitarian families who were variously connected by family and marriage. Yet we know that these social occasions were not exclusively Unitarian gatherings because of an early faux pas they made in setting the date for what Drennan described as 'a small large party'.

> We had fixed it on Friday and had sent several cards without once thinking it was Good Friday, a thing not to be thought odd in Presbyterians who are not even in possession of an almanac, so we were obliged immediately to issue a second set inviting for Thursday, but this it seems was out of the frying pan into the fire, for old Mrs. Bruce told Mrs. Hincks her sorrow that she did not inform us that it was Holy Thursday and that it would displease all our Catholic visitors. We could not issue a third set of cards and as for the Catholics I believe there will be but two of that persuasion, young men who do not regard that much rigor in religion.[18]

Just as Sarah was showing the first signs of her pregnancy, Drennan was called at six o'clock one morning to the home of Doctor Emmet to attend his daughter Mary Anne whose husband Robert Holmes had been recently released from Newgate. He was there until ten at night. When he arrived home, he was almost immediately called out again to another female patient with whom he was obliged to sit until 10 am the next morning. When he finally finished this almost thirty-hour shift he found he had missed a call from William Godwin (1756–1836), the philosopher and novelist and widower of Mary Wollstonecraft. Godwin was in Dublin at the invitation of John Philpot Curran and was staying at his home in Ely Place.

Drennan invited Godwin and Curran to dinner and he also invited nine others including Robert Holmes and Robert Orr. The food was good and Drennan gave them as much claret as they chose to drink. He thought Godwin 'not illuminated in conversation' and it is clear that he was no admirer: 'A plain, simple mannered looking man, his eyes set to downcast, though evidently ambitious of singular fame, I never liked his books, and *St Leon* his late novel, is I think very stupid, with much fine writing thrown away on meagre fact. He is a literary libertine, perhaps unconsciously.'[19]

On the other hand, he found Curran, whom he usually apparently loathed, on this occasion to be 'brilliant and had all sufficient meat, drink and exercise of tongue'.[20]

In the same letter in which he told Martha of his dinner with Godwin and Curran, the only public news he had was that an informer who had murdered a man was executed at Newgate 'amidst the shouts and acclamations of an amazing number of people'. He was obviously referring to Jemmy O'Brien, the notorious murderer and burglar whom Major Sirr[21] had recruited as a 'bloodhound'. Curran had once said of O'Brien: 'Here is a wretch that would dip the Evangelists in blood.'[22] W.J. Fitzpatrick, the nineteenth-century historian, tells us that 'to track O'Brien's bloody progress through the reign of terror would prove a repulsive task'.[23] Fitzpatrick also gave an account of the murder that led to O'Brien's execution. O'Brien had climbed a fence to scrutinise a group of men who were playing a football match at Stevens' Lane. He was helped by an old man called Hoey. When the cry of 'O'Brien the informer' went up, the people fled, and O'Brien illogically wrecked his vengeance by stabbing and killing Hoey his accomplice. Despite Major Sirr lauding his informant at the trial, O'Brien was sentenced to death.[24] Of the many public executions in Dublin in the year 1800, this was probably the only one we know of which gave rise to gallows humour and was enjoyed by the people of the city. Fitzpatrick gives a graphic description of the event which he claimed was recounted to him by a witness fifty-four years later:

A vast ocean of people surged around the prison and under the gallows. A delay occurred; the populace became impatient, and finally uneasy, lest the government had yielded to the memorial which was known to have been presented in his favor. A multitudinous murmur gradually gave place to a loud boom of popular indignation. The delay was caused by the cowardice of O'Brien, who shrank from his approaching doom. Prostrate on his knees, he begged intervals of indulgence according as the turnkey reminded him 'that his hour had come'. At length Tom Galvin the hangman a person of barbarous humor accosted him, saying, Ah Misther O'Brien, long life to you sir, come out on the balcony an' don't keep the people in suspense; they are mighty uneasy entirely under the swing-swong.[25]

The Act of Union was passed on 1 August 1800 and Drennan thought it a strange coincidence that the day his 'country died' should have been the happiest day which he 'had spent on this earth'. For that was the day he was told he was to become a father. In fact, the 'death' of his country seemed to have been a liberation for him for he told his mother:

> My country is now contracted to the limit of this house. I have done my duty to <u>that</u> parent [Ireland], without much pleasure or advantage, and now that she has died without a groan or a struggle, I should not wish to be employed in writing her epitaph. I cannot praise her character or her conduct, her morality or her spirit. We now have no country.[26]

Such were his financial circumstances that in this letter to his mother to inform her she was about to have her first grandchild, he was obliged to ask if he could borrow another £100 as he had not received a professional fee in three months.[27]

At about this time, Jane Emmet and her brother John Patten and Jane's three children arrived in Belfast on their way to visit and stay with Jane's husband, Thomas Addis Emmet, at the prison in Fort George. Martha met with and was impressed by Jane whom she found to be a prettyish, unaffected, affable woman. However, Martha took a distinct dislike to Jane's eight-year-old son Robert. She thought him the boldest, most ill-bred boy she ever saw and that 'in jail with his father is the very place for him, he is indeed a liberty boy'.[28]

Louisa O'Connor and her brother Roderick arrived in Belfast having spent some time visiting their father Roger (1762–1834) and their uncle Arthur who were incarcerated at Fort George. Louisa spent a morning with Martha discussing her future. Roger O'Connor was a wealthy man but did not wish to send Louisa to boarding school as his son had met with insults and the other students would not speak to him on account of his father's association with the United Irish Society. At first, Martha thought it might be convenient for Louisa to lodge with William and Sarah in Dublin but then she called to mind that Louisa was an 'O'Connor' and she thought the better of it. It would not be the last time that Martha would warn William and Sarah against giving refuge to a female with a notorious republican surname. Five years later, when Catherine [Kitty] Emmet was in need of refuge after the execution of her uncle Robert and the deaths of all the other Emmets on this side of the Atlantic, Martha warned her brother not to take her in as 'her name in your house will rivet calumny'.[29]

32

LET IRISHMEN REMAIN SULKY

William and Sarah's first child was born on 24 April 1801. Thomas Hamilton Drennan was named Thomas for his grandfather Reverend Drennan and Hamilton for Hamilton Young, a cousin of William who had died in 1799. Drennan expected eventually to inherit Hamilton Young's fortune from the deceased's aged sister Miss Martha Young. Hamilton Young had died intestate and his sister faced legal difficulties securing her inheritance which were not finally resolved until May 1801. Both Drennan and Martha were confident that if the old woman could be prevailed upon to make her will then William and Sarah's financial difficulties would be at an end. However, in spite of repeated hints from Martha, old 'Miss Young' was reluctant to finalise the matter.

Drennan was obliged to borrow money to meet his growing living costs. One of those he borrowed from was Robert Mercer, a wealthy merchant who had made his fortune in India. Yet Drennan had mixed feelings about his friend. Mercer had been asked by Arthur O'Connor to give evidence for the defence at his trial. When Mercer had declined to go and when Drennan had agreed to travel he felt 'he had a rise on him'. He also felt that the old man would not have been capable of giving cool and collected evidence.[1] In March 1799, when the Chancellor had amended the Rebellion Act so that anyone suspected of treason could be taken up, Drennan said of the old man:

> Mercer is without exception the most imprudent man in conversation in the King's dominions, though I don't think the most courageous, and I am of the opinion that this amendment to the rebellion Bill will strike panic into people who thought that great wealth and round age would protect them while they egged on younger and poorer men by their vehemence and by other means.[2]

Reverend James Porter, Unitarian Minister at Greyabbey, was hanged outside his Meeting House on 2 July 1798, leaving his widow Anna with seven young children. He had taken no part in the Rebellion but had earned the unbridled enmity of Lord Londonderry, Castlereagh's father, as Reverend Porter was the author who satirised his Lordship in the *Northern Star* in a column entitled *Billy Bluff and the Squire*. Porter's other crime was that at a fast-day sermon entitled *Wind and Weather*, which he delivered in February 1797, he had treated his congregation to a 'tour de force of ironic political analyses' against the war with France and 'the anti-democratic thrust of church–state collaboration'.[3] When Martha reported that old Mercer had left £300 in his will to *Wind and Weather*'s widow Anna, she gave the credit to Mercer's lawyers, Robert Holmes and Robert Orr, for doing justice to that family.[4]

In August, the Drennans left four-month-old baby Tom with a childminder for a few hours and went into the country to visit their friends, the Emmet family. They found Dr Emmet tolerably recovered from a severe indisposition. The Emmets had been in a little alarm as Major Sirr had recently raided the printer John Stockdale and seized a copy of *Beauties of the Press*. This book was a compound of the best writing that had appeared in the *Press* in late 1797 and early 1798 before it was suppressed. *Beauties* runs to more than 600 pages, not including speeches and writings by Arthur O'Connor which are appended to the volume. The Emmets were alarmed because Mary Anne's husband, Robert Holmes, sometimes frequented Stockdale's printing works and because Holmes was, at first, thought to be on Sirr's list for arrest. His name had been mistaken for a neighbour of Stockdale's whose name was Hope. The title page of *Beauties* claims that the book was published in London in 1800 but gives no details of the printer.[5] Stockdale had been the printer of the *Press* and had served six months in prison on that account. Drennan and his sister both had their own copies of *Beauties* and knew that it contained *Erin* and the *Wake of William Orr* and more of Drennan's work.[6] Drennan had himself been deeply involved with Stockdale in the past but prudently omitted mention of this when he told Martha of the alarm of the Emmet family.

Martha expressed the hope that if baby Thomas lived, he would see better times than his father and his aunt had lived through. She thought it possible that Bruce had been right when he foretold that 'every virtuous effort in favour of Ireland only tend to rivet her chains and point them into fangs for those who sacrificed all, life, and everything dear in it'. There is little doubt that Martha had Lord Castlereagh in mind when she declared that 'cold blooded traitors not only escape but mount into higher and safer seats, rewarded by the country to which they sold us'. She urged her brother that his son should be educated in these matters and expressed the hope that: 'Let Irishmen remain sulky, grave, prudent and watchful, not subdued into tame servility, poverty, and contempt, not satisfied until time blunts their chains and feelings, but ardent to seize the possible moment of national revenge, never to lose hope of it till obtained, and then in proud and glorious safety scorn it.'[7]

It is clear from his correspondence towards the end of 1801 that the advent of the Act of Union and the total failure or refusal of the Irish people to mount any effective resistance to it, had changed everything for Drennan. When Pitt suddenly left office and was replaced by Henry Addington (1757–1844), Drennan predicted that there would be peace with France and he suggested that Addington had been appointed for that purpose. When his prediction came true he found himself deeply conflicted:

As a man and a citizen of the world I ought to rejoice at this general peace. As an Irishman who has lost his country without much hope of redemption, it is more becoming to be silent. It is a most lamentable thing to be obliged to seek for our purposes through the most terrible consequences of war and to dread peace as the consummation of our calamities.[8]

This is a very significant statement. He had opposed this war from the beginning. It was a 'merely personal' war and had been launched, in his view, because the English monarch had been wounded and alarmed by the treatment of Louis. Edmund Burke, whose eloquence was pensioned to 'trumpet forth the necessity of a coalition of kings' to attack the revolution, is likened by Drennan to Milton's fallen angel Moloch. Moloch was the 'horrid king, besmeared with blood of human sacrifice and parents' tears' who demanded the sacrifice of children. Pitt, according to Drennan, had been enlisted by the fulsome flattery of his great abilities but in later years persisted with the war to stick with his master rather than because he expected to be able to win it.[9]

Drennan believed wrongly that the peace would endure. There was now no possibility of a French intervention in Ireland. This was calamitous for the prospects of the Irish ever becoming a free people. With the advent of peace he even doubted that Bonaparte would pay any attention to the groans of Ireland. He was unlikely to give protection to those in Ireland who had supported the French and who might want to emigrate to that country. Drennan next went on to make a most revealing statement.

On the whole I am however inclined as a *Briton* [emphasis added] that peace will bring about a reform, much more readily than war could effectuate a revolution and that England will become what France really is, a reformed monarchy. The military power which the war, of necessity increased to a magnitude not only to cope with, but to keep down the people, left no alternative but silent submission or rebellion (as the event has made it properly termed), and it now appears that the strength against reform is superlatively strongest in time of war, it leads to hope that the principles and the practice of peace will dispose both nations to do what they should have done at first, to make a common cause of public liberty, public economy, and public, or political justice to different sects of religion and even different parties in politics.[10]

He clearly understood that as long as wartime conditions existed, the government could keep the people down and resist all pressure for reform. He mistakenly predicted that with Pitt out of office, his principles would not continue to be prevalent and that Catholic Emancipation would be granted. He hoped that the new governor of Ireland might endeavour, 'by a modification of tithes, a proper plan of national education and suspension of scandalising newspapers, to bring about a reconciliation of the parties in this country'.[11] His misplaced optimism arose from the conviction that such an approach was 'the surest means of consolidating the British Empire'. Drennan might have called it so wrongly because the British Government had no desire to improve conditions or effect a reconciliation in Ireland. The peace did not endure and the war resumed and continued until the battle of Waterloo in 1815. Catholic Emancipation and parliamentary reform were postponed years beyond Drennan's life time.

Drennan had made it his life works to create an Irish nation by forging a unity amongst Catholic, Protestant and Dissenter. As far back as *Orellana*, he had insisted that if a people wish to be free, it must show that it is determined not only to gain freedom but to maintain that freedom when achieved. The Act of Union had definitively proved to him that the Irish people had shown no determination either to achieve or maintain freedom. There was now for him no Irish nation and he could ever after only speak as a citizen of the world or as a Briton. Fundamental as this shift in his thinking was there remained a coherent consistency in his political objectives. Ever after, he continued to advocate the United Irish agenda by advocating an end to the British war of aggression against France, a more equal representation of the people in parliament and Catholic Emancipation.

Drennan and Sarah's second child, William, was born on 15 March 1802. His correspondence with Martha at this period is dominated by domestic issues such as the poor health of his ageing mother and his financial difficulties. He found he needed about £380 per annum to live comfortably but his income was never more than £200. He was forced to borrow to make ends meet. Innocuous as these letters were, the authorities continued to open and examine everything they sent through the post.[12]

When Dr Alexander Haliday (1728–1802) lay dying in Belfast, Martha urged her brother to prepare an obituary for publication in the Belfast papers when the time came.[13] Drennan put a great deal of effort into this character sketch. It was not just because Haliday had been a life-long family friend but because Drennan wished to identify himself with Haliday's 'private worth, consistent public spirit and high professional reputation'.[14] Another reason why Haliday's reputation was of the greatest significance to Drennan is that he was the son of Reverend Samuel Haliday, who had stood side by side with Drennan's father Thomas in the first non-subscription crisis described in Chapter 2.

Martha also believed the obituary might help her brother to get over the false notion that he had been connected with rebellion and invasion. Drennan commenced his panegyric by stressing Haliday's professional merits and his 'virtuous independence and dignified impartiality'. His summary of Haliday's political principles gives a clue into how his own thinking was evolving:

> In his political principles he was a genuine Whig, not understanding by that denomination the mere factionary of a powerful party, but the hearty hater of arbitrary power whether exercised by individuals or parties, the zealous yet judicious advocate of civil and religious freedom, the strong upholder of those popular principles which form the living spirit of the British Constitution, and which, at different periods, have called forth all the heroism of British story ... If the British Constitution be a medium between republicanism and absolute government I will not scruple to assert that Haliday approached nearer to the former than the latter extreme.[15]

Drennan goes on to claim that Haliday's principles had gained him the confidence of 'that good and great man Grattan' and led him to regard Charles J. Fox as the 'titular genius of the British Constitution'.[16] However, in all this fulsome praise of an old friend, Drennan cannot resist making a thinly veiled side swipe at some old adversaries. He proclaimed that Haliday's principles were those of the venerable Camden, the amiable Charlemont, the untitled Stewart and the unpensioned Burke. The reference to the untitled Stewart refers to Castlereagh's grandfather who, unlike his son and grandson, had remained a Whig and a Protestant

Dissenter whereas Lord Londonderry and Castlereagh had betrayed their Whig and Protestant dissenting principles for titles and political office. Burke had likewise sold out his Whig principles to gain his pension.

Drennan had long held admiration for Napoleon Bonaparte whom he once described as the great avenger of the world's wrongs.[17] He saw the Corsican as 'a monarch who reigned with the sanction and acquiescence of public opinion'. In Drennan's view, Napoleon had abandoned wisely for his country the design of republicanising the world but if he lived he would reform the governments of Europe.[18] From early 1799, Drennan hung a finely framed and glazed print of his hero on the bedroom wall.[19] However, he completely revised his opinion when he heard that Napoleon had ordered the restoration of slavery to Saint Domingo in May 1802. The print was not removed, Drennan simply reversed it leaving the First Consul's heels where his head had been.[20] Martha could never understand how her brother had been so long blind to Bonaparte, who for her was a man that had 'damned the fairest fame, blasted the purest hope and shamed fortune who had made him her darling'.[21] Drennan eventually expressed a very negative opinion of Napoleon when he said:

> Who could have imagined that one little man could operate such a counter revolution as to place France pretty nearly as it was, only changing the dictator and the dynasty, and that philosophy, patriotism, rights of humanity, etc., should became terms of ridicule and even disgust not only there, but in all surrounding nations. Mr. Pitt should now, if he has the spirit of rivality, turn democrat, for Bonaparte, I think threatens to subjugate the world.[22]

The peace with France did not last and Drennan's hopes that peace would bring reform were not fulfilled. However, the Treaty of Amiens did result in the freedom of the Fort George prisoners, most of whom were ordered to Hamburg and banned from returning to Ireland under the Banishment Act. In June 1802, Thomas Addis Emmet wrote from Hamburg to Dublin instructing that his property be converted into money and his Dublin-based children be sent to him. Emmet intended moving with his wife and family to the United States. Drennan believed that 'Emmet's abilities of head and heart would push him forward perhaps in a political line under the presidency of Thomas Jefferson.'[23] Thomas Russell, who intended to go to France, wrote to Martha and many other of his friends pleading with them to help to support his penniless sister Margaret (1752–1834).

In December 1802, Drennan's old friend Dr Robert Emmet died. The old man's funeral was altogether private, possibly because his son Robert Emmet junior had secretly slipped back into Ireland the previous October. The family probably felt badly that Drennan, whom they knew to be a good friend of the Doctor, had been excluded from the funeral for they sent him some of the deceased's scarves and his hat band as a memento. Drennan was aware of young Robert's return to Ireland but did not think he intended to stay.[24]

In April 1803, Martha paid a visit to Dublin and brought Thomas back to Belfast with her, as Sarah was advanced in pregnancy and expecting her third child. Thomas was a delight to Martha and the rest of the family and he thrived in the North. A daughter Marianne was born on 2 June but lived only until September.

In May, the Treaty of Amiens broke down when Britain declared war on France and Drennan felt it would be wonderful if England were to be invaded.[25] However, he believed that if the French did not invade England within a few weeks, she was safe. When United Irish rebels, still active in the Wicklow mountains, destroyed a military barracks in the Glen of Imaal in June, Drennan saw it as them 'sending up a rocket to be seen in France'.[26] Martha had heard rumours that her dear friend Thomas Russell had been calling on several old friends in the North. Russell's presence in Ireland was a breach of the Banishment Act and he was therefore facing the death penalty if apprehended. It is not surprising that the letter in which Martha mentioned Russell's activity in the North went by private hands rather than through the post office.[27] In fact, Russell had come to Dublin at the beginning of April. He had stayed for a time at Robert Emmet's secret headquarters at Butterfield Lane in Rathfarnham County Dublin. Since then, he had been working with Emmet to raise a rebellion which would coincide with a hoped-for French invasion of England in the autumn.

33

THE EMMET FAMILY TRAGEDY

On 23 July 1803, Drennan wrote to his sister saying he had booked his seat on the mail coach to travel North to visit his mother for a time and then to bring his son, Thomas, home to Dublin. However, later that evening, Robert Emmet's Rebellion broke out in various parts of the city. Drennan reported 'this strange disturbance'. Sarah suggested he delay as she did not want him to travel at such a time. He feared that people would misinterpret his motives for going North 'into something political'.[1]

Three days later, Drennan hurried the short distance from Marlborough Street to Summerhill to collect Sarah 'with reports at his heels that rebels were rushing into the city from all quarters'. Within a few hours, the panic into which the city had been thrown abated and everything was quiet in Dublin. Regiments of regulars were pouring into the city and Drennan believed that within a few days, it might be safe for him to travel North. However, his friend Robert Holmes had been taken into custody. Drennan believed it was not because of any involvement in the Rebellion but because the authorities wanted to question him about his brother-in-law Robert Emmet. Within a few days, Emmet was named in *Faulkner's Weekly Journal* as the director of the Rebellion.[2]

At the end of August, Drennan reported that 'young Emmet is taken and many others daily'. When Martha heard that Thomas Russell's friend Dr James MacDonnell (1763–1845) had subscribed forty guineas to help in his capture, she thought him 'a contemptable cold-blooded Judas'.[3] By late August, it seemed to Drennan that the insurrection was 'quite trampled and trodden under foot'.

> The yeomanry are on permanent duty, and a striking contrast does their full-fed, masculine and even martial appearance make to the squalid sickly miserable wretches they affect to fear. One of them is executed almost daily ... it is said that young Emmet, the only one of any higher rank supposed at present to be actually concerned in this mad business, will be tried on

Monday next. His mother knows not yet of his arrest and I believe they wish to get her to Wales as soon as possible lest she should get to hear of it. Of Holmes I hear not a syllable but should suppose he would be liberated after the trials.[4]

The reference to this being a mad business should not be taken as an indication that Drennan was out of sympathy with Emmet or the objectives of his Rebellion. As Drennan was not informed of what young Emmet was about, it must have appeared to him like a street riot with no serious purpose. In fact, Emmet believed he had been promised French aid and that no fewer than nineteen counties would have risen if he had managed to capture Dublin.

Whatever about his attitude to the Rebellion, Drennan remained deeply loyal to and supportive of the Emmet family. He attended old Mrs Emmet, who died of an inflammation of the bowel ten days before her son was executed, never having been told of his capture. Martha was almost pleased that the old woman had died without knowing the full extent of her family's misfortunes. She urged her brother to do all he could to help Mary Anne Emmet now that her husband was incarcerated and her brother facing execution. She observed 'what a family tragedy is the Emmet's story'.[5]

However, at this point, a family tragedy unfolded for William and Sarah. Their baby daughter Marianne who had thrived and never been ill in her first four months of life was suddenly attacked by a complaint in her bowel. She bled profusely and despite Drennan's best efforts, she breathed her last on the night of 16 September.

Just three days after the death of Marianne, Robert Emmet came to trial. As he offered no defence, a guilty verdict and a death sentence were inevitable. When the prosecution's case was concluded, Emmet's counsel Leonard McNally addressed the court: 'My lord, Mr. Emmet says he does not intend to call any witnesses, or to take up the time of the court by his counsel stating any case, or making observations upon the evidence; and, therefore, I presume the trial is now concluded on both sides.'[6]

However, the prosecuting counsel William Plunket, a one-time friend of Thomas Addis Emmet, rose to his feet and delivered 'a most masterful performance' as he berated and insulted the prisoner. Plunket had been regarded as a reformer and had defended the Sheares brothers in 1798. Now, however, he had changed sides and was determined to please his new masters in Dublin Castle. He derided Emmet's character accusing him of luring the illiterate with his ambition and arrogance with promises of a better alternative system. Plunket mocked the working-class background of some of Emmet's associates. He said the leaders of the insurrection 'stretched all the way to the bricklayer, to the baker, the old clothes man, the hodman and the hostler'.[7] Maeve Ryan suggests that Plunket was pursuing a twofold strategy: 'Emmet had to be seen to be the clear driving force and the extent to which the corrupting influence of conspiracy had taken hold had to be built up to the status of grave public threat particularly the possibility of foreign invasion. At the same time the rebels themselves had to be shown as contemptable.'[8]

The tone and vehemence of Plunket's attack shocked many, not only those well-disposed to the accused. Martha, who knew Plunket's family, was disgusted and exclaimed afterwards, 'why did Plunket speak? If to shine, it is not in my eyes, I like him not in that speech. Had I been he, I would be ashamed of, a servile disgusting imitation.'[9]

The allegation that Plunket had made a vicious, cruel and unnecessary attack on a doomed man, to please the authorities, hung over him for the rest of his life and since. On two occasions, he successfully sued for libel when accused of having dishonoured Emmet's father at whose table it is alleged he had often dined. For his part, he denied ever being a friend of the Emmets. McNally, who cannot be regarded as a reliable source, said that Robert Emmet was furious with Plunket and said if he had not been interrupted by Lord Norbury he would have crushed 'the head of the reptile that had stung [him]'.[10]

Plunket's father, Reverend Thomas Plunket, who died in 1776, had been a Unitarian Minister at Great Strand Street and he had been mentioned in very positive terms by Drennan in his obituary for Doctor Haliday in early 1802. The Great Strand Street baptismal register shows that Addis Emmet, Mary Anne Holmes, née Emmet and William Plunket had their children baptised at Great Strand Street.

Both Drennan and Martha had been appalled at what they perceived as the betrayal by Doctor MacDonnell when he had offered a reward for the capture of his friend Thomas Russell. Drennan felt that Plunket's speech at Emmet's trial was a betrayal of a similar nature. He composed what he described as a severe epigram on the business. Much play had been made in the loyalist press about the savagery of the rebels who had piked Lord Kilwarden to death in Thomas Street on the night of the Rebellion. Drennan portrayed Plunket's behaviour as savagery of a similar nature:

Prostrate, unarmed, no more alive,
Had ceased Kilwarden's breath

The savage strife was then to give
A death-wound after death
When Emmet self-convicted stood,
In fate already hung
Plunket still longed to taste the blood
And piked him with his tongue.
Now which of these barbarians say
Waged the most cruel war
The savage of the bloody fray
Or savage of the bar?[11]

Thomas Russell was captured in Dublin on 9 September and Martha begged her brother for any well-attested information regarding him. She also begged him to write something on Russell's behalf which might result in saving his life even if it meant he might be sent to Botany Bay. She always clung to the belief that her petition to General Nugent in 1798 had saved the life of Joe Crombie (1776–1806). Martha was clearly now clutching at straws for she knew that no one in authority would pay attention to anything her brother would write and she knew also that Russell would be executed quickly after sentence.

It caused her great distress to think of Russell when on the run, lying in hovels and ditches and not approaching her habitation or involving any friend in his troubles. She had heard that when he approached Mrs Ferguson's window near Antrim and asked for a drink, he had staggered through weakness; she assumed him drunk and refused. Russell replied, 'Your eyes deceive you.' Martha was a little comforted when she heard of the conspicuous fortitude with which Russell had faced his execution:

I rejoice in it and that whatever it was, enthusiasm, fortitude or error, that it bore him up to the last. Few, few have I known like him. Heart, and enthusiasm is laughed to scorn now and fares the same fate of patriotism, yet the two former we may presume will have a place in heaven though so dangerous here.[12]

Martha told her brother that Dr MacDonnell, who had subscribed to the reward for the capture of Russell, had advertised in the papers regarding the loss of a cow. She had tried to write a ballad about it but had found it too difficult. Her brother, although by this time engaged in writing his epic poem Glendalloch, obliged her:

Epitaph– on the Living

Stop passenger, awhile attend
If business will allow
Here lives a man who sold his friend
And lately lost his cow
Here lives a man who could subscribe
To hang that friend at last
Whom future history will describe
The Brutus of Belfast
Here lives a man whose country's claim
Has proved by such a test
Whom felt affection a mere shame
And friendship but a jest
Brutus for father and for friend
His feelings warm could smother
And here's a man who for that end
Could sacrifice his mother
This is the man that wears no masque
Who serves no selfish end
Though the sly Quaker well might ask
Would thee have such a friend?
Let this man live, live and mind his trade
But in unbounded space
Should he e're chance on Russell's shade
O let him hide his face.[13]

The sly Quaker question was what John Hancock, a Lisburn Quaker, had put to a priest who had praised McDonnell for putting public good before private friendship. Hancock would work with Drennan on many projects in the years after Drennan's return to Belfast in 1807. John Templeton, Ireland's pre-eminent botanist and a founder member of the Belfast Literary Society, had withdrawn from society as he refused to meet McDonnell because of his treachery. Templeton did not speak to McDonnell for twenty-two years. It was not until 1825 that a reconciliation of sorts came about and even after all that time, Templeton still had raw feelings about what had happened. He recorded in his diary:

> April 25. Funeral of Mr. William Dickey at Randalstown. Today Dr. McDonnell and I met and shook hands. This renewal of our intercourse

was brought about by my sister Eliza. Disagreeable sensation yet pass across my mind when I recollect the deed of 1803, and with what affection, yes apparently brotherly affection, Russell looked upon McDonnell.[14]

When Robert Holmes was arrested in July 1803, Drennan assumed wrongly that his friend would soon be liberated. He was not finally released until February of the following year. He was released just in time for the birth of his son. Baby Hugh was baptised by Reverend John Moody at Great Strand Street on 2 February and Robert Holmes signed the register as his father. The child's mother, Mary Anne, was going through a most terrible time. Her brother, Thomas Addis, had been banished from Ireland on his release from Fort George. Both her parents had died within nine months of each other. Within days of the death of her mother, her much-loved younger brother had been publicly hanged and beheaded.

When her husband was incarcerated, she was pregnant and looking after her own two daughters and her orphaned niece [Catherine] Kitty. Kitty was the daughter of her brother Christopher Temple who had died in 1789 when Kitty was four years old. Her mother Anne outlived her husband by four months and passed away in the same year.[15] Kitty had been subject to nervous attacks which Drennan reported had increased much since her Uncle Robert's lamentable end.[16] William and Sarah took Kitty Emmet into their home for a time and Kitty became very fond of Sarah. As Mary Anne's health deteriorated, Sarah began to plan for Kitty's long-term welfare. At first, she hoped that Kitty would continue to live with the Drennans at Marlborough Street. However, Martha was very opposed to this idea as she believed that Kitty's illness was of such a dreadful nature that she would be difficult to care for. Martha also thought Kitty should change her surname as the Emmet name would 'rivet calumny' to the Drennan household.[17]

The remainder of Mary Anne's short life continued to be marked by sickness, tragedy and death. Baby Hugh died in September aged just nine months and Drennan remarked that both parents were looking poorly at this point. Early in the new year, Drennan remarked:

The Emmets are, I think a striking instance of suffering. Mrs Holmes I am pretty certain, will not survive long. I saw her today and her strength is failing and many bad symptoms occurring, yet she is not sensible to her situation as she was some months ago. Her husband pays her every attention. Her deafness at all times great, has much increased, and she has few female friends she can bear. Mr Holmes thinks that now she does not even relish

259

Sarah's company whom she always seemed to like, and wished to be with her some hours in the morning ... It is a long winter to the Emmet family.[18]

Drennan attended Mary Anne's bedside almost every day before her death on 9 March 1805. Mary Anne did not seem to realise she was dying and she did not have much pain at the end. Drennan thought this some compensation for the suffering of both mind and body which she had endured for so long.[19]

Robert Holmes now had charge of his two surviving daughters and his niece Kitty. Sarah Drennan hoped that Holmes and his girls would come and live at Marlborough Street. However, Holmes decided against this plan but he must have sought Sarah's help in securing a refuge for Kitty, who was now twenty years old and suffering from epilepsy. Kitty went to Sarah's home town of Wem in Shropshire where she lodged for the rest of her life with the redoubtable Unitarian minister Reverend William Hazlitt, father of the celebrated essayist of the same name.

34

LETTER TO CHARLES FOX

The Drennans' fourth child and third son, John, was born in June 1804 but, as in the sad case of his sister Marianne, he did not survive his first year; he died in March 1805 and was interred with his little sister. Martha thought it might help the bereaved parents if she brought their son Tom down to Dublin on a visit. She came in April and stayed for four months during which time Sarah went to England for a time to visit her family at Wem. Martha and Tom had become very close and the family had to decide Tom's future. At last it was agreed that Tom would stay in Dublin with his parents and his younger brother, William, would return to Belfast with Martha.[1] However, Tom could not settle in Dublin and in September, Martha was delighted when Drennan brought Tom back to the North and took William home to Dublin.

There were two nights of illuminations in Dublin in November to celebrate Nelson's victory at Trafalgar. Several of Drennan's Unitarian friends including Daniel and Joseph Hutton and old Mrs Bruce had their windows smashed for not showing enough enthusiasm for the British victory. Drennan wished that the victory might bring peace and healing but he was enough of a realist to know that the pretensions of both sides would prevent peace for some time.

The divisions in Dublin between the loyalists and those who opposed the war led to the blackening of King William's statue in College Green on 3 November, the eve of the King's birthday. The loyalist faction rectified the matter and it was soon adorned with more orange ribbons than ever for the birthday ceremony. Drennan had always thought King William the best of men and he thought this instigation of bigotry was a disgrace to his name. He felt moved to transcribe word for word a contrast composed by Thomas Somerville between William and Charles II.

In the character of Charles II, we are struck with the brilliancy of his wit and gracefulness of manners, destitute of one ingredient of principle or virtue with politeness affability, gaiety good humour, everything that captivates imagination or gives delight at the moment. In the character of William, we turn our eyes to sterling merit, naked and unadorned, to stern integrity, incorruptible patriotism, unshaken fidelity, but no splendid dress or gaudy trappings to arrest the attention of the superficial observer.[2]

Somerville goes on to assert that Charles, with all his vices, was beloved when he lived and lamented when he died, whereas William, with all his virtues, never obtained the affection of his subjects. Martha knew that her brother's regard for King William had a great deal to do with his belief that he himself was a person of stern integrity, incorruptible patriotism, unshaken fidelity who could not easily win affection. She remarked wryly that such a character becomes a king better than a private individual who had to make his fortune amongst equals.[3]

At the close of 1805, Martha reported that her ageing mother was very weak. She was rising for only two hours each night, and sleeping and eating were her only comforts. The old woman would be pleased to go.[4] She was very well looked after by Nancy and she finally passed away on 25 January 1806 in her eighty-eighth year. Sad as Drennan was at her passing, he regarded it as a blessing for Nancy whose faithful and unremitting attention over the years had helped her mother to reach 'such a great age with so few calamities'.[5] He also knew that as he would be the main beneficiary of his mother's will, his long years of financial insecurity were over.

William Pitt died in the same week as Mrs Drennan and his passing raised new political possibilities. Drennan was amused that the man had 'after embroiling the world these past twenty years', declared on his death bed that 'he died in peace with all of mankind not excepting Bonaparte'. Martha described Pitt's last words as the 'unmeaning cant of vulgarity'. She described them as the sort of thing the murderer says under the gallows. Far better for Pitt if he could have said 'I hope or believe I have not an enemy as I am not sensible of having deserved one.'[6]

Drennan's assessment of Pitt was that he had come into high office too young before he had any settled principles of action. Pitt was not himself corrupt but 'this was poor praise as he had connived with others' (who presumably were). Pitt's pride had led him to employ new and incapable men for his underlings. Drennan must have been referring to the long war when he observed that Pitt could never distinguish between perseverance and obstinacy. He thought that perhaps Castlereagh would take over and that there would be a blind adherence to the same system. He concluded rather optimistically as it turned out that 'this face cannot continue for long'.[7]

In fact, Castlereagh did not inherit Pitt's place and a new 'Ministry of all the Talents' was formed under Lord Grenville with a place in the cabinet for Charles J. Fox. Martha strongly urged her brother that this was the time to return to political writing. She advised him to 'command the notice of those who will now preside. Now or never, and forever establish on honorable and safe ground the consistency and accredited justness of your political character. Write somewhat for the purpose, which will raise expectation, at the time the press is yet dumb, take care to answer it by important matter, manly truths, energetic glowing style, just praise and softened censure'.[8]

Drennan responded that, while the temperature of the times had considerably cooled, so had his zeal which he felt would carry him no further than a letter to the new viceroy. If he were to write, he would explain as an independent Whig how the people of the North had been driven into exaggerated principles and exasperated passions. He would suggest that a return to genuine Whiggish principles was the best safeguard of the peoples' rights and the citadel of the constitution. In the event, Bernard Trotter (1774–1818), a friend of Drennan and the editor of the *Evening Herald*, a new paper in Dublin, was called to England to work as Charles J. Fox's private secretary. Martha suggested that his letter should be addressed and sent to Charles J. Fox via Trotter.

Drennan started work at once, though at the time he was involved in a laborious attendance on a very sick woman and child. He managed to save the woman but not the child. Yet he produced a forty-page letter to Fox which he sent to Trotter and he sent an advertisement to the newspapers and the sheets to some friends to have it published in London. He thought his efforts on this occasion dull and dry but Sarah, who read some of it, did not agree.

Soon thereafter Drennan received a note from John Bernard Trotter:

> I received your letter with true pleasure as it showed you had not forgotten me ... and gratified the wish I had immediately formed on seeing your pamphlet announced in the Irish papers. I shall myself put it in Mr. Fox's hand. I have read it with much pleasure and sympathise with its whole tenor. Ireland has in truth been the victim under Mr. Pitt's administration of all the worst passions, of the worst men she had.[9]

Drennan began his letter with his assertion that the country and particularly the North, had been 'driven into exaggerated principles and exasperated passions'.

He next suggests the need for a return to genuine Whiggish principles as the safeguard of the peoples' rights and the citadel of the constitution.[10]

Drennan greatly admired Fox, whom he held to be 'an impregnable stronghold of honesty and honour'.[11] He had once hailed him as 'the tutelary genius of the British Constitution'.[12] Fox had always opposed the war with France. In 1798, both men had agreed to give evidence at the trial in Kent of their mutual friend Arthur O'Connor. Fox detested the way the Rebellion had been put down and expressed his great affection for his first cousin Lord Edward Fitzgerald, Drennan's friend who had died in the Rebellion.[13]

Drennan was clearly pleased that Fox was coming into office at an 'auspicious period when men are no longer nicknamed out of their livelihoods'.[14] He opened with a bitter attack on the Irish administration, accusing it of 'such ministerial denunciations, such privileged slander and vulgar calling of names by people in high station [which] contaminated and corrupted as it descended through the different classes of society'.[15]

Drennan introduced himself to Fox as an independent Whig and a Protestant Dissenter. He assures Fox that the Protestant Dissenters of the North, many of whom have the mixed occupation of farmers and weavers, are also Whigs. Their reformed Presbyterianism is supported on two pillars – the inalienable right to private judgement and an inflexible resistance to religious authority in matters of religion between God and man.[16]

Drennan then turns to the question of the *Regium Donum* which he asserts turns ministers of religion into government pensioners. He suggests that it is a slow poison poured into the Protestant Dissenting church.[17] Perhaps Drennan was hoping for Fox's help to undermine Castlereagh's *Regium Donum* scheme which we have seen previously was designed to change the temper of the Presbyterian Synod.

Looking back over several administrations in the reign of George III, Drennan assures Fox that the sentiments of the North of Ireland were in opposition for the whole of the reign. 'Lord Bute (1713–1792) had trenched on the liberty of the subject and Lord North (1732–1792) trenched on our fellow subjects in America.' When the Tory administration waged war on America, it confirmed the attachment of the North to Whig principles.[18]

Drennan reminded Fox that he had pronounced the way the Union had been accomplished was most disgraceful. However 'the Union could be restored only when the people were restored to a fair representation'.[19] Drennan goes on to explain what had happened in Ireland and how the Tories had caused an unnecessary war with France by their panic reaction to the French Revolution. In the process, Drennan directs his barbs at Castlereagh for the discord in Ireland and at Edmund Burke for the long and continuing war with France.

In relation to Ireland, Drennan identifies 'the defection of the popular leaders from the cause of the people as the primary source of the civil discord and general disaffection'.[20]

> No particular event was the cause of greater irritation and more deeply graved in the memory than the defection of a young man of a much-loved Whig family,[21] whose election had been gained by the indefatigable exercise and activity of popular agents but who shortly thereafter threw off his coat of patriotism ... for his name is immortalised as an Irishman in and by the degradation and extinction of his country.[22]

Recalling Fox's own warm welcome for the French Revolution, Drennan remarked how, at its origins, the revolution had 'gladdened everything that was great in human nature'.[23] The Tory administration had soon grown jealous and had raised a panic while the cornucopian eloquence of Burke became the trumpet of war.[24] Frequent disappointment regarding reform bred a distaste for the constitution which was the primary cause of civil discord and general disaffection in Ireland.[25] 'The whole propertied community set itself in party hostility against the mass of the inhabitants.'[26] Drennan then gave Fox an account of the emergence of the United Irish society:

> A new set of popular leaders from the middling ranks [emerged]. It was chiefly by the agency, by the good sense and liberality of these men ... a conquest was made of the religious antipathies long prevalent amongst the Presbyterians of the North and a correspondence entered into with their Catholic countrymen on the footing of a common country and a common right to its civil and political blessings.[27]

Drennan goes on to claim his authorship of the United Irish test but manages to do so without naming the body for which it was written. He tells Fox that the Tory administration began a system of vituperation in which, 'the veriest hireling of the press, the lowest cur of office deemed himself a chosen guardian of the State'.[28] The popular leaders became desperate and were impelled into a foreign intrigue and their followers into a rebellion.[29]

Drennan next adopts an optimistic tone when he says much is promised and doubtless more will be performed.[30] He believes the race of informers will perish in infamy and famine, the prison doors will be unbarred and that the unfortunate emigrants will be pardoned and allowed to return.[31] He believed he would see the papistical spirit of the Protestant Ascendancy put out of countenance. The press would be free again and the condition of the lower orders would be ameliorated through education. The Catholics would find their way to complete emancipation.[32] Despite this optimism, he still had fears. Tory principles were dominant for years past. A Whig majority in the House of Commons could only be achieved by an equal representation of the people in Parliament.[33]

Drennan's confidence and optimism were feigned for effect for, even as he wrote in March 1806, he knew that Fox was in poor health and he predicted that after Fox's death 'things will revert to the usual Toryism'.[34] Drennan was not at all surprised when Charles J. Fox died on 13 September 1806. Denys Scully (1773–1830), a Catholic barrister, had been meeting with Fox pressing him to support a petition in favour of the Catholics. He had kept Drennan fully informed of Fox's health. He also told him of the difficulties under which Fox laboured when he had been forced into office in a cabinet which would resist all notion of reform and concentrate all its efforts prosecuting the war against Napoleon. Scully told Drennan that when Fox met him, 'he never saw a man so embarrassed acting a part assigned to him against his own convictions'.[35]

Things did indeed revert to the usual Toryism after Fox's death, as Drennan predicted, and the race of informers did not perish in infamy and famine but rather died in their beds often unexposed and still in receipt of their pensions. Most of the unfortunate emigrants died in exile.[36] The battle for a free press went on and nothing was done to educate the lower orders. Catholics were denied the right to sit in parliament for another twenty-three years.

Within weeks of Fox's death, the Catholics of Dublin were again considering a petition and asked for Drennan's help with the wording. Drennan believed that the current administration would act like the former which could think of nothing but Napoleon. He read their draft and made a number of suggestions but felt those Catholics who were for pressing ahead with their demands had more zeal than ability if they were reduced to asking him to look at their intended petition. Even so, Drennan always responded positively to requests for assistance in seeking political rights for Catholics.

35

THE NATURAL LEADERS

William Drennan had never enjoyed his work in Dublin, nor had he ever managed to develop a practice which generated enough fees to meet the needs of his growing family. However, in 1807 he became financially independent following the death of Miss Young who bequeathed him a substantial legacy. Within a few months, he and his family moved to Belfast where he lived henceforth in moderate affluence. He was unburdened at last from the drudgery of his less than lucrative medical duties. Yet he had no intention of retiring quietly from public affairs to enjoy his new-found prosperity. The public spirit of the North seemed to him 'dead and rotting like their flax when steeping in holes and ditches'. This he attributed 'to the literary talents of Belfast displayed in their vapid newspapers etc'.[1] When Drennan returned to his home town, he was a man with a mission.

He quickly gravitated towards a formidable coterie of committed radicals who were involved in a set of projects and endeavours all of which were linked to their reform agenda. He joined the Society for Promoting Knowledge, he founded the *Belfast Monthly Magazine* and the Belfast Academical Institution and helped to found the Historic Society and the Friends of Civil and Religious Liberty. From the outset, Drennan's energy and talent commanded a position of pre-eminence amongst his associates and Ian McBride tells us Presbyterian radicalism rediscovered its most articulate voice.

The notables Drennan worked with included former Volunteers and veteran reformers, John Barnett and James Munfoad. In the circle also were John Hancock and John Templeton both of whom we have encountered in relation to the Thomas Russell and Dr McDonnell affair. William Tennent, the former United Irishman and State prisoner, and his brother Robert were also involved. A.H. Thornton has described this group as a faction who 'assumed the office of dictators of the people and directors of public opinion declaring themselves at one point to be "the natural leaders of the people"'.[2]

For all Drennan's varied involvement in the civic affairs of Belfast, there was one society he shunned. He had received an invitation from William Bruce to join the Belfast Literary Society. He held aloof not only because, as he told his sister, 'it is now composed only of Bruce, Cupples[3] of Lisburn, Joy, McDonnell and Stephenson, and I hear they do not do much good in any way'.[4] Rather, 'he did not want to publicly ally himself with the moderates who formed the core of its membership'.[5] Bruce had founded his Literary Society in 1801. As we have seen, John Templeton, who was a founder member, withdrew because he no longer wanted to associate with Dr McDonnell. Given the sentiment which Drennan expressed in *Epitaph – on the living*, it is likely he would have had a similar aversion to McDonnell's company.

The Belfast Society for Promoting Knowledge was a subscription library established in 1788 and is commonly known today as the Linen Hall Library. Thomas Russell was appointed Librarian in 1794 and carried out his pleasant if not very arduous duties until September 1796 when Lord Castlereagh arrived in town. His Lordship carried warrants for the arrest of Russell, Samuel Neilson, Henry Joy McCracken and five other prominent board members of the society. The library was broken open in the search for Russell and Neilson, who eventually surrendered, and they were taken in chains to Kilmainham. Despite the subsequent executions of McCracken and Russell, the library was not suppressed perhaps because, in the absence of the imprisoned radicals, William Bruce came into the ascendancy, becoming president in February 1798.[6] Bruce had joined the Yeomanry and was known to be loyal to government and this perhaps saved the society from suppression. Drennan became involved with the society in 1807 and 'gave valuable service as both a committee member and a benefactor'.[7]

Within a few weeks of his arrival in Belfast, Drennan embarked on what was to prove the most successful and enduring of his public projects, the founding of the Belfast Academical Institution. He had long regarded a national education system as important. In September 1807, he responded to an advertisement calling a meeting to discuss the establishment of a new academy. He was anxious to do what public service he could 'to the interest of education' in his 'native country and town'.[8] The meeting which Drennan attended at the Exchange rooms was a follow-on from a gathering at the same venue the previous year when a group of merchants agreed that: 'the extending commerce and extending population of Belfast render a high-class school expedient and necessary. The general outline only is stated. The object is said to have first been stated by the unfortunate Thomas Russell in the preceding century and now in 1806 it was brought to an issue by a few Belfast merchants.'[9]

This meeting took place in June, just thirty-two months after Thomas Russell had been publicly executed at Downpatrick as a traitor. It is clear that some of the respectable and opulent citizens of Belfast retained a great affection for his memory and were apparently not afraid to put it on the public record. No doubt Drennan would have felt at home in such company. The second meeting which Drennan attended appointed a committee of twenty-two to carry on the business and, within a few days, they had collected a sum of £5,728 by public subscription.[10] The committee was delighted and issued a florid statement that was most likely composed by Drennan:

> We do not want to indulge in fanciful expectation, yet the preset occasion authorises to cherish a well-grounded hope, that instead of sending our youth to procure the necessary qualifications for a learned profession in foreign universities, a seminary now is about to be raised amongst ourselves which will revive the ancient spirit of learning that this town may be a center from which the lessons of science may emanate, not only illuminating the scholar and speculative philosopher, but enlightening the husbandman, the manufacturer, and the artisan, and guiding their steps to new discoveries and improvements in every path of human knowledge.[11]

The Marquis of Donegall granted eight statute acres of very well-located land and the foundation stone was laid in July 1810.

The Belfast Academical Institution project was 'astonishingly ambitious'.[12] The school, which came to be known colloquially as the 'Inst', was opened as a grammar school in 1814. When it enrolled collegiate students the following year, it became the first university to be established in the British Isles since Trinity College Dublin was founded at the end of the sixteenth century.[13]

The school was founded and, to some extent, run by former United Irishmen and their sympathisers.[14] Drennan worked with William Tennent (1760–1832) and Robert Simms (1761–1843), former state prisoners, and Robert Caldwell and William Simms (1763–1843), former proprietors of the *Northern Star*, Dr Robert Tennent, William's brother, and the Reverend Henry who was suspected of complicity in the Rebellion.[15]

Arthur Wellesley (1769–1852), despite 'pressing engagements in the [Iberian]Peninsula had become chief Secretary to the Lord Lieutenant in 1808'.[16] He denounced the school even before it opened its doors as a 'democratical establishment' which would be pervaded by 'the republican spirit of the Presbyterians'.[17] Lord Castlereagh and Robert Peel, the Irish chief secretary, were very concerned at the influence Drennan and the other democrats wielded in the management of the new venture.[18] Castlereagh was mainly concerned about the link between the Institution and the Synod. As the former was to have the power of granting certificates of qualification to the Presbyterian ministry, he regarded this as 'a deep-laid scheme by Dr. Drennan and his associates to bring the Presbyterian Synod into the ranks of democracy'.[19] He wanted the link broken and the 'Inst' remodelled to give the government a right of veto over the appointment of teachers.[20]

Bruce and Black were also hostile from the outset. Bruce, who was principal of the Belfast Academy, saw it as unwelcome competition to his own school, and Black was contemptuous of the 'classical republican' governance structure, which he remarked, reminded him of the French Constitution.[21] In spite of the hostility of these influential ministers, the Synod welcomed the new college because aspiring ministers no longer needed to travel to Scotland to train for the ministry.[22] When, in 1815, the Synod formally agreed to a connection with the Inst, the college secured an annually renewable grant from a very reluctant government.[23]

The formal opening took place on 1 February 1814. George Benn tells us that 'Dr Drennan was the principal speaker and addressed the audience with his accustomed eloquence and power.'[24] Drennan used the occasion to define the progressive ethos of the new establishment.[25] He told his listeners that the new college would be a place where 'liberal ingenious men, uniting their labours, without regard to nation, sect, or party in one grand pursuit alike interesting to all, by which mental prejudice may be worn off, the youth entrusted to their care will be stimulated to the pursuit of knowledge and the practice of virtue'.[26]

Drennan went on to thank the public for its support and identified them as the new school's best patron.[27] He promised that 'the mysterious veil that makes one knowledge for the learned and another for the vulgar ... would be torn down'. The fees would be 'as low as possible and some [students be] admitted gratuitously'.[28] The admission of scholars would be 'perfectly unbiased by religious distinctions'.[29] Example rather than coercion would be the order of the day as 'motives of the mind are better for education that pains inflicted on the body, that example should teach better than manual correction or corporal punishment'.[30]

Robert Tennent was chairman of the 'Inst' board. On the eve of Saint Patrick's Day 1816, he presided at a radical dinner which was attended by some members of the staff, management and board of visitors of the school. Tennent spoke of passing on to a new generation the spirit of 1782 and 1792. The former relates to the hey-day of the Volunteers and the latter to that of the United Irishmen. Tennent's speech was followed by many 'unashamedly radical toasts'.[31]

Drennan, William Tennent and John Hancock were saluted for their skills and libertarian principles as well as their services to the cause of parliamentary reform and Catholic emancipation.[32] The French and South American revolutions were toasted but probably most controversial of all, was the salute to the United Irish exiles in America. The revellers lifted their glasses to 'The Exiles of Erin – may they find that protection under the wing of the republican eagle, which was denied them by the monarchical lion.'[33]

This provided just the opportunity the government and the enemies of the 'Inst' needed 'to put the reformers in their place'.[34] A few days after the festivities, an account of the event was published in the *Belfast Commercial Chronicle*. However, no names were mentioned. This anonymity was a source of great indignation to a correspondent to the *Belfast Newsletter* on 29 March. Although he himself hid behind the pseudonym '*A Detester of Faction*', he called for those present to be named.[35] He railed against United Irish exiles as 'traitors whom the mercy of a too lenient government had allowed to escape ... treason, damned spotted treason was the God of their idolatry ... Mr Editor a foul stigma has been cast on our town of Belfast'.[36]

Sir George Hill MP (1763–1839), who had initially been a supporter of the Inst, told the House of Commons that the principles of Paine and Priestley were being openly taught in Belfast.[37]

Drennan believed that Bruce and others in the Synod were the secret prompters of government in the affair.[38] When Bruce attacked the Inst using the pen name 'Presbyter', Drennan's response was scathing. He accused Bruce of attempting to:

> Create a rupture between the Synod and the Institution by giving credit to suspicions (in want of proofs) of disaffection, anarchy, religious and political confusion, in order to alarm the Reverend Body which has given its sanction to the Institution ... to prejudice the government against the continuation of the annual grant for there, there is the fountain from which these bitter waters flow.[39]

Castlereagh exerted considerable pressure on the proprietors of the 'Inst' and he was not placated when Robert Tennent, the visitors and managers who had attended the dinner were persuaded to resign. The Saint Patrick's Eve dinner affair was the excuse he was looking for but he overplayed his hand. The

271

proprietors of the 'Inst' were prepared to compromise but would not give in to Castlereagh's demand for the right of government to appoint two honorary visitors. He therefore withdrew the grant and threatened the Synod that it would lose the *Regium Donum* if it continued to support the 'Inst'.[40]

The Synod defied Castlereagh and appointed Reverend Samuel Hanna as Synod approved professor of Church History. Had Castlereagh followed through with his threat, his policy to use the *Regium Donum* to create 'a considerable internal fermentation' and 'a schism to change the temper' of the Synod would have been in ruins. He backed down and while the 'Inst' lost its grant, the Synod continued to receive the *Regium Donum*.[41]

The loss of the government grant was not fatal for the prospects of the 'Inst' due to the support received from Lord Moira (1754–1826), who was at that time Governor General of India. He had been one of the Whig members of Parliament who had been sympathetic to the Volunteer and United Irish movements.[42] He helped to raise £5,000 and the Belfast public reacted by making further subscriptions.[43] Some of the democrats saw the outcome of the Saint Patrick's Eve affair as a victory. In resisting Castlereagh, the Presbyterians had 'again revealed the spirit of defiance and democracy which had characterised their eighteenth-century forbears' and one enthusiastic commentator declared, 'the people of Belfast can claim ... they are themselves again'.[44] Ian McBride has interpreted the Saint Patrick Eve event as 'the most celebrated episode in the history of Presbyterian radicalism after the [1798] rebellion'.[45]

Despite the hostility of government, Castlereagh and his allies, Drennan and his radical friends succeeded in their two main objectives. They created a great college of higher education and a place where candidates for the Presbyterian ministry could be educated in Ulster. The education of Presbyterian ministers continued for more than thirty years until the opening of Queen's University, at which time, many of the academic staff transferred to the new institution. The 'Inst' continues as a great and much beloved school in the centre of Belfast, open to boys[46] of all creeds and backgrounds. On the notice board at the school gate, William Drennan's name is on proud display. This is one of four places where this author has seen Drennan's name in Belfast. There is a plaque at his birth place at First Presbyterian Rosemary Street, his headstone is in Cliftonville cemetery and he is the subject of a down-at-heel mural in the nationalist New Lodge Road.

36

BELFAST MONTHLY MAGAZINE

The Belfast Academical Institute stands as the most enduring of Drennan's lifetime achievements yet the *Belfast Monthly Magazine* (*BMM*), which he founded with John Hancock and Robert Tennent in 1808, must have required his greatest input of effort and energy. There is little doubt that his writing work gave him great pleasure. The *BMM* was a mammoth production and was published monthly for more than five years. The archive runs to thirteen volumes of over four hundred pages each. The first issue appeared in September 1808. Readers were promised that in its forthcoming issues 'pleasure would be rendered subsidiary to improvement' and that 'theological and intemperate political discussion would be excluded'.[1] The facts which give rise 'to those political differences which agitate the public mind must be recorded but if they require explanation these shall be always dictated by the spirit of true constitutional patriotism'.[2] The format of the magazine included biographical sketches, book reviews, ancient and modern literature, poetry, discoveries in art and manufacture, agricultural reports and a monthly retrospective on politics.

The monthly retrospective gave Drennan the scope to indulge his passion for political questions as did, to a lesser extent, the biographical sketches and book reviews. Drennan's contributions to the *BMM* were unswerving in support for reform and reformers in England. He published articles on John Horne Tooke, Major John Cartwright, Francis Burdett and other leading English reformers.[3]

J.J. Wright has described the *BMM* as 'the house journal of the natural leaders', his term for Drennan's radical circle. Drennan, early on, told his readers that:

We are not discouraged by the ill success which has attended the French Revolution, from wishing well to the cause of liberty and rational reform nor are we inclined to be led aside from our even steady course by loading the present French ruler [Napoleon] with abuse. We cannot but cherish the hope that if the people are true to themselves our political situation will be further amended.[4]

Through the nearly six years of the magazine's existence, Drennan was remarkably consistent in his polemics and priorities. The failure of the government to grant Catholic political rights loomed large, as did the folly of the ongoing war with France. Other regular themes were the need for a general education system,[5] freedom of the press[6] and the abolition of the slave trade.[7] The magazine often voiced its opposition to the Orange Order and Orangeism. The 1798 Rebellion was rarely mentioned and we shall see that on one occasion, when it was, the rebels were portrayed in a positive light.

Drennan always held the view that the way the Union had been foisted on Ireland was a disgrace but, in the *BMM*, he expressed the view that Ireland could be reconciled to the Union only if Catholic emancipation was conceded:

> If her manacles are shaken off, and she feels the British constitution maketh the sun to act with equal light and heat, she will become an ally of immense importance; if she is depressed and experience exclusion and coldness, no statesman can calculate on future times, and the neglect of home concerns may eventually turn the scale of things in the world.[8]

Henry Grattan was applauded for presenting a petition to the British House of Commons on behalf of the Catholics in 1810.[9] In the same issue, the *BMM* reasserted Drennan's long-held view that:

> The Catholics have long been in a state of proscription in these countries contrary to the principles of justice and sound policy. They have proven themselves capable of being good subjects and peaceable citizens. Speculative points of theology have little influence on conduct and the State ought to have no authority over opinions ... complete emancipation is their right.[10]

However, the *BMM* now argued that the concession of Catholic emancipation could serve to assimilate Catholics into the British constitution and thereby eliminate Catholic distinctiveness and the Irish feeling that still burns under the ashes of national independence. Drennan wrote that 'the fondest wish of our hearts may be obliterated, and we may say at least say to each of our children – Be Britons with all your souls – and forget that your father called himself an Irishman'.[11]

This is Drennan at his propagandist best. While proclaiming that Irish independence is the fondest wish of his heart, he assures the opponents of Catholic emancipation that the concession of it is the best way to end Catholic distinctives and any lingering desire for Irish independence. This is not to suggest he was insincere in his view that if equal constitutional rights were conceded that Irish radicals such as himself would not be more than happy to be assimilated into a free British Society.

The war with France had dragged on from 1793 with a few brief pauses but continued for most of the lifetime of the *BMM*. Drennan never ceased to denounce the war as a wasteful folly with no purpose.[12] This position was shared by most radical opinion in England at the time.[13] When the Common Council of Dublin blamed the ill-effects of the Union for bankruptcies in Dublin, Drennan strongly rejected their claim:

> Bankruptcies are no less frequent in England and other parts of Ireland confessedly not injured by the Union ... Whether this measure was good or bad in itself, the means by which it was brought about will stamp with disgrace on the actors in the page of history. The Common Council of Dublin must look further than the Union. The cause will be found in war.[14]

These and other similar comments by Drennan in the *BMM* have been taken as indicating that he was developing a nascent Unionism.[15] He had clearly come around to a tentative acceptance of the Union and recognised that it had 'a tendency to allay party feuds, and relieve us of some of the rough riding of our Irish unprincipled jockeys'. He argued that 'calls for repeal were misguided as it would create division amongst reformers in the two islands, they should join forces with their British allies to seek parliamentary reform as they had done at the time of the Volunteers'.[16]

The *BMM* attacked the Orangemen by stealing their clothes and claiming to be in the true Williamite tradition: 'We too are Orangemen but not of the modern tribe who adopt that appellation and who appear to be bred in the school of the furious and fanatical James, rather than the mild and magnanimous William. We are such Orangemen as good William would approve, hearty enemies to arbitrary power in any person, any party or religious persuasion.'[17]

Drennan was concerned about the pernicious effects of Orangeism upon social harmony and justice. On the other hand, he also had fears 'that Catholics might decide to pursue their own community interests while ignoring the greater goal of creating a common civil society'.[18] When, in 1811, a new Dublin newspaper published a prospectus which promised to cater for a specifically Catholic interest, Drennan regarded this as a negative development. The *BMM* warned the Catholics against 'cooperating with the errors, the follies and the crimes of past and present administrations in perpetuating a distinctness; a separating instead of an associating spirit'.[19]

There is, nowhere in the *BMM*, any indication that William Drennan had moderated his politics or regretted his past involvements. There is a discernible development of his thinking in that he came around to the view that the Union could develop in a positive way only if Roman Catholics could fully enjoy the freedoms of the British Constitution. He rarely mentioned dead United Irishmen but old comrades who were still living were always portrayed in a positive light.[20] For instance, in December 1816, *BMM* published letters which the great English reformer Dr John Jebb had addressed to Archibald Hamilton Rowan in 1784. Rowan, having been pardoned, had returned to Ireland in 1806 and was now living in comfort and prosperity between his three residences in Dublin, Kildare and his ancestral castle at Killyleagh in County Down. Drennan clearly felt that after thirty-two years, Jebb's advice to Rowan was still relevant to his readers and he was willing to allow the *BMM* to be publicly associated with the name of a notorious United Irishman who was known to have escaped the gallows only by escaping lawful custody.

One reference to the Rebellion appears in volume four, 1810, and takes the form of an address to the commanding officer of a district which had been under rebel control in 1798. 'Can we blame the trodden worm? It is said that they formed a conspiracy for a general massacre. No such disposition was apparent these two days that we of this town were entirely in their power ... They offered no injury to the officers' wives in my house nor the sick soldiers or officers' servants.'[21]

In February 1811, the *BMM* established a fund to support the imprisoned radical journalist Peter Finnerty. This story has been told in an earlier chapter and though Drennan insisted that the issue at stake was press freedom, it may have been his attempt to repay a debt of gratitude to Finnerty for his loyalty in 1798.

In July 1813, an Orange march was attacked by stone throwers when returning from Lisburn to Belfast. The marchers fired on their attackers shooting four people and killing two. J.J. Wright suggests that the attackers were Catholics but this is unlikely as the two dead men were Protestants.[22] Most likely the victims were Belfast Presbyterians who were at this point antagonistic to Orangeism. Drennan and his friends demanded a town meeting to discuss the situation. Thomas Verner, the town sovereign and himself an Orangeman, assisted by the Reverend Edward May, a former sovereign, tried to prevent a discussion of the matter by first adjourning a meeting in July and attempting to adjourn a second meeting in August. When Robert Tennent placed his hand on May's arm at the second meeting, he was dragged off to the Black Hole and was sentenced to three months in prison for assault. However, before Tennent's case came to court, the matter was complicated when he was asked for advice by the husband of one Jane Barnes, who wished to pursue a case against Verner for the alleged rape of his wife. According to the *BMM*, the prosecution tried to prejudice the jury against Tennent by publishing a biased account of Tennent's involvement in the rape case in the *Belfast News Letter* and taking care to ensure the jury members read it before the trial.[23]

Verner and May succeeded in their case against Tennent but the *BMM* published the details of the trial and the attempts to smear a man renowned for his peaceable quiet and remonstrative character. This was clearly a politically motivated prosecution. One good that came from the trial, according to the *BMM*, was that it 'established the right of the inhabitants of a town or other districts to meet for public purposes, if they do not act illegally the chief magistrate has no authority to dissolve the meeting at his pleasure'. However, Drennan was disgusted that when Tennent was released from Carrickfergus gaol there was no public demonstration or dinner in his honour. He lamented that some were spreading the contagion of timidity to destroy public spirit.[24]

Though Drennan had promised from the first that his comments on politics would be in the spirit of constitutional patriotism, this did not mean that he had become a moderate much less a loyalist. When the *BMM* reported on plans for a public dinner to celebrate the fiftieth anniversary of George III's coronation, Drennan wrote a short paragraph which neatly captures his view of the government he had lived under for the greater part of his life:

> The aldermen and other bloated capitalists who feel little of the weight of taxation ... may feast if they wish and shew their loyalty and eat their turtle at the same time, why call upon the people to rejoice? This has been a disastrous reign: – are we to rejoice at the separation of America by unwise councils; the abridgment of liberty, or the dreadfully oppressive increase in national debt, arising from the wars that have occupied half of the last 50 years?[25]

The last issue of *BMM* appeared in December 1814. It is not clear if its demise resulted from loss of public interest or whether Drennan and his friends could not sustain the vigour and intellectual energy required to regularly produce such a substantial body of work. Perhaps they were distracted by their attempts to appoint and attract scholars to staff their new university. In March 1815, Drennan published *Fugitive Pieces* in Belfast but it was also sold in Dublin and London.

37

LAST LETTERS AND DEATH

William Drennan became seriously ill with a liver complaint in late 1819. Shortly before being struck down with illness, he wrote two letters which give us a clear exposition of his political outlook as he moved nearer to the end of his days. Each letter dealt with an issue most dear to Drennan's heart. The first was addressed to Daniel O'Connell and dealt with the question of political rights for Catholics. The second was addressed to Martha in the aftermath of the Peterloo Massacre, an event which has come to be seen as a major turning point in the campaign for the reform of parliament in Britain.

His letter to O'Connell of 30 January 1819 was in the context of Drennan's belief that negotiations between the Irish Roman Catholic hierarchy and the British government were likely to lead to an agreement.[1] In return for the government having a veto over the appointment of Roman Catholic bishops, Catholic political rights would be secured and a *Regium Donum* scheme would be introduced for the Catholic clergy. He began by telling O'Connell that 'the whole matter is settled. The veto in operation already. Well you must balance the much you will receive against the comparatively little you will lose. The Catholic *Regium Donum* would[2] follow the Presbyterian *Regium Donum* but the love of laymen for liberty will overcome and quench the ecclesiastical proneness for prostration.'[3]

For years, Drennan had condemned the practice of the State pouring its 'slow poison' of the *Regium Donum* into the Protestant Dissenting churches, turning its clergy into placemen and government hacks. He was now warning O'Connell that the government was attempting to attach the Roman Catholic clergy to the state in a similar fashion. He expressed his confidence that the laymen could overcome the clergy on this matter. Drennan went on to compliment O'Connell and offer his support but also warned:

You will always act the honest part, not the poor spirited and aspiring character of the day. I would not condescend to compliment you or anyone without grounds, but I sincerely think that you possess many of the characteristics of Charles Fox in his manly spirit openness and candor, his ability and perhaps his gullibility, the weak part of an otherwise impregnable stronghold of honesty and honour. I was going to say to you odd as it might sound. Beware the goodness of your heart.[4]

He tried to put O'Connell on his guard and advised him to be wary of 'juggling and leger-de-main speculating politicians' but expressed his confidence that O'Connell would achieve his objectives and his name would be recorded in history.[5] To compare any political figure to his hero Charles Fox 'the titular genius of the British constitution' was praise indeed from William Drennan. His view that the state should have no role in any Christian church was a core Unitarian principle imbibed at his father's knee.

The last letter which Drennan sent to Martha is undated but is concerned with the massacre of working people by the 15th Hussars which took place at Saint Peter's Field in Manchester on 16 August 1819. A peaceful pro-reform meeting of some 70,000 working people had been attacked by drunken cavalry who killed several people and wounded as many as 700. Four years after the battle of Waterloo, the 'Peterloo' massacre became a major defining event in the emergence of the English working class.[6] Drennan had been reading the newspaper reports and expressed strong views about how the radicals should respond to the massacre:

> Sir F. Burdett seems to me to have sounded the tocsin, and to have urged the military to join the people in pretty plain language. If the law officers do not prosecute immediately, it shows the ministry are panic struck, and probably in that case a division will take place in the cabinet previous to the dissolution of the administration.

> If the meeting had not taken place at Smithfield the people would have lost ground. Cartwright was quite wrong. He has grown too old – most patriots and heroes live too long. The meeting challenged ministry, and they durst not repeat the Manchester mode of dispersion. Hence the conclusion must be (not withstanding the thanks of the Regent) that they repent of the steps taken, which was done, merely because they thought anything might be done, *in terrorem* against the lowest order. It is this contempt for the populace which will be the ruin of the gentry. The ministry would overlook anything that passed in a room but what happens on a heath or common,

or in a square, this they dread, and how can millions of people assemble but under a canopy of kites and crows.

Sir F. Burdett has come forward and, probably, the Whig leaders (Bedford, etc.) will appear at the Westminster meeting. This may give an impulse to the whole country, which, bye the bye, is as yet in greater part a looker-on, and if there be any relaxation on the part of the reformers, they, then the host of neutrality, will quietly go over to the ministry, who perhaps wish the Whigs to take a lead in order to keep the radicals down in public opinion, and this last meeting been given, I would I think be over with them.

A great meeting will take place at Liverpool today in a square of the moderate reformers, under umbrellas. Shepard, a clergyman and an excellent mob orator, is to be chairman. He is the son of a shoemaker. One reverend may counterbalance the three reverend ministers of the gospel who composed the active part of the Manchester magistracy. But with all these meetings there will only be words, no blows, unless there be listening to Burdett on the part of the army – that indeed would be a Hounslow Heath shout,[7] which would horrify all the Stewart race, here and elsewhere – but it will not happen. The resistance to taxes is the strongest arm of the people – stronger than pikes or poniards. The radicals should instantly join Burdett, not indulge in suspicions of him or call him down as desirous to run away with the game which they have hunted to the death – for this they have done, however abused. Yet Burdett's party is great and will add great strength. Disunion will lead to dispersion – Hunt ought to shake the hand of all who can help him. All is uncertain, and particularly whether we may not in November be glad of the shelter of the cabin rather than run to the capital.[8]

Francis Burdett MP (1770–1844) was a life-long reformer, who, like Drennan, had opposed the war with France from the beginning. He was a supporter of adult male suffrage, Catholic emancipation and had always opposed the slave trade. Burdett had been a very close friend of Arthur O'Conner and had helped Thomas Paine financially when he needed funds to emigrate to the United States of America. Drennan had followed Burdett's career with interest and had written many supportive articles in the *BMM*. In the event, Burdett was prosecuted for what Drennan described as his 'sounding the tocsin'[9] but Drennan was dead before the case came to court in March 1820.

Major John Cartwright (1740–1824) published his pro-reform pamphlet *Take your Choice* as early as 1779 and, in time, would come to be known as 'The Father of Reform'. He was also the subject of many favourable articles in the *BMM*. It is not clear why Drennan thought Cartwright was wrong on this occasion but it may have been that in February 1819, Cartwright had publicly attacked Burdett in what Cartwright's own biographer has described as a 'naïve, self-righteous and almost simple minded' fashion.[10]

It was to arrest Henry 'the Orator' Hunt (1773–1835), the Wiltshire gentleman farmer turned radical agitator, that the Manchester magistrates had ordered the attack on the unarmed citizens at Peterloo. The government stood by the drunken sabre-wielding murderers and the Prince Regent thanked the magistrates. Hunt, who was to spend two years in jail, was the only person charged over the affair.

Drennan's warning that at 'any relaxation on the part of the reformers, the host of neutrality, will quietly go over to the ministry' proved all too accurate.[11] John Belcham tells us:

> The moral and propaganda triumph of Peterloo proved a pyrrhic victory. Back in control the government asserted its power. Parliament was specially convened to pass Six Acts, an attempt to return to the narrow political participation of the eighteenth century: 'taxes on knowledge' were imposed on the press, and the right to public meetings was limited by a series of measures, prohibiting banners and flags and restricting attendance to those actually resident in a parish.[12]

His Peterloo letter to Martha was very probably the last that Drennan ever wrote. It is undated but was most likely written in September 1819 a few weeks before he became ill. Drennan retained his political radicalism to the end of his days. He is in sympathy with the most radical section of the British reform movement but realises that, for it to make progress, it must unite with the moderates. The theme of the need for the strength that comes from union and the need to avoid disunion was a constant from when he first joined the Volunteers through his involvement with the Society of United Irishmen. His sympathy for the lowest order of the people had always been evident from his earliest political writing to his last.

Drennan's son William tells us his father was never a robust man and that in the winter of 1819, his health began to seriously decline. He removed to Martha's house in Belfast where, after considerable suffering, he passed away on 5 February 1820.

The Belfast Newsletter, which had often published Drennan's writings, carried this report of his death.

Dr. William Drennan M.D.

It is our painful duty to record the death of this very honorable gentleman which took place at the home of his sister Mrs McTier on Saturday last in the 65th year of his age. We shall not now presume to portray his character but cannot let the opportunity pass without paying our sincere tribute of respect to his memory.

Possessed of an ardent and disinterested love of his native country, he fearlessly advocated her cause in the worst of times and those who might differ from him in opinion on public affairs the admiration [word unclear] which evinced on every occasion the accomplished scholar the well-bred gentlemen and the conscientious patriot.

His attachment to his native town was shown in his zeal for its public establishments to which he devoted much of his time and occupied much of his attention until the last moments of his existence. Though we have seen him at his fire-side excising all the aimable perfection of social life we must leave to those who are better acquainted the duty of displaying his inestimable qualities as a husband, father, a friend in which he was equally distinguished as in public life.[13]

William Drennan was taken to the New Burial ground in Belfast on Tuesday 8 February. On the way, the procession stopped for a few minutes at the gates of the Belfast Academical Institution in accordance with his dying wish. His long-standing request that his remains be carried to the grave by six Catholics and six Protestants was complied with. The *Newsletter* reported that clergymen of every denomination attended along with a very large and respectable assembly of friends and inhabitants. William Drennan junior observed that no carriages were present but there was a large attendance of people of the lower orders.

CONCLUSION:
REVOLUTION, REFORM AND VIOLENCE

All his adult life William Drennan walked with the ghost of his father. The beckoning spectre of Reverend Thomas Drennan had a significant influence over his son's religious and political principles and practice. They both agreed that there is no earthly authority in religious matters and no one should suffer civil penalties for their religious opinions. These guiding values inspired William Drennan's activities within the United Irish movement and sustained his energy in the cause of political rights for Catholics. However, the Catholic question, while important for Drennan, was but an aspect of what for him was the fundamental issue. His main political objective was to achieve a more equal representation of the people in parliament. This objective had long been shared by Protestant Dissenters and radical Whigs in both Ireland and England.

William Drennan was a more advanced republican and had many more radical views than he was usually prepared to expound in print. As a student, he and his friends wished that 'all the tyrants in Europe had but one neck, that neck laid on the block and one of us appointed executioner'.[1] Among his 'ancestral ghosts' were Marcus Brutus, who had assassinated the would-be tyrant Julius Caesar, John Milton, who had hailed the execution of Charles I, and Algernon Sydney and William Lord Russell, executed for treason against Charles II.[2] Another of his heroes was John Hampden who died on the battlefield fighting for Parliament in the English Civil War. Drennan and some of his Belfast associates celebrated the anniversary of the execution of Charles I and toasted that the tyrant may tremble at the day.[3] These sentiments may have been shared by other radicals who were steeped in the tradition of the Real Whigs or Commonwealthmen.

However, Drennan had an attitude towards and a concern for the common people which was unusual for its time. To Edmund Burke the hard-working common people were the swinish multitude, to Francis Higgins they were a beggary of no value or estimation. Even Henry Grattan asked the Volunteers when they allowed working people to join if they were now the armed beggary of Ireland? Drennan, from his earliest writing, expressed enthusiasm for the revolutionary potential of the lower orders and clearly expressed sympathy for their suffering and had always advocated that their living conditions be improved. He repeated time and again throughout his life that the lower orders should have access to education. He always deprecated 'the mysterious veil' which posits 'one sort of knowledge for the learned and another for the vulgar'.[4] Nor did he have any horror of the common people engaging in violence on their own behalf. He felt the mob, unless motivated by religion, usually only engaged in violence when such violence was necessary.

When Drennan wrote, he did so as a literary propagandist and not as a political philosopher. Whether writing as a Volunteer, United Irishman or Natural Leader he usually adopted his polemic to a heterodox audience in order to promote a unity of purpose which he believed increased the power of the people. He always strove to avoid division amongst those he was addressing. Although he was himself an enthusiastic supporter of the American cause, he advised the Volunteers not even to speak of the American question. He knew of the potential for disunion between those Volunteers who thought like himself and others who had joined the ranks to defend their country against invasion by America's allies, France and Spain.

By 1789, the prospects for a more equal representation of the people in parliament looked decidedly bleak. The heady days of what Drennan called the Revolution of '79 had given way to despondency and disappointment. The Whig opposition had deserted the cause of reform and the Castle administration was not inclined and felt no need to grant concessions. The Volunteers had become politically irrelevant due to the timidity of Charlemont. Then came news from Paris, in August 1789, which Wolfe Tone said changed everything in an instant. It certainly changed William Drennan's state of mind.

The French Revolution shook Drennan out of his ennui and set him off in a much more active direction. He concluded there could be no reform, no freedom in Ireland without separation from Britain. He planned to set up a secret institution 'to assassinate the tyrant Britain' and he stated that 'reform to be anything must be revolution and revolution must be reform'. Nothing short of a convulsion would throw off the incumbency of national political and civil grievances. Nor would Drennan shirk from violence for he declared 'the people can seldom be mistaken in their judgement and if they are violent it is because violence is necessary'.[5]

This, however, was set down in a private letter to his friend William Bruce. His public writing polemics and addresses never mentioned revolution, separation or violence by the people. Drennan had established a formidable reputation as a writer in the radical cause long before he attended his first committee meeting of the Dublin United Irish Society. He came to that meeting with a carefully worded test that he had obviously taken time and care in preparing. His test required the members of the new Society to strive for an impartial and adequate representation of the Irish nation in Parliament and to forward a brotherhood of affection amongst Irishmen of every creed.

When this test was adopted unanimously, it placed Drennan in a very influential position within the Society. It is clear from the reports of the informer Collins that, from the beginning, the bulk of the Dublin Society's addresses, statements, leaflets, resolutions and letters thereafter came from Drennan's 'dangerous' pen.[6] Careful and prudent as he tried to be, Drennan's pen exposed himself and others, including Thomas Muir and Archibald Hamilton Rowan, to prosecution. On one occasion, in 1792, when he threw caution to the wind and drafted a Bastille Day address to the National Assembly of France from the Citizens-Soldiers of Belfast, his pen posed a great danger to his native town.

At that time, the Duke of Brunswick was leading his Prussian and Austrian troops towards Paris threatening the city's destruction while pike-wielding sans culottes swarmed into the Tuileries to threaten their King. In adopting Drennan's address, Belfast's citizen soldiers wished success to the armies of France and denounced the impudent despots of Europe. King George was about to join the impudent despots in a war of annihilation against the Revolution. Within a few weeks of Britain entering the war in early 1793, Belfast was dragooned and occupied by government troops.

Many of the reformers in Ireland and England who welcomed the French Revolution were appalled by the September massacres of prisoners in Paris and the execution of the King. While Drennan would have openly condemned the murders, he tacitly approved of them because he felt they were necessary to protect the citizens of Paris and the Revolution. Not only did Drennan support the execution of the King, he advocated it as a desirable necessity if the Revolution was to be saved.

Claims that Drennan was severely chastened by his night in prison and trial cannot be sustained. There is no evidence that after his trial Drennan had developed 'a distaste for the more extreme views in politics'.[7] He had promised not to risk himself where he did not see it as 'absolutely necessary'.[8] Yet, within a short time, he wrote an open letter to Lord Fitzwilliam in which he declared himself a United Irishman, even though that body had very recently been raided and dispersed by the sheriffs. If, after his trial, he appeared to be standing 'aloof from the radicals' that was probably because he 'was well aware that any involvement on his part [if it were known] would have been suicidal'.[9] His avoidance of 'petty plotting' and 'mole work' should not be taken as an indication, as has been alleged, of 'his growing disaffection with the United Irish movement as armed revolution supplanted literary propaganda'.[10] In reality, there was no supplanting of literary propaganda by the United Irish movement. In the months leading up to the Rebellion, the propaganda continued in the pages of the *Press* and *Paddy's Resource*. We know that Drennan was involved. The question is now how deeply involved was he? The evidence adduced here suggests that he was 'Marcus', the author of a 'malicious and seditious' libel against the Earl of Camden.[11] The authorities tried hard but failed to identify Marcus. If Drennan was indeed Marcus, he was as committed to the Rebellion as any of his comrades.

Drennan was proud to acknowledge his authorship of *Erin* and *The Wake of William Orr* in later and safer times. It is also clear that he had a great deal of contact with William Sampson in the weeks before the *Press* was suppressed. Francis Higgins and the other informers' reports of Drennan's involvements and activities before the Rebellion may be fabrications. No one has ever suggested that Francis Higgins was anything other than well-informed. Further, we know that Higgins' information about Finnerty and Stockdale's involvement with the *Press* and Drennan's and Sampson's authorship of some of the material in *Paddy's Resource* was accurate. It is safe to say that Dublin Castle always regarded Higgins as a good source so perhaps the question that remains relates to why was Drennan not arrested in 1798.

The Castle administration was expecting a French invasion. The authorities had unleashed a reign of terror on the common people to provoke a premature rebellion and their gaols were overflowing with those they considered dangerous leaders of the conspiracy. Informers were inundating the Castle with information. It may have been, as Tom Bartlett suggests, that Dublin Castle was suffering from information overload.[12] However, another possibility strongly suggests itself. Higgins had been giving the Castle detailed information about the meetings of the Directory at the heart of the conspiracy and often named Fitzgerald, O'Connor, Bond, the Sheares brothers, Jackson and Sampson as being present. He never placed Drennan at any of these key meetings. All he ever accused Drennan of was drafting a letter to the Northern Presbyterians, involvement in establishing the *Press* and contributing to *Paddy's Resource*. As nobody at the time identified William Drennan as Marcus, it might have been Drennan's good fortune that he was able to deceive the Castle just as he has managed to mislead historians regarding his activities in early 1798.

The charges against Drennan of anti-Catholic bigotry and racism do not stand up to scrutiny. Drennan resented and mistrusted some members of the Catholic Committee. However, from 1784 until his death thirty-six years later, there is an abundance of evidence to sustain Drennan's claim that, in him, the Catholics of Ireland 'had not a more constant friend'.[13]

We have seen that when Drennan returned to Belfast, he rapidly emerged as the most articulate voice of Presbyterian radicalism. He became the leading figure amongst a coterie of radicals and former United Irishmen whom J.J. Wright has dubbed the Natural Leaders. Through their broad range of activities including the establishment of the 'Inst' and the *BMM*, the Natural Leaders continued to vigorously pursue their reform agenda.

Ulster Presbyterianism was riven by internal dispute and controversy in the aftermath of the 1798 Rebellion. The tensions manifested as organisational and Church governance issues, such as the distribution of as the *Regium Donum*. We have seen that the *Regium Donum* dispute was a deliberate attempt by Castlereagh to bring about a schism which he hoped would damage what he called the democratic party. His allies Robert Black and William Bruce worked hard for Castlereagh without necessarily knowing his motives. Their promotion of the *Regium Donum* and their opposition and hostility to the Belfast Academical Institution had little to do with Church governance, religion or education and everything to do with politics. Specifically, the undercurrent of these disputes was about the differing attitudes of loyalists and democrats to the Rebellion. The slow poison which Castlereagh and his allies poured into the Synod finally produced the desired schism long after Castlereagh, Black and Drennan were dead. It is a strange irony that the schism which drove the democrats from the Synod in 1826 took the form of a theological debate about Socinianism. The loyalism of William Bruce did not protect him from expulsion from the Synod along with his fellow Unitarians.

Through his writings in the *BMM*, it is possible to discern a pattern of consistency and to trace how Drennan's thought developed in the last decade of his life. He was consistent in his support for reform and reformers and Catholic rights as well as in his opposition to the war and the slave trade. However, while the way the Union was brought about was continually denounced, he always rejected calls for a campaign for repeal of the Union.

In the early 1790s, Drennan had expressed privately the wish for a revolution to separate Ireland from England. In the *BMM*, he accepted that the fondest wish of his heart had been obliterated and the best way forward was to join with the English reformers in pursuit of parliamentary reform and to extend the rights of the British constitution to all the citizens of these islands. He deplored the rise of Orangeism and viewed the emergence of a distinct Catholic interest as a very negative development.

Drennan made his life's work the forwarding of a brotherhood of affection, the attainment of Catholic rights and a more equal representation of the people in parliament. He did not live to see any of this come to pass. Catholic emancipation finally came about in 1828, far too late for it to have had any potential to decrease religious animosity in Ireland. While the great Reform Bill of 1832 made some changes for the better, it would take the mass mobilisation of the English working class by the Chartists in the 1840s to bring about adult male suffrage.

The union of Irishmen which Drennan advocated evaporated as Orange Unionism and Catholic Nationalism went their separate ways in mutual animosity. Two hundred years have passed since William Drennan's death. In all that time, Drennan's home town of Belfast has known sectarian hatred and intercommunal tension, often exploding into murder and mayhem. The brazen walls of separation are no longer just the elegant metaphor honed by William Drennan. No, they are an ugly physical construct called with, no sense of irony, 'The Peace Wall'. These brazen walls of separation have been erected at the request of residents on both sides, to keep Belfast's most deprived citizens apart.

SOURCES

Primary Sources

Agnew, Jean, *The Drennan-McTier Letters*, 3 vols (Dublin, 1998, 1999).
Vane, Charles (ed.), *Memoirs and Correspondence of Viscount Castlereagh*, 13 vols (London, 1848–54).

Royal Irish Academy, Dublin

Special list/Liosta speiseialta AO36-The Dublin Unitarian Church Collection.

Trinity College Library

Letter to the Right Honorable William Pitt (Dublin, 1799).
Letter to the Right Honorable Charles J. Fox (Dublin, 1806).
The Belfast Monthly Magazine, 13 vols (1808–1814).
Trial of Mr. Peter Finerty: late printer of the Press, for a libel against his excellency Earl Camden, Lord Lieutenant of Ireland: in a letter signed Marcus in that paper (Dublin, 1798).

Public Record Office of Northern Ireland

Duffin, Brian, *The Gentle Jacobin* (unpublished, 1977), PRONI T/965.

BIBLIOGRAPHY

Books

Barrington, J., *Personal Sketches and Recollections of His Own Times* (Dublin, 1997).

Bartel, R., *Liberty and Terror in England: Reactions to the French Revolution* (Boston, 1965).

Bartlett, T. (ed.), *Theobald Wolfe Tone: Memoirs, journals and political writings, compiled and arranged by William T.W. Tone* (Dublin, 1998).

——— (ed.), *Revolutionary Dublin 1795–1801: The Letters of Francis Higgins to Dublin Castle* (Dublin, 2004).

Bartlett, T., Dickson, D., Keogh D., Whelan, K. (eds), *1798: A Bicentenary Perspective* (Dublin, 2003).

Belchem, J., *Popular Radicalism in Nineteenth Century Britain* (London, 1996).

Benn, G., *A History of the Town of Belfast from 1799–1810*, 2 vols (Belfast, 1880).

Bew, J., *The Glory of Being Britons* (Dublin, 2009).

——— *Castlereagh: Enlightenment, War and Tyranny* (London, 2011).

Brooke, P., *Ulster Presbyterianism: The Historical Perspective 1610–1970* (Dublin, 1987).

Brown, M., *The Irish Enlightenment* (Cambridge, 2016).

Burke, R., *Empire and Revolution* (Princeton, 2015).

Byrne, P., *Lord Edward Fitzgerald* (London, 1955).

Champion, J., *Republican Learning: John Toland and the Crisis of Christian Culture* (Manchester, 2003).

Carroll, D., *The Man from God Knows Where: Thomas Russell 1767–1803* (Dublin, 1995).

———*Unusual Suspects: Twelve Radical Clergy* (Dublin, 1998).

Chart, D.A., *The Drennan Letters* (Belfast, 1931).

Clifford, B. (ed.), *William Drennan: Selected Writings*, vols I, II (Belfast, 1998).

Connolly, S.J. (ed.), *Political Ideas in Eighteenth-Century Ireland* (Dublin, 2000).

——— *Divided Kingdom: Ireland 1630–1800* (Oxford, 2008).

Cookson, J.E., *The Friends of Peace: Anti-War Liberalism in England 1793–1815* (London, 1982).

Curtin, N.J., *The United Irishmen: Popular Politics in Ulster and Dublin 1791–1798* (Oxford, 1998).

Dawson, K.L., *The Belfast Jacobin: Samuel Neilson and the United Irishmen* (Kildare, 2017).

Derry, J.W., *Castlereagh* (Edinburgh, 1976).

Dickson, D., Keogh, D. and Whelan, K., *The United Irishmen: Republicanism, Radicalism and Rebellion* (Dublin, 1993).

Dolan A., *Reinterpreting Emmet: Essays on the Life and Legacy of Robert Emmet* (Dublin, 2007).

Drennan, W., *The Wake of William Orr, 1797* (Dublin, 1938).

Drummond, W.H., *The Autobiography of Archibald Hamilton Rowan* (Dublin, 1840).

Elliott, M., *Wolfe Tone: Prophet of Irish Independence* (Yale, 1989).

Fisher, J.R., *Royal Belfast Academical Institution* (Belfast, 1913).

Fitzpatrick, W.J., *The Secret Service under Pitt* (London, 1892).

——— *The Sham Squire and the Informers of 1798* (Dublin, 1865).

Geoghegan, P., *Robert Emmet: a Life* (Dublin, 2002).

Hall, G.R., *Ulster Liberalism, 1778–1876* (Dublin, 2011).

Hayter Hames, J., *Arthur O'Connor: United Irishman* (Cork, 2001).

Hill, J., *From Patriots to Unionists: Dublin Civic Politics and Irish Protestant Patriotism, 1660–1840* (Oxford, 1997).

Holmes, F., *The Presbyterian Church in Ireland: A Popular History* (Dublin, 2000).

Jacob, R., *The Rise of the United Irishmen* (Dublin, 1937).

Johnston, K.R., *Unusual Suspects: Pitt's Reign of Alarm and the Lost Generation of the 1790s* (Oxford, 2013).

——— *Joy Henry, Bruce William. Belfast Politics* (*Belfast*, 2010).

Keane, J., *Tom Paine: A Political Life* (London, 2009).

Kelly, R., *Bard of Erin: The Life of Thomas Moore* (Dublin, 2008).

Keogh, D., *The French Disease: The Catholic Church and Irish Radicalism* (Dublin, 1993).

Killen, J., *A History of the Linen Hall Library 1788–1988* (Belfast, 1990).

Larkin, J., *The Trial of William Drennan* (Dublin, 1991).

Lecky, W.H.E., *Ireland in the Eighteenth Century* (London, 1892).

Lock, F.P., *Edmund Burke:1784-1797*, vol. II (Oxford, 2009).

McDonagh, O., *O'Connell: The life of Daniel O'Connell* (London, 1991).

McBride, I.R., *Scripture Politics: Ulster Presbyterianism and Irish Radicalism in the Late Eighteenth Century* (Oxford, 1998).

——— *Eighteenth Century Ireland* (Dublin, 2009).

McDowell, R.B., *Proceedings of the Dublin Society of United Irishmen* (Dublin, 1998).

Madden, R.R., *The United Irishmen: Their Lives and Times* (Dublin, 2007).

McFarland E.W., *Ireland and Scotland in the Age of Revolution* (Edinburgh, 1994).

McGuiness P., *John Toland's Christianity Not Mysterious: Text, Associated Works and Critical Essays* (Dublin, 1997).

Mac Giolla Easpaig, S.N., *Tómás Ruiséil* (Baile Atha Cliath, 1957).

McMillan, William, 'Presbyterian Ministers in the Ulster Rising' in Swords, Liam (ed.), *Protestant, Catholic & Dissenter: The Clergy and 1798* (Dublin, 1997).

Millin S.S., *History of the Second Congregation of Protestant Dissenters in Belfast* (Belfast, 1900).

Mitchell, L.G., *Charles James Fox* (London, 1992).

Moody, T.W., McDowell, R.B. and Woods, C.J., *The Writings of Theobald Wolfe Tone, 1763–98*, 3 vols (Oxford, 2007).

Moore, Thomas, *The Life and Death of Lord Edward Fitzgerald* (London, 1832).

Murphy S., *Forgotten Patriot: Charles Lucas 1717–1771* (Bray, 2009).

Newsinger, J., *United Irishman: The Autobiography of Jemmy Hope* (London, 1992).

Norman, J., *Edmund Burke: Philosopher, Politician, Prophet* (London, 1988).

O'Donnell, R., *Robert Emmet and the Rebellion of 1798* (Dublin, 2003).

——— *Robert Emmet and the Rising of 1803* (Dublin, 2003).

Osborne, J.W., *John Cartwright* (London, 1972).

Power, P.C., *The Court Martials of 1798–99* (Kilkenny, 1997).

Quinn, J., *Soul on Fire: A life of Thomas Russell* (Dublin, 2002).

Robbins, C., *The Eighteenth-Century Commonwealth Man* (Harvard, 1959).

Roylance, K.C.B., *The English Radicals: A Historical Sketch* (New York, 1971).

Small, S., *Political Thought in Ireland 1776–1798* (Oxford, 2002).

Smyth, J., *Revolution, Counter-revolution and Union: Ireland in the 1790s* (Cambridge, 2000).

Stewart, A.T.Q., *A Deeper Silence: The hidden Origins of the United Irishmen* (Belfast, 1993).

Swords, L., *Protestant Catholic & Dissenter: The Clergy and 1798* (Dublin, 1997).

——— *A Stable Unseen Power* in *Essays Presented to Michael Roberts* (Belfast, 1976).

Tillyard, S., *Citizen Lord: Edward Fitzgerald 1763–1798* (London, 1998).

Walker C., *Reason and Religion in Late Seventeenth Century England* (London 2013).

Whelan, F., *Dissent into Treason: Unitarians, King-killers and the Society of United Irishmen* (Brandon, 2010).

——— *God Provoking Democrat: The Remarkable Life of Archibald Hamilton Rowan* (Dublin, 2015).

Witherow, T., *Historical and Literary Memorials of Presbyterianism in Ireland* (Belfast, 1879).

Woods, C.J., *The Diaries and Memoirs of Thomas Russell 1791–95* (Dublin, 1991).

Wright, J.J., *The 'Natural Leaders' and their World* (Liverpool, 2012).

Journals and Articles

Maher, M., 'Oliver Bond' in *Dublin Historical Record*, vol. xi (Dublin, 1950).

Metscher Thomas, 'Between 1789 and 1798: The "Revolution in the Form of Thought" in Ireland', *Études Irlandaises*, n°14-1, 1989.

Appendix 1
Pamphlets, Letters and Publications by William Drennan

A letter to Edmund Burke (1780).

An Address to the Volunteers of Ireland by the Author of an address to Edmund Burke (1781).

Letters of Orellana, an Irish Helot, to the seven northern counties not represented in the National Assembly of Delegates, held in Dublin, 1784, for obtaining a more equal representation of the people in the Parliament of Ireland (created 1785).

Letter to His Excellency Earl Fitzwilliam (1795).

Letter to the Right Honorable William Pitt (1799).

Second letter to the Right Honorable William Pitt (1799).

A Protest from one of the people of Ireland against a union with Great Britain (1800).

Letter to the Right Honorable Charles James Fox (1806).

Fugitive pieces in verse and prose (1815).

A Courteous Reply to the Remarks of Presbyter Relative to the Belfast Academical Institution (1816).

ENDNOTES

Introduction

1　Thomas Metscher, 'Revolution in the Form of Thought', *Études Irlandaises*, n°14-1, 1989, pp. 139–46, written between 1789 and 1798.

2　William Bruce and Henry Joy, *Belfast Politics: Thoughts on the British Constitution* (hereafter *Belfast*) (Belfast, 1794), p. 134.

3　William Drennan to McTier, January 1793, in Jean Agnew, *The Drennan-McTier Letters 1776–1819* (hereafter *Drennan-McTier*) , vol. II (Dublin, 1998, 1999), p. 460.

4　L.M. Cullen, 'The Internal Politics of the United Irishmen' in Dickson et al., *The United Irishmen: Republicanism, Radicalism and Rebellion* (hereafter *Republicanism, Radicalism and Rebellion*) (Dublin, 1993), pp. 179–80; Dáire Keogh, *The French Disease: The Catholic Church and Irish Radicalism* (hereafter *French Disease*) (Dublin, 1993), p. 103; D.A. Chart, *The Drennan Letters* (hereafter *The Letters*) (Belfast, 1931), p. 228; Jonathan J. Wright, *The 'Natural Leaders' and their World* (hereafter *Natural Leaders*) (Liverpool, 2012), p. 68.

5　James McGuire and James Quinn, *Dictionary of Irish Biography: From Earliest Times to 2002* (hereafter *DIB*) (Dublin, 2009), vol. III, p. 461.

6　Chart, *The Letters*, p. viii.

7　*Drennan-McTier*, vol. I, p. xxi.

8　Drennan to McTier, 21 March 1798, *Drennan-McTier*, vol. II, p. 380.

9　Drennan to McTier, 24 January 1799, *Drennan-McTier*, vol. II, p. 454.

10　W. Drennan to A. Drennan 13 August 1799, *Drennan-McTier*, vol. II, p. 517.

11　Drennan to McTier, 14 March 1796, *Drennan-McTier*, vol. II, p. 210; and William Drennan, *Letter to Charles J. Fox* (Dublin, 1806).

12　Drennan to McTier, 14 March 1796, *Drennan-McTier*, vol. II, p. 210.

13　John Larkin, *The Trial of William Drennan* (hereafter *Trial*) (Dublin, 1991), p. 125.

14　Drennan to McTier, 21 January 1794, *Drennan-McTier*, vol. II, p. 5.

15　Drennan to McTier, 18 April 1796, *Drennan-McTier*, vol. II, p. 227.

16　Charles Vane (ed.), *Memoirs and Correspondence of Viscount Castlereagh*, vol. IV, (London, 1848–54), pp. 224–6, Castlereagh to Addington, 21 July 1802.

17　Drennan to McTier, 9 August 1800, *Drennan-McTier*, vol. II, p. 619.

18　This was the coalition administration formed after the death of William Pitt in 1806.

19　*Drennan-McTier*, vol. III, p. xxv.

20　Gerald R. Hall, *Ulster Liberalism, 1778–1876* (Dublin, 2011), p. 59.

21　Ibid.

22　Peter Brooke, *Ulster Presbyterianism: The Historical Perspective 1610–1970* (hereafter *Ulster Presbyterianism*) (Dublin, 1987), p. 139.

Chapter 1

1   William Drennan (Junior), *William Drennan, Selected Writings: The United Irish years 1791–1798*, vol. II (Belfast, 1998), p. 11.

2   'Drennan, William', *Dictionary of National Biography* (hereafter *DNB*) (Oxford, 2004).

3   *Drennan-McTier*, vol. I, p. xi.

4   George Benn, *A History of the town of Belfast: From Earliest Times to the close of the Eighteenth-Century* (Belfast, 2008) (hereafter *Town of Belfast*), vol. I, p. 407.

5   A.T.Q. Stewart, *A Deeper Silence: The Hidden Origins of the United Irishmen* (hereafter *Deeper Silence*) (Belfast, 1993), p. 73.

6   Ibid.

7   Ibid.

8   Ibid.

9   Caroline Robbins, *The Eighteenth Century Commonwealthman* (Harvard, 1959), p. 3.

10 Ibid., p. 163.

11 *Drennan-McTier*, vol. I, p. xi.

12 S. Shannan Millin, *History of the Second Congregation of Protestant Dissenters in Belfast* (Belfast, 1900), p. 9.

13 *Drennan-McTier*, vol. I, p. xi.

14 Ibid., p. 114.

15 Brian Duffin, *The Gentle Jacobin* (hereafter *Jacobin*) (unpublished, 1977), PRONI, T/965, p. 3.

16 *Drennan-McTier*, vol. 1, p. xii.

17 Stewart, *Deeper Silence*, p. 114.

18 Duffin, *Jacobin*, p. 4.

19 *Drennan-McTier*, vol. 1, p. xi.

20 Duffin, *Jacobin*, p. 4.

21 Stewart, *Deeper Silence*, p. 49.

22 Duffin, *Jacobin*, p. 2.

23 Ibid.

24 Stewart, *Deeper Silence*, p. 67.

25 Larkin (ed.), *Trial*, p. 124.

26 *Duffin, Jacobin, p. 6.*

27 Drennan to McTier, 16 March 1776, *Drennan-McTier*, vol. I, p. 5.

28 Drennan to McTier, 3 April 1776, *Drennan-McTier*, vol. I, p. 8.

29 Ibid.

30 John Swanwich Drennan, *Glendalloch and other Poems by the late Dr Drennan* (Dublin, 1859).

31 Arthur Herman, *The Scottish Enlightenment: The Scots' Invention of the Modern World* (hereafter *The Scots*) (London, 2001), p. 69.

32 Ian McBride, 'William Drennan and the Dissenting Tradition', in D. Dickson, D. Keogh and K. Whelan, *The United Irishmen: Republicanism, Radicalism and Rebellion* (Dublin, 1993), p. 60.

33 K. R., Johnston, *Unusual Suspects: Pitt's Reign of Alarm and the Lost Generation of the 1790s* (Oxford, 2013), p. 146.

34 Herman, *The Scots*, p. 232.

35 Ibid.

36 Drennan to McTier, 20 January 1778, *Drennan-McTier*, vol. I, p. 32.

37   Ibid., p. 7.
38   *Drennan-McTier*, vol. I, p. xi.
39   Drennan to McTier, 20 January 1778, *Drennan-McTier*, vol. I, p. 33.
40   McTier to Drennan, 16 November 1777, *Drennan-McTier*, vol. I, p. 25.
41   Drennan to McTier, 13 December 1777, *Drennan-McTier*, vol. I, p. 29.
42   Ibid., vol. I, p. 368.
43   Ibid., vol. I, p. 35.
44   Drennan to McTier, 1 March 1778, *Drennan-McTier*, vol. I, p. 41.
45   McTier to Drennan, 30 January 1793, *Drennan-McTier*, vol. I, p. 475.
46   The name given to Louis XVI of France after he was dethroned and prior to his execution.
47   Drennan to McTier, 3 December 1792, *Drennan-McTier*, vol. I, p. 443.
48   Chart, *Letters*, p. 111.
49   Drennan-McTier, vol. I, p. 50.

Chapter 2

1   Stewart, *Deeper Silence*, p. 75.
2   Ibid., p. 76.
3   Thomas Witherow, *Historical and Literary Memorials of Presbyterianism in Ireland* (Belfast, 1879), p. 276.
4   Christopher Walker, *Reason and Religion in Late Seventeenth-Century England: The Politics and Theology of Radical Dissent* (hereafter *Reason and Religion*) (London, 2013), p. 153.
5   John H. McLachlan, *Socinianism in Seventeenth-Century England* (hereafter *Socinianism*) (Oxford, 1951), p. 10.
6   Walker, *Reason and Religion*, p. 102.
7   McLachlan, *Socinianism*, p. 11.
8   Walker, *Reason and Religion*, p. 153.
9   Robert P. Kraynak, 'John Locke: From Absolutism to Toleration', *The American Political Science Review*, vol. 74, no. 1 (March 1980), p. 55.
10   John Locke, *A Letter Concerning Toleration* (London, 1689), p. 57.
11   McLachlan, *Socinianism*, p. 328.
12   J.C.D. Clarke, *English Society 1660–1832* (Cambridge 2000), p. 338.
13   Ibid.
14   Philip McGuiness, et al. (eds), *John Toland's Christianity Not Mysterious: Text, Associated Works and Critical Essays* (hereafter *John Toland*) (Dublin, 1997), p. 208.
15   Ibid.
16   Justin Champion, *Republican Learning: John Toland and the Crisis of Christian Culture, 1696–1722* (hereafter *Republican Learning*) (Manchester, 2003), p. 70.
17   McGuiness, *John Toland*, p. 224.
18   *Republican Learning*, p. 77.
19   Ibid.
20   Ibid.
21   Stewart, *Deeper Silence*, p. 113.
22   Thomas Emlyn, *A True Narrative of the Proceedings of the Dissenting Ministers of Dublin against Mr. Thomas Emlyn* (hereafter *Narrative*) (London, MDCCXIX), p. xvii.
23   Stewart, *Deeper Silence*, p. 110.
24   Emlyn, *Narrative*, p. xxx.

25 Ibid.
26 Stewart, *Deeper Silence*, p. 111.

Chapter 3

1 Drennan to McTier, 21 January 1794, *Drennan-McTier*, vol. II, p. 5.
2 Paul Frame, *Liberty's Apostal: Richard Price his Life and Times* (Cardiff, 2015), p. 161.
3 Drennan to McTier, 21 January 1794, *Drennan-McTier*, vol. II, p. 5.
4 E.P. Thompson, *The Making of the English Working Class* (London, 1963), p. 105.
5 Ibid.
6 Drennan to McTier, 21 January 1794, *Drennan-McTier*, vol. II, p. 5.
7 His friend William Bruce had been preaching against Paine at Rosemary Lane and perhaps Drennan expected Bruce to publish his sermons.
8 Drennan to McTier, 20 October 1795, *Drennan-McTier*, vol. II, p. 207.
9 Ibid.
10 *Drennan-McTier*, vol. II, p. 530.
11 Drennan to McTier, 18 April 1794, *Drennan-McTier*, vol. II, p. 227.
12 Drennan to McTier, February 1792, *Drennan-McTier*, vol. I, p. 390.
13 Ibid.
14 Ibid. p. 391.
15 Castlereagh to Addington, 22 July 1802, *Memoirs of Viscount Castlereagh*, Charles Vane (ed.), 12 vols (London, 1848–54), vol. I, pp. 224–6.
16 Ibid.
17 Ibid.
18 Drennan to McTier, 9 August 1800; *Drennan-McTier*, vol. II, p. 619.
19 McTier to Drennan, 6 January 1800, *Drennan-McTier*, vol. II, p. 556–7.
20 Drennan to McTier, 12 December 1800, *Drennan-McTier*, vol. II, p. 659.
21 Ibid. p. 620.
22 McTier to Drennan, 15 October 1800, *Drennan-McTier*, vol. II, p. 637.
23 McTier to Drennan, 19 October 1800, *Drennan-McTier*, vol. II, p. 639.
24 Drennan to McTier, 21 January 1794, *Drennan-McTier*, vol. II, p. 5.

Chapter 4

1 Drennan to McTier, 6 April 1778, *Drennan-McTier*, vol. I, p. 44.
2 Duffin, *Jacobin*, p. 15.
3 Vincent Morley, *Irish Opinion and the American Revolution, 1760–1783* (hereafter *Irish Opinion*) (Cambridge, 2002), p. 190.
4 Ian McBride, *Scripture Politics: Ulster Presbyterianism and Irish Radicalism in the Late Eighteenth Century* (hereafter *Scripture Politics*) (Oxford, 1998), p. 123.
5 Ibid.
6 Drennan to McTier, 7 July 1778, *Drennan-McTier*, vol. I, p. 48.
7 Stewart, *Deeper Silence*, p. 61.
8 Drennan's descendant, Brian Duffin, suggests that he introduced a scheme for inoculation against smallpox there, Duffin, *Jacobin*, p. 15.

9   R.W.W. Strain, *Belfast and its Charitable Society: A story of urban social development* (Belfast, 1961), p. 80.

10   Brendan Clifford (ed.), *William Drennan: Selected Writings* (hereafter *Selected Writings*) (Belfast, 1998), vol. I, p. 51.

11   Richard Burke, *Empire and Revolution* (hereafter *Empire*) (Princeton, 2015), p. 374.

12   William Drennan, *A Letter to Edmund Burke Esq; by birth an Irishman by adoption an Englishman. Containing some reflections on patriotism, party-spirit, and the union of free nations* (hereafter *Letter to Edmund Burke*) (Belfast, 1780), p. 4.

13   Jonathan Bardon, *A History of Ulster* (Belfast, 1992), p. 214.

14   *Letter to Edmund Burke*.

15   Ibid., p. 6.

16   Ibid., p. 13.

17   Ibid., p. 16.

18   Burke lost the Bristol seat in September 1780.

19   *Letter to Edmund Burke*, p. 14.

20   Ibid.

21   Ibid.

22   Edmund Burke, *Reflections on the Revolution in France* (London, 1791).

23   Ibid., p. 18.

24   Ibid., p. 66.

25   Ibid., p. 12.

26   Burke, *Empire*, p. 400.

27   Ibid.

28   Ibid., p. 401.

29   Ibid.

30   Ibid.

31   Larkin, *Trial*, p. 126.

32   Ibid.

33   *Letter to Edmund Burke*, p. 8.

34   Burke, *Empire*, p. 403.

35   *Letter to Edmund Burke*, p. 36.

36   Burke, *Empire*, p. 403.

37   Ibid.

38   William Drennan, *An Address to the Volunteers of Ireland by the Author of a Letter to Edmund Burke Esquire containing Reflections on Patriotism, Party Spirit and the Union of Free Nations* (Dublin, 1781), p. 3.

39   Ibid.

40   Ibid., p. 20.

41   Ibid.

42   Ibid.

43   Morley, *Irish Opinion*, p. 306.

44   Ibid.

45   Drennan, *Letter to William Bruce*.

46   Stewart, *Deeper Silence*, p. 62.

47   Ibid., p. 63.

48   M. McTier to S. McTier, 2 October 1778, *Drennan-McTier*, vol. I, p. 65.

49   Stewart, *Deeper Silence*, p. 37.

50   Clifford, *Selected Writings*, vol. I, p. 37.

51   Ibid.
52   Ibid., p. 41.
53   Danny Mansergh, *Grattan's Failure: Parliamentary Opposition and the People in Ireland, 1779–1800* (hereafter *Grattan's Failure*) (Dublin, 2005), p. 72.
54   Clifford, *Selected Writings*, p. 41.
55   Mansergh, *Grattan's Failure*, p. 81.
56   Clifford, *Selected Writings*, p. 42
57   *Drennan-Bruce Letters*, PRONI, D/553, f 4.

Chapter 5

1   S. McTier to M. McTier, January 1783, *Drennan-McTier*, vol. I, p. 115.
2   Ibid.
3   Ibid·
4   William McMillan, 'Presbyterian Ministers and the Ulster Rising' in Liam Swords (ed.), *Protestant, Catholic and Dissenter: The Clergy and 1798* (Dublin, 1997), p. 113.
5   Drennan to McTier, 1 January 1783, *Drennan-McTier*, vol. I, p. 69.
6   McTier to Drennan, 1783, *Drennan-McTier*, vol. I, p. 74.
7   Drennan to McTier, 1783, *Drennan-McTier*, vol. I, p. 88.
8   Drennan to McTier, 1783, *Drennan-McTier*, vol. I, p. 100.
9   William Drennan, *Letters of Orellana: an Irish Helot to the seven northern counties not represented in the National Assembly of Delegates, held in Dublin, 1784, for obtaining a more equal representation of the people in the Parliament of Ireland* (hereafter, *Orellana*) (Dublin, 1785), p. 6.
10   McTier to McTier, 2 June 1783, *Drennan-McTier*, vol. I, p. 106.
11   Ibid., p. 109.
12   Enclosed in Ann Drennan to Martha McTier, 2 July 1783, *Drennan-McTier*, vol. I, p. 120.
13   Haliday to McTier, 17 June 1783, *Drennan-McTier*, vol. I, p. 111.
14   Ann Drennan to McTier, 2 July 1783, *Drennan-McTier*, vol. I, p. 120.
15   H. Montgomery Hyde, *The Londonderrys: A Family Portrait* (London, 1979), p. 4.
16   McTier to Drennan, 1783, *Drennan-McTier*, vol. I, p. 125.
17   Drennan to McTier, (undated) 1783, *Drennan-McTier*, vol. I, p. 128.
18   Ibid., p. 127.
19   McTier to Drennan, 1783, *Drennan-McTier*, vol. I, p. 128.
20   Ibid., p. 131.
21   Ibid., p. 130.
22   Mansergh, *Grattan's Failure*, pp. 84–8.
23   Ibid., p. 90.
24   Ibid., p. 93.
25   Ibid., p. 94.
26   Clifford, *Selected Writings*, Drennan to Bruce, Letter no. 23.
27   Stewart, *Deeper Silence*, p. 133. This is a direct quote from Stewart. Bruce had moved to Great Strand Street by this time.
28   Stewart , *Deeper Silence*, p. 135.
29   Johnston, *Unusual Suspects*, p. 147.
30   Drennan, *Orellana*, p. 6.
31   Ibid., letter, p. 35.

32   Ibid., letter 5.
33   Michael Brown, *The Irish Enlightenment* (Cambridge, 2016), pp. 388–91.
34   Ibid.
35   Ibid.
36   Drennan to McTier, 1784, *Drennan-McTier*, vol. I, p. 186.
37   Clifford, *Selected Writings*, p. 16.
38   McTier to Drennan, (undated) 1784, *Drennan-McTier*, vol. I, p. 184.
39   Ibid.
40   As quoted in James Kelly, 'Parliamentary Reform in Irish Politics' in David Dickson et al.,
      The United Irishmen: Republicanism, Radicalism and Rebellion (Dublin, 1993), p. 81.
41   Drennan to McTier, 1784, *Drennan-McTier*, vol. I, p. 166.
42   *Drennan, Orellana*, letter 5, p.38.
43   When a proposal to end a property qualification for the franchise was carried by a reform
      Committee of the Dublin United Irishmen in early 1793, by eleven votes to nine, Drennan
      voted with the minority.
44   Drennan to McTier, (undated) 1785, *Drennan-McTier*, vol. I, p. 193.
45   Ibid.
46   William Hamilton Drummond, *The Autobiography of Archibald Hamilton Rowan, Esq*
      (hereafter *Rowan*) (Dublin, 1840), p. 117.
47   Muzzleloading flintlock.
48   Drummond, *Rowan*, p. 117.
49   Sean Murphy, *Forgotten Patriot: Charles Lucas 1717–1771* (Bray, 2009), p. 24.
50   Drummond, *Rowan*, p. 130.
51   Ibid.
52   Benn, *Town of Belfast*, p. 639.
53   Drummond, *Rowan*, p. 139.
54   Clifford, *Selected Writings*, vol. II, p. 13.
55   Drummond, *Rowan*, p. 127.
56   Drennan to McTier, 1784, *Drennan-McTier*, vol. I, p. 320.
57   Ibid., p. 219.
58   William Drennan to Willian Bruce, 7 February 1784, PRONI: D 553/20.

Chapter 6

1   Benn, *Town of Belfast*, pp. 640–1.
2   Clifford, *Selected Writings,* vol. II, p. 15.
3   Stewart, *Deeper Silence*, p. 141.
4   William Drennan to William Bruce, January 1786, no. 57, Clifford, *Selected Writings*, vol. I,
     p. 127.
5   Ibid., p. 135.
6   Ibid., p. 158.
7   *Orellana*, letter 5, p. 38.
8   L.M. Cullen, 'The Internal Politics of the United Irishmen', pp. 179–80; Dáire Keogh, *The
     French Disease: The Catholic Church and Irish Radicalism* (Dublin, 1993), p. 103; Chart, *The
     Letters*, p. 228; Wright, *The Natural Leaders*, p. 68.
9   I have not found this term in the literature but several of the Professor's former students have
     stated that 'the Wretched Drennan' was a term coined by Professor Cullen.

10   Clifford, *Selected Writings*, vol. II, p. 237.

11   National Archives, Rebellion Papers, 620/10/121/35.

12   Drennan, *Orellana*, p. 38.

13   See *Letter to Fitzwilliam*, p. 3.

14   Drennan, *Orellana*, p. 38.

15   Drennan to McTier, January 1793, *Drennan-McTier*, vol. I, p. 461.

16   Clifford, *Selected Writings*, vol. II, p. 237.

17   For details of Wolfe Tone see, Marianne Elliott, *Wolfe Tone: Prophet of Irish Independence* (hereafter *Tone*) (Yale, 1989); Thomas Bartlett (ed.), *Theobald Wolfe Tone: Memoirs, journals and political writings* (hereafter *The Life of Tone*), compiled and arranged by William T.W. Tone (Dublin, 1988).

18   Elliott, *Tone*, p. 127.

19   Drennan to McTier, 31 August 1796, *Drennan-McTier*, vol. II, p. 256.

20   Johnston, *Unusual Suspects*, p. 154.

21   Drennan to McTier, 14 March 1796, *Drennan-McTier*, vol. II, p. 211.

22   Drennan to McTier, 31 August 1796, *Drennan-McTier*, vol. II, p. 256.

23   Ibid.

24   Drennan never acquired a Roman Catholic patient until March 1802; see *Drennan-McTier*, vol. III, p. 16.

25   Drennan to McTier, 21 March 1798, *Drennan-McTier*, vol. II, p. 379.

26   Keogh, *French Disease*, p. 103.

27   E.W. McFarland, *Ireland and Scotland in the Age of Revolution* (Edinburgh, 1994), p. 148.

28   Drennan to McTier, 8 April 1795, *Drennan-McTier*, vol. II, p. 145.

29   Chart, *The Letters*, p. x.

30   Drennan to McTier, 14 March 1796, *Drennan-McTier*, vol. II, p. 210.

31   Chart, *The Letters*, p. 170.

32   R.B. McDowell, *Burke and Ireland*, in Dickson, *Republicanism, Radicalism and Rebellion*, p. 108.

33   Bartlett, *The Life of Tone*, p. 90.

34   Drennan to McTier, 20 July 1796, *Drennan-McTier*, vol. II, p. 252.

35   Drennan to Samuel McTier, December 1791, *Drennan-McTier*, vol. I, p. 376.

36   Wright, *Natural Leaders*, p. 68.

37   A.T.Q. Stewart, 'A Stable Unseen Power', *Essays presented to Michael Roberts* (Belfast, 1976), pp. 86–7.

38   McTier to Drennan, March 1805, *Drennan-McTier*, vol. III, p. 330.

39   Drennan to McTier, 13 March 1805, *Drennan-McTier*, vol. III, p. 334.

40   Drennan to McTier, 17 April 1807, *Drennan-McTier*, vol. III, pp. 595–9.

41   Ibid.

42   *Belfast Monthly Magazine* (hereafter *BMM*), 1809, vol 3, p. 13.

43   McBride, *Scripture Politics*, p. 214.

44   This letter is quoted verbatim in Oliver MacDonagh, *O'Connell: The life of Daniel O'Connell* (London, 1991), p. 166.

45   Clifford, *Selected Writings*, vol. II, p. 237.

46   William Drennan, *Letter to His Excellency Earl Fitzwilliam* (hereafter, *Letter to Fitzwilliam*) (Dublin, 1795), p. 25.

47   Drennan to McTier, January 1798, *Drennan-McTier*, vol. II, p. 358.

48   DNB.

Chapter 7

1   Drennan to McTier, 1799, *Drennan-McTier*, vol. I, p. 339.
2   Drennan to McTier, December 1789, *Drennan-McTier*, vol. 1, p. 342.
3   Ibid., p. 344.
4   Ibid.
5   Drennan to McTier, February 1790, *Drennan-McTier*, vol. I, p. 344.
6   Stewart, *Deeper Silence*, p. 102.
7   Ibid., p. 35.
8   Thomas Witherow, *Historical and Literary Memorials of Presbyterianism in Ireland* (Belfast, 1879), p. 127.
9   Ibid.
10 Lord Henry Fitzgerald (1761–1829), MP for Dublin City and brother of the 2nd Duke of Leinster.
11 Travers Hartley had not sought re-election.
12 The dangerous common people of Tory imagination.
13 Drennan to McTier, May 1790, *Drennan-McTier*, vol. I, p. 348.
14 W.H.E. Lecky, *Ireland in the Eighteenth Century* (London, 1892), vol. III, p. 230.
15 Fergus Whelan, *God Provoking Democrat: The Remarkable Life of Archibald Hamilton Rowan* (hereater *Provoking Democrat*) (Dublin: New Island, 2015), p. 233.
16 Whelan, *Dissent*, p. 237.
17 Drennan to McTier, 5 February 1791, *Drennan-McTier*, vol. I, p. 356.
18 Clifford, *Selected Writings*, vol. I. pp. 175–6.
19 Drennan to McTier, 2 January 1791, *Drennan-McTier*, vol. I, p. 354.
20 Ian McBride, *Eighteenth Century Ireland* (Dublin, 2009), p. 416.
21 Sir Richard Musgrave, *Memoirs of the Irish Rebellion of 1798*, 4th edition (Indiana, 1995), pp. 51–3.
22 Ibid.
23 Drennan to McTier, 2 January 1791, *Drennan-McTier*, vol. I, p. 356.
24 Thomas H.D. Mahony, *Edmund Burke and Ireland* (London, 1960), p. 161.
25 Ibid.
26 Thomas Bartlett, 'Ireland during the Revolutionary and Napoleonic Wars' in James Kelly (ed.), *The Cambridge History of Ireland*, vol. II (Cambridge 2018), p. 76.
27 Ibid.

Chapter 8

1   Clifford, *Selected Writings*, vol. I, p. 23.
2   Bartlett, *Life of Tone*, p. 39.
3   Ibid.
4   Ibid.
5   The greatest happiness of the greatest number was originally formulated by Francis Hutcheson.
6   Drennan to McTier, 21 May 1791, *Drennan-McTier*, vol. I, p. 357.
7   Nancy J. Curtin, *The United Irishmen: Popular Politics in Ulster and Dublin 1791–1798* (Oxford, 1998), p. 43.
8   McTier to Drennan, 2 July 1791, *Drennan-McTier*, vol. I, p. 360.

9   Ibid.
10 Ibid.
11 Ibid.
12 Drennan to McTier, 3 July 1791, *Drennan-McTier*, vol. I, p. 360.
13 In Greek mythology, the dog who guards the gates of Hades to prevent escape.
14 Drennan to McTier, 3 July 1791, *Drennan-McTier*, vol. I, p. 361.
15 Ibid.
16 Ibid.
17 T.W. Moody, R.B. McDowell and C.J. Woods, *The Writings of Theobald Wolfe Tone*, vol. I (Oxford, 2007), p. 108.
18 The editor of the *Belfast Newsletter*.
19 Perhaps the defeat of Wolfe Tone's resolution.
20 McTier to Drennan, 1791, *Drennan-McTier*, vol. I, p. 365.
21 Ibid.
22 T.W. Moody et al. (eds), *The Writings of Theobald Wolfe Tone, 1763–1798*, vol. I (Oxford, 2007), p. 129.
23 Drennan to McTier, November 1791, *Drennan-McTier*, vol. I, p. 371.
24 Ibid., p. 374.
25 Ibid.
26 Ibid.

Chapter 9

1   McTier to Drennan, (undated) 1792, *Drennan-McTier*, vol. I, p. 393.
2   Henry Joy and William Bruce, *Belfast Politics with thoughts on the British Constitution* (hereafter *Belfast Politics*) (Belfast, 2010), p. 134.
3   Drennan to McTier, 28 January 1792, *Drennan-McTier*, vol. I, p. 388.
4   Ibid.
5   Ibid.
6   Ibid., vol. I, p. 395.
7   Ibid.
8   Joy and Bruce, *Belfast Politics*, p. 135.
9   Oscar Wilde said this of Edward Carson QC when he acted against Wilde in his case against the Marquis of Queensbury.
10 Joy and Bruce, *Belfast Politics*, p. 135.
11 Ibid.
12 Ibid., p. 137.
13 Ibid.
14 Ibid., p. 145.
15 Drennan to McTier, February 1792, *Drennan-McTier*, vol. I, p. 393.
16 Joy and Bruce, *Belfast Politics*, p. 149.
17 Ibid., p. 153.
18 Rosamond Jacob, *The Rise of the United Irishmen* (hereafter *United Irishmen*) (London, 1937), p. 80.
19 Drummond, *Rowan*, p. 165.
20 Elliott, *Tone*, p. 162.
21 Drennan to McTier, February 1792, *Drennan-McTier*, vol. I, p. 396.

22 Drennan to McTier, 2 April 1792, *Drennan-McTier*, vol. I, p. 403.
23 Bartlett, *The Life of Tone*, p. 50.
24 Ibid.
25 Drennan to McTier, 3 March 1792, *Drennan-McTier*, vol. I, p. 404.
26 Ibid., p. 398.
27 Bartlett, *The Life of Tone*, p. 50.

Chapter 10

1   Drennan to McTier, 13 December 1777, *Drennan-McTier*, vol. 1, p. 29.
2   Burke, *Empire*, p. 322.
3   Ibid., p. 316.
4   Ibid., p. 451.
5   Ibid., p. 317.
6   Jesse Norman, *Edmund Burke: Philosopher, Politician, Prophet* (hereafter *Burke*) (London, 1988), p. 73.
7   Ibid., p. 425.
8   Ibid.
9   Ibid.
10 E. Burke, *Letter to Sir Hercules Langrishe*, 3 January 1792.
11 Burke, *Empire*, p. 425.
12 Conor Cruise O'Brien, *The Great Melody: A Thematic Biography and a Commented Anthology of Edmund Burke* (London, 1993), p. 409.
13 E. Burke, *Speech on the Petition of the Unitarians* (11 May 1792).
14 Burke, *Empire*, p. 743.
15 Eamon O'Flaherty, 'Edmund Burke', *DIB*.
16 Stuart Andrews, *Unitarian Radicalism: Political Rhetoric, 1770–1814* (hereafter *Unitarian Radicalism*) (London, 2003), p. 8.
17 Jenny Uglow, *In these Times: Living in Britain Through Napoleon's Wars, 1793–1815* (London, 2014), p. 13.
18 Richard Price, A *Discourse on the Love of our Country* (London, 1789).
19 Ibid.
20 William Morgan, 'Memoirs of the Life of the Rev. Richard Price', *Enlightenment and Dissent*, no. 22, 2003, p. 82.
21 John Keane, *Tom Paine: A Political Life* (hereafter *Paine*) (London, 2009), p. 289.
22 Ibid., p. 111.
23 Ibid.
24 Andrews, *Unitarian Radicalism*, p. ix.
25 Bartlett, *Life of Wolfe Tone*, p. 29.

Chapter 11

1   Jenny Uglow, *The Lunar Men: The Friends who made the Future* (London, 2003), p. 446.
2   Ibid.
3   Ibid., p. 444.
4   Johnston, *Unusual Suspects*, p. 55.

5   Ibid., p. 442.
6   Roland Bartel (ed.), *Liberty and Terror in England: Reactions to the French Revolution* (Boston, 1965), p. 58.
7   *Northern Star*, 24 April 1792.
8   Burke, *Empire*, p. 769.
9   Andrews, *Unitarian Radicalism*, p. 81.
10   Drennan to McTier, March 1794, *Drennan-McTier*, vol. II, p. 15.
11   R.B. McDowell, *The Proceedings of the Dublin Society of United Irishmen* (hereafter *Proceedings*) (Dublin, 1998), p. 8.
12   Drennan to McTier, (undated) 1794, *Drennan-McTier*, vol. II, p. 33.
13   Stephen Small, *Political Thought in Ireland, 1776–1798: Republicanism, Patriotism and Radicalism* (Oxford, 2002), p. 233.
14   McDowell, *Proceedings*, p. 120.
15   Drennan to McTier, 1803, *Drennan-McTier*, vol. III, p. 102.
16   Craig Nelson, *Enlightenment, Revolution, and the Birth of Modern Nations* (hereafter *Enlightenment*) (London, 2006), p. 225.
17   Ibid., p. 203.
18   Keane, *Paine*, p. 320.
19   Ibid.
20   Nelson, *Enlightenment*, p. 204.
21   Ibid., p. 227.
22   McDowell, *Proceedings*, p. 22.
23   Keane, *Paine*, p. 341.
24   Nelson, *Enlightenment*, p. 228.
25   Keane, *Paine*, p. 341.
26   Ibid.
27   Bartlett, *Life of Tone*, p. 701.
28   Norman, *Burke*, p. 181.
29   Nelson, *Enlightenment*, p. 230.
30   Keane, *Paine*, p. 343.
31   Andrews, *Unitarian Radicalism*, p. 151.
32   Drennan to McTier, 8 February 1805, *Drennan-McTier*, vol. III, p. 320.
33   *BMM*, iv, 1810, p. 117.

Chapter 12

1   Norman, *Burke*, p. 87.
2   R.B. McDowell, 'Burke and Ireland' in Dickson, *Republicanism, Radicalism and Rebellion*, p. 108.
3   Ibid.
4   F.P. Lock, *Edmund Burke* (hereafter *Edmund Burke*), vol. II (Oxford, 2009), p. 412.
5   Burke, *Empire*, p. 784.
6   Ibid., p. 802.
7   Henry Dundas (1742–1811), later 1st Viscount Melville, home secretary, *DNB*; Marianne Elliott, *Wolfe Tone: Prophet of Irish Independence* (London, 1989), p. 154.
8   Lock, *Edmund Burke*, p. 412.
9   Drennan to McTier, 1791, *Drennan-McTier*, vol. I, p. 374.

10   Ibid.
11   Elliott, *Tone*, p. 155.
12   Burke, *Empire*, p. 798.
13   Drennan to McTier, January 1792, *Drennan-McTier*, vol. I, p. 384.
14   Drennan to McTier, 28 January 1792, *Drennan-McTier*, vol. I, p. 388.
15   Elliott, *Tone*, p. 156.
16   Lock, *Edmund Burke*, p. 401.
17   Elliott, *Tone*, p. 155.
18   Lock, *Edmund Burke*, p. 400.
19   Bartlett, *Life of Tone*, p. 164.
20   Drennan to McTier, 25 November 1792, *Drennan-McTier*, vol. I, p. 428.
21   Ibid.

Chapter 13

1   Drennan to S. McTier, 21 June 1792, *Drennan-McTier*, vol. I, p. 409.
2   Ibid.
3   Brendan Clifford, *Belfast in the French Revolution* (hereafter *French Revolution*) (Belfast, 1989), pp. 61–2.
4   David Lawday, *Danton* (London, 2009), p. 116.
5   Clifford, *French Revolution*, pp. 59–60.
6   T.W. Moody et al. (eds), *The Writings of Wolfe Tone, 1763–98* (hereafter *Writings of Tone*), vol. I (Oxford, 2007), p. 216.
7   Ibid.
8   Clifford, *French Revolution*, p. 63.
9   Drennan, *Letter to Fitzwilliam*, p. 33.
10   Joy and Bruce, *Belfast Politics*, p. 38.
11   Ibid.
12   Drennan to McTier, 3 March 1792, *Drennan-McTier*, vol. I, p. 411.
13   Reay Tannahill (ed.), *Paris in the Revolution: A collection of eye-witness accounts* (hereafter *Paris in the Revolution*) (London, 1969), p. 56.
14   Drennan to S. McTier, 18 August 1792, *Drennan-McTier*, vol. I, p. 411.
15   Ibid.
16   Drennan to McTier, 3 March 1792, *Drennan-McTier*, vol. I, p. 411.
17   George Rudé, *Revolutionary Europe 1783–1815* (London, 1964), p. 131.
18   Drennan to S. McTier, 18 August 179, *Drennan-McTier*, vol. I, p. 412.
19   Ibid.
20   Ibid., p. 414.
21   Treason against the nation.
22   Ibid., p. 415.
23   Tannahill, *Paris in the Revolution*, p. 68.
24   Ibid.
25   Moody, *Writings of Tone*, p. 319.
26   Alan Blackstock, *Double Traitors: The Belfast Volunteers and Yeomen, 1778–1828* (Belfast, 2000), p. 9.
27   Drennan to McTier, 1 November 1792, *Drennan-McTier*, vol. I, p. 420.
28   Ibid., p. 418.

29   Drennan to McTier, 30 October 1792, *Drennan-McTier*, vol. I, p. 421.
30   Drummond, *Rowan*, p. 150.
31   Moody, *Writings of Tone*, p. 318.
32   Ibid.
33   Drennan to McTier, 8 November 1792, *Drennan-McTier*, vol. I, p. 423.
34   Ibid.
35   Drennan to McTier, 20 November 1792, *Drennan-McTier*, vol. I, p. 427.

Chapter 14

1   McTier to Drennan 1792, *Drennan-McTier*, vol. I, p. 424.
2   McTier to Drennan, 25 November 1792, *Drennan-McTier*, vol. I, p. 429.
3   McDowell, *Proceedings*, p. 40.
4   John Brims, 'Scottish Radicalism and the United Irishmen' in Dickson et al. (eds), *The United Irishmen: Republicanism, Radicalism and Rebellion* (Dublin, 1993), p. 156.
5   McDowell, *Proceedings*, p. 43.
6   Drennan to McTier, 20 November 1792, *Drennan-McTier*, vol. I, p. 427.
7   Drennan to McTier, 19 December 1792, *Drennan-McTier*, vol. I, p. 447.
8   Jacob, *United Irishmen*, p. 129.
9   Ibid.
10   Drennan to McTier, 24 November 1792, *Drennan-McTier*, vol. I, p. 428.
11   Ibid.
12   Drennan to McTier, 1 December 1792, *Drennan-McTier*, vol. I, p. 435.
13   Ibid., p. 428.
14   Jacob, *United Irishmen*, p. 121.
15   Drennan to McTier, 8 December 1792, *Drennan-McTier*, vol. I, p. 442.
16   Ibid.
17   Drennan to McTier, 10 December 1792, *Drennan-McTier*, vol. I, p. 445.
18   Ibid.
19   Elliott, *Tone*, p. 211.
20   Drennan to McTier, 10 December 1792, *Drennan-McTier*, vol. I, p. 445.
21   Ibid.
22   McDowell, *Proceedings*, p. 47.
23   The anniversary of the Dungannon Convention of 1782.
24   Jacob, *United Irishmen*, p. 152.
25   Drennan to McTier, 10 December 1792, *Drennan-McTier*, vol. I, p. 444.
26   Drennan to McTier, 10 December 1792, *Drennan-McTier*, vol. I, p. 445.
27   Ibid.
28   Ibid., p. 446.
29   McDowell, *Proceedings*, p. 54.
30   Elliott, *Tone*, p. 201.
31   Drennan to S. McTier, 19 December 1792, *Drennan-McTier*, vol. I, p. 446.
32   Ibid.
33   Kenneth L. Dawson, *The Belfast Jacobin: Samuel Neilson and the United Irishmen* (hereafter *Samuel Neilson*) (Dublin, 2017), p. 47.
34   Drennan to McTier, 19 December 1792, *Drennan-McTier*, vol. I, p. 455.
35   Ibid.

36 Ibid.
37 Ibid., p. 449.
38 Ibid.

Chapter 15

1   Drennan to McTier, 28 December 1792, *Drennan-McTier*, vol. I, p. 454.
2   Ibid.
3   Ibid.
4   Elliott, *Tone*, p. 203.
5   Ibid.
6   Ibid.
7   Drennan to McTier, January 1793, *Drennan-McTier*, vol. I, p. 465.
8   Drennan to McTier, 28 December 1792, *Drennan-McTier*, vol. I, p. 454.
9   Thomas Moore, *The Life and Death of Lord Edward Fitzgerald* (Glasgow, circa 1880), p. 103.
10 Jacob, *United Irishmen*, p. 130.
11 *Drennan-McTier,* vol. I, p. 485.
12 McTier to Drennan, 30 January 1793, *Drennan-McTier*, vol. I, p. 475.
13 Dawson, *Samuel Neilson*, p. 49.
14 *Finn's Leinster Journal*, February 1793.
15 Presumably Simon Butler, Thomas Addis Emmet and Leonard McNally.
16 Drennan to McTier, 28 January 1793, *Drennan-McTier*, vol. I, p. 472.
17 Ibid.
18 Ibid.
19 Ibid.
20 Drennan to McTier, February 1793, *Drennan-McTier*, vol. I, p. 479.
21 McTier to Drennan, 30 January 1793, *Drennan-McTier*, vol. I, p. 475.
22 Ibid., p. 472.
23 Stella Tillyard, *Citizen Lord: Edward Fitzgerald, 1763–1798* (hereafter *Lord Edward*) (London, 1997), p. 139.
24 Ibid.
25 Drennan to McTier, 1 February 1793, *Drennan-McTier*, vol. I, p. 476.
26 Tillyard, *Lord Edward*, p.157.
27 Drennan to McTier, February 1793, *Drennan-McTier*, vol. I, p. 480.

Chapter 16

1   Jacob, *United Irishmen*, p. 134.
2   Drennan to McTier, February 1793, *Drennan-McTier*, vol. I, p. 493.
3   McDowell, *Proceedings*, p. 67.
4   Jacob, *United Irishmen*, pp. 142–3.
5   D.A. Fleming, A.P.W. Malcolmson, *A Valley of Execrations: The Letters and Papers of John Fitzgibbon, Earl of Clare* (hereafter *Excretions*) (Dublin, 2005), p. 161.
6   McTier to Drennan, 30 January 1793, *Drennan-McTier*, vol. I, p. 475.
7   McTier to Drennan, February 1793, *Drennan-McTier*, vol. I, p. 481.
8   Ibid.

9   Drennan to McTier, February 1793, *Drennan-McTier*, vol. I, p. 484.
10   Tillyard, *Lord Edward*, p. 157.
11   The letter was postmarked 8 February.
12   McTier to Drennan, 17 February 1793, *Drennan-McTier*, vol. I, p. 491.
13   Ibid.
14   Drennan to McTier, February 1793, *Drennan-McTier*, vol. I, p. 493.
15   *Finn's Leinster Journal*, 2 March 1793.
16   Drennan to McTier, (undated) 1778, *Drennan-McTier*, vol. I, p. 43.
17   Agrarian secret society.
18   Drennan to McTier, 25 February 1793, *Drennan-McTier*, vol. I, p. 494.
19   Ibid., p. 495.
20   Fleming and Malcolmson, *Excretions*, p. 172.
21   Ibid.
22   Drennan to McTier, 4 March 1793, *Drennan-McTier*, vol. I, p. 498.
23   Ibid., p. 501.
24   Drennan to McTier, 6 March 1793, *Drennan-McTier*, vol. I, p. 499.
25   Ibid., p. 500.
26   Fleming, Malcolmson, *Excretions*, p. 162.
27   Drennan to McTier, 9 March 1793, *Drennan-McTier*, vol. I, p. 501.
28   Ibid.
29   *Finn's Leinster Journal*, 2 March 1793.
30   Ibid., p. 24.

Chapter 17

1   McTier to Drennan, March 1793, *Drennan-McTier*, vol. I, p. 503.
2   Benn, *Town of Belfast*, p. 651.
3   Ibid.
4   McTier to Drennan, 1 April 1793, *Drennan-McTier*, vol. I, p. 509.
5   McTier to Drennan, March 1793, *Drennan-McTier*, vol. I, pp. 502–3.
6   Ibid.
7   Reverend William Bristow (1736–1808), vicar of Belfast, burgess and sovereign.
8   McTier to Drennan, 24 March 1793, *Drennan-McTier*, vol. I, p. 505.
9   Ibid.
10   Drennan to McTier, 26 March 1793, *Drennan-McTier*, vol. I, p. 505.
11   Ibid., p. 507.
12   Ibid., p. 506.
13   Ibid., p. 508.
14   Ibid., p. 506.
15   Jefferies was the judge who sentenced Algernon Sidney to death in the aftermath of the Rye House plot in 1683.
16   Drennan to McTier, 30 March 1793, *Drennan-McTier*, vol. I, p. 508.
17   Drennan to McTier, 25 February 1805, *Drennan-McTier*, vol. III, p. 324.
18   Drennan to McTier, 27 March 1793, *Drennan-McTier*, vol. I, p. 508.
19   McDowell, *Proceedings*, p. 70.
20   Ibid.
21   Ibid.

22   Drennan to McTier, 26 March 1793, *Drennan-McTier*, vol. I, p. 506.

23   McDowell, *Proceedings*, pp. 72–6.

24   Rowan's trial did not go ahead until January 1794.

25   McDowell, *Proceedings*, p. 71.

26   Ibid., p. 126.

27   Drennan to McTier, 12 April 1793, *Drennan-McTier*, vol. I, pp. 511–12.

28   Ibid. p. 512.

29   Ibid.

30   Elliott, *Tone*, p. 204.

31   Ibid., p. 205.

32   Drennan to McTier, (undated) 1793, *Drennan-McTier*, vol. I, p. 519.

33   Ibid.

34   Ibid.

Chapter 18

1   Ibid., p. 513

2   Ibid.

3   *Freeman's Journal*, 21 March 1793.

4   McTier to McTier, 20 April 1793, *Drennan-McTier*, vol. I, p. 516.

5   Jacqueline Hill, p. 178. *From Patriots to Unionists: Dublin Civic Politics and Irish Protestant Patriotism, 1660–1840* (hereafter *Patriots to Unionists*) (Oxford, 1997).

6   Wolfe Tone's father had been unsuccessful in the coach building business and Thomas Russell would tease Tone by calling him Hutton. Tone used the name Hutton when referring to himself in his diaries. The coach which Elizabeth II used to attend the opening of Parliament until 2014 was built by the Hutton family in the mid-nineteenth century.

7   Hill, *Patriots to Unionists*, p. 250.

8   *Report of the trial of Archibald Hamilton Rowan, Esq. on an information, filed, ex officio, by the attorney general, for the distribution of a libel* (Dublin, 1794), p. 36.

9   Ibid., p. 256.

10   Jonah Barrington, *Personal Recollections and Sketches of His Own Time* (Dublin, 1997), p. 155.

11   S. McTier to M. McTier, 22 April 1793, *Drennan-McTier*, vol. I, p. 518.

12   Ibid.

13   Ibid., p. 519.

14   Ibid.

15   Ibid., p. 524.

16   McDowell, *Proceedings*, p. 76.

17   Ibid.

18   McDowell, *Proceedings*, p. 81.

19   (d. 1799) Sister of Daniel Mussenden of Larchfield; see *Drennan-McTier*, vol. I, p. 132.

20   Anne, widow of Reverend Alexander Orr, matron of the Dublin lying-in hospital; see Agnew, vol. I, p. 190.

21   M. McTier to S. McTier, 2 April 1793, *Drennan-McTier*, vol. I, p. 526.

22   Ibid., p. 516.

23   Ibid., p. 528.

24   Ibid., p. 526.

25   Ibid., p. 52.
26   Ibid., p. 541.
27   Ibid., p. 542.
28   *Dublin Evening Post*, May 1793.
29   McDowell, *Proceedings*, p. 74.
30   See Thomas Bartlett (ed.), *Revolutionary Dublin 1795–1801; The Letters of Francis Higgins to Dublin Castle* (hereafter *Revolutionary Dublin*) (Dublin, 2004); W.J. Fitzpatrick, *The Secret Service under Pitt* (London, 1892); W.J. Fitzpatrick, *The Sham Squire and the Informers of 1798* (hereafter *Informers*) (Dublin 1865).
31   *Freeman's Journal*, May 1793.
32   Bartlett, *Life of Tone*, p. 300.
33   Ibid.
34   Drennan to McTier, 2 May 1793, *Drennan-McTier*, vol. I, p. 534.
35   Ibid., p. 531.
36   *Freeman's Journal*, May 1793.
37   Harold Nicolson, *The Desire to Please: A Story of Hamilton Rowan and the United Irishmen* (hereafter *Desire*) (New York, 1943), p. 115.
38   Maura Maher, 'Oliver Bond' in *Dublin Historical Record*, No. 4 (Dublin, 1950), p. 100.
39   Drennan to McTier, 2 May 1793, *Drennan-McTier*, vol. I, p. 535.
40   Drennan to McTier, 1 September 1793, *Drennan-McTier*, vol. I, p. 559.
41   Ibid., p. 536.
42   *Freeman's Journal*, May 1793.

Chapter 19

1   Drennan to McTier, 17 July 1793, *Drennan-McTier*, vol. I, p. 555.
2   Drennan to McTier, 20 July 1793, *Drennan-McTier*, vol. I, p. 556.
3   McDowell, *Proceedings*, p. 85.
4   Drennan to McTier, 16 August 1793, *Drennan-McTier*, vol. I, p. 558.
5   McDowell, *Proceedings*, p. 85.
6   Ibid.
7   Drennan to McTier, 16 August 1793, *Drennan-McTier*, vol. I, p. 558.
8   Ibid., p. 561.
9   Ibid.
10   Ibid.
11   Ibid., p. 560.
12   Ibid.
13   Ibid.
14   Ibid.
15   Ibid., p. 563.
16   Ibid., p. 568.
17   E.P. Thompson, *The Making of the English Working Class* (London, 1963), p. 135.
18   Ibid.
19   Drennan to McTier, 11 October 1793, *Drennan-McTier*, vol. I, p. 568.
20   Drummond, *Rowan*, p. 171.
21   Ibid.
22   Drennan to McTier, 11 October 1793, *Drennan-McTier*, vol. I, p. 569.

23   John Fitzgibbon was a lawyer.
24   Nicolson, *Desire*, p. 108.
25   Drummond, *Rowan*, p. 174.
26   Ibid., p. 179.
27   Reverend Palmer was a Unitarian minister and a friend of Rowan from their Cambridge days.
28   Drennan to McTier, 8 November 1793, *Drennan-McTier*, vol. I, p. 571.
29   Ibid., p. 572.
30   McDowell, *Proceedings*, p. 94.
31   Drumond, *Rowan*, p. 174.
32   John Willoughby Cole, Viscount Cole, later 2nd Earl of Enniskillen (1768–1820).
33   McTier to Drennan, 16 November 1793, *Drennan-McTier*, vol. I, p. 573.
34   Ibid., p. 577.

Chapter 20

1   McDowell, *Proceedings*, p. 98.
2   Ibid.
3   Ibid., p. 95.
4   Drummond, *Rowan*, p. 188.
5   Drennan to McTier, 17 January 1794, *Drennan-McTier*, vol. II, p. 2.
6   Ibid.
7   Drummond, *Rowan*, p. 442.
8   Drennan to McTier, 21 January 1794, *Drennan-McTier*, vol. II, p. 5.
9   Reverend Dr John Moody, minister, Strand Street and brother of Boyle; Reverend Philip Taylor (1747–1830), minister, Eustace Street, Dublin.
10   Drennan to McTier, 21 January 1794, *Drennan-McTier*, vol. II, p. 5.
11   Ibid., p. 6.
12   Thomas Paine, Helen Maria Williams and Mary Wollstonecraft were sympathetic to the Girondists and when Archibald Hamilton Rowan was on board a French ship fleeing to America in 1795, he translated Manon Roland's trial speech into English for his wife.
13   Drennan to McTier, 21 January 1794, *Drennan-McTier*, vol. II, p. 6.
14   Ibid., p. 7.
15   Nicolson, *Desire*, p. 110.
16   Drummond, *Rowan*, p. 189.
17   Drennan to S. McTier, 27 January 1794, *Drennan-McTier*, vol. II, p. 9.
18   Drummond, *Rowan*, p. 189.
19   Drennan to S. McTier, 27 January 1794, *Drennan-McTier*, vol. II, p. 9.
20   Ibid., p. 201.
21   Drennan to S. McTier, 3 February 1794, *Drennan-McTier*, vol. II, p. 13.
22   See Royal Irish Academy, Dublin Unitarian connection, STR 3 final page.
23   Drennan to McTier, 3 February 1794, *Drennan-McTier*, vol. II, p. 15.
24   Drennan to McTier, 12 February 1794, *Drennan-McTier*, vol. II, p. 16.
25   Ibid., p. 17.
26   Ibid.
27   Drennan to McTier, 19 February 1794, *Drennan-McTier*, vol. II, p. 18.
28   Drennan to McTier, 22 February 1794, *Drennan-McTier*, vol. II, p. 20.

Chapter 21

1　Drennan to McTier, 25 February 1794, *Drennan-McTier*, vol. II, p. 23.
2　Drennan to McTier, 22 February 1794, *Drennan-McTier*, vol. II, p. 20.
3　Drennan to McTier, 25 February 1794, *Drennan-McTier*, vol. II, p. 23.
4　Francis Joseph Bigger, *William Orr*, Facsimile reprint (Dublin, 1998), p. 19.
5　Ibid.
6　Ibid., p. 76.
7　Larkin, *Trial*, p. 13.
8　Pollock to McTier, 10 March 1794, *Drennan-McTier*, vol. II, p. 36.
9　Ibid.
10　Fitzpatrick, *Informers*, pp. 253–5.
11　Ibid.
12　Fitzpatrick, *Informers*, pp. 253–5.
13　Drennan to McTier, 16 February 1794, *Drennan-McTier*, vol. II, p. 18.
14　Drennan to McTier, 8 July 1800, *Drennan-McTier*, vol. II, p. 610.
15　McDowell, *Proceedings*, p. 119.
16　Ibid.
17　*Drennan-McTier*, vol. II, p. 43.
18　McDowell, *Proceedings*, p. 124.
19　Bartlett, *Life of Tone*, p. 231.
20　Drennan to McTier, 3 May 1794, *Drennan-McTier*, vol. II, p. 46.
21　McDowell, *Proceedings*, p. 125.
22　Drennan to McTier, 3 May 1794, *Drennan-McTier*, vol. II, p. 47.
23　Drennan to McTier, 28 May 1794, *Drennan-McTier*, vol. II, p. 60.
24　On 12 May 1794, Drennan was arrested on the lesser charge of sedition.
25　See Jacob, *United Irishmen*, p. 232.
26　Drennan to McTier, 3 May 1794, *Drennan-McTier*, vol. II, p. 47.
27　*Faulkner's Weekly*, May 1794.
28　Drennan to McTier, 3 May 1794, *Drennan-McTier*, vol. II, p. 47.
29　*Freeman's Journal*, May 1794.
30　Whelan, *Provoking Democrat*, p. 87.
31　Drennan to McTier, 28 May 1794, *Drennan-McTier*, vol. II, p. 60.
32　Drummond, *Rowan*, p. 218.

Chapter 22

1　Drennan to McTier, 3 May 1794, *Drennan-McTier*, vol. II, p. 48.
2　*Freeman's Journal*, May 1794.
3　McDowell, *Proceedings*, p. 126.
4　Drennan to McTier, 16 May 1794, *Drennan-McTier*, vol. II, p. 54.
5　Drennan to McTier, 14 May 1794, *Drennan-McTier*, vol. II, p. 50.
6　Ibid.
7　Ibid.
8　Ibid., p. 53.
9　Ibid.
10　Ibid., p. 53.

11   Ibid., p. 56.
12   Ibid., p. 58.
13   Ibid., p. 54.
14   Ibid., p. 58.
15   McDowell, *Proceedings*, p. 128.

Chapter 23

1   Ibid., p. 66.
2   Ibid., p. 61.
3   Drennan to McTier, 28 May 1794, *Drennan-McTier*, vol. II, p. 61.
4   Drennan to McTier, 16 June 1794, *Drennan-McTier*, vol. II, p. 63.
5   *Freeman's Journal*, 3 June 1794.
6   Drennan to McTier, 1788, *Drennan-McTier*, vol. I, p. 307.
7   Ibid., p. 24.
8   S. McTier to M. McTier, 26 June 1794, *Drennan-McTier*, vol. II, p. 67.
9   Larkin, *Trial*, p. 32.
10   Ibid.
11   Tommy Graham, 'The Transformation of the Dublin Society of United Irishmen into a mass-based revolutionary organisation, 1791–6', in Thomas Bartlett et al. (eds), 1798: *A Bicentenary Perspective* (Dublin, 2003), p. 145.
12   Chart, *Letters*, p. viii.
13   Johnston, *Unusual Suspects*, p. 147.
14   Ibid., p. 152.
15   When the *Wake of William Orr* was published in the *Press* in January 1798, Drennan's name did not appear. When Drennan's songs were published in *Paddy's Resource*, in 1798 and 1803, his name did not appear. It will be argued below that Drennan sometimes used the pseudonym 'Marcus'. When writing for the *BMM* he rarely, if ever, signed his work.
16   Drennan to Drennan, 26 June 1794, *Drennan-McTier*, vol. II, p. 69.
17   McTier to Drennan, 30 June 1794, *Drennan-McTier*, vol. II, p. 74.
18   Drennan to McTier, 14 July 1794, *Drennan-McTier*, vol. II, p. 83.
19   William Drennan, *Fugitive pieces in verse and prose* (Belfast, 1815), pp. 192–3.
20   Larkin, *Trial*, p. 124.
21   Stewart, *Deeper Silence*, p. 71.
22   Larkin, *Trial*, p. 128.
23   Maiah Towgood, *The Dissenting Gentleman's Answer to Mr White* (Newry, 1816), p. 22.
24   Ibid., p. 27.
25   Ibid., p. 30.
26   Drennan to McTier, 21 March 1806, *Drennan-McTier*, vol. III, p. 446.

Chapter 24

1   Ibid., p. 81.
2   Ibid.
3   Ibid., p. 95.

4   For details of Thomas Russell see James Quinn, *Soul on Fire: a Life of Thomas Russell* (Dublin, 2002); S.N. Mac Giolla Easpaig, *Tómás Ruiseil* (Baile Atha Cliath, 1957); C.J. Woods, *The Diaries and Memoirs of Thomas Russell, 1791–95* (Dublin, 1991); Denis Carroll, *The Man from God Knows Where: Thomas Russell, 1767–1803* (Dublin, 1995).

5   For details of McNally's treachery see W.J. Fitzpatrick, *The Secret Service Under Pitt* (London, 1892), p. 180.

6   Thomas Bartlett, *Revolutionary Dublin,* p. 103, n. 55. 'Drennan declares hatred of the Catholics, charges them with duplicity and ingratitude', J.W. to Cooke, 26 September 1796; NA, RP 629/10/121/35.

7   Henry Jackson (1750–1817).

8   Either Henry Sheares (1755?–1798) or his brother, John Sheares (1766?–1798); see their entries in *DIB*.

9   *Drennan-McTier*, vol. II, p. 92.

10   See 'Butler, Simon' by James Quinn, *DIB*.

11   Drennan to McTier, August 1794, *Drennan-McTier*, vol. II, p. 93.

12   Ibid.

13   Ibid.

14   McTier to Drennan, 3 September 1794, *Drennan-McTier*, vol. II, p. 95.

15   McTier to Drennan, October, 1794, *Drennan-McTier*, vol. II, p. 99.

16   Drennan to McTier [undated], *Drennan-McTier*, vol. II, p. 112.

17   For details of Thomas Hardy and his trial, see C.B. Roylance Kent, *The English Radicals: an Historical Sketch* (New York, 1971), pp. 147–55.

18   Drennan to McTier, 24 October, *Drennan-McTier*, vol. II, p. 105.

19   Drennan to McTier, October, *Drennan-McTier*, vol. II, p. 109.

20   Ibid.

21   Drennan to S. McTier, 12 January 1795, *Drennan-McTier*, vol. II, p. 119.

22   Ibid., p. 3.

23   Ibid.

24   Ibid.

25   Keane, *Paine*, p. 347.

26   E.W. McFarland, *Ireland and Scotland in the Age of Revolution* (Edinburgh, 1994), p. 105.

27   *Letter to Fitzwilliam*, p. 5.

28   Ibid., p. 21.

29   Ibid.

30   The Defenders were a Roman Catholic secret society; see Liam Kelly, *A Flame now Unquenched: Rebels and Frenchmen in Leitrim, 1793–98* (Dublin, 1998).

31   *Letter to Fitzwilliam*, p. 24.

32   Ibid., p. 25.

33   Ibid.

34   Ibid., p. 42.

35   McTier to Drennan, 17 August 1795, *Drennan-McTier*, vol, II, p. 121.

36   Drennan to McTier, 12 January 1795, *Drennan-McTier*, vol. II, p. 119.

37   McTier to Drennan, March 1794, *Drennan-McTier*, vol. II, p. 138.

38   Thomas Addis Emmet (1764–1827).

39   Drennan to McTier, January 1795, *Drennan-McTier*, vol. II, p. 120.

40   For biographical accounts of Lord Edward Fitzgerald see Patrick Byrne, *Lord Edward Fitzgerald* (London, 1955); Thomas Moore, *The Life and Death of Lord Edward Fitzgerald* (London 1832); Stella Tillyard, *Citizen Lord: Edward Fitzgerald, 1763–1798* (London, 1998).

41 Drennan to McTier, January 1795, *Drennan-McTier*, vol. II, p. 122.
42 Drennan to McTier, 1 April 1795, *Drennan-McTier*, vol. II, p. 144.
43 Bartlett, *Revolutionary Dublin*, p. 74.
44 John Jeffreys Pratt, 2nd Earl of Camden.
45 Bartlett, *Revolutionary Dublin*, p. 74.
46 Fitzwilliam had alleged that a British desire for a legislative union with Ireland lay behind his dismissal. See ibid., p. 79, n. 45.
47 Ibid., p. 79.
48 Ibid.
49 Drennan to McTier, *Drennan-McTier*, vol. II, p. 119.
50 Ibid.
51 Ibid.
52 Drennan to McTier, 5 February 1791, *Drennan-McTier*, vol. I, p. 356.
53 Drennan to McTier, 5 February 1795, *Drennan-McTier*, vol. II, p. 134.
54 Drennan to McTier, 8 April 1795, *Drennan-McTier*, vol. II, p. 147; Elliott, *Tone*, p. 249, puts the number in attendance at 4,000.
55 Ibid.
56 Ronan Kelly, *Bard of Erin: The Life of Thomas Moore* (Dublin, 2008).
57 Bartlett, *Revolutionary Dublin*, p. 76.
58 Elliott, *Tone*, p. 249.
59 Ibid., p. 250.
60 Drennan to McTier, 22 February 1798, *Drennan-McTier*, vol. II, p. 371.

Chapter 25

1 Ibid., p. 82.
2 Jonah Barrington, *Personal Sketches and Recollections of his Own Time* (Dublin, 1997), p. 237.
3 Drennan to McTier, 30 April 1795, *Drennan-McTier*, vol. II, p. 149.
4 Ibid.
5 Ibid.
6 McTier to Drennan, October 1795, *Drennan-McTier*, vol. II, p. 189.
7 McTier to Drennan, 7 August 1795, *Drennan-McTier*, vol. II, p. 168.
8 Ibid., p. 165.
9 *Drennan-McTier*, vol. I, p. xx.
10 *Drennan-McTier*, vol. II, p. 164.
11 McTier to Drennan, 7 August 1795, *Drennan-McTier*, vol. II, p. 166.
12 Drennan to McTier, 20 October 1795, *Drennan-McTier*, vol. II, p. 190.
13 McTier to Drennan, 1795, *Drennan-McTier*, vol. II, p. 192.

Chapter 26

1 Libraryireland.com, Edmund Burke Irish Biography.
2 Ibid.
3 Burke, *Empire*, p. 537.
4 Word unclear.

5   Drennan to McTier, 5 November 1796, *Drennan-McTier*, vol. II, p. 273.
6   Ibid., p. 210.
7   Ibid.
8   Ibid., p. 211.
9   Ibid.
10   Ibid.
11   Drennan to McTier, 31 August 1795, *Drennan-McTier*, vol. II, p. 178.
12   Ibid., p. 212.
13   Ibid., p. 216.
14   Drennan to McTier, 24 March 1796, *Drennan-McTier*, vol. II, p. 216.
15   Bartlett, *Revolutionary Dublin*, p. 92, n. 99.
16   Jane Hayter Hames, *Arthur O'Connor, United Irishman* (hereafter *Arthur O'Connor*) (Cork, 2001), p. 208.
17   Ibid., p. 130.
18   Ibid., p. 222.
19   Drennan to McTier, September 1796, *Drennan-McTier*, vol. II, pp. 258–9.
20   Ibid.
21   Ibid.
22   Ibid.
23   McTier to Drennan, 19 September 1796, *Drennan-McTier*, vol. II, p. 263.
24   Ibid.
25   Ibid.
26   Bartlett, *Revolutionary Dublin*, p. 103.
27   Drennan to McTier, October 1796, *Drennan-McTier*, vol. II, p. 270.
28   Dorothea, wife of Denis George, Baron of the Exchequer and Recorder of Dublin.
29   Drennan to McTier, 5 November 1796, *Drennan-McTier*, vol. II, p. 273.
30   Drennan to McTier, 17 November 1796, *Drennan-McTier*, vol. II, p. 278.
31   Ibid., p. 276.
32   Drennan to McTier, 17 November 1796, *Drennan-McTier*, vol. II, p. 278.
33   Ibid., p. 280.
34   Martha mentioned his prison visit to Russell and Nielson in her letter of 13 January 1797, *Drennan-McTier*, vol. II, p. 286.
35   Ibid., p. 278.

Chapter 27

1   Ibid., p. 298.
2   Drennan to McTier, 14 January 1797, *Drennan-McTier*, vol. II, p. 288.
3   Ibid., p. 298.
4   Ibid., p. 297.
5   Ibid.
6   Ibid.
7   John Newsinger (ed.), *United Irishman: The Autobiography of Jemmy Hope* (London, 1992), p. 48.
8   McTier to Drennan, February 1796, *Drennan-McTier*, vol. II, p. 299.
9   Maura Maher, 'Oliver Bond' in *Dublin Historical Review*, vol xi (Dublin, 1950), p. 106.

10   The Pill Lane King Killers was one of the many humorous titles which Higgins attached to the now underground Dublin United Irishmen. King-killer was a term of abuse which was often levelled at Protestant Dissenters and referred to the role of their republican and Leveller ancestors in the execution of Charles I.

11   Bartlett, *Revolutionary Dublin*, p. 130.

12   Fitzgerald's wife Pamela was Égalité's daughter.

13   Hayter Hames, *Arthur O'Connor*, p. 121.

14   Ibid., p. 135.

15   Ibid.

16   McTier to Drennan, 3 January 1797, *Drennan-McTier*, vol. II, p. 285.

17   Hayter Hames, *Arthur O'Connor*, p. 137.

18   McTier to Drennan, 2 January 1797, *Drennan-McTier*, vol. II, p. 284.

19   Drennan to McTier, 14 January 1797, *Drennan-McTier*, vol. II, p. 287.

20   Ibid.

21   Ibid.

22   McTier to Drennan, 15 January 1797, *Drennan-McTier*, vol. II, p. 289.

23   Ibid., p. 291.

24   Ibid.

25   Ibid., p. 292.

26   Hayter Hames, *Arthur O'Connor*, p. 279.

27   McTier to Drennan, 17 March 1797, *Drennan-McTier*, vol. II, p. 303.

28   Drennan to McTier, 1797, *Drennan-McTier*, vol. II, p. 313.

29   Ibid.

30   Ibid.

31   A.T.Q. Stewart, *The Summer Soldiers: The 1798 Rebellion in Antrim and Down* (hereafter *Summer Soldiers*) (Belfast, 1995), p. 41.

32   Drennan to McTier, (undated) 1797, *Drennan-McTier*, vol. II, p. 316.

33   Ibid.

34   National Archive, Rebellion Papers, 620/1817/6.

35   McTier to Drennan, 16 June 1797, *Drennan-McTier*, vol. II, p. 320.

36   Ibid.

37   McTier to Drennan, 19 June 1797, *Drennan-McTier*, vol. II, p. 320.

Chapter 28

1   Ibid., p. 329.

2   Ibid., p. 331.

3   Drennan to McTier, (undated) 1797, *Drennan-McTier*, vol. II, p. 337.

4   Stewart, *Summer Soldiers*, p. 47.

5   John Killen, *The Decade of the United Irishmen Contemporary Accounts 1791–1801* (Belfast, 1997), p. 106.

6   Stewart, *Summer Soldiers*, p. 49.

7   Ibid.

8   Drennan to McTier, 29 September 1797, *Drennan-McTier*, vol. II, p. 339.

9   Ibid.

10   Hayter Hames, *Arthur O'Connor*, p. 156.

11 *Trial of Mr Peter Finerty: late printer of the press, for a libel against his excellency Earl Camden, Lord Lieutenant of Ireland: in a letter signed Marcus in that paper* (hereafter *Finerty Trial*) (Dublin, 1798), p. 1.

12 Bartlett, *Revolutionary Dublin*, 2004, p. 184.

13 Ibid.

14 William Orr (b. 1766) was hanged at Carrickfergus on 14 October 1797, *DIB*.

15 *Finerty Trial*, p. 6.

16 The *Press*, 26 October 1797, no. 13.

17 Ibid.

18 Ibid.

19 Drennan, *Letter to Fitzwilliam*, p. 34.

20 Ibid.

21 See 'Peter Finnerty', *DIB*.

22 Bartlett, *Revolutionary Dublin*, p. 210.

23 *Letter to Fitzwilliam*, p. 62.

24 Ibid.

25 Ibid.

26 Richard R. Madden, *The United Irishmen: their lives and times*, 2nd edition (Dublin, 1858), pp. 259–62.

27 Johnston, *Unusual Suspects*, p. 147.

28 Drennan to McTier, January 1797, *Drennan-McTier*, vol. II, p. 292.

29 Drennan to McTier, August 1797, 9 October 1797, January 1797, *Drennan-McTier*, vol. II, pp. 337, 340, 342, 361.

30 Ian McBride in Dickson, *Republicanism, Radicalism and Rebellion*, pp. 50–7.

31 Ibid.

32 W. Drennan, *Fugitive Pieces*, p. 173.

33 See Benn *Town of Belfast*, vol I, p. 640.

34 Ibid.

35 Drennan to Sam McTier, 14 July 1794, *Drennan-McTier*, vol. II, p. 83.

36 Drennan, *Letter to Fitzwilliam*, p. 40.

37 The *Press*, 2 January 1798, 'Letter to the People of Ireland'.

38 Ibid.

39 Drennan to McTier, 20 November 1797, *Drennan-McTier*, vol. II, p. 349.

40 Ibid.

41 Ibid.

42 Ibid.

43 Johnston, *Unusual Suspects*, p. 144.

44 Wright, *Natural Leaders*, p. 75.

45 Ibid.

46 Drennan to McTier, March 1797, *Drennan-McTier*, vol. II, p. 374.

47 Ibid.

48 *DIB*.

49 William Sampson, *Memoirs of William Sampson: Including particulars of his adventures in various parts of Europe* (Leesburg Virginia, 1817), p. 20.

50 Drennan to McTier, 21 March 1798, *Drennan-McTier*, vol. II, p. 379.

51 Ibid.

52 Ibid.

53 Ibid.

54 Ibid.
55 Bartlett, *Revolutionary Dublin*, p. 233.
56 M.H. Thuente, *The Harp Re-strung: The United Irishmen and the Rise of Literary Nationalism* (hereafter *Literary Nationalism*) (New York, 1994), p. 110.
57 *Drennan-McTier*, vol. II, p. 328.
58 Ibid., p. 331.
59 Thuente, *Literary Nationalism*, p. 111.
60 Ibid., p. 153.
61 Ibid., p. 111.
62 Ibid.
63 Ibid.

Chapter 29

1   Fleming, Malcomson, *Excretions*, p. 298.
2   Drennan to McTier, 23 April 1798, *Drennan-McTier*, vol. II, p. 392.
3   Ruán O'Donnell, *Robert Emmet and the Rebellion of 1798* (Dublin, 2003), p. 66.
4   Ibid.
5   Drennan to McTier, 23 April 1798, *Drennan-McTier*, vol. II, p. 392.
6   Ibid., p. 995.
7   Drennan to McTier, 22 February 1798, *Drennan-McTier*, vol. II, p. 392. From Shakespeare's *Julius Caesar*; Cinna the poet was stabbed by mistake for Cinna the conspirator.
8   Ibid., p. 395.
9   Drennan to McTier, 7 May 1798, *Drennan-McTier*, vol. II, p. 399.
10 Drennan to McTier, May 1798, *Drennan-McTier*, vol. II, p. 403.
11 Ibid., p. 408.
12 Ibid.
13 Ibid.
14 R. O'Donnell, *Robert Emmet and the Rising of 1803* (hereafter *Emmet in 1893*) (Dublin, 2003), p. 71.
15 Bacon was a tailor who had made the uniforms for Rowan's short-lived National Battalion of Volunteers. See Bartlett, *Revolutionary Dublin*, p. 247.
16 O'Donnell, *Emmet in 1803*, pp. 82–5.
17 Ibid., p. 85.
18 Bruce and Crombie were attached to First Church Rosemary Lane as was Martha.
19 McTier to Drennan, 25 September 1798, *Drennan-McTier*, vol. II, p. 414.
20 Martha McTier to General Nugent, draft petition [1798] (PRONI, D/531/4).
21 W. Drennan to Nancy Drennan, 26 August 1798, *Drennan-McTier*, vol. II, p. 412.
22 Drennan to McTier, 15 October 1798, *Drennan-McTier*, vol. II, p. 414.
23 Drennan to McTier, 8 November 1798, *Drennan-McTier*, vol. II, p. 422.
24 Ibid., p. 425.

Chapter 30

1   Drennan to McTier, 15 January 1799, *Drennan-McTier*, vol. II, p. 452.
2   Ibid., p. 454.

3   Stewart, *Summer Soldiers*, p. 134.

4   Ibid.

5   Francis Dobbs, *Five Propositions for Tranquilising the Country* (Dublin, 1799).

6   McTier to Drennan, May 1799, *Drennan-McTier*, vol. II, p. 507.

7   Bartlett, *Revolutionary Dublin*, p. 275.

8   Drennan to McTier, March 1799, *Drennan-McTier*, vol. II, p. 481.

9   Ibid.

10   Ibid.

11   Ibid.

12   *Drennan-McTier*, vol. I, p. xxi.

13   Drennan to McTier, 21 January 1794, *Drennan-McTier*, vol. II, p. 454.

14   William Drennan, *Letter to the Right Honorable William Pitt* (hereafter *Letter to Pitt*) (Dublin, 1799), p. 4.

15   Ibid.

16   Ibid., p. 3.

17   Ibid., p. 4.

18   Ibid.

19   McTier to Drennan, 22 January 1799, *Drennan-McTier*, vol. II, p. 459.

20   *Letter to Pitt*, p. 9.

21   Ibid.

22   Ibid., p. 17.

23   Ibid., p. 18.

24   Ibid., p. 19.

25   McTier to Drennan, 22 January 1799, *Drennan-McTier*, vol. II, p. 459.

26   Ibid.

27   Drennan to McTier, January 1799, *Drennan-McTier*, vol. II, p. 45.

28   William Drennan, *A Second Letter to William Pitt* (Dublin, 1799), p. 13.

29   Ibid.

30   Johnston, *Unusual Suspects*, p. 151.

31   Ibid., p. 329.

32   William Drennan, 'A Protest on behalf of One of the People of Ireland against an Union with Great Britain' (Dublin, 1800), p. 5.

33   Ibid., p. 9.

34   Drennan to McTier, 2 January 1800, *Drennan-McTier*, vol. II, p. 556.

35   Ibid.

Chapter 31

1   McTier to Drennan, 6 June 1799, *Drennan-McTier*, vol. II, p. 508.

2   McTier to Drennan, 12 May 1799, *Drennan-McTier*, vol. II, p. 500.

3   W. Drennan to A. Drennan, 13 August 1799, *Drennan-McTier*, vol. II, p. 517.

4   The marriage certificate forms part of the Dublin Unitarian Church collection held in the Royal Irish Academy.

5   Drennan to McTier, 13 February 1800, *Drennan-McTier*, vol. II, p. 576.

6   Drennan to McTier, June 1798, *Drennan-McTier*, vol. II, p. 406.

7   *Dublin Journal*, July 1798.

8   Maura Maher, 'Oliver Bond', in *Dublin Historical Record*, vol. xi (Dublin 1950), p. 98. Maher tells us that the Bonds were married in 1791 and had four children called Thomas, Henry Jackson, Elizabeth and Harvey Margaret.

9   Drennan to McTier, 25 May 1799, *Drennan-McTier*, vol. II, p. 505.

10   Drennan to McTier, 13 February 1800, *Drennan-McTier*, vol. II, p. 576.

11   Drennan to McTier, March 1800, *Drennan-McTier*, vol. II, p. 585.

12   Drennan to McTier, 16 May 1800, *Drennan-McTier*, vol. II, p. 597.

13   McTier to Drennan, Friday, 30 May 1800, *Drennan-McTier*, vol. II, p. 598.

14   This must refer to the repayments of the loan to Mrs Ann Drennan.

15   S. and W. Drennan to McTier, 30 June 1800, *Drennan-McTier*, vol. II, p. 605.

16   Eleanor Bond née Jackson was related through marriage to William Tennent of the Rosemary Lane Unitarian congregation Belfast.

17   Mrs Stapleton was a cousin of Sarah's and Bethia Hincks, and a sister of Mrs John Hutton. See *Drennan-McTier*, p. 570, n. 36.

18   Drennan to McTier, Saturday 5 March [*sic* but 5 April postmark], *Drennan-McTier*, vol. II, p. 586.

19   Drennan to McTier, 22 July 1800, *Drennan-McTier*, vol. II, p. 612.

20   Ibid.

21   Henry Charles Sirr (1764–1841), chief of Dublin police. See *Drennan–McTier*, vol. II, p. 719, n. 132.

22   Fitzpatrick, *Informers*, pp. 185–6.

23   Ibid.

24   Ibid.

25   Ibid.

26   W. Drennan to A. Drennan, 4 August 1800, *Drennan-McTier*, vol. II, p. 616.

27   Ibid., p. 617.

28   Ibid., p. 618.

29   McTier to Drennan, 23 February 1805, *Drennan-McTier*, vol. III, p. 324.

Chapter 32

1   Drennan to McTier, May 1798, *Drennan-McTier*, vol. II, p. 406.

2   Drennan to McTier, 11 March 1799, *Drennan-McTier*, vol. II, p. 482.

3   Denis Carroll, *Unusual Suspects: Twelve Radical Clergy* (Dublin, 1998), pp. 50–1.

4   McTier to Drennan, 1 August 1801, *Drennan-McTier*, vol. II, p. 719.

5   A copy of *Beauties of the Press* in the N.L.I. notes in the British library suggest that it was privately printed by John Stockdale and carries an inscription 'Found at John Stockdale's 62 Abbey Street 10th August 1801 Henry Sirr'.

6   Drennan to McTier, 13 August 1801, *Drennan-McTier*, vol. II, p. 719.

7   McTier to Drennan, 2 April 1801, *Drennan-McTier*, vol. II, p. 693.

8   Drennan to McTier, 27 October 1801, *Drennan-McTier*, vol. II, p. 733.

9   Ibid., p. 734.

10   Ibid., p. 733.

11   Ibid.

12   McTier to Drennan, 20 March 1802, *Drennan-McTier*, vol. III, p. 24.

13   Ibid., p. 15.

14   Ibid., pp. 25–31.

15   Ibid.
16   Ibid.
17   Drennan to McTier, December 1798, *Drennan-McTier*, vol. II, p. 442.
18   Drennan to McTier, February 1802, *Drennan-McTier*, vol. III, p. 13.
19   Drennan to McTier, March 1799, *Drennan-McTier*, vol. II, p. 476.
20   Drennan to McTier, 25 May 1802, *Drennan-McTier*, vol. III, p. 44.
21   McTier to Drennan, 3 June 1802, *Drennan-McTier*, vol. III, p. 49.
22   Drennan to McTier, 8 February 1805, *Drennan-McTier*, vol. III, p. 321.
23   Drennan to McTier, 16 June 1802, *Drennan-McTier*, vol. III, p. 51.
24   Drennan to McTier, 14 December 1802, *Drennan-McTier*, vol. III, p. 87.
25   Drennan to McTier, 15 July 1803, *Drennan-McTier*, vol. III, p. 127.
26   Drennan to McTier, June 1803, *Drennan-McTier*, vol. III, p. 123.
27   McTier to Drennan, 13 June 1803, *Drennan-McTier*, vol. III, p. 120.

Chapter 33

1   Ibid. p. 129.
2   O'Donnell, *Emmet and 1803*, p. 11.
3   McTier to Drennan, October 1803, *Drennan-McTier*, vol. III, p. 158.
4   Drennan to McTier, September 1803, *Drennan-McTier*, vol. III, p. 141.
5   McTier to Drennan, September 1803, *Drennan-McTier*, vol. III, pp. 144–8.
6   P. Geoghegan, *Robert Emmet a Life* (Dublin, 2002), p. 239.
7   Maeve Ryan 'The Reptile that had Stung Me: William Plunket and the Trial of Robert Emmet', (hereafter 'The Reptile') in A. Dolan et al., *Reinterpreting Emmet: Essays on the Life of Robert Emmet* (Dublin, 2007), p. 84.
8   Ibid.
9   McTier to Drennan, 28 September 1803, *Drennan-McTier*, vol. III, p. 153.
10   Ryan, 'The Reptile', p. 96.
11   Drennan to Mctier, 18 October 1803, *Drennan-McTier*, vol. III, p. 157.
12   Ibid., p. 159.
13   Ibid., p. 170.
14   J. Killen, *A History of the Linen Hall Library, 1788–1988* (hereafter *Linen Hall*) (Belfast, 1990), p. 47.
15   Madden, *The United Irishmen*, p. 20.
16   Drennan to McTier, 11 February 1893, *Drennan-McTier*, vol. III, p. 198.
17   McTier to Drennan, 23 February 1805, *Drennan-McTier*, vol. III, p. 324.
18   Drennan to McTier, 31 January 1805, *Drennan-McTier*, vol. III, p. 317.
19   Drennan to McTier, 13 March 1803, *Drennan-McTier*, vol. III, p. 333.

Chapter 34

1   Ibid., p. xix.
2   Drennan to McTier, 10 November 1805, *Drennan-McTier*, vol. III, p. 386.
3   McTier to Drennan, 18 November 1805, *Drennan-McTier*, vol. III, p. 392.
4   Ibid., p. 409.
5   Ibid.

6   McTier to Drennan, 10 February 1806, *Drennan-McTier*, vol. III, p. 426.
7   Drennan to McTier, 29 January 1806, *Drennan-McTier*, vol. III, p. 420.
8   Ibid., p. 425.
9   Drennan to McTier, 4 April 1806, *Drennan-McTier*, vol. III, p. 455.
10   Drennan to McTier, February 1806, *Drennan-McTier*, vol. III, p. 429.
11   O. MacDonagh, *O'Connell: The life of Daniel O'Connell* (London, 1991), p. 166.
12   Drennan to McTier, March 1800, *Drennan-McTier*, vol. III, p. 28.
13   L.G. Mitchell, *Charles James Fox* (London, 1992), p. 156.
14   *Letter to the Right Honorable Charles James Fox* (hereafter *Letter to C.J. Fox*) (Dublin, 1806), p. 3.
15   Ibid., p. 4.
16   Ibid., p. 8.
17   Ibid., p. 10.
18   Ibid., p. 12.
19   Ibid., p. 10.
20   Ibid., p. 13.
21   Robert Stewart, later Lord Castlereagh.
22   *Letter to C.J. Fox*, p. 15.
23   Ibid., p. 15.
24   Ibid.
25   Ibid., p. 13.
26   Ibid., p. 16.
27   Ibid., p. 17.
28   Likely a reference to Francis Higgins in the *Freeman's Journal* attack on the United Irishmen.
29   *Letter to C.J. Fox*, p. 21.
30   Ibid., p. 26.
31   Ibid., p. 27.
32   Ibid., p. 32.
33   Ibid.
34   Drennan to McTier, 21 March 1806, *Drennan-McTier*, vol. III, p. 447.
35   Drennan to McTier, 27 October 1800, *Drennan-McTier*, vol. III, p. 537.
36   One exception was Archibald Hamilton Rowan who returned home and was pardoned in 1805. Drummond, *Rowan*, p. 377.

Chapter 35

1   Drennan to McTier, 17 April 1807, *Drennan-McTier*, vol. III, p. 595.
2   Jonathan Jeffrey Wright, *The 'Natural Leaders' and the World* (hereafter *Natural Leaders*) (Liverpool, 2012), p. 49.
3   Reverend Dr Snowden Cupples (1750–1835), rector of Lisburn, Orangeman, later Vicar General of Down and Connor. See *Drennan-McTier*, vol. III, p. 628.
4   Drennan to McTier, September 1807, *Drennan-McTier*, vol. III, p. 628.
5   Wright, *'Natural Leaders'*, p. 146.
6   Ibid., p. 177.
7   Killen, *Linen Hall*, p. 48.
8   Drennan to McTier, September 1807, *Drennan-McTier*, vol. III, p. 628.
9   Benn, *Town of Belfast*, vol. II, p. 102.
10   Ibid., p. 103.
11   Ibid.
12   Brooke, *Ulster Presbyterianism*, p. 139.

13 Ibid.
14 Ibid., p. 141.
15 Ibid.
16 J.R. Fisher, *Royal Belfast Academical Institution* (hereafter *Belfast Academical*) (Belfast, 1913); p. 39.
17 Ibid.
18 I.R. McBride, *Scripture Politics: Ulster Presbyterians and Irish Radicalism in the late Eighteenth Century* (hereafter *Scripture Politics*) (Oxford, 1998), p. 211.
19 Ibid.
20 Brooke, *Ulster Presbyterianism*, p. 144.
21 McBride, *Scripture Politics*, p. 212.
22 Brooke, *Ulster Presbyterianism*, p. 141.
23 Ibid., p. 143.
24 Benn, *Town of Belfast*, vol. II, p. 106.
25 Ibid.
26 Fisher, *Linen Hall*, p. 203.
27 Ibid., p. 204.
28 Ibid., pp. 204–5.
29 Ibid.
30 Ibid.
31 Wright, 'Natural Leaders', p. 86.
32 Ibid.
33 Ibid.
34 Ibid., p. 87.
35 *BNL*, 29 March 1816.
36 Ibid.
37 McBride, *Scripture Politics*, p. 213.
38 Drennan to McTier, 13 May 1816, *Drennan-McTier*, vol. III, p. 684.
39 William Drennan, *A Courteous Reply to the Remarks of Presbyter Relative to the Belfast Academical Institution* (Belfast, 1816), p. 10.
40 Wright, 'Natural Leaders', p. 88.
41 Ibid.
42 Brooke, *Ulster Presbyterianism*, p. 144.
43 Fisher, *Linen Hall*, p. 70.
44 Wright, 'Natural Leaders', p. 88.
45 McBride, *Scripture Politics*, p. 211.
46 Drennan and his group at first wanted to open the college to women and Benn suggests this was perhaps the earliest aspiration expressed for the higher education of women. Benn, *Town of Belfast*, vol. II, p. 120.

Chapter 36

1 *MM*, no. 1, September 1808.
2 Ibid.
3 Wright, *Natural Leaders*, p. 68.
4 *BMM*, III, 1809, p. 67.
5 For education, see *BMM*, IV, January 1810, p. 5 and III, September, 1809, p. 302.

6   For press freedom, see *BMM*, IV, February 1810, p. 150 and III, 1809, p. 71.
7   For anti-slavery material, see *BMM*, IV, 1810, pp. 117–23 and II, 1810, p. 474.
8   *BMM*, III, p. 67.
9   Ibid., p. 225.
10 Ibid.
11 Wright, '*Natural Leaders*', p. 75.
12 *BMM*, IV, January 1810, p. 117 and III, November 1809.
13 J.E. Cookson, *The Friends of Peace: Anti-War Liberalism in England, 1793–1815* (London, 1982).
14 *BMM*, July 1810, p. 18.
15 Wright, '*Natural Leaders*', p. 72.
16 Hall, *Ulster Liberalism*, p. 59.
17 *BMM*, III, 1809, p. 68.
18 Hall, *Ulster Liberalism*, p. 62.
19 Ibid.
20 *BMM*, 13 December 1816, pp. 447–9.
21 *BMM*, V, July 1810, p. 17.
22 A. Blackstock, *Loyalism in Ireland 1789–1829* (Woodbridge, 2007), p. 166.
23 Wright, '*Natural Leaders*', p. 83.
24 Ibid., p. 63.
25 *BMM*, III, 1809, p. 231.

Chapter 37

1   This letter is quoted verbatim in Oliver McDonagh, *O'Connell: The life of Daniel O'Connell* (hereafter *O'Connell*) (London, 1991), p. 166.
2   *Letter to C.J. Fox.*
3   McDonagh, *O'Connell*, p. 166.
4   Ibid.
5   Ibid.
6   John W. Osborne, *John Cartwright* (hereafter *Cartwright*) (Cambridge, 1972), p. 129.
7   James II's army camped on Hounslow Heath cheered the acquittal of the seven bishops prosecuted by the King for seditious libel in 1688.
8   Drennan to McTier, Monday morning, 1819, *Drennan-McTier*, vol. III, p. 708.
9   Ibid.
10 Osborne, *Cartwright*, p. 126.
11 Drennan to McTier, 1819, *Drennan-McTier*, vol. III, p. 708.
12 John Belchem, *Popular Radicalism in Nineteenth Century Britain* (London, 1996), pp. 48–9.
13 *BNL*, February 1820.

Conclusion

1   Drennan to McTier, 1 March 1778, *Drennan-McTier*, vol. I, p. 41.
2   Ian McBride in Dickson, *Republicanism, Radicalism and Rebellion*, pp. 56–7.
3   Drennan to McTier, 30 January 1778, *Drennan-McTier*, vol. I, p. 35.
4   Fisher, *Belfast Academical*, p. 39.

5   Clifford, *Selected Writings*, vol. I, p. 176.
6   McDowell, *Proceedings*, p. 95.
7   Chart, *Letters*, p. VIII.
8   Drennan to McTier, August 1794, *Drennan-McTier*, vol. II, p. 93.
9   *Drennan-McTier*, vol. I, p. xx.
10   Mary Helen Thuente, *The Harp Re-strung: The United Irishmen and the Rise of Literary Nationalism* (New York, 1994), p. 111.
11   *Finerty Trial*.
12   Bartlett, *Revolutionary Dublin*, p. 66.
13   Drennan to McTier, 20 July 1796, *Drennan-McTier*, vol. II, p. 252.

INDEX